S0-CEX-286

STOP!

This is the back of the book.
You wouldn't want to spoil a great ending!

This book is printed "manga-style," in the authentic Japanese right-to-left format. Since none of the artwork has been flipped or altered, readers get to experience the story just as the creator intended. You've been asking for it, so TOKYOPOP® delivered: authentic, hot-off-the-press, and far more fun!

DIRECTIONS

If this is your first time reading manga-style, here's a quick guide to help you understand how it works.

It's easy... just start in the top right panel and follow the numbers. Have fun, and look for more 100% authentic manga from TOKYOPOP®!

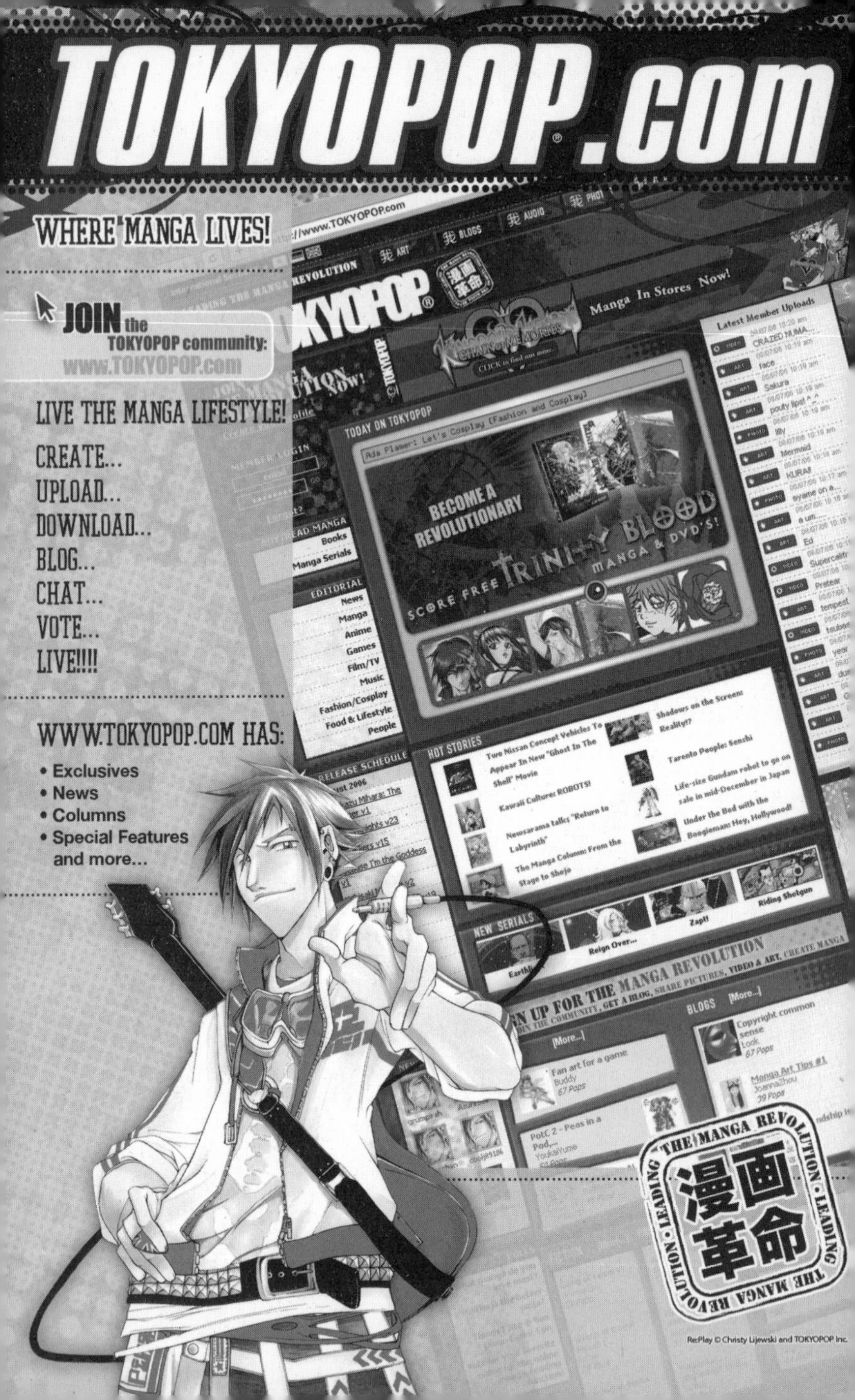
TOKYOPOP®.com
WHERE MANGA LIVES!
JOIN the TOKYOPOP community:
www.TOKYOPOP.com
LIVE THE MANGA LIFESTYLE!
CREATE...
UPLOAD...
DOWNLOAD...
BLOG...
CHAT...
VOTE...
LIVE!!!!
WWW.TOKYOPOP.COM HAS:
• Exclusives
• News
• Columns
• Special Features and more...
THE MANGA REVOLUTION • LEADING • 漫画革命
Re:Play © Christy Lijewski and TOKYOPOP Inc.

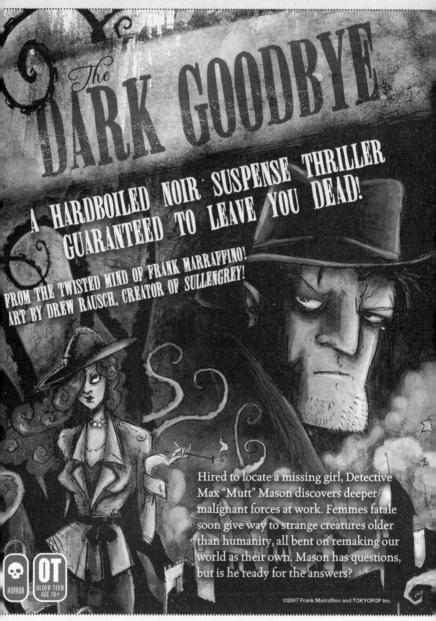

Shojo showers bring April Flowers!
Shojo manga that doesn't miss a beat.
DRAMACON
TOKYOPOP
2
Created by Svetlana Chmakova
Dramacon © Svetlana Chmakova and TOKYOPOP Inc.

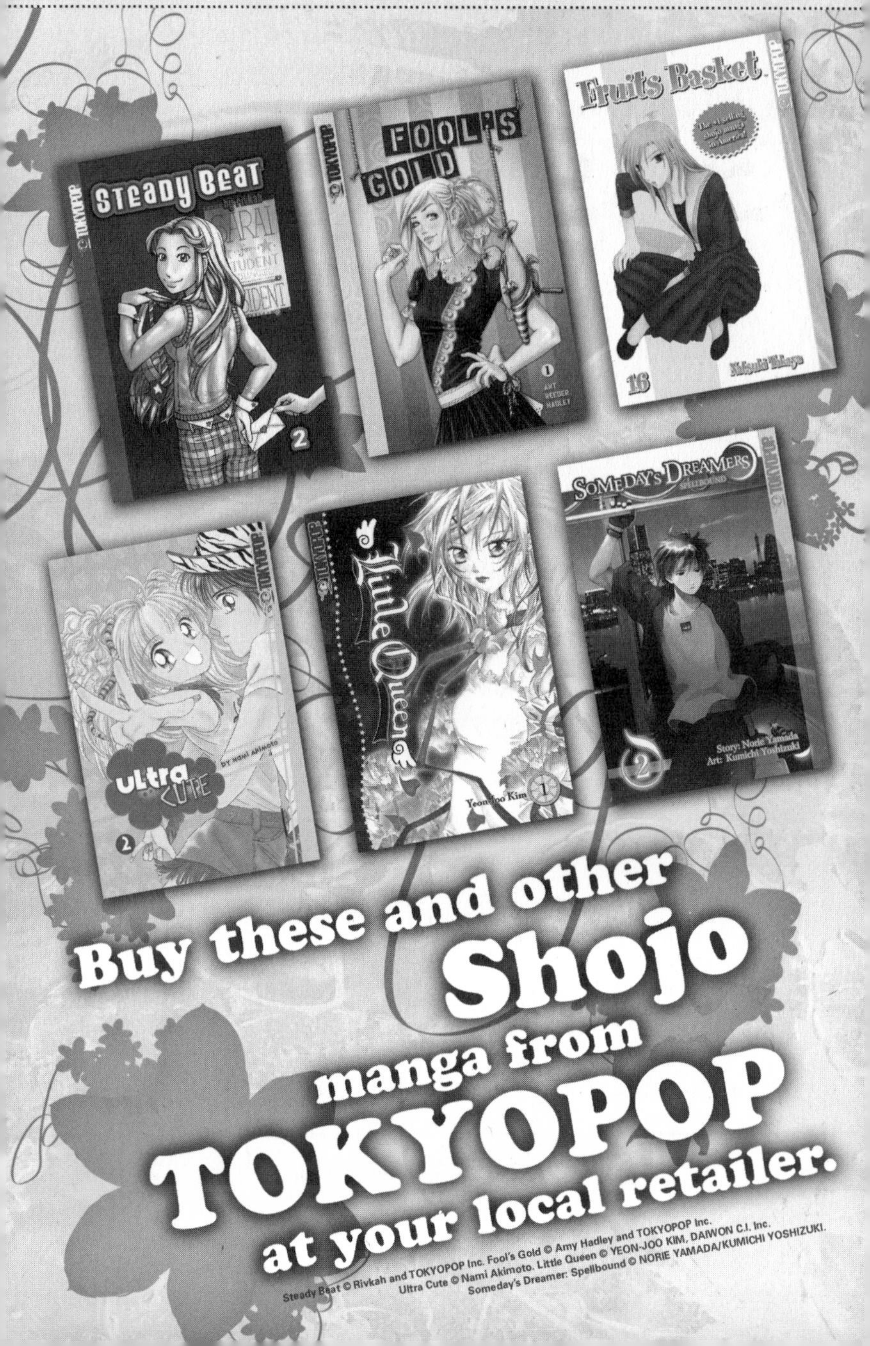

Steady Beat
2
Fool's Gold
1
Amy Reeder Hadley
Fruits Basket
Natsuki Takaya
16
Ultra Cute
By Nami Akimoto
2
Little Queen
Yeon-Joo Kim
1
Someday's Dreamers
Spellbound
Story: Norie Yamada
Art: Kumichi Yoshizuki
2
Buy these and other
Shojo
manga from
TOKYOPOP
at your local retailer.
Steady Beat © Rivkah and TOKYOPOP Inc. Fool's Gold © Amy Hadley and TOKYOPOP Inc.
Ultra Cute © Nami Akimoto. Little Queen © YEON-JOO KIM, DAIWON C.I. Inc.
Someday's Dreamer: Spellbound © NORIE YAMADA/KUMICHI YOSHIZUKI.

In the next Volume of...

SATISFACTION GUARANTEED

Shima gets bullied into having his fortune read by a gorgeous Tarot whiz, but soon he wishes he hadn't. Prospects look sinister for our stubby Sherlock. Could the foul omen in Shima's future be...babysitting?

SATISFACTION GUARANTEED

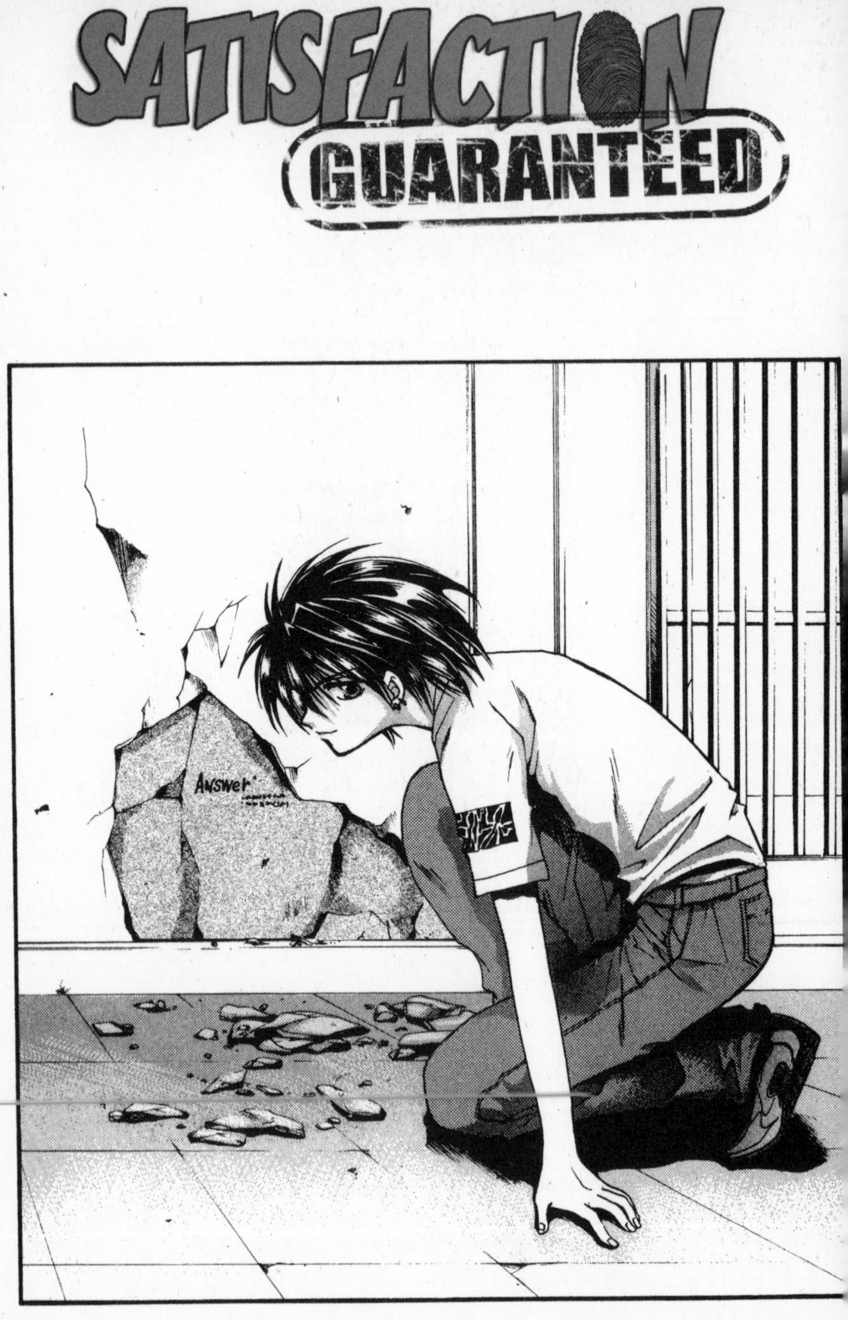
Answer

Satisfaction Guaranteed Volume 3
Created by Ryo Saenagi

Translation - Monica Seya Chin
English Adaptation - Matt Yamashita
Retouch and Lettering - Star Print Brokers
Production Artist - Mike Estacio
Cover Design - Louis Csontos

Editor - Hope Donovan
Digital Imaging Manager - Chris Buford
Pre-Production Supervisor - Erika Terriquez
Art Director - Anne Marie Horne
Production Manager - Elisabeth Brizzi
Managing Editor - Vy Nguyen
VP of Production - Ron Klamert
Editor-in-Chief - Rob Tokar
Publisher - Mike Kiley
President and C.O.O. - John Parker
C.E.O. and Chief Creative Officer - Stuart Levy

A  Manga

TOKYOPOP and 🐾 are trademarks or registered trademarks of TOKYOPOP Inc.

TOKYOPOP Inc.
5900 Wilshire Blvd. Suite 2000
Los Angeles, CA 90036

E-mail: info@TOKYOPOP.com
Come visit us online at www.TOKYOPOP.com

ISBN: 978-1-59816-534-0

First TOKYOPOP printing: March 2007
10 9 8 7 6 5 4 3 2 1
Printed in the USA

SATISFACTION GUARANTEED

Volume 3
by
Ryo Saenagi

HAMBURG // LONDON // LOS ANGELES // TOKYO

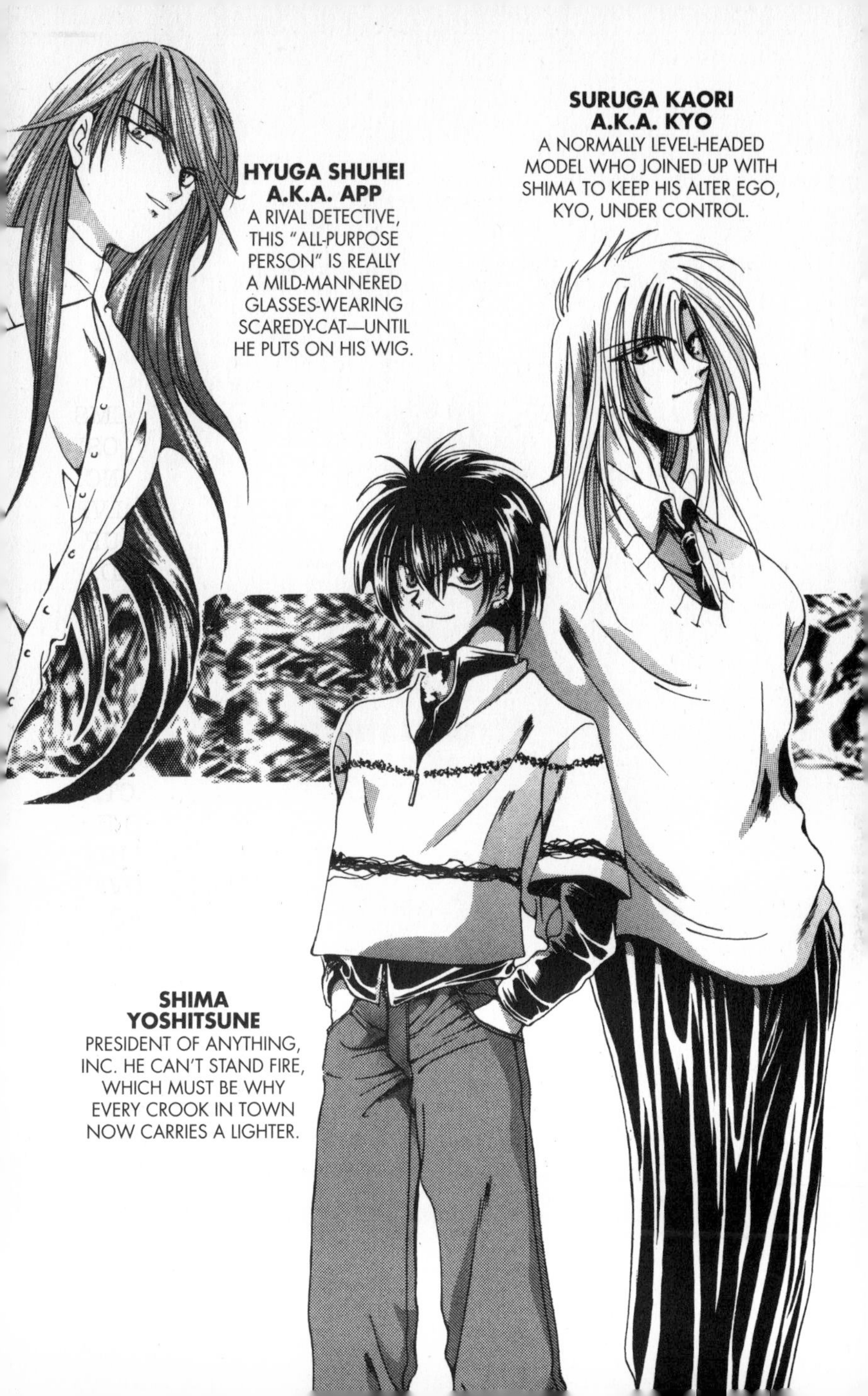
SURUGA KAORI A.K.A. KYO
A NORMALLY LEVEL-HEADED MODEL WHO JOINED UP WITH SHIMA TO KEEP HIS ALTER EGO, KYO, UNDER CONTROL.
HYUGA SHUHEI A.K.A. APP
A RIVAL DETECTIVE, THIS "ALL-PURPOSE PERSON" IS REALLY A MILD-MANNERED GLASSES-WEARING SCAREDY-CAT—UNTIL HE PUTS ON HIS WIG.
SHIMA YOSHITSUNE
PRESIDENT OF ANYTHING, INC. HE CAN'T STAND FIRE, WHICH MUST BE WHY EVERY CROOK IN TOWN NOW CARRIES A LIGHTER.

LAST TIME

SHIMA YOSHITSUNE IS AN ENTERPRISING
YOUNG MAN WITH A KNACK FOR SOLVING PROBLEMS.
HE'S ALSO THE PRESIDENT OF HIS OWN ALL-PURPOSE
ODD JOBS AND DETECTIVE AGENCY, ANYTHING, INC.
IN HIS MIND, THE WORST CRIME IS ONE LEFT UNSOLVED,
SO HIS PERSONAL DIRECTIVE IS TO NEVER GIVE UP
ON A CASE, NO MATTER HOW TOUGH OR TWISTED.

BUT SHIMA'S RAMBUNCTIOUSNESS MASKS INNER
PAIN. THE RECENT LOSS OF HIS PARENTS TO AN ARSONIST'S
FIRE HAS TRAUMATIZED HIM, AND HE CAN'T STAND BEING
AROUND EVEN THE TINIEST BIT OF FLAME WITHOUT
BREAKING DOWN. UNTIL KAORI CAME INTO HIS LIFE, THAT
IS. KAORI, A POPULAR FASHION MODEL, CONTRACTED
SHIMA TO NAB A SNEAKY STALKER, BUT ENDED UP
ASKING THE JUNIOR DETECTIVE TO HELP KEEP HIS
PROFESSIONAL ALTER EGO, KYO, FROM TAKING OVER.
SHIMA, WHO WAS INSTANTLY PUT AT EASE BY KAORI'S
KIND SMILE AND CALM DEMEANOR, AGREED, EVEN
LETTING KAORI JOIN HIM AS A PARTNER
AT ANYTHING, INC.

CONTINUING TO TAKE ON CASES OF THE
UNSOLVABLE, INCOMPREHENSIBLE AND
REPREHENSIBLE, ANYTHING, INC. GUARANTEES
SPECTACULAR RESULTS -- OR YOUR
MONEY BACK!

CONTENTS

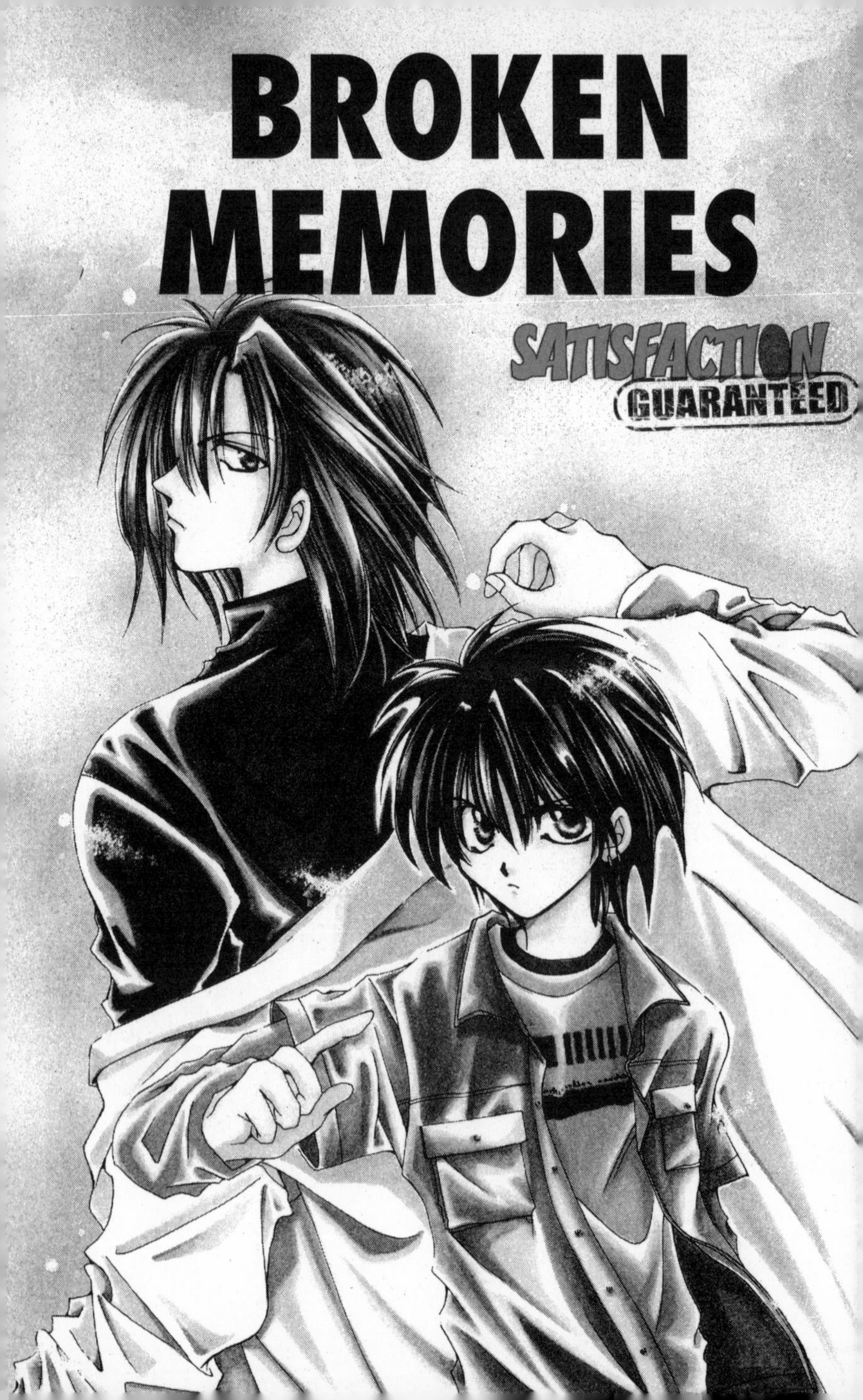
BROKEN MEMORIES
SATISFACTION GUARANTEED

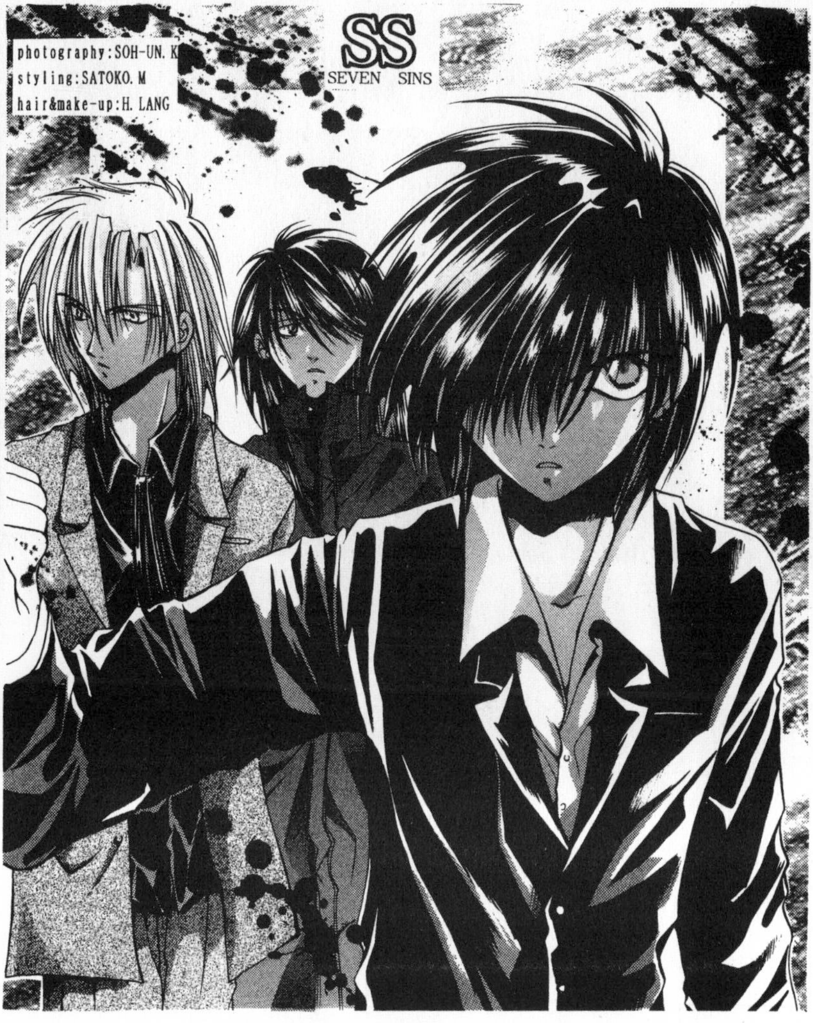
SS
SEVEN SINS
photography:SOH-UN.K
styling:SATOKO.M
hair&make-up:H.LANG

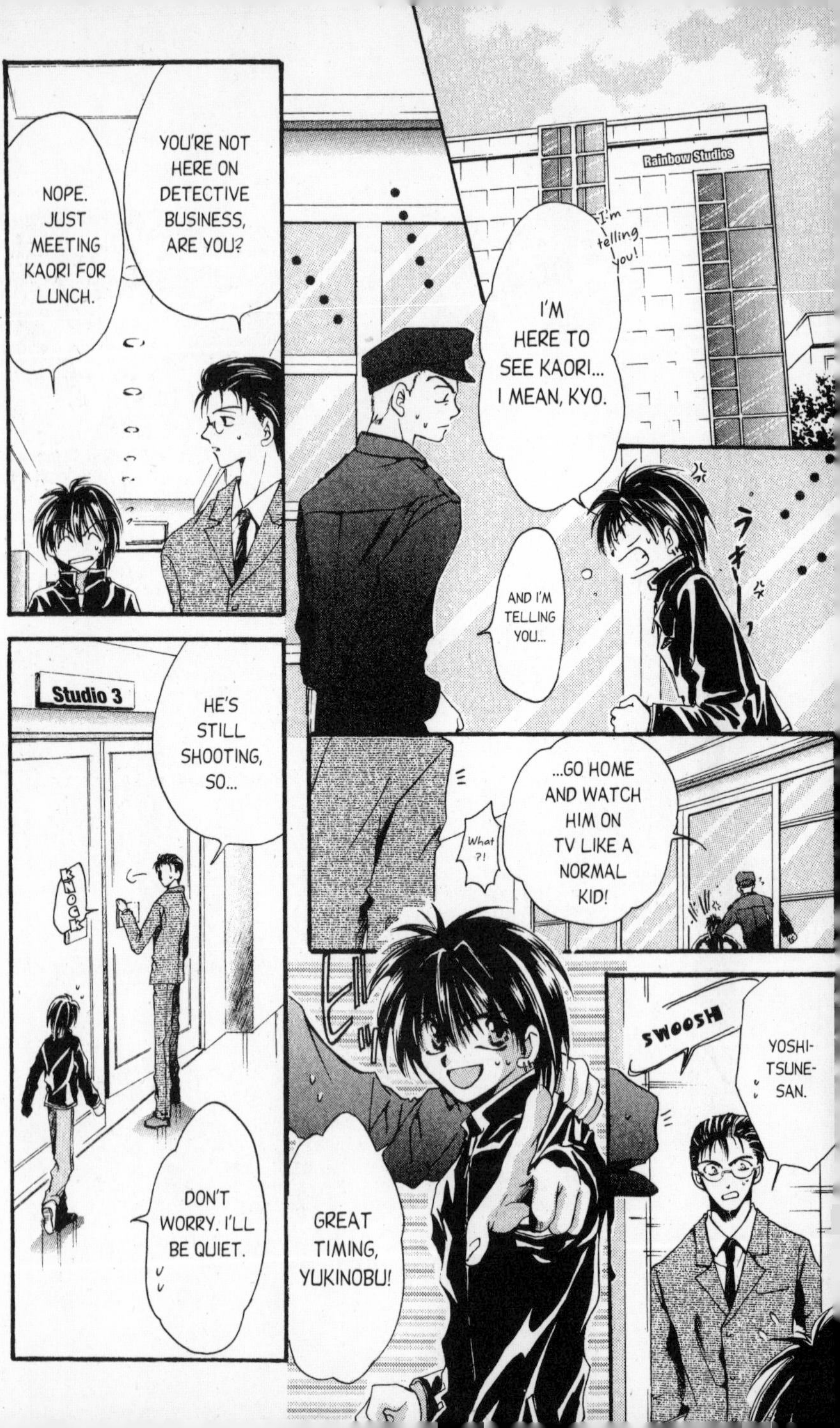
Rainbow Studios
I'm telling you!
I'M HERE TO SEE KAORI... I MEAN, KYO.
AND I'M TELLING YOU...
...GO HOME AND WATCH HIM ON TV LIKE A NORMAL KID!
What?!
SWOOSH
YOSHI-TSUNE-SAN.
GREAT TIMING, YUKINOBU!
YOU'RE NOT HERE ON DETECTIVE BUSINESS, ARE YOU?
NOPE. JUST MEETING KAORI FOR LUNCH.
Studio 3
HE'S STILL SHOOTING, SO...
KNOCK
DON'T WORRY. I'LL BE QUIET.

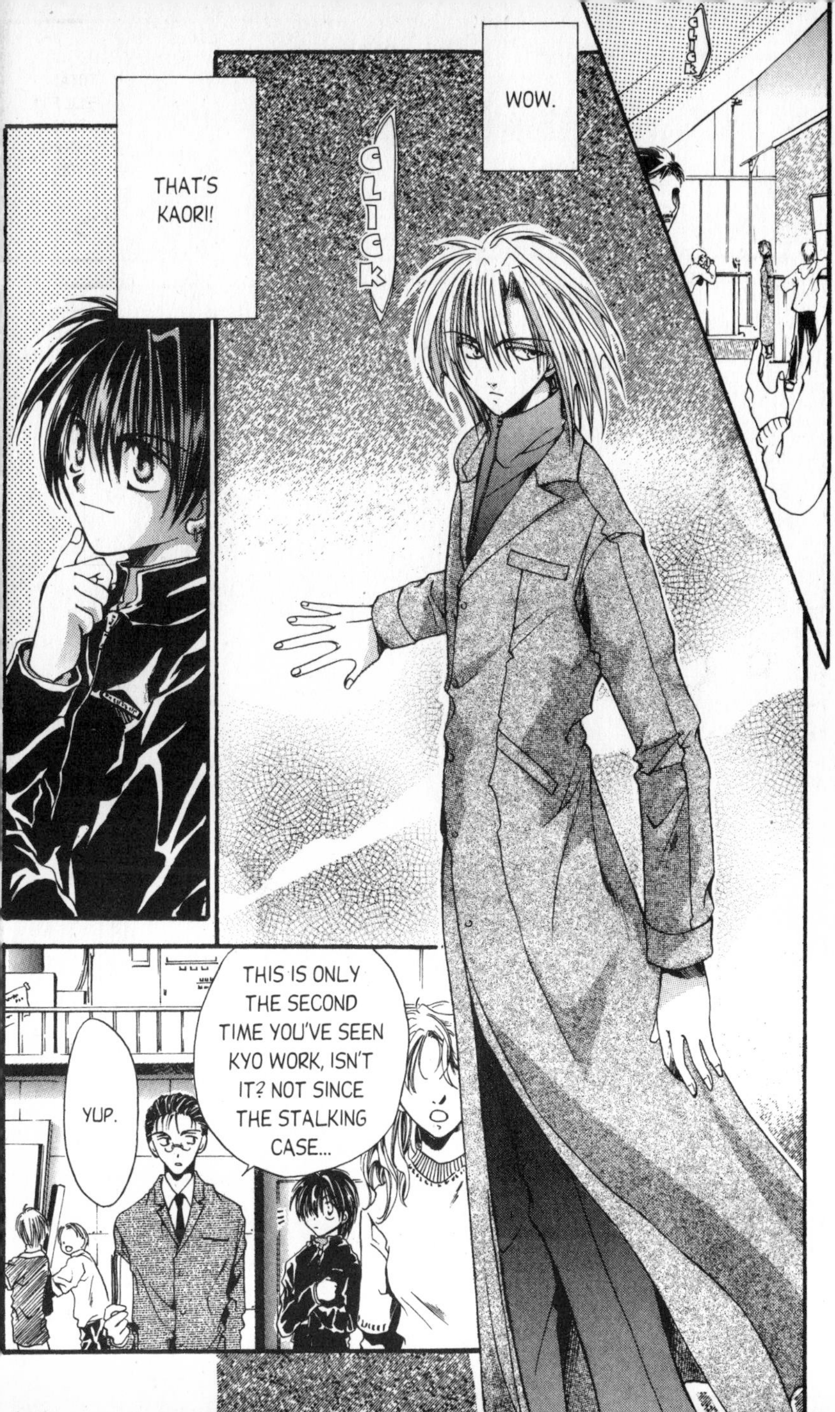
CLICK
WOW.
CLICK
THAT'S KAORI!
THIS IS ONLY THE SECOND TIME YOU'VE SEEN KYO WORK, ISN'T IT? NOT SINCE THE STALKING CASE...
YUP.

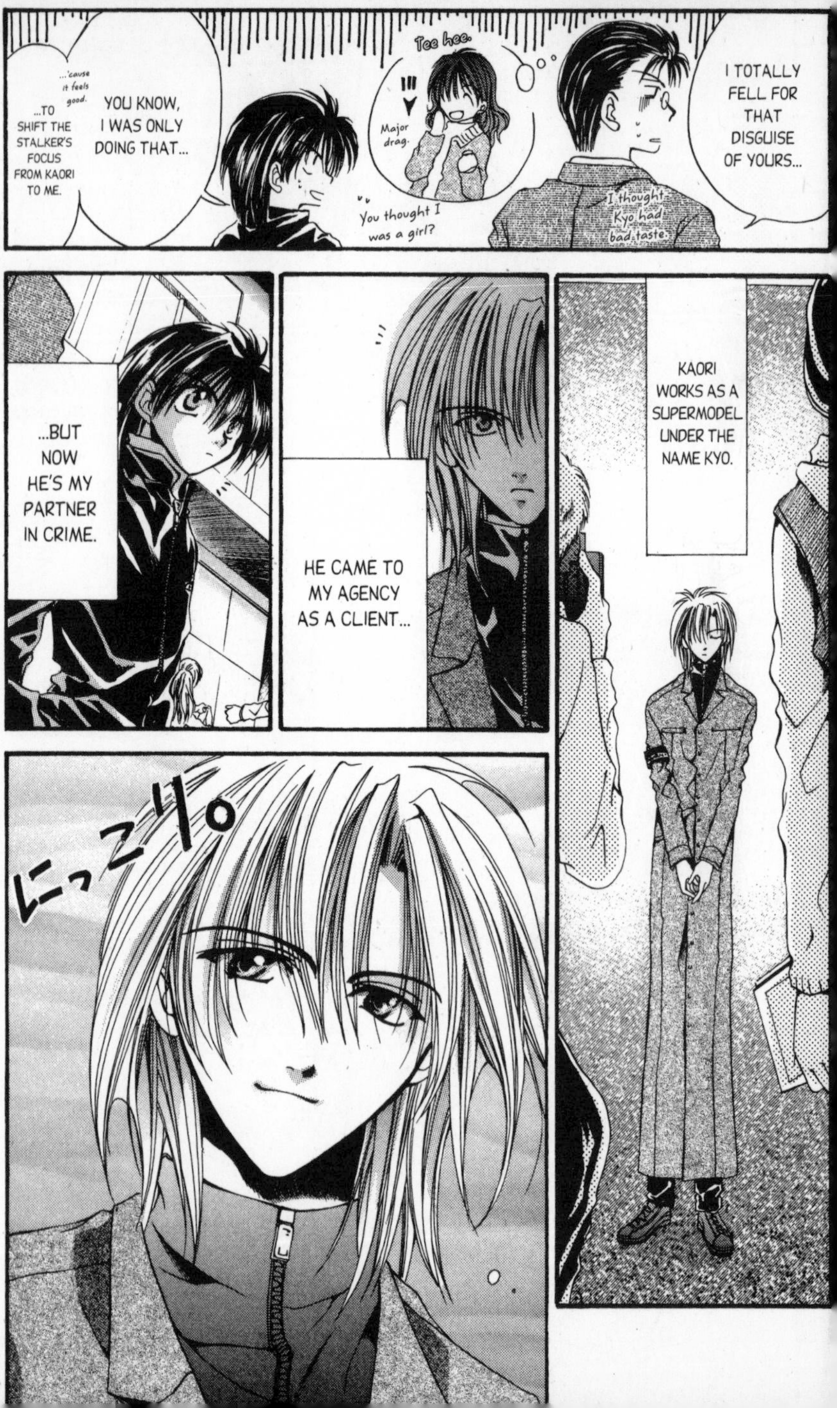
I TOTALLY FELL FOR THAT DISGUISE OF YOURS...
I thought Kyo had bad taste.
Tee hee.
Major drag.
You thought I was a girl?
YOU KNOW, I WAS ONLY DOING THAT...
...TO SHIFT THE STALKER'S FOCUS FROM KAORI TO ME.
...'cause it feels good.
KAORI WORKS AS A SUPERMODEL UNDER THE NAME KYO.
HE CAME TO MY AGENCY AS A CLIENT...
...BUT NOW HE'S MY PARTNER IN CRIME.
にっこり。

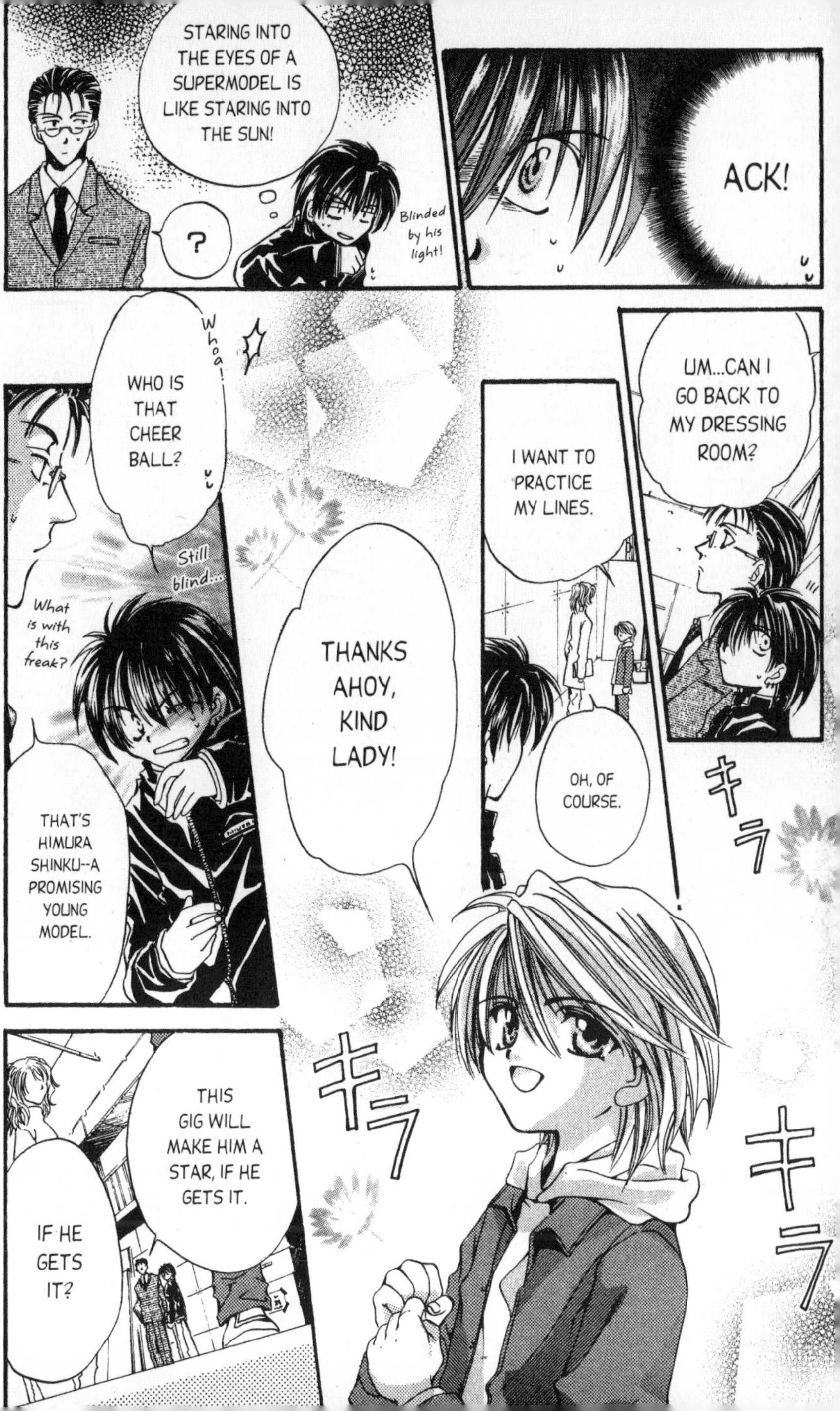
ACK!
STARING INTO THE EYES OF A SUPERMODEL IS LIKE STARING INTO THE SUN!
Blinded by his light!
?
UM...CAN I GO BACK TO MY DRESSING ROOM?
I WANT TO PRACTICE MY LINES.
OH, OF COURSE.
キラ
THANKS AHOY, KIND LADY!
キラ
キラ
Whoa!
WHO IS THAT CHEER BALL?
Still blind...
What is with this freak?
THAT'S HIMURA SHINKU--A PROMISING YOUNG MODEL.
THIS GIG WILL MAKE HIM A STAR, IF HE GETS IT.
IF HE GETS IT?

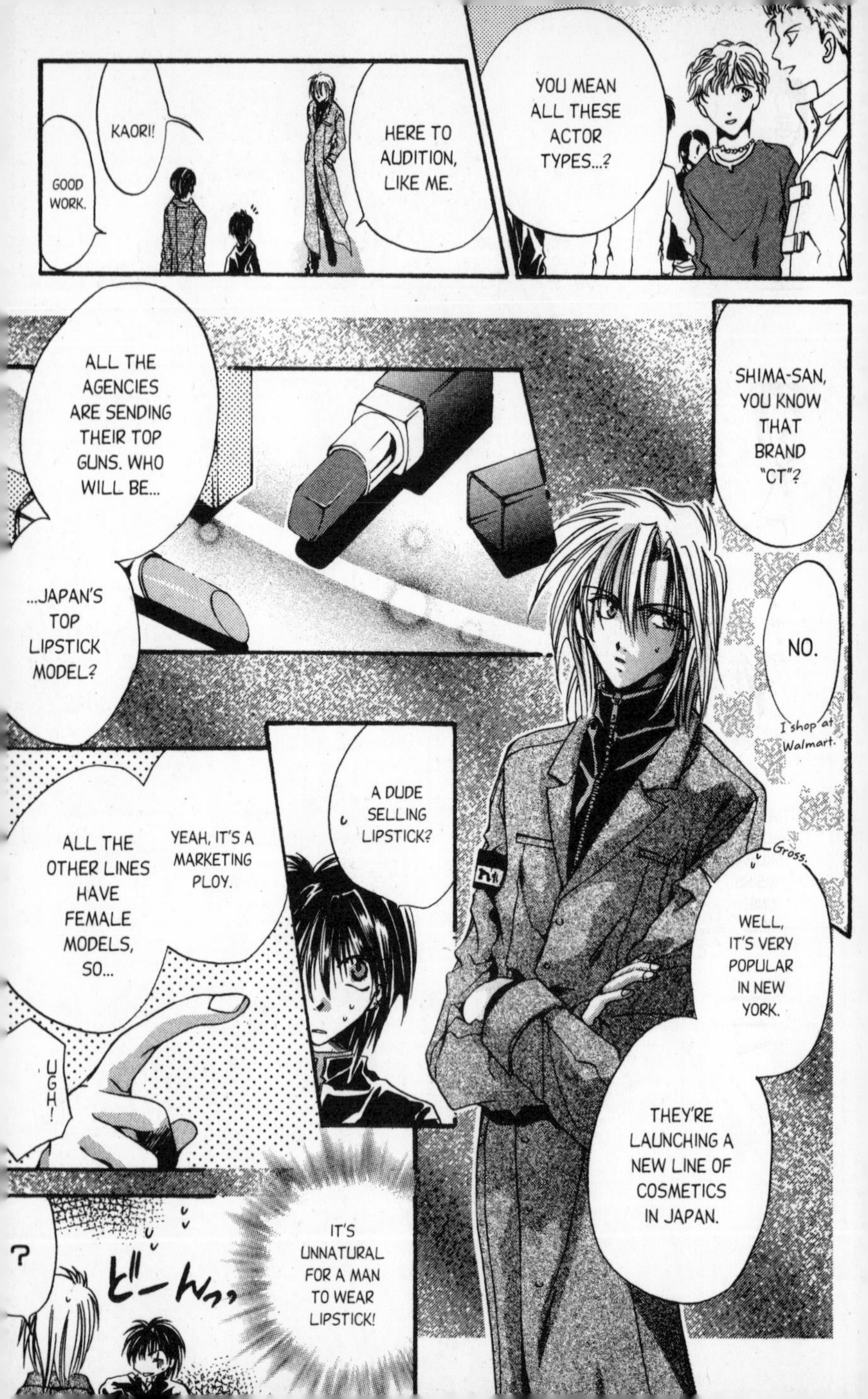
YOU MEAN ALL THESE ACTOR TYPES...?
HERE TO AUDITION, LIKE ME.
KAORI!
GOOD WORK.
SHIMA-SAN, YOU KNOW THAT BRAND "CT"?
NO.
I shop at Walmart.
Gross.
WELL, IT'S VERY POPULAR IN NEW YORK.
THEY'RE LAUNCHING A NEW LINE OF COSMETICS IN JAPAN.
ALL THE AGENCIES ARE SENDING THEIR TOP GUNS. WHO WILL BE...
...JAPAN'S TOP LIPSTICK MODEL?
A DUDE SELLING LIPSTICK?
YEAH, IT'S A MARKETING PLOY.
ALL THE OTHER LINES HAVE FEMALE MODELS, SO...
UGH!
IT'S UNNATURAL FOR A MAN TO WEAR LIPSTICK!
?
どーんっ

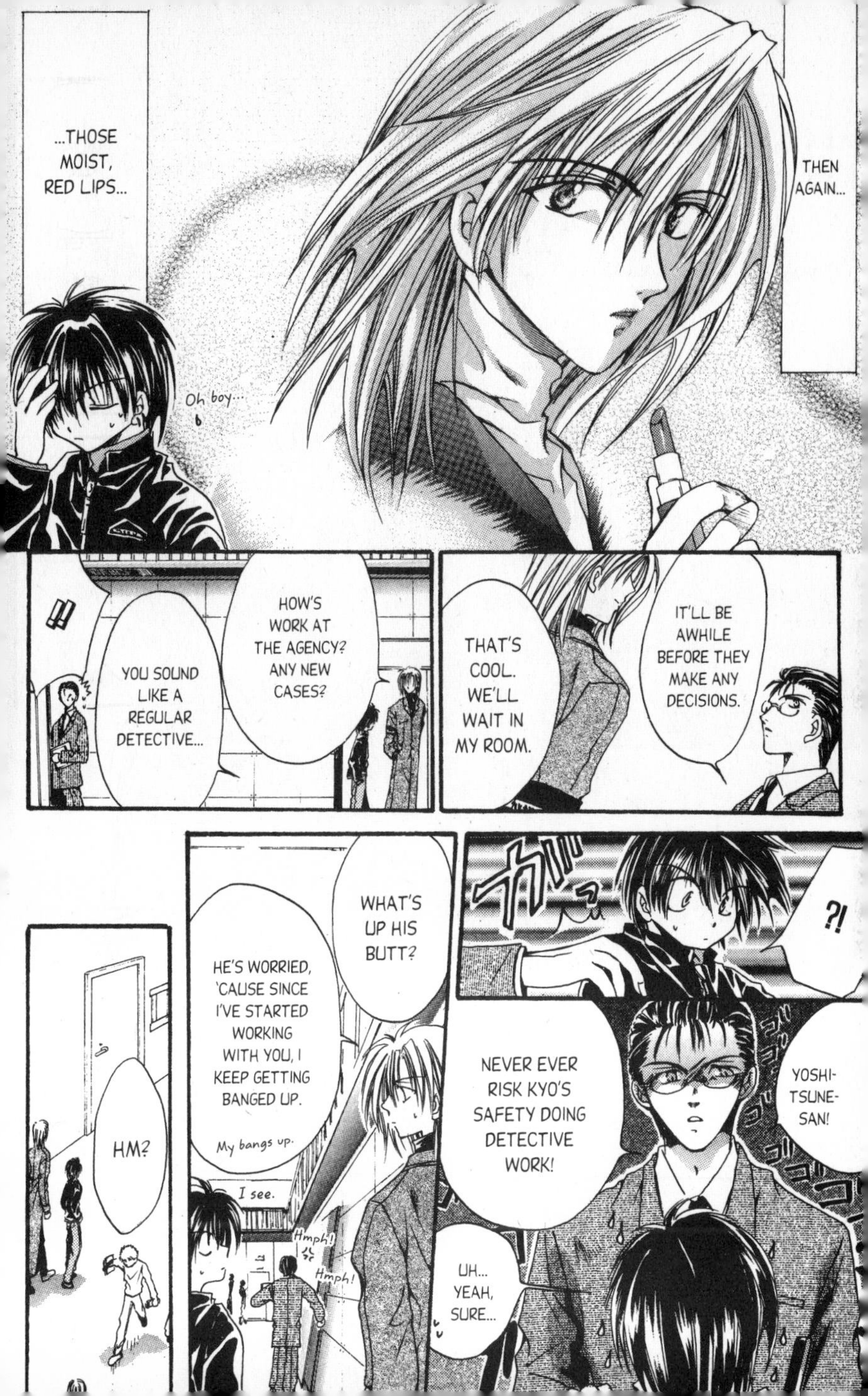
THEN AGAIN...
...THOSE MOIST, RED LIPS...
Oh boy...
IT'LL BE AWHILE BEFORE THEY MAKE ANY DECISIONS.
THAT'S COOL. WE'LL WAIT IN MY ROOM.
HOW'S WORK AT THE AGENCY? ANY NEW CASES?
YOU SOUND LIKE A REGULAR DETECTIVE...
!!
?!
YOSHI-TSUNE-SAN!
NEVER EVER RISK KYO'S SAFETY DOING DETECTIVE WORK!
UH... YEAH, SURE...
WHAT'S UP HIS BUTT?
HE'S WORRIED, 'CAUSE SINCE I'VE STARTED WORKING WITH YOU, I KEEP GETTING BANGED UP.
My bangs up.
I see.
Hmph!
Hmph!
HM?

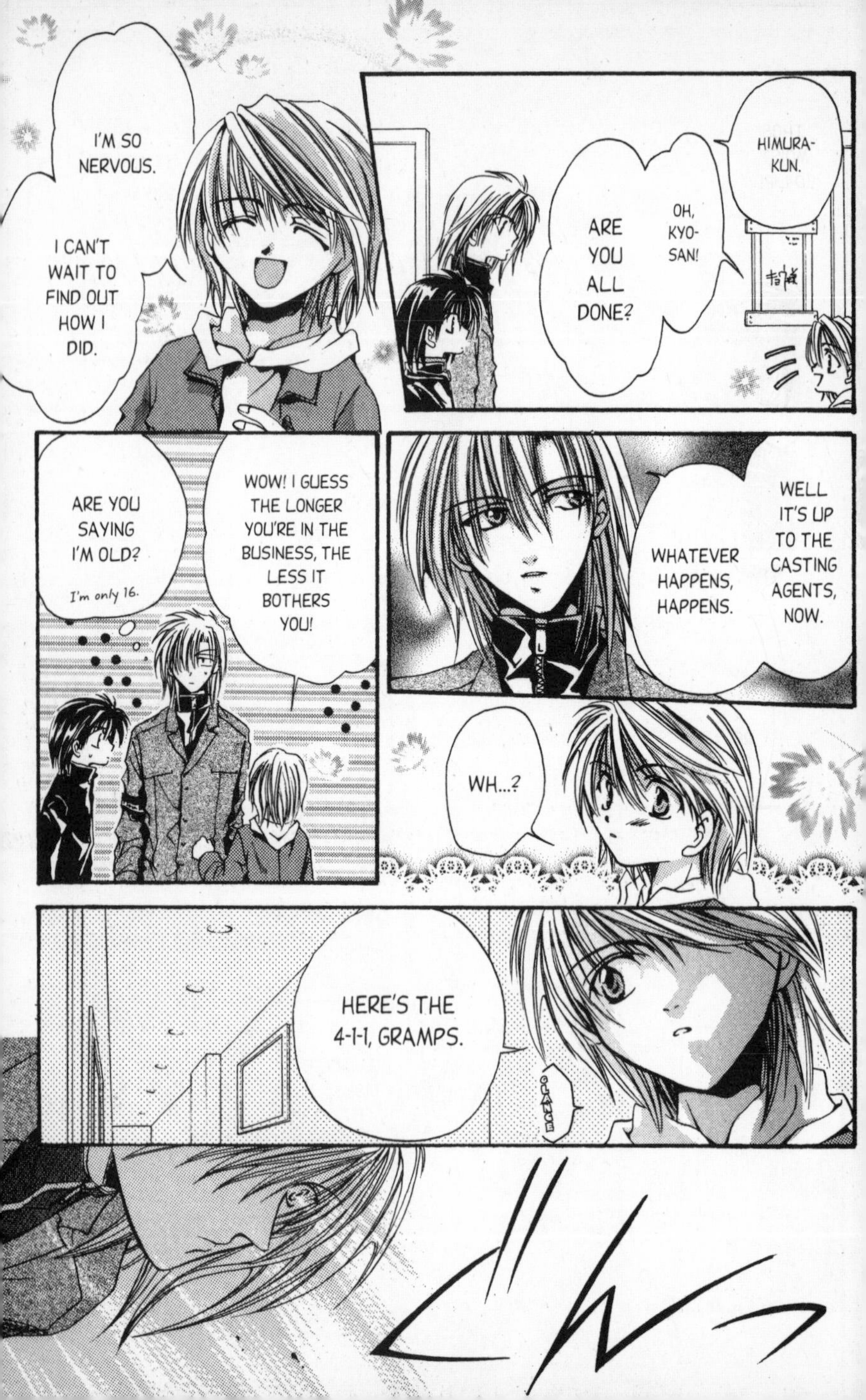

HIMURA-KUN.
OH, KYO-SAN!
ARE YOU ALL DONE?
I'M SO NERVOUS.
I CAN'T WAIT TO FIND OUT HOW I DID.
WELL IT'S UP TO THE CASTING AGENTS, NOW.
WHATEVER HAPPENS, HAPPENS.
WH...?
WOW! I GUESS THE LONGER YOU'RE IN THE BUSINESS, THE LESS IT BOTHERS YOU!
ARE YOU SAYING I'M OLD?
I'm only 16.
HERE'S THE 4-1-1, GRAMPS.
GLANCE

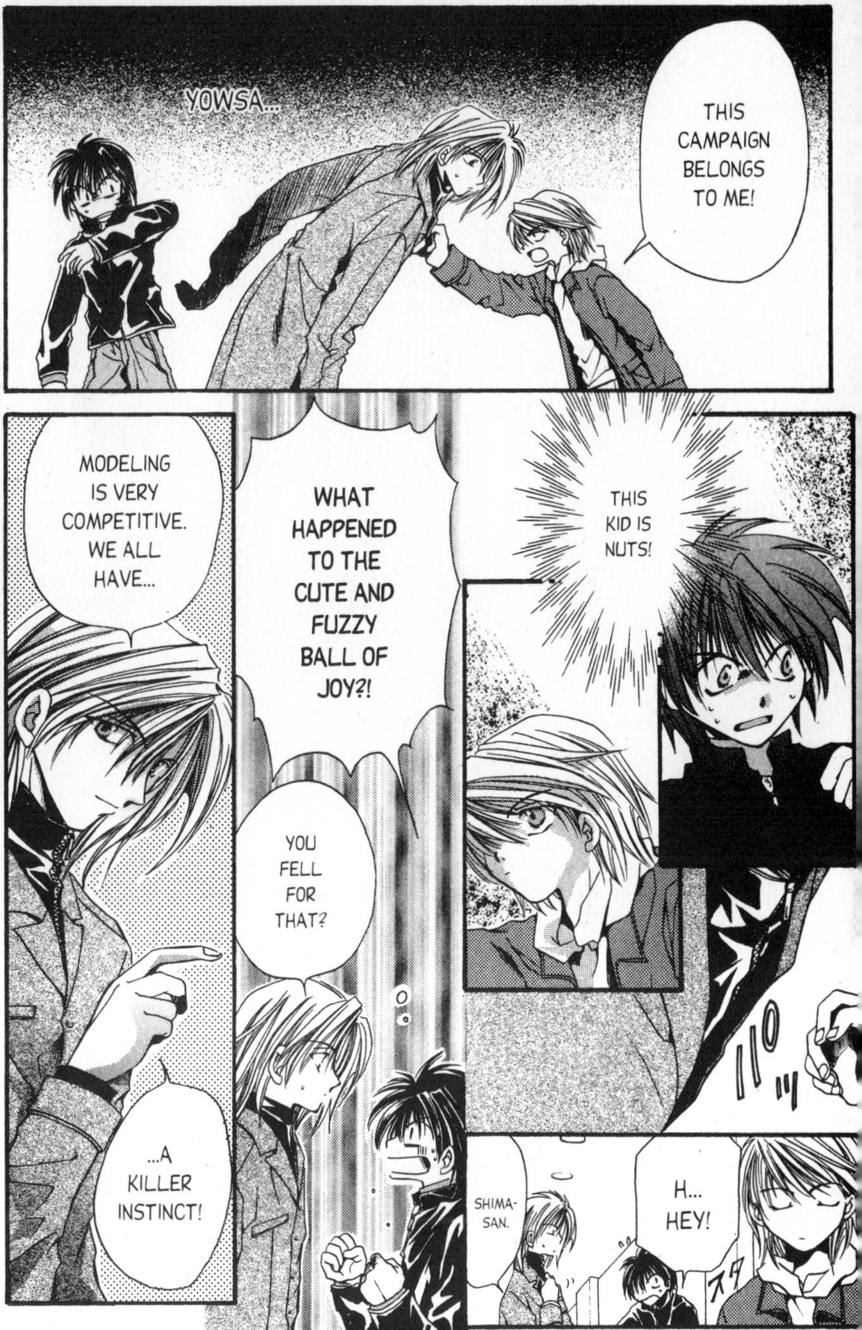
THIS CAMPAIGN BELONGS TO ME!
YOWSA...
THIS KID IS NUTS!
パッ
H... HEY!
スタ
SHIMA-SAN.
WHAT HAPPENED TO THE CUTE AND FUZZY BALL OF JOY?!
YOU FELL FOR THAT?
MODELING IS VERY COMPETITIVE. WE ALL HAVE...
...A KILLER INSTINCT!

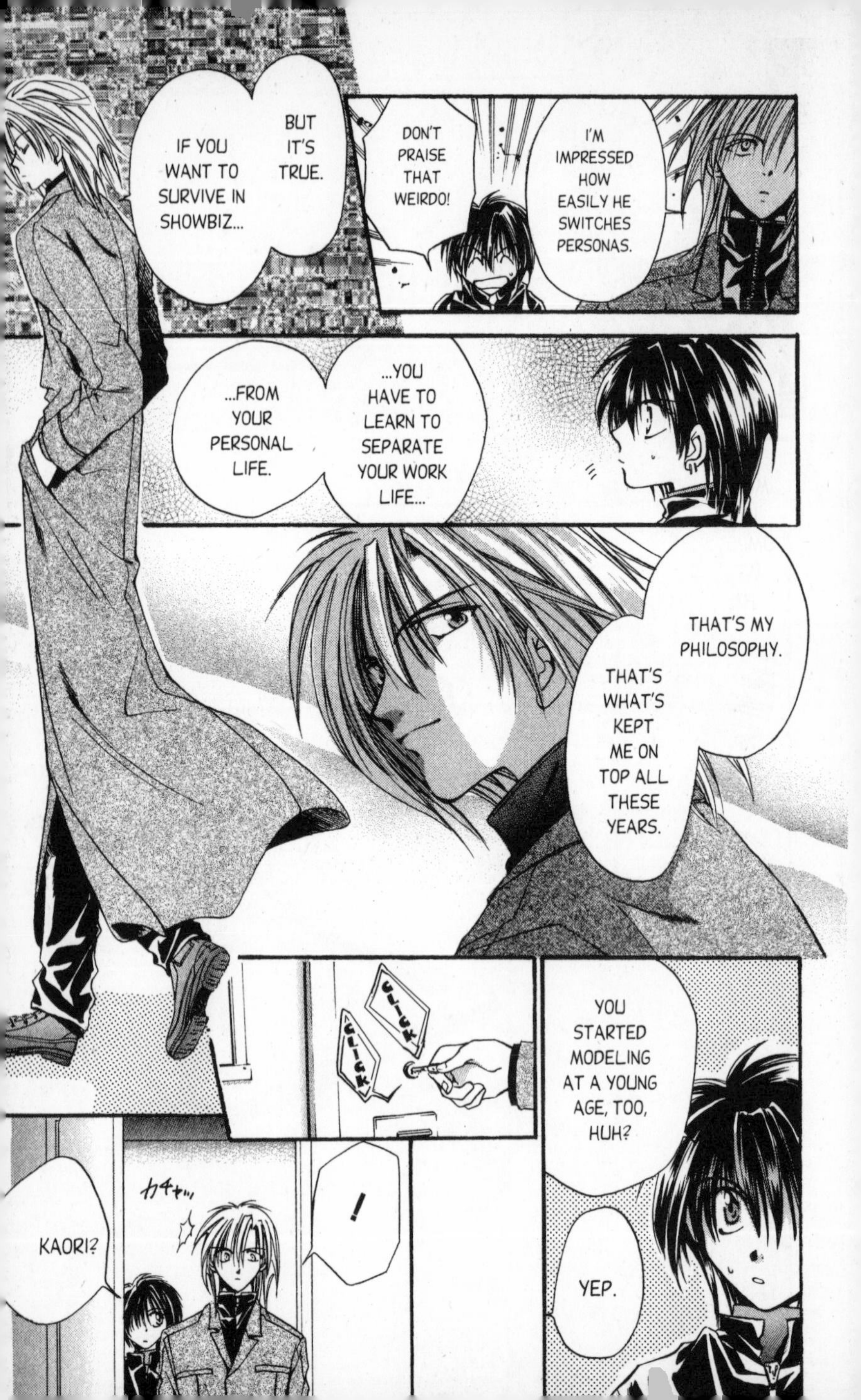
I'M IMPRESSED HOW EASILY HE SWITCHES PERSONAS.
DON'T PRAISE THAT WEIRDO!
BUT IT'S TRUE.
IF YOU WANT TO SURVIVE IN SHOWBIZ...
...YOU HAVE TO LEARN TO SEPARATE YOUR WORK LIFE...
...FROM YOUR PERSONAL LIFE.
THAT'S MY PHILOSOPHY.
THAT'S WHAT'S KEPT ME ON TOP ALL THESE YEARS.
YOU STARTED MODELING AT A YOUNG AGE, TOO, HUH?
YEP.
CLICK
CLICK
!
カチャッ
KAORI?

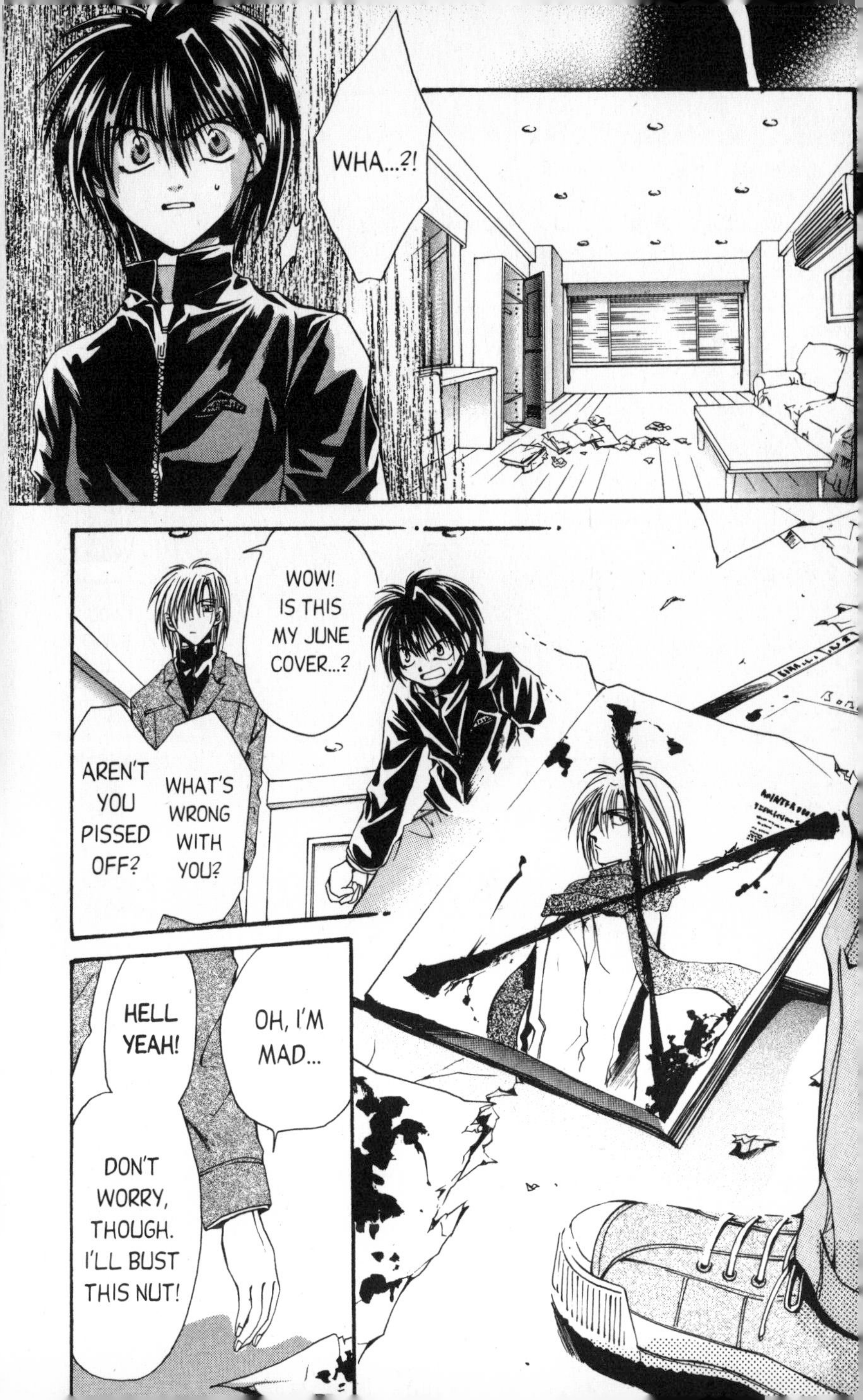
WHA...?!
WOW! IS THIS MY JUNE COVER...?
WHAT'S WRONG WITH YOU?
AREN'T YOU PISSED OFF?
OH, I'M MAD...
HELL YEAH!
DON'T WORRY, THOUGH. I'LL BUST THIS NUT!

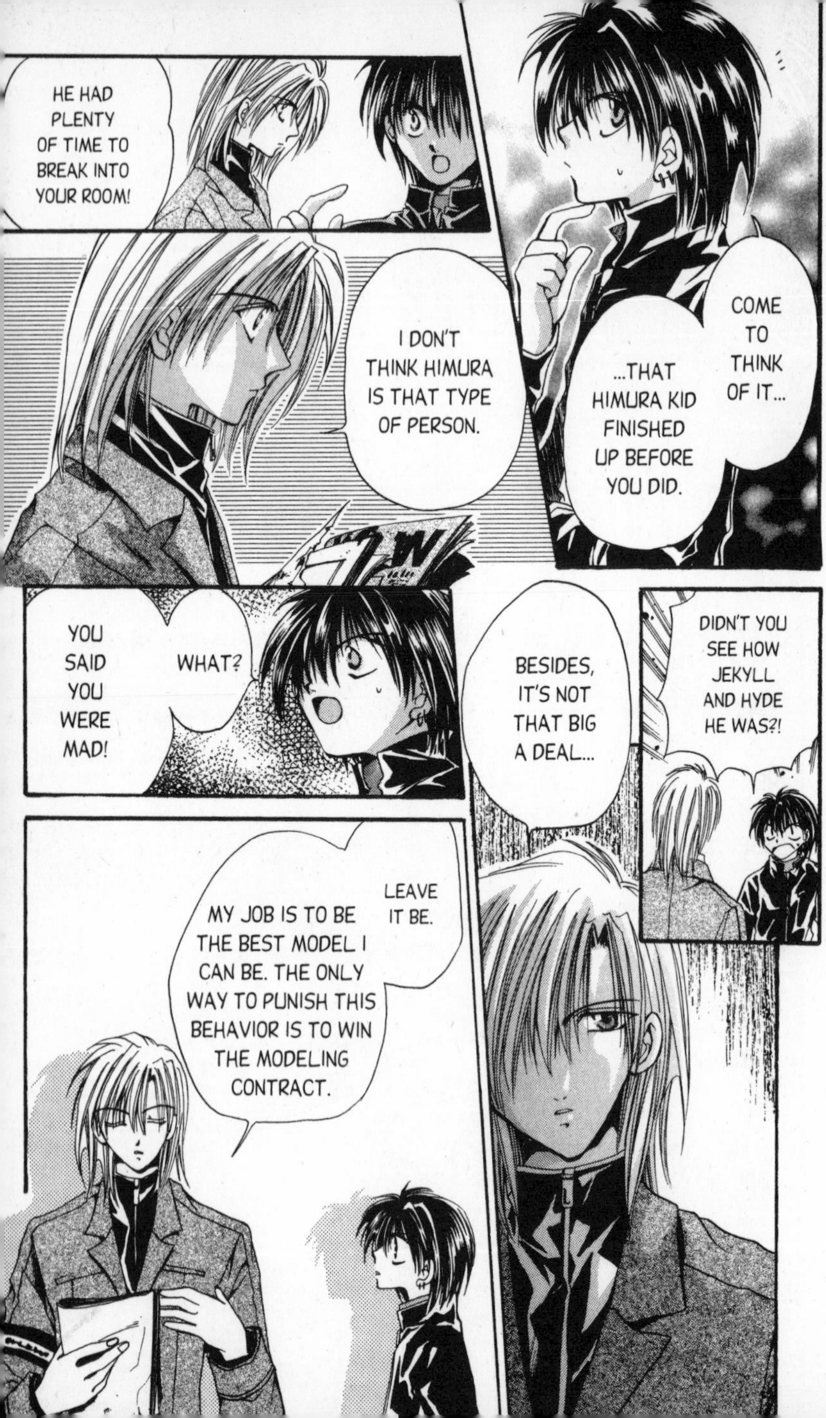
COME TO THINK OF IT...
...THAT HIMURA KID FINISHED UP BEFORE YOU DID.
HE HAD PLENTY OF TIME TO BREAK INTO YOUR ROOM!
I DON'T THINK HIMURA IS THAT TYPE OF PERSON.
DIDN'T YOU SEE HOW JEKYLL AND HYDE HE WAS?!
BESIDES, IT'S NOT THAT BIG A DEAL...
WHAT?
YOU SAID YOU WERE MAD!
LEAVE IT BE.
MY JOB IS TO BE THE BEST MODEL I CAN BE. THE ONLY WAY TO PUNISH THIS BEHAVIOR IS TO WIN THE MODELING CONTRACT.

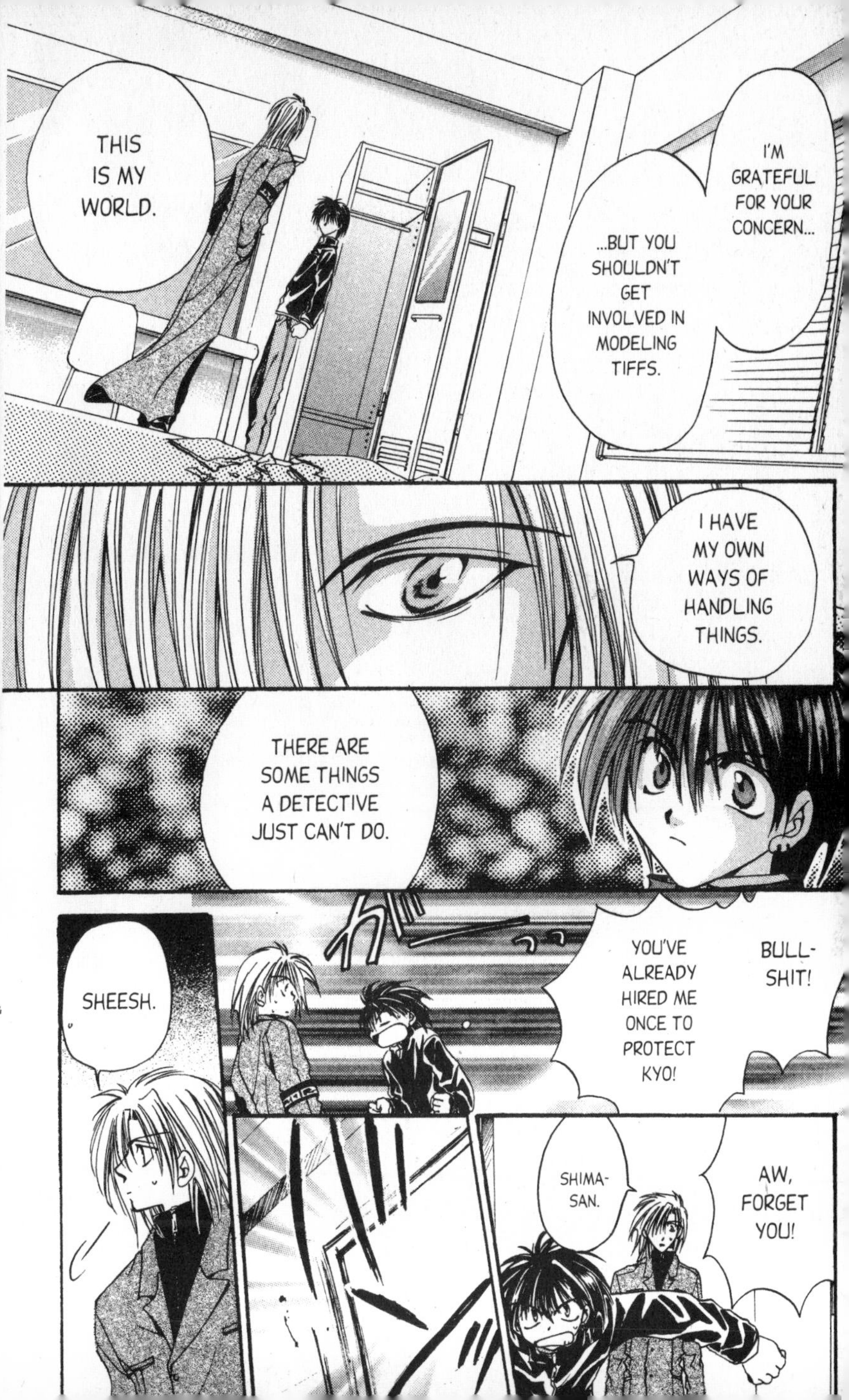
I'M GRATEFUL FOR YOUR CONCERN...
...BUT YOU SHOULDN'T GET INVOLVED IN MODELING TIFFS.
THIS IS MY WORLD.
I HAVE MY OWN WAYS OF HANDLING THINGS.
THERE ARE SOME THINGS A DETECTIVE JUST CAN'T DO.
BULL-SHIT!
YOU'VE ALREADY HIRED ME ONCE TO PROTECT KYO!
AW, FORGET YOU!
SHIMA-SAN.
SHEESH.

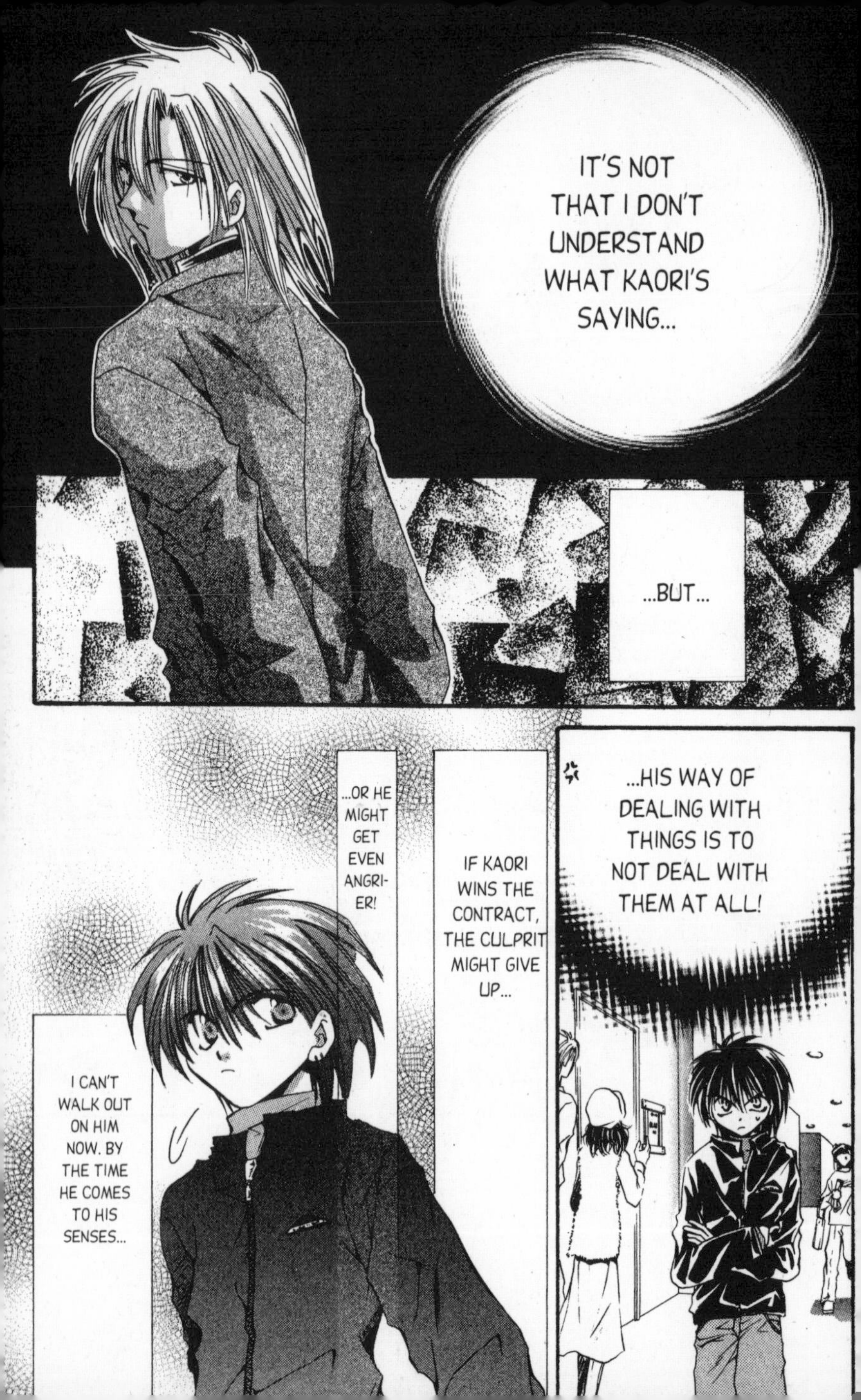
IT'S NOT THAT I DON'T UNDERSTAND WHAT KAORI'S SAYING...
...BUT...
...HIS WAY OF DEALING WITH THINGS IS TO NOT DEAL WITH THEM AT ALL!
IF KAORI WINS THE CONTRACT, THE CULPRIT MIGHT GIVE UP...
...OR HE MIGHT GET EVEN ANGRI-ER!
I CAN'T WALK OUT ON HIM NOW. BY THE TIME HE COMES TO HIS SENSES...

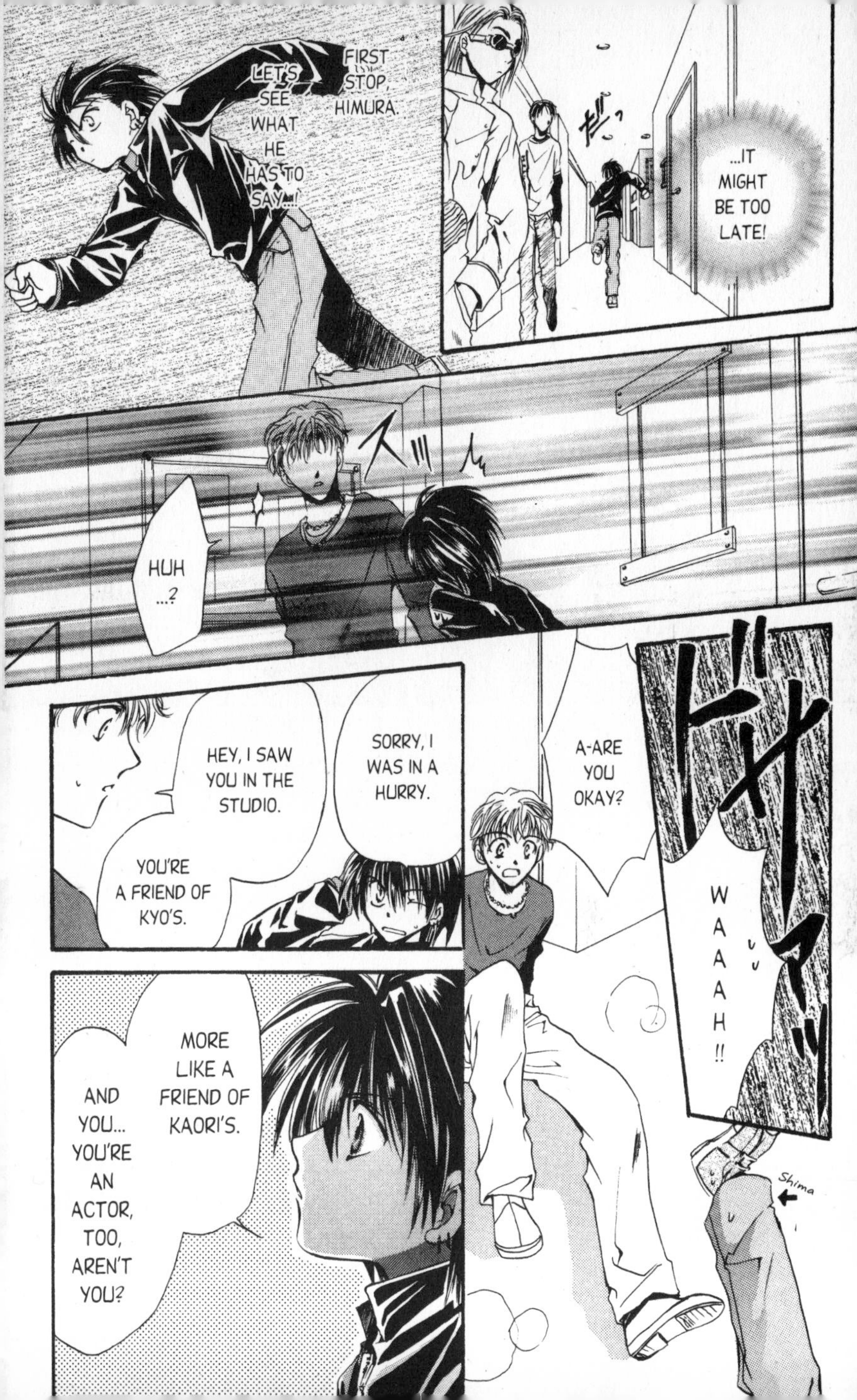
...IT MIGHT BE TOO LATE!
FIRST STOP, HIMURA.
LET'S SEE WHAT HE HAS TO SAY...!
HUH ...?
A-ARE YOU OKAY?
WAAAAH!!
Shima
SORRY, I WAS IN A HURRY.
HEY, I SAW YOU IN THE STUDIO.
YOU'RE A FRIEND OF KYO'S.
MORE LIKE A FRIEND OF KAORI'S.
AND YOU... YOU'RE AN ACTOR, TOO, AREN'T YOU?

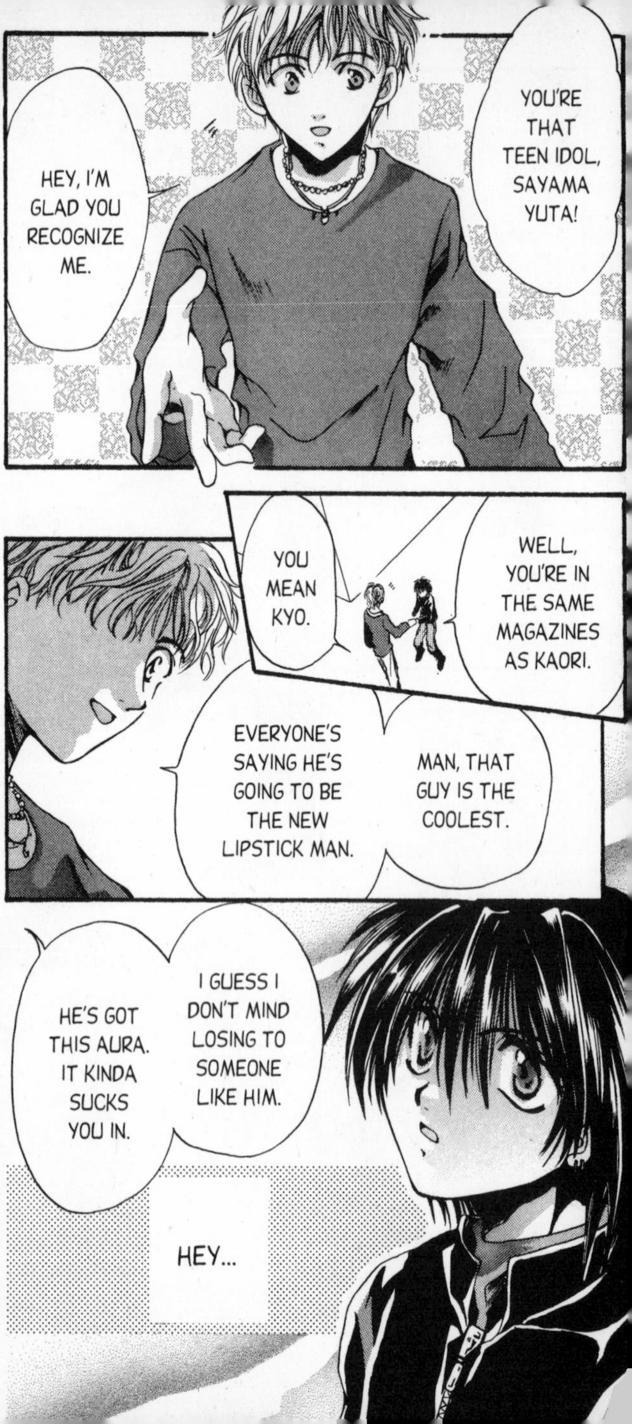
YOU'RE THAT TEEN IDOL, SAYAMA YUTA!
HEY, I'M GLAD YOU RECOGNIZE ME.
WELL, YOU'RE IN THE SAME MAGAZINES AS KAORI.
YOU MEAN KYO.
MAN, THAT GUY IS THE COOLEST.
EVERYONE'S SAYING HE'S GOING TO BE THE NEW LIPSTICK MAN.
I GUESS I DON'T MIND LOSING TO SOMEONE LIKE HIM.
HE'S GOT THIS AURA. IT KINDA SUCKS YOU IN.
HEY...

Hi ho! Ryo Saenagi here. Welcome to volume 3! Two books was cool--three books is an additional 50% rockin'! The back cover for this book is Kaori and APP. At first, I wanted to draw Kaori alone, but then I wanted to put APP in there too, so I did it! (Hee hee!) Come on, I don't get to draw in color that much, anyway! A lot of you have been asking about Kaori's hair color. To be honest, I'm just not sure... For now, let's say it's greenish. (Gray is cool, too.) A while back, SMAP's Katori-kun's hair was dyed a similar color, and I thought that was the closest color ever. Kaori's eyes are green too, so when he stands next to Shima, he totally looks like a Japanese leprechaun. When *Satisfaction Guaranteed* was first printed in the magazines, they offered to let me draw the preview page in color. At that time, I didn't think too much about hair color or anything. Live and learn.

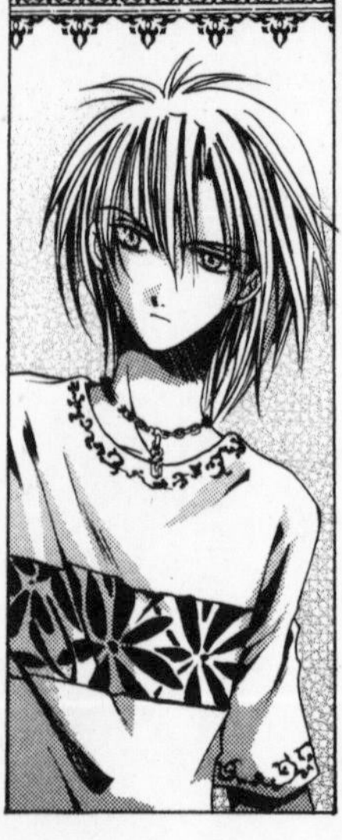

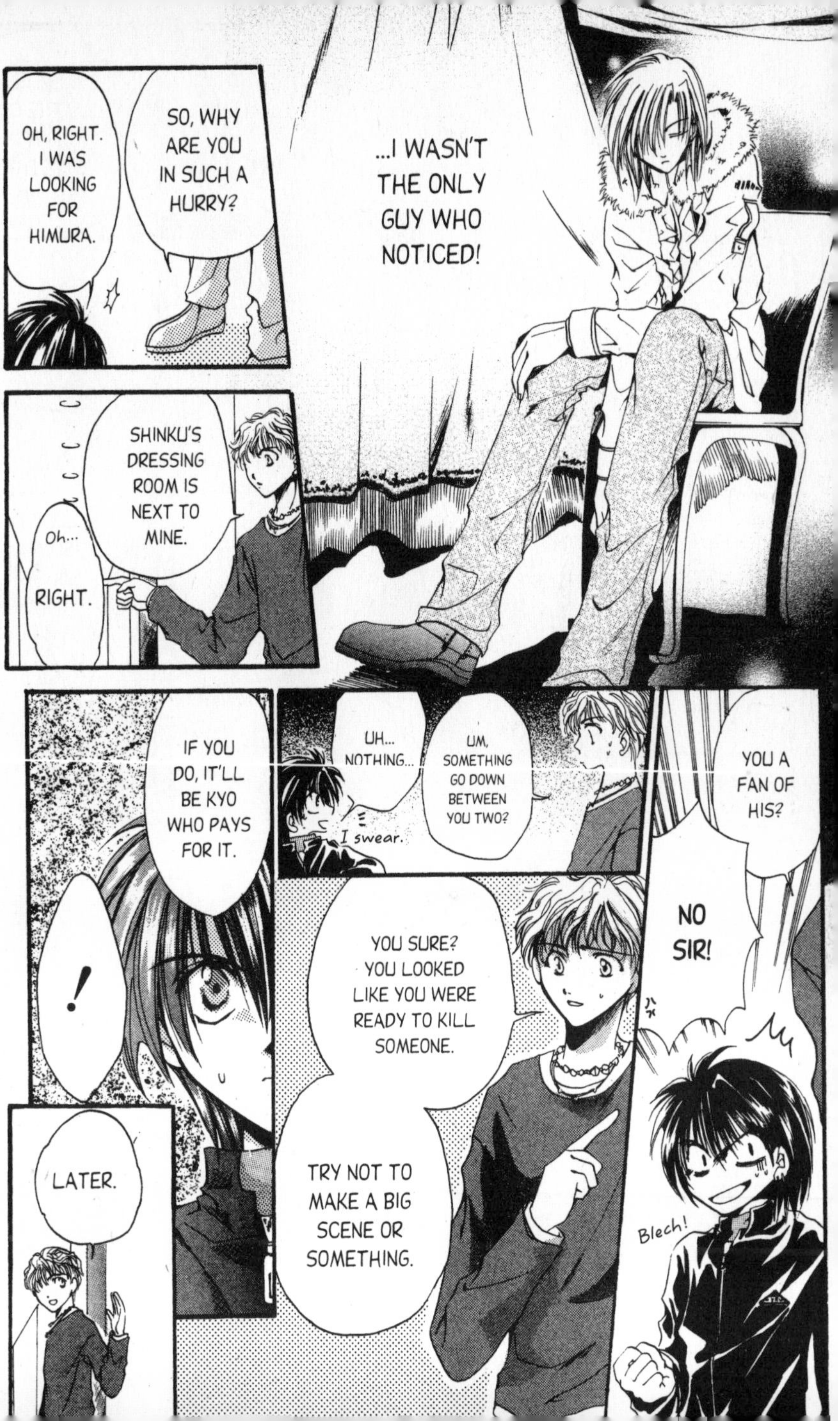
...I WASN'T THE ONLY GUY WHO NOTICED!
SO, WHY ARE YOU IN SUCH A HURRY?
OH, RIGHT. I WAS LOOKING FOR HIMURA.
SHINKU'S DRESSING ROOM IS NEXT TO MINE.
Oh...
RIGHT.
YOU A FAN OF HIS?
NO SIR!
Blech!
UM, SOMETHING GO DOWN BETWEEN YOU TWO?
UH... NOTHING...
I swear.
YOU SURE? YOU LOOKED LIKE YOU WERE READY TO KILL SOMEONE.
TRY NOT TO MAKE A BIG SCENE OR SOMETHING.
IF YOU DO, IT'LL BE KYO WHO PAYS FOR IT.
!
LATER.

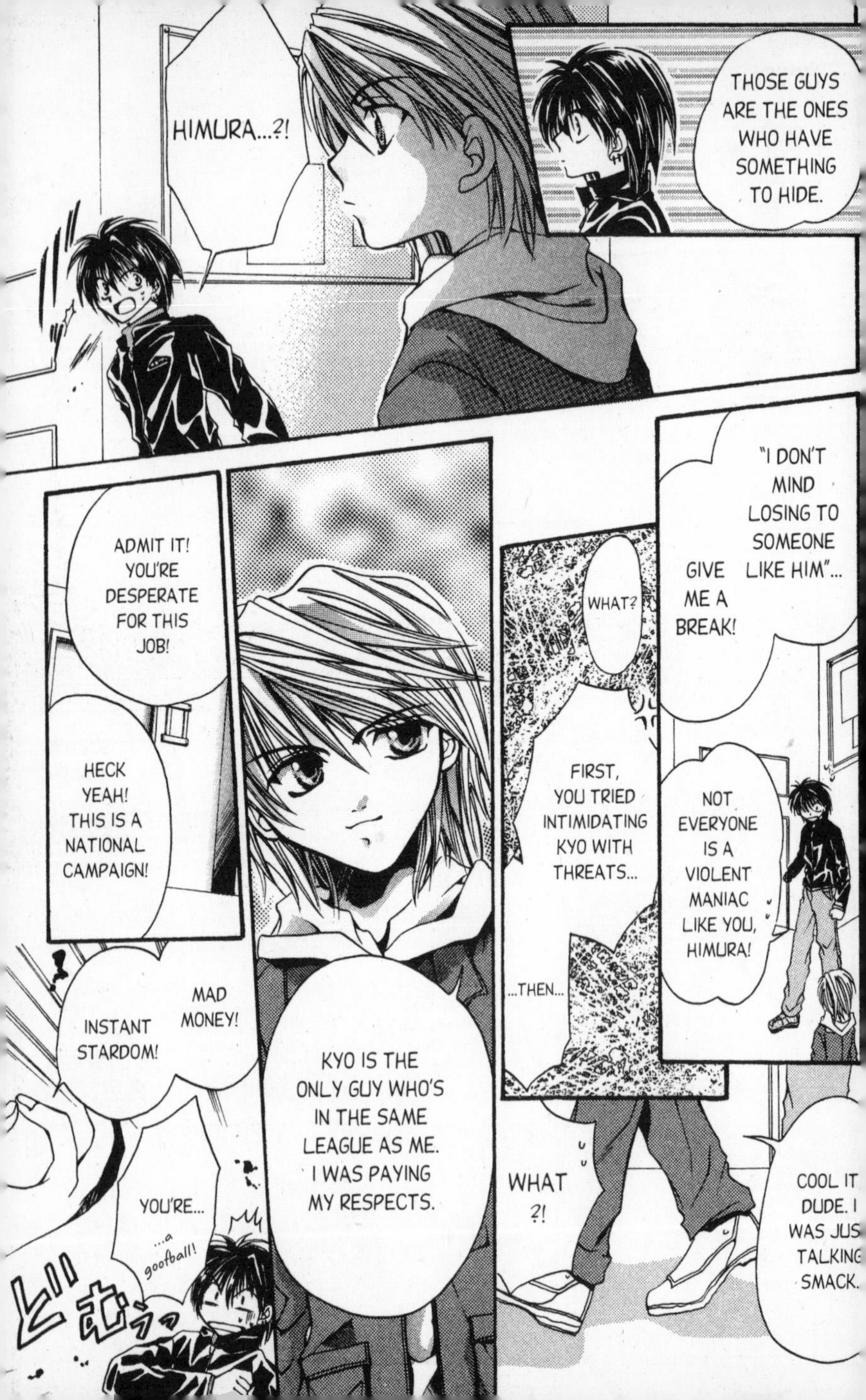

THOSE GUYS ARE THE ONES WHO HAVE SOMETHING TO HIDE.
HIMURA...?!
"I DON'T MIND LOSING TO SOMEONE LIKE HIM"...
GIVE ME A BREAK!
NOT EVERYONE IS A VIOLENT MANIAC LIKE YOU, HIMURA!
COOL IT DUDE. I WAS JUS TALKING SMACK.
WHAT ?!
WHAT?
FIRST, YOU TRIED INTIMIDATING KYO WITH THREATS...
...THEN...
KYO IS THE ONLY GUY WHO'S IN THE SAME LEAGUE AS ME. I WAS PAYING MY RESPECTS.
ADMIT IT! YOU'RE DESPERATE FOR THIS JOB!
HECK YEAH! THIS IS A NATIONAL CAMPAIGN!
MAD MONEY!
INSTANT STARDOM!
YOU'RE...
...a goofball!

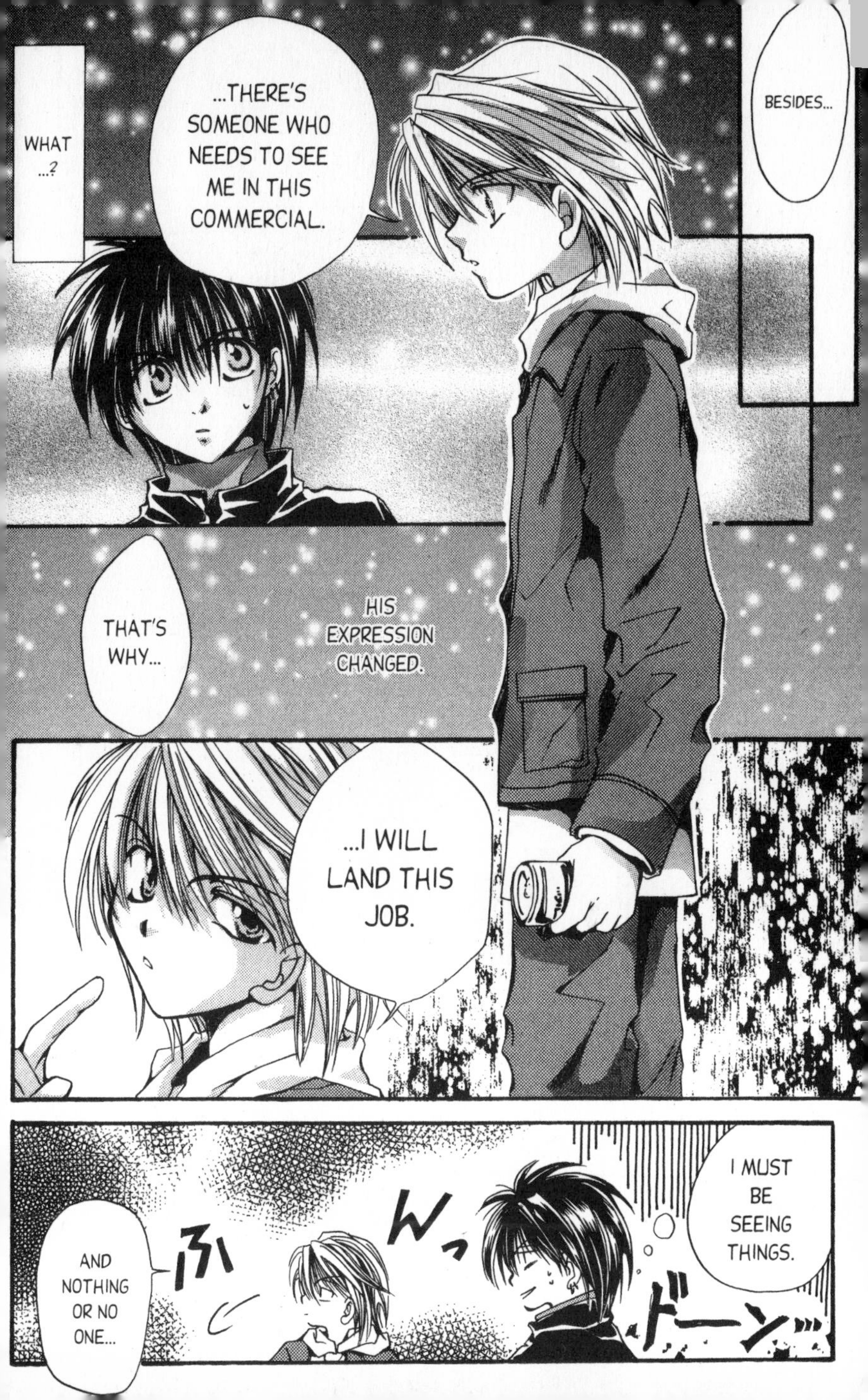
BESIDES...
...THERE'S SOMEONE WHO NEEDS TO SEE ME IN THIS COMMERCIAL.
WHAT ...?
HIS EXPRESSION CHANGED.
THAT'S WHY...
...I WILL LAND THIS JOB.
I MUST BE SEEING THINGS.
ドーン
んっ
ふ
AND NOTHING OR NO ONE...

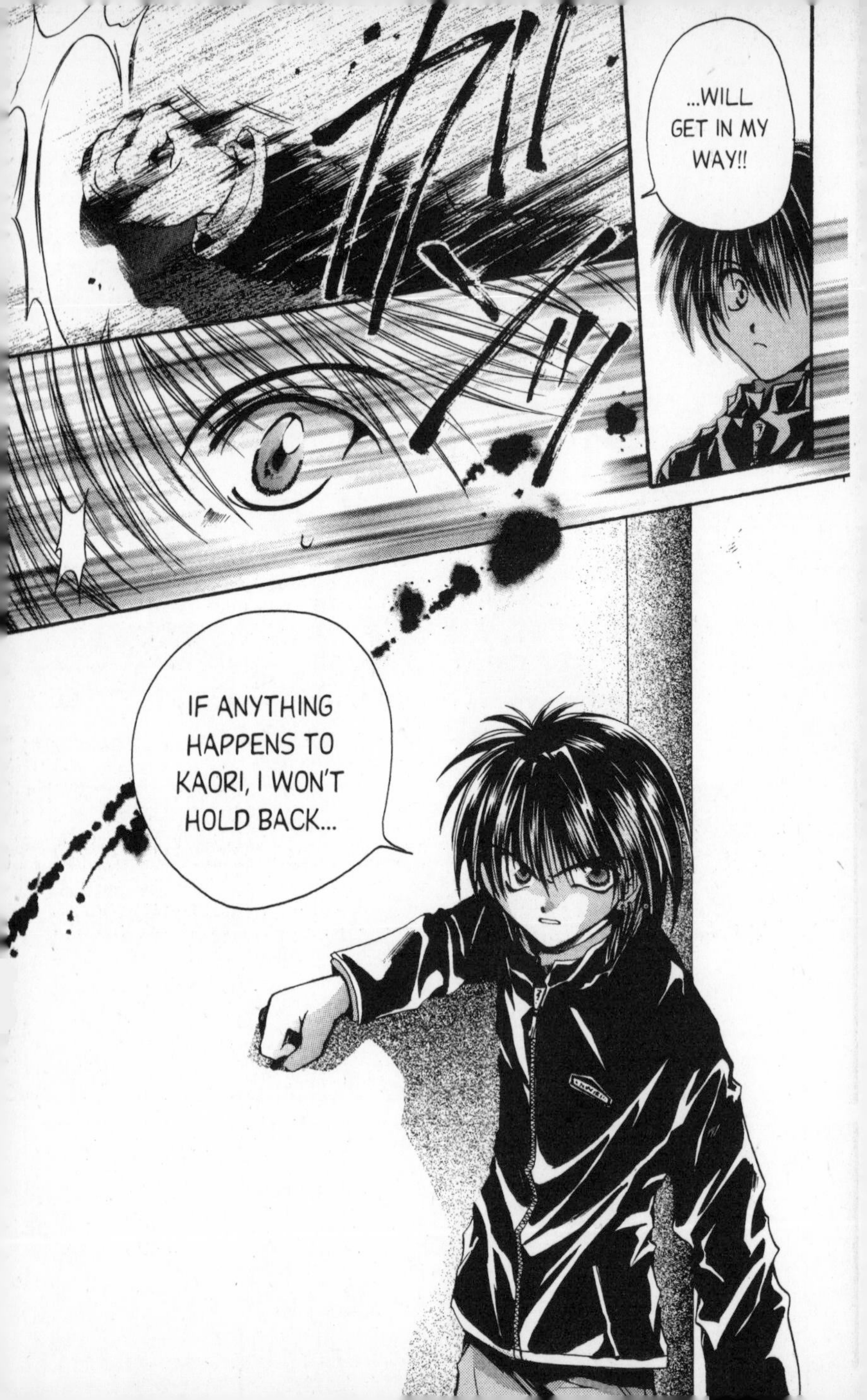
...WILL GET IN MY WAY!!
IF ANYTHING HAPPENS TO KAORI, I WON'T HOLD BACK...

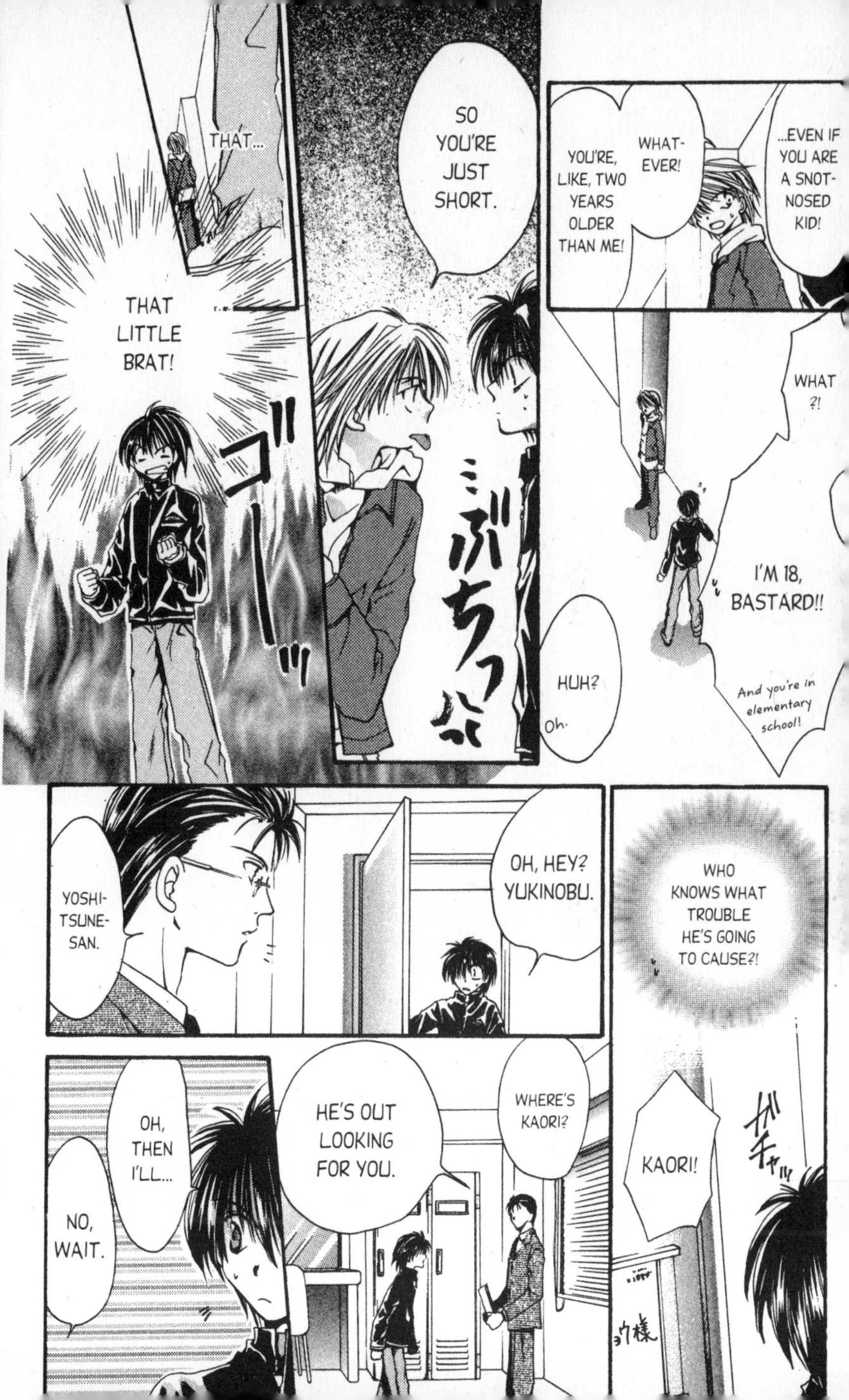
...EVEN IF YOU ARE A SNOT-NOSED KID!
WHAT-EVER!
YOU'RE, LIKE, TWO YEARS OLDER THAN ME!
WHAT?!
I'M 18, BASTARD!!
And you're in elementary school!
HUH?
Oh.
SO YOU'RE JUST SHORT.
ぶちっ
THAT...
THAT LITTLE BRAT!
ゴーッ
WHO KNOWS WHAT TROUBLE HE'S GOING TO CAUSE?!
ガチャ
KAORI!
OH, HEY? YUKINOBU.
YOSHI-TSUNE-SAN.
WHERE'S KAORI?
HE'S OUT LOOKING FOR YOU.
OH, THEN I'LL...
NO, WAIT.

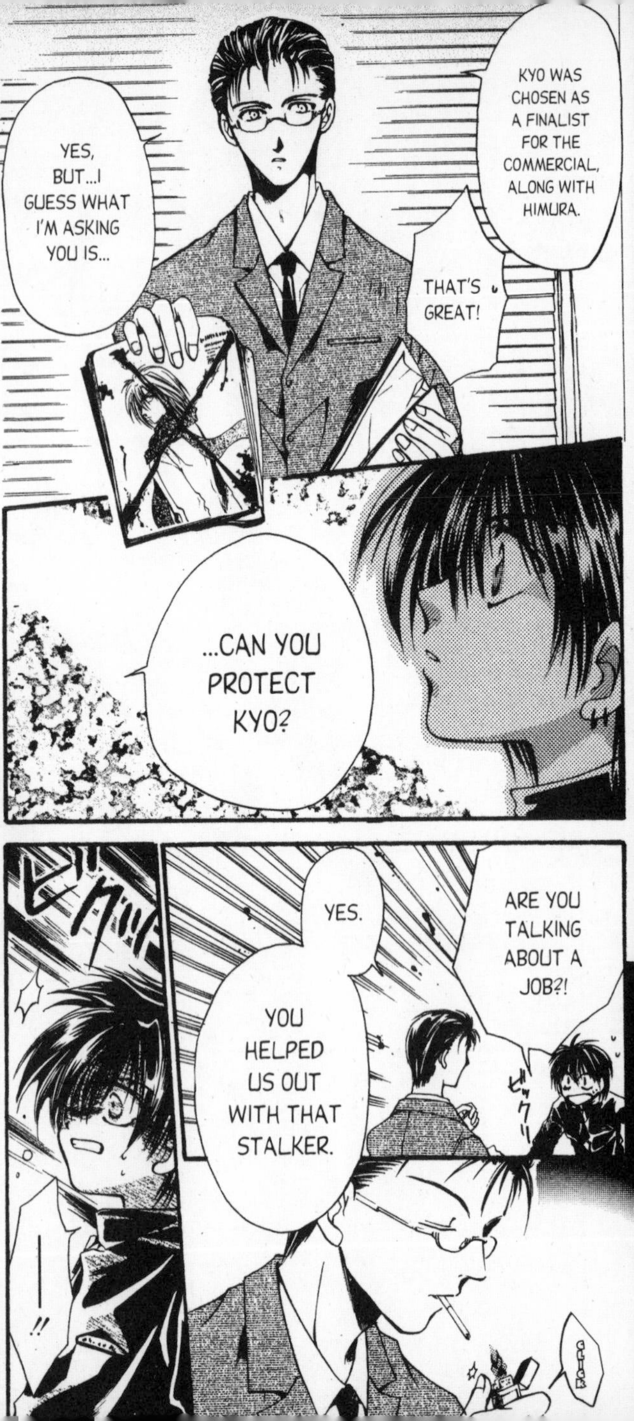
KYO WAS CHOSEN AS A FINALIST FOR THE COMMERCIAL, ALONG WITH HIMURA.
THAT'S GREAT!
YES, BUT...I GUESS WHAT I'M ASKING YOU IS...
...CAN YOU PROTECT KYO?
ARE YOU TALKING ABOUT A JOB?!
YES.
YOU HELPED US OUT WITH THAT STALKER.
!!
CLICK

I never really did color illustrations until one of my classmates got me started. She was much better than me, so I considered her the master of coloring! If it wasn't for Master, I never would've learned how to color properly. (Not that I'm perfect now, either.) Thank you, Master Kazuki. It's crazy, but I didn't start doing "manga" seriously until high school. Before that, I barely touched a pen.

All I ever did was just doodle in my notebook with a pencil. I started this manga series that I kept working on 'til...well, I guess I never stopped. Luckily, I don't have time to draw it much anymore. Only a handful of people know about it, thank goodness!

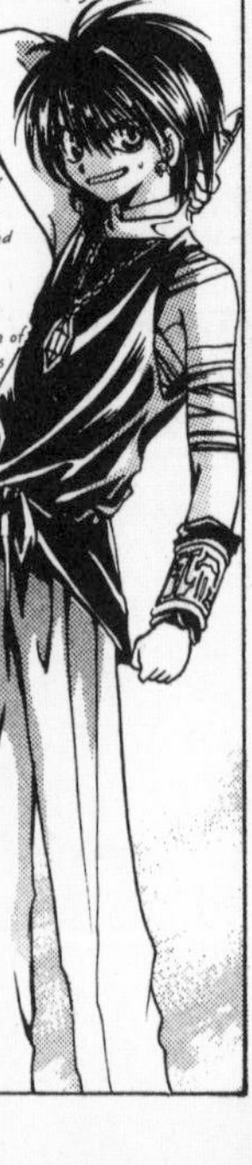

The main character of my notebook manga looked kinda like Shima...or exactly like! This was one of the costumes he wore.

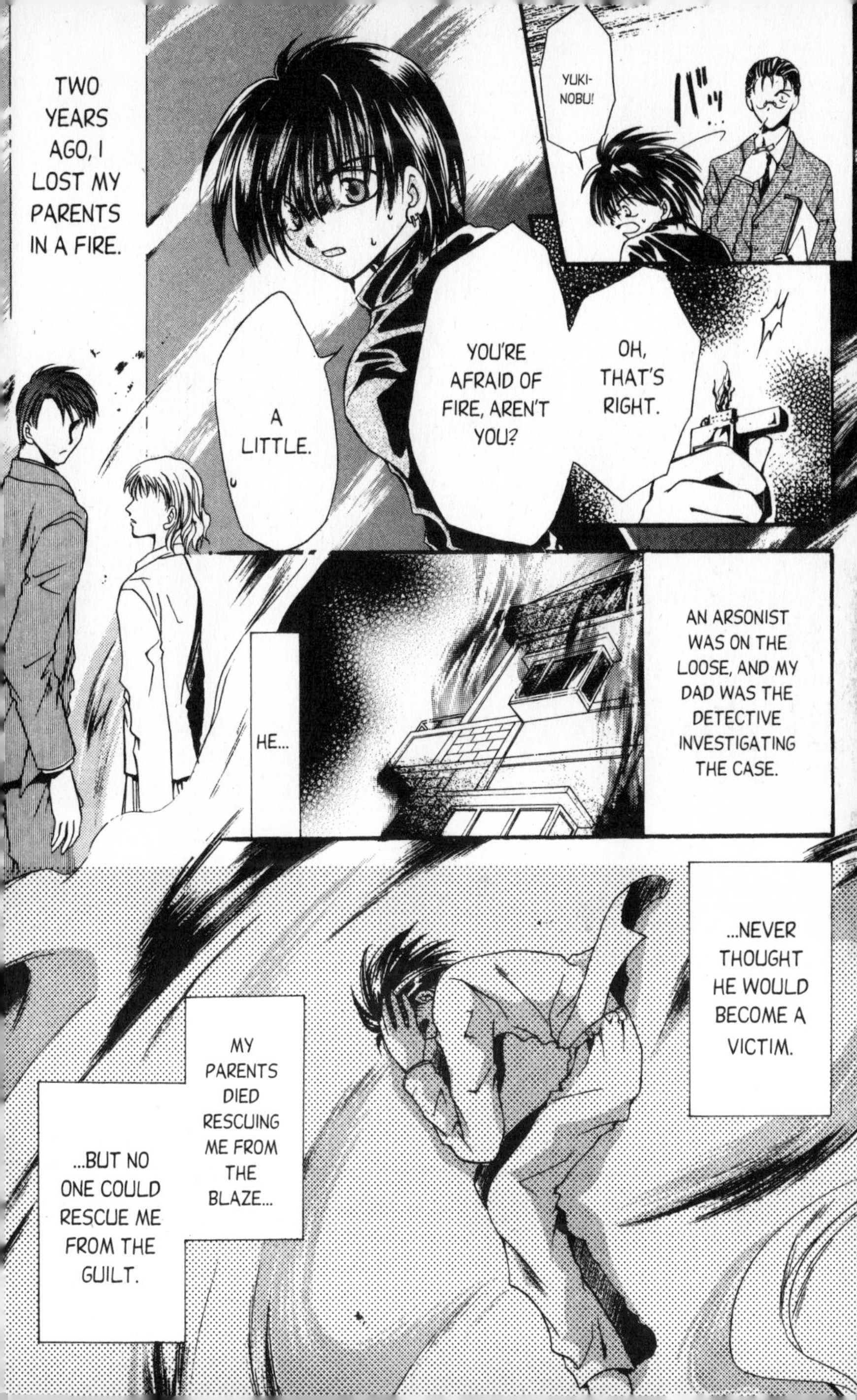
YUKI-NOBU!
バッ
OH, THAT'S RIGHT.
YOU'RE AFRAID OF FIRE, AREN'T YOU?
A LITTLE.
TWO YEARS AGO, I LOST MY PARENTS IN A FIRE.
AN ARSONIST WAS ON THE LOOSE, AND MY DAD WAS THE DETECTIVE INVESTIGATING THE CASE.
HE...
...NEVER THOUGHT HE WOULD BECOME A VICTIM.
MY PARENTS DIED RESCUING ME FROM THE BLAZE...
...BUT NO ONE COULD RESCUE ME FROM THE GUILT.

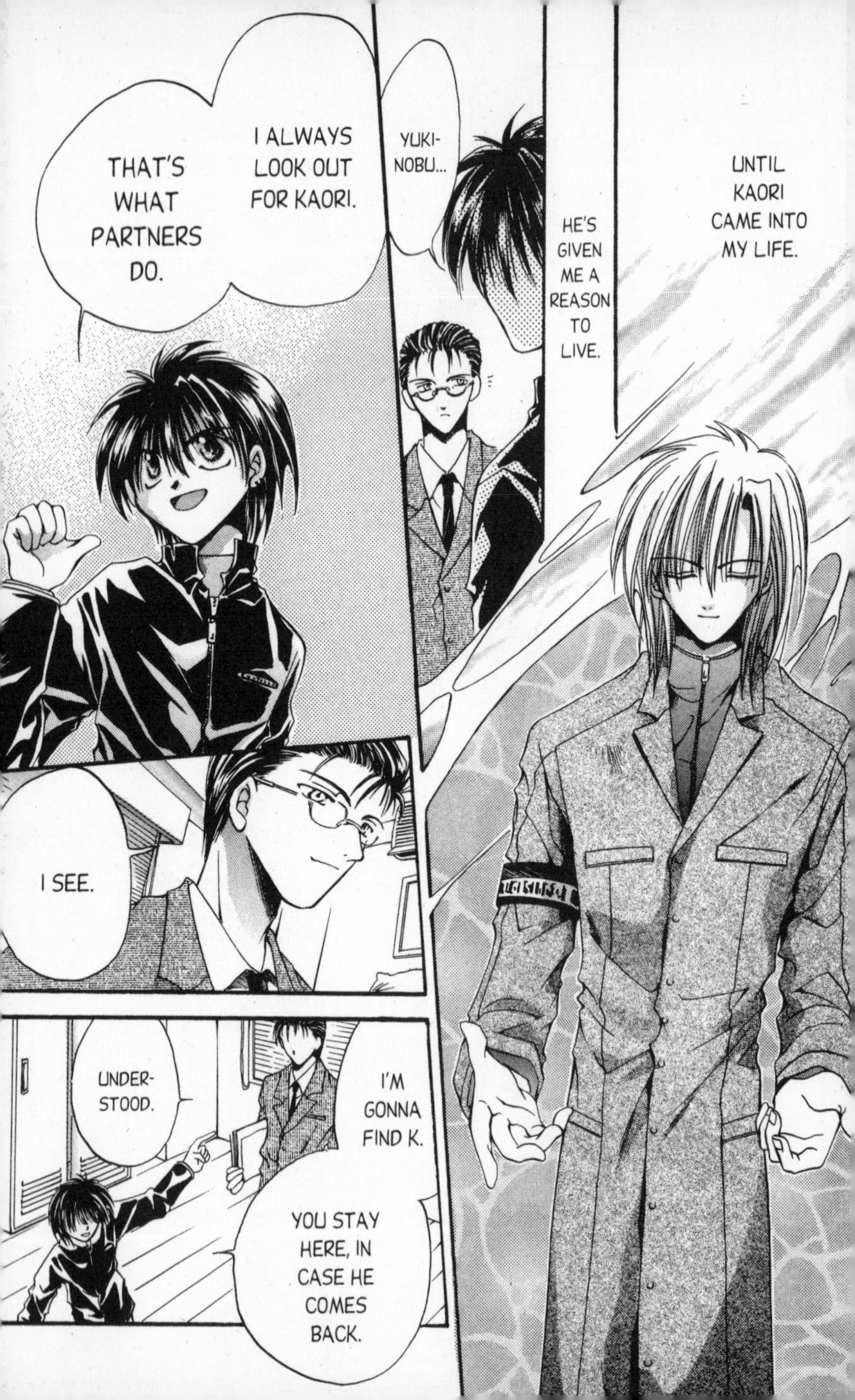
UNTIL KAORI CAME INTO MY LIFE.
HE'S GIVEN ME A REASON TO LIVE.
YUKI-NOBU...
I ALWAYS LOOK OUT FOR KAORI.
THAT'S WHAT PARTNERS DO.
I SEE.
I'M GONNA FIND K.
YOU STAY HERE, IN CASE HE COMES BACK.
UNDER-STOOD.

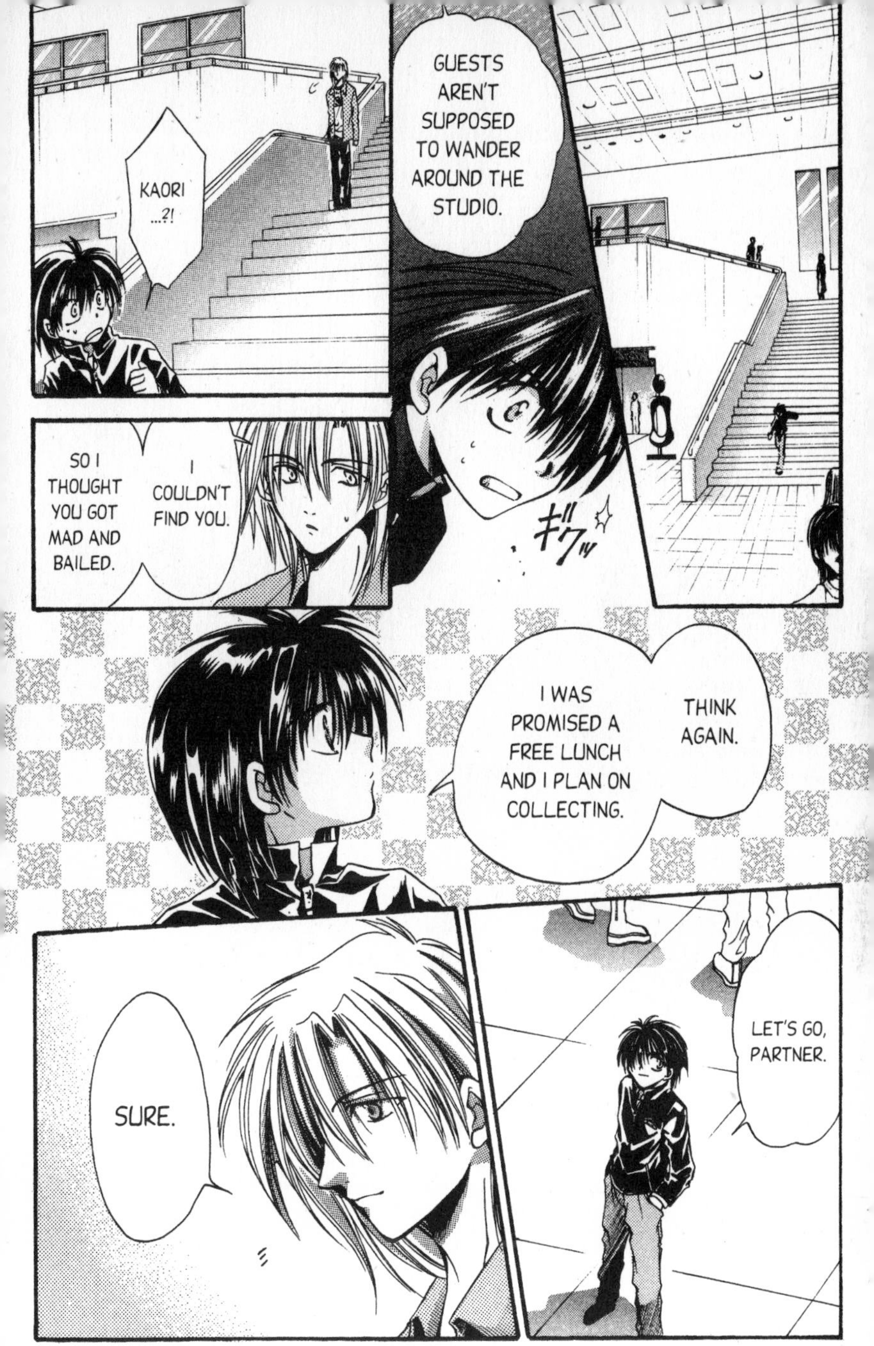
GUESTS AREN'T SUPPOSED TO WANDER AROUND THE STUDIO.
ギクッ
KAORI ...?!
I COULDN'T FIND YOU.
SO I THOUGHT YOU GOT MAD AND BAILED.
THINK AGAIN.
I WAS PROMISED A FREE LUNCH AND I PLAN ON COLLECTING.
LET'S GO, PARTNER.
SURE.

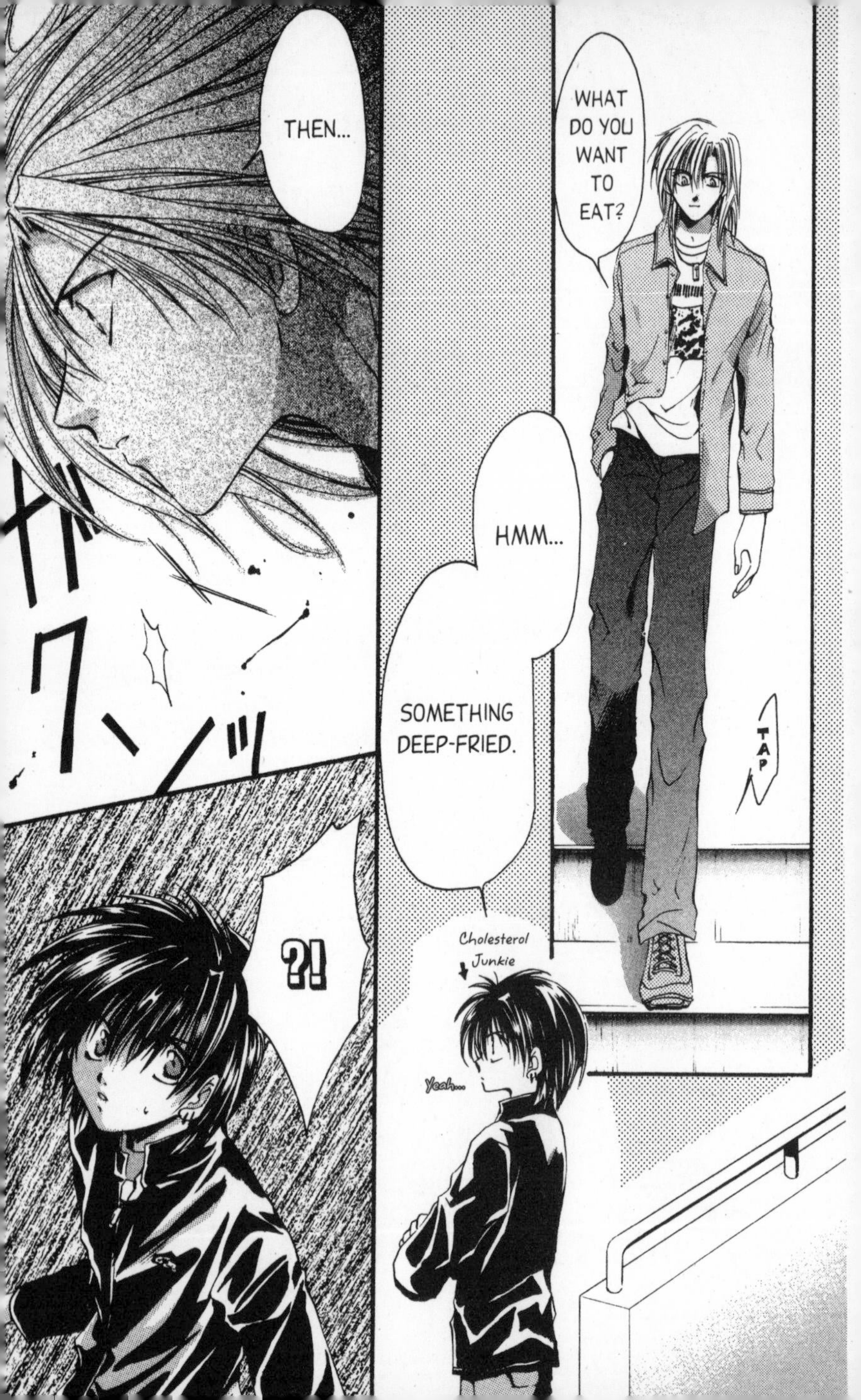
WHAT DO YOU WANT TO EAT?
HMM...
SOMETHING DEEP-FRIED.
TAP
Cholesterol Junkie
Yeah...
THEN...
?!

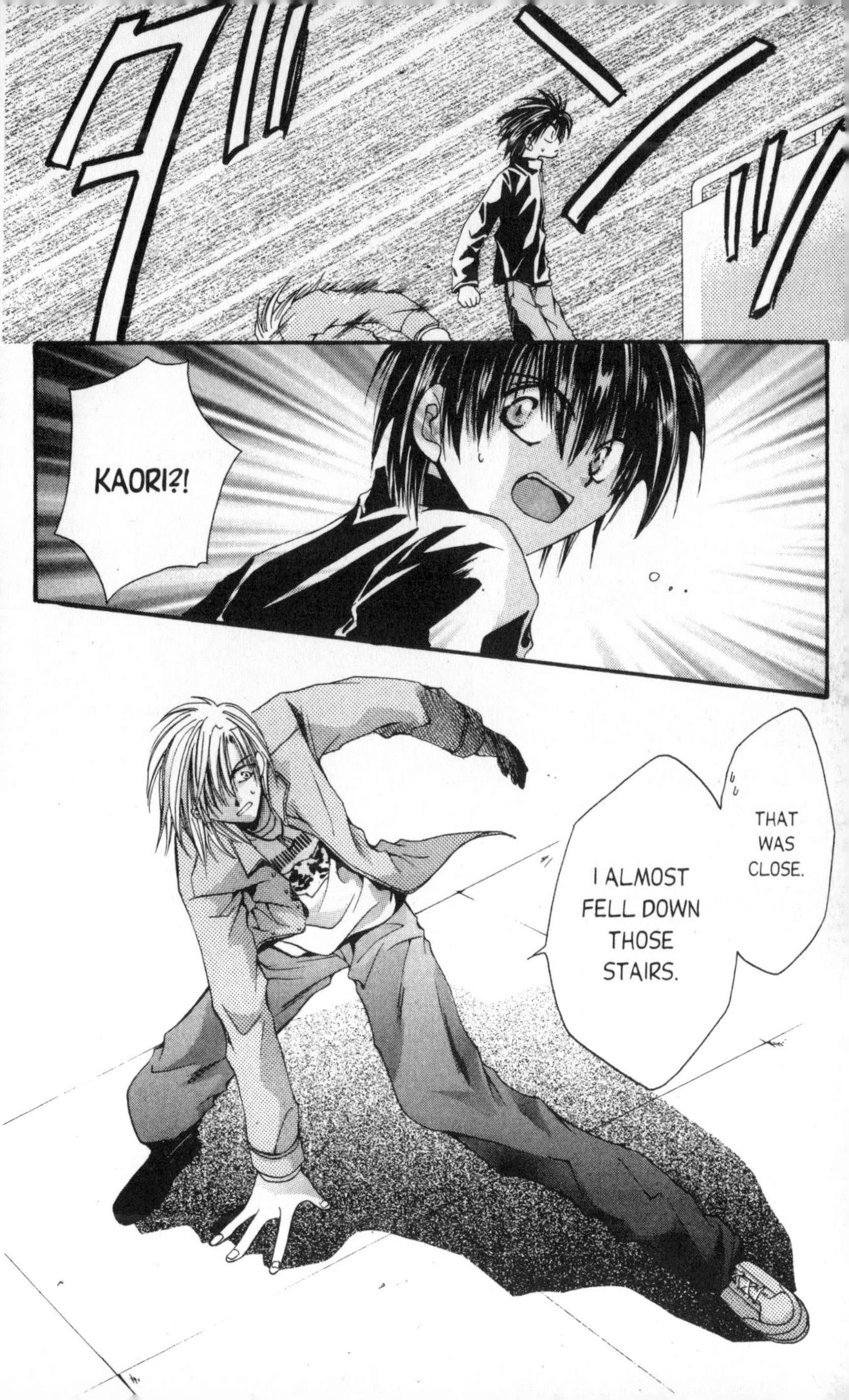
KAORI?!
THAT WAS CLOSE.
I ALMOST FELL DOWN THOSE STAIRS.

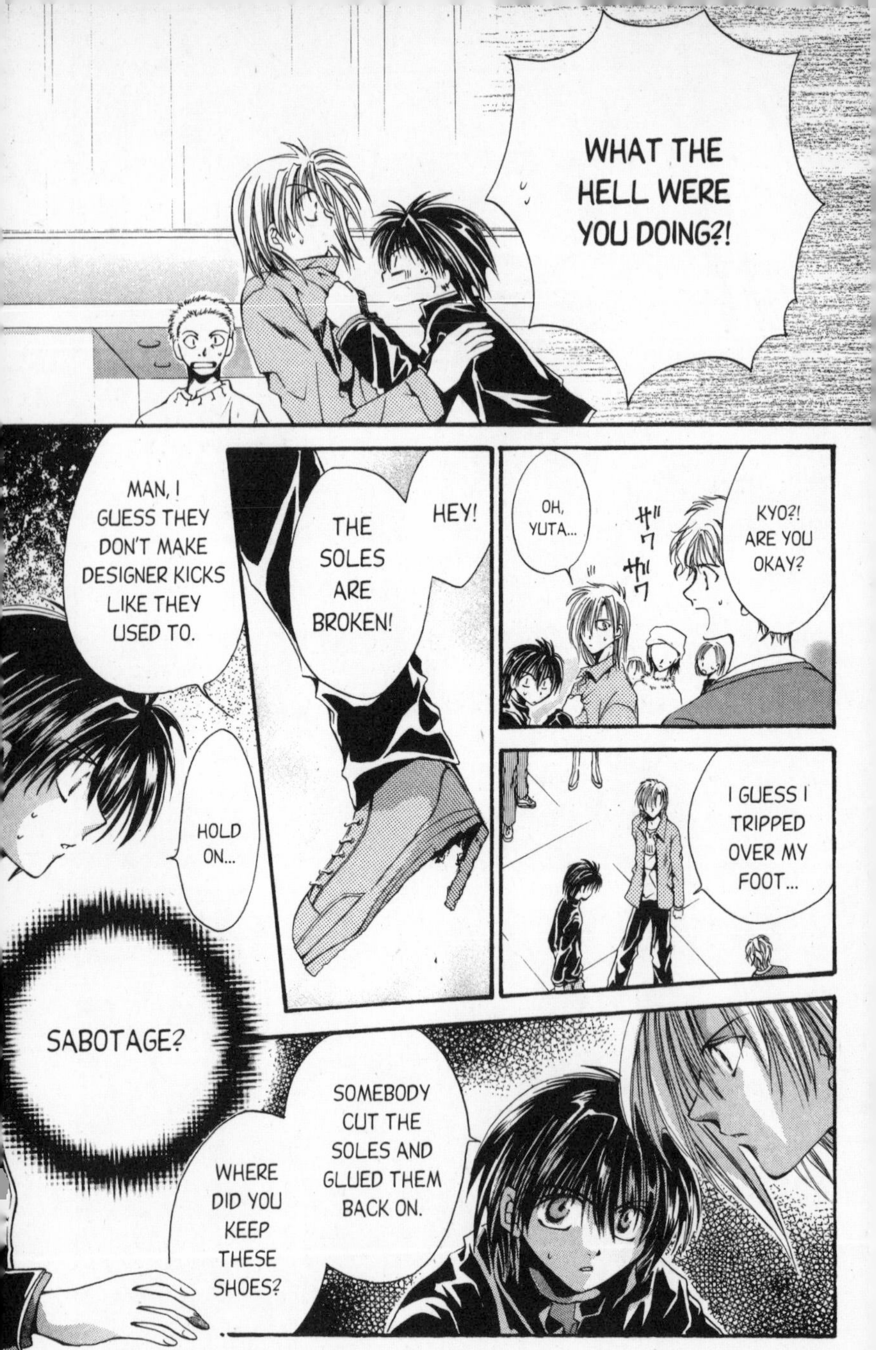
WHAT THE HELL WERE YOU DOING?!
KYO?! ARE YOU OKAY?
ザワザワ
OH, YUTA...
I GUESS I TRIPPED OVER MY FOOT...
HEY!
THE SOLES ARE BROKEN!
MAN, I GUESS THEY DON'T MAKE DESIGNER KICKS LIKE THEY USED TO.
HOLD ON...
SABOTAGE?
SOMEBODY CUT THE SOLES AND GLUED THEM BACK ON.
WHERE DID YOU KEEP THESE SHOES?

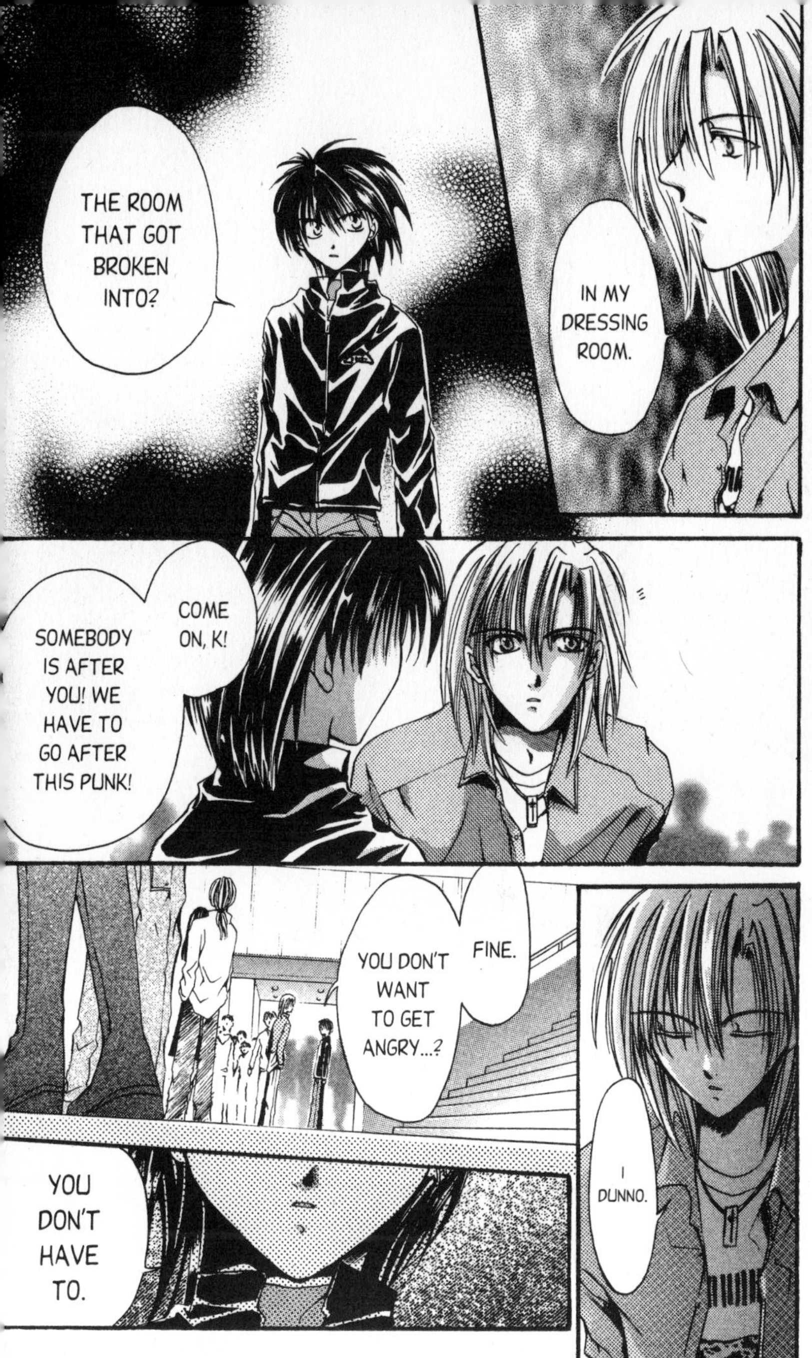
IN MY DRESSING ROOM.
THE ROOM THAT GOT BROKEN INTO?
COME ON, K!
SOMEBODY IS AFTER YOU! WE HAVE TO GO AFTER THIS PUNK!
I DUNNO.
FINE.
YOU DON'T WANT TO GET ANGRY...?
YOU DON'T HAVE TO.

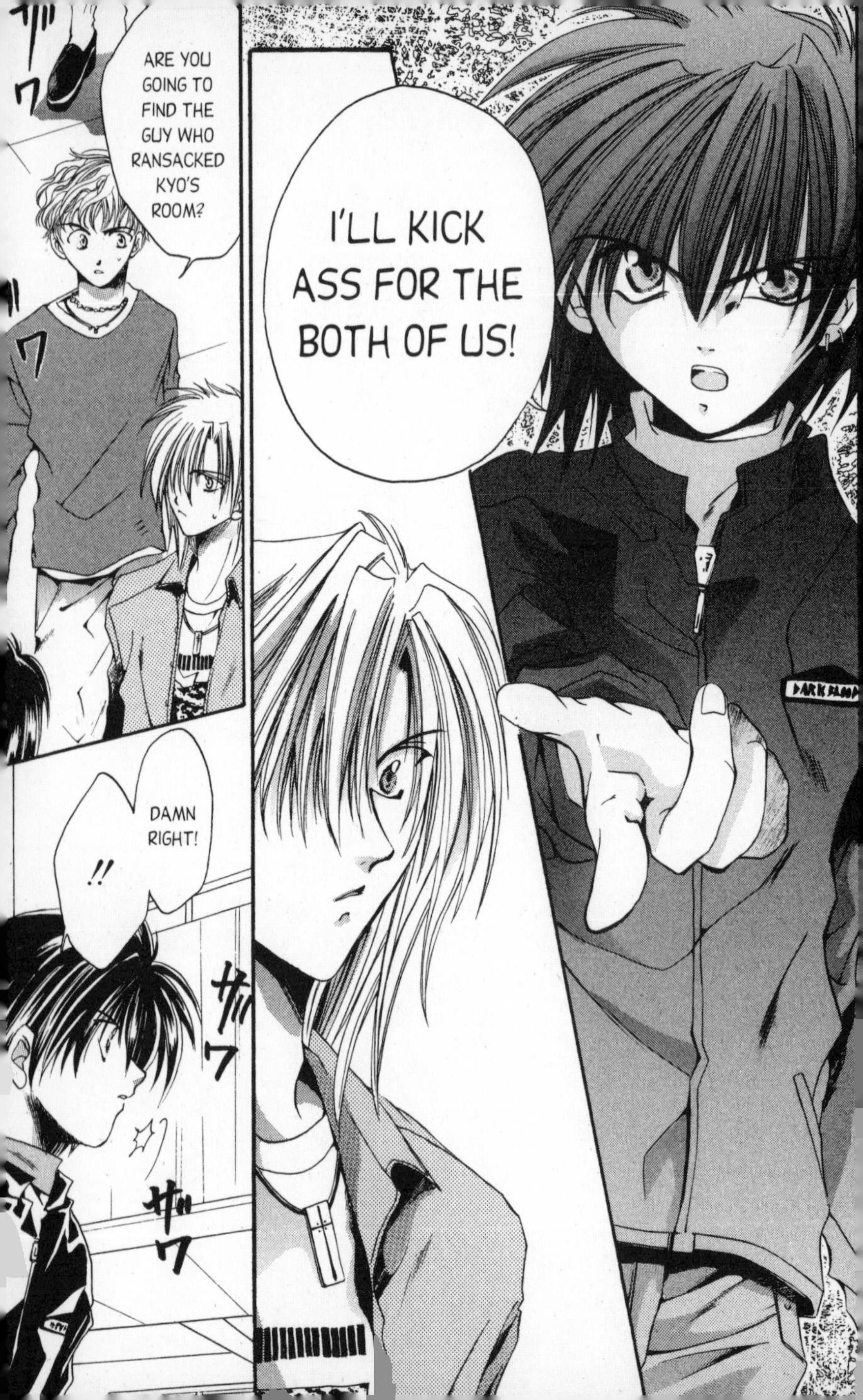
I'LL KICK ASS FOR THE BOTH OF US!
ARE YOU GOING TO FIND THE GUY WHO RANSACKED KYO'S ROOM?
ザワ
DAMN RIGHT!
!!
ザワ
ザワ

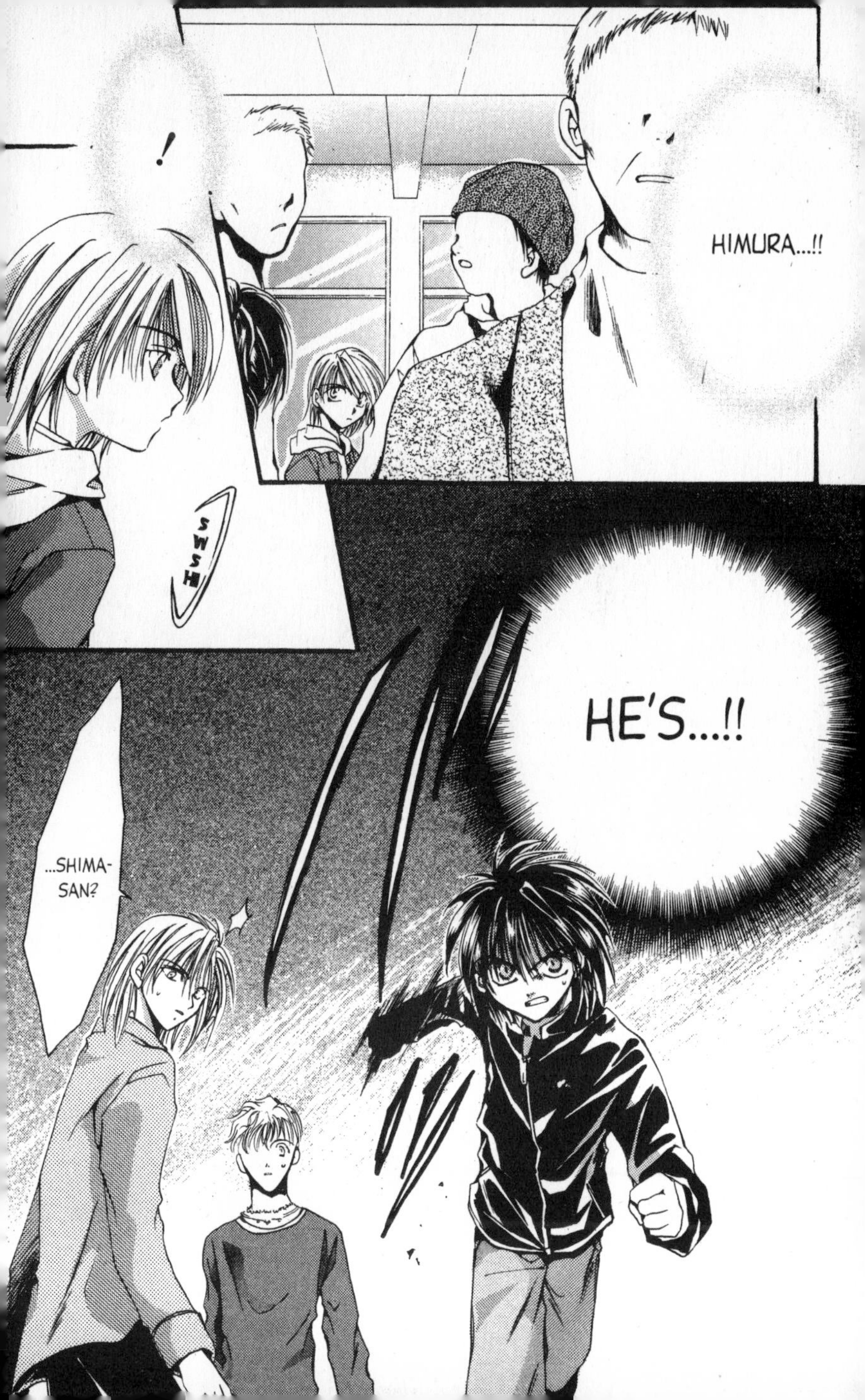
HIMURA...!!
!
SWSH
HE'S...!!
...SHIMA-SAN?

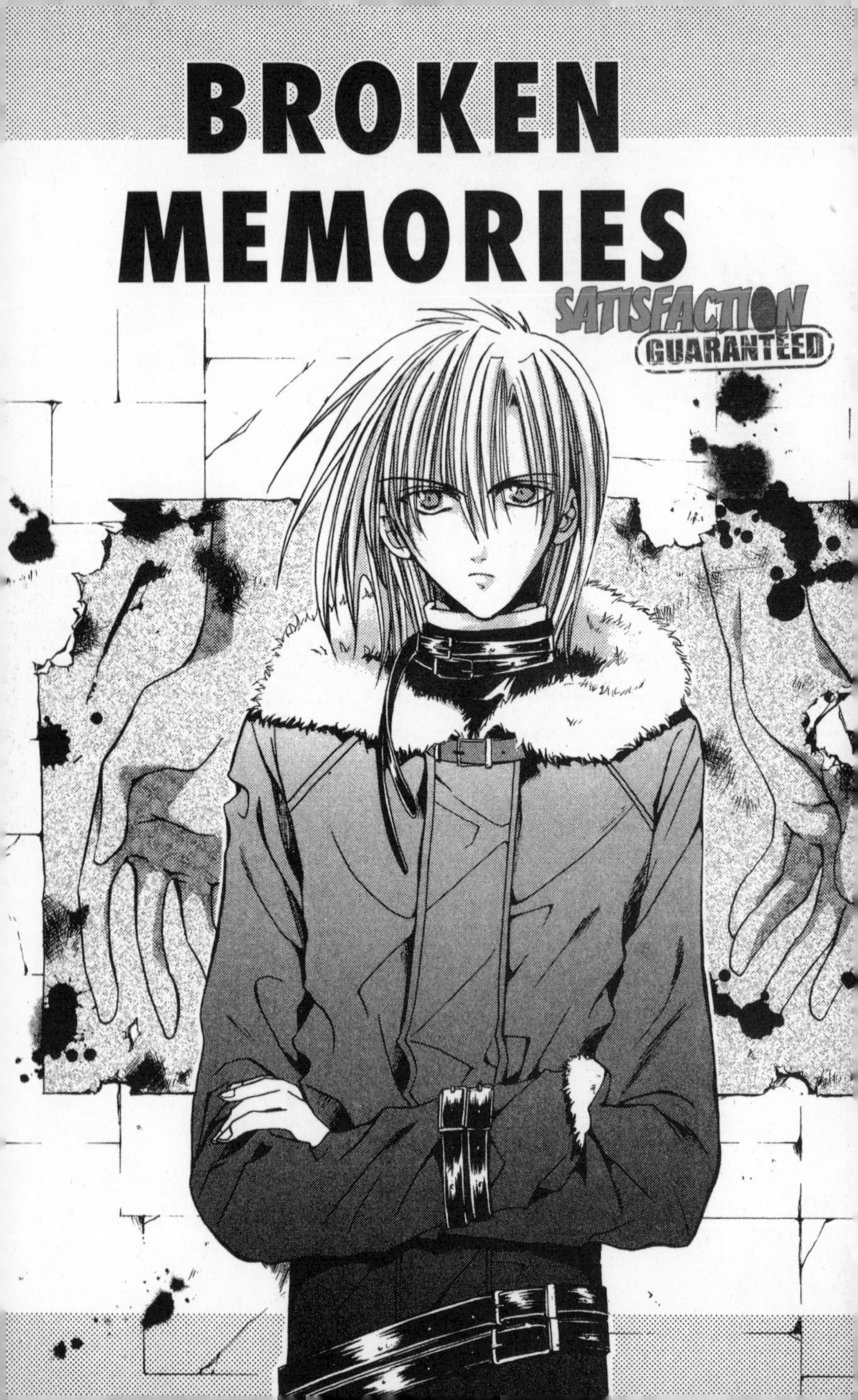
BROKEN MEMORIES
SATISFACTION GUARANTEED

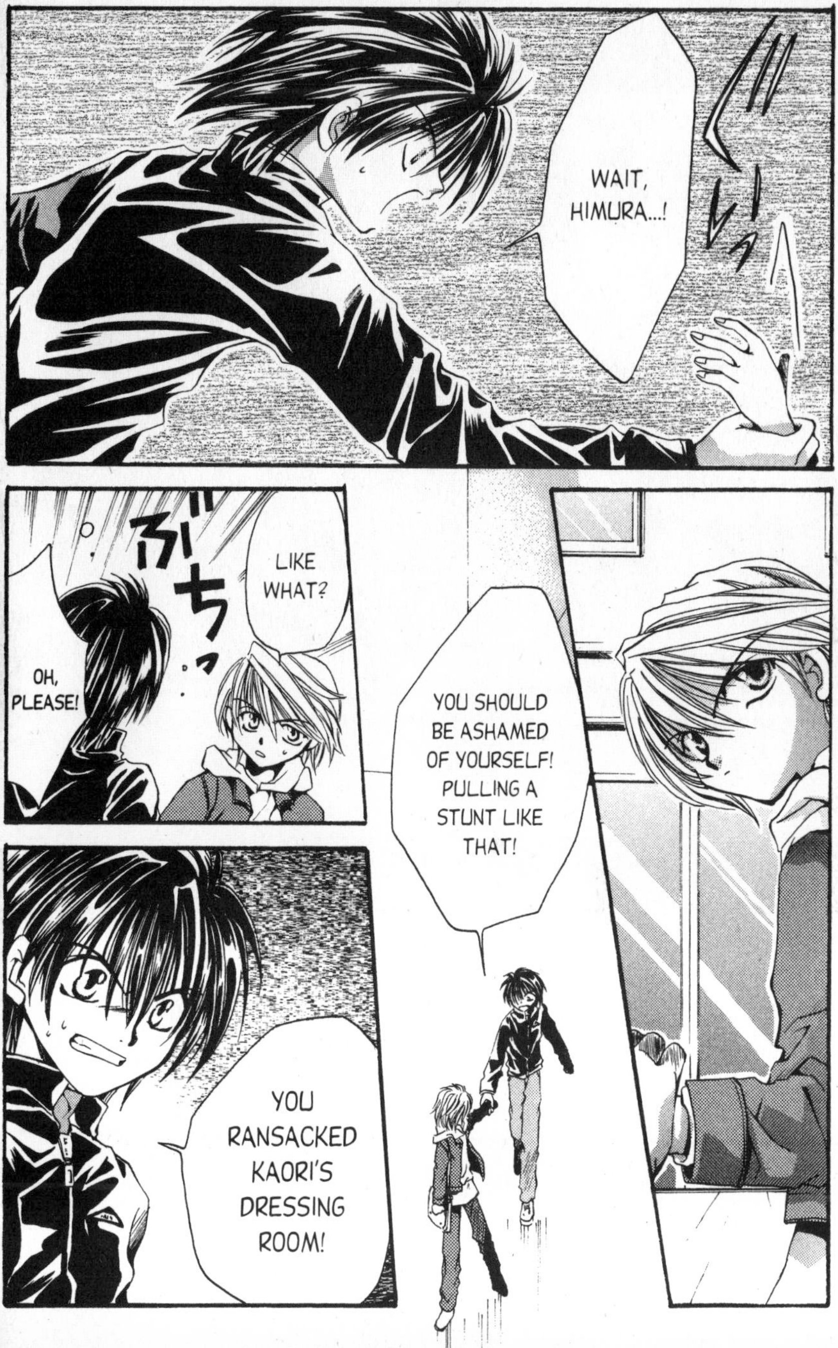
WAIT, HIMURA...!
YOU SHOULD BE ASHAMED OF YOURSELF! PULLING A STUNT LIKE THAT!
LIKE WHAT?
ぶちっ
OH, PLEASE!
YOU RANSACKED KAORI'S DRESSING ROOM!

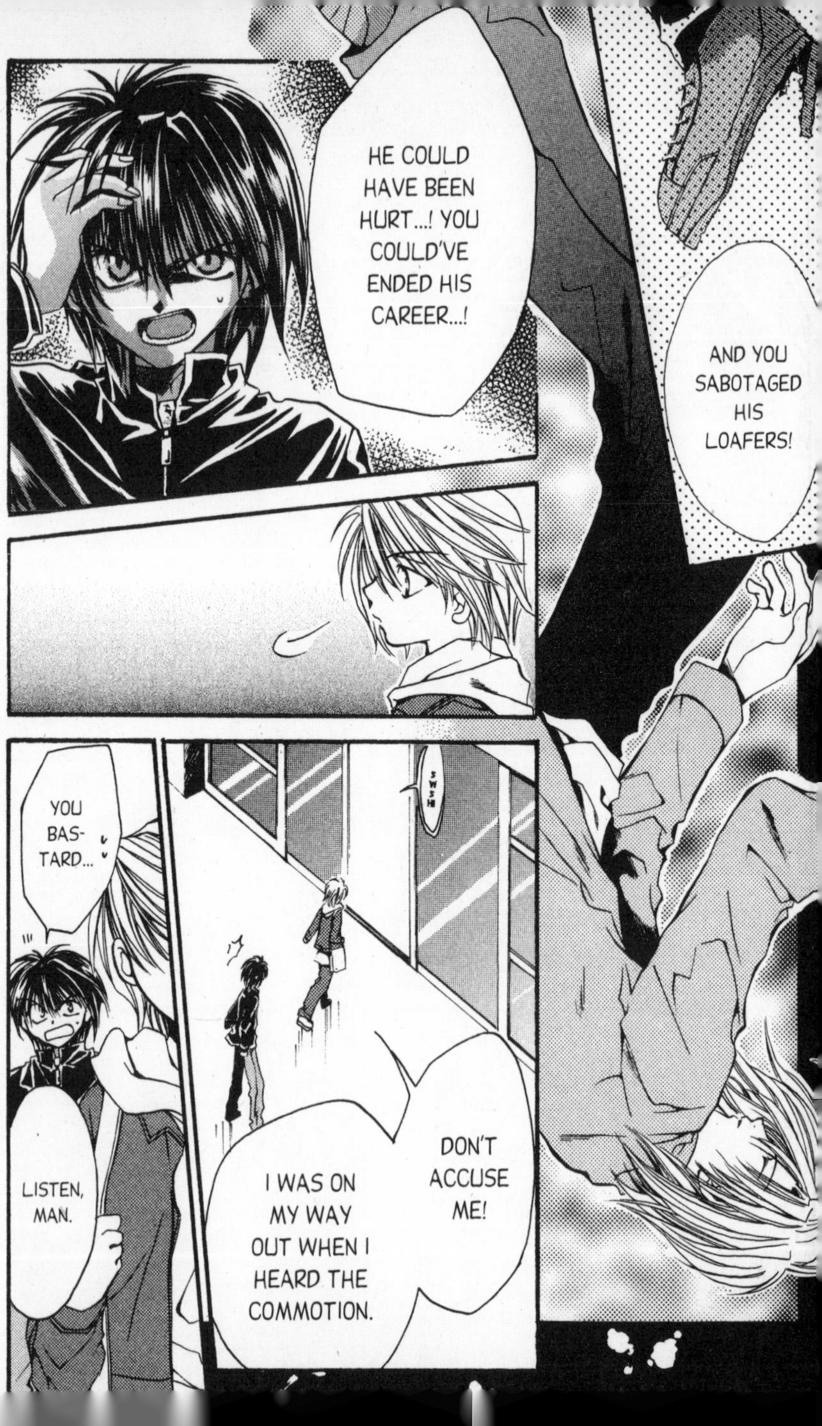
AND YOU SABOTAGED HIS LOAFERS!
HE COULD HAVE BEEN HURT...! YOU COULD'VE ENDED HIS CAREER...!
SWSH
DON'T ACCUSE ME!
I WAS ON MY WAY OUT WHEN I HEARD THE COMMOTION.
YOU BASTARD...
LISTEN, MAN.

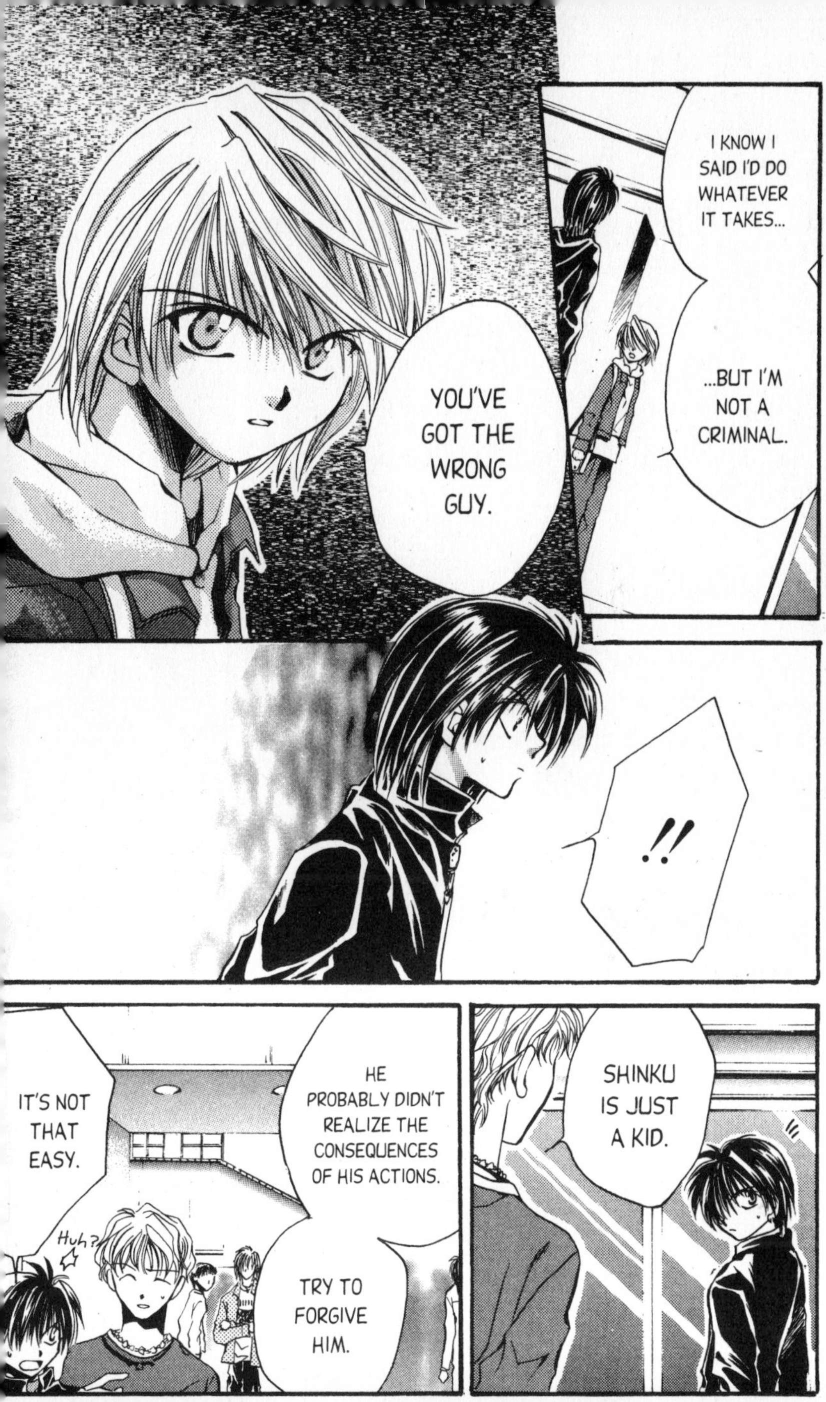
I KNOW I SAID I'D DO WHATEVER IT TAKES...
...BUT I'M NOT A CRIMINAL.
YOU'VE GOT THE WRONG GUY.
!!
SHINKU IS JUST A KID.
HE PROBABLY DIDN'T REALIZE THE CONSEQUENCES OF HIS ACTIONS.
TRY TO FORGIVE HIM.
IT'S NOT THAT EASY.
Huh?

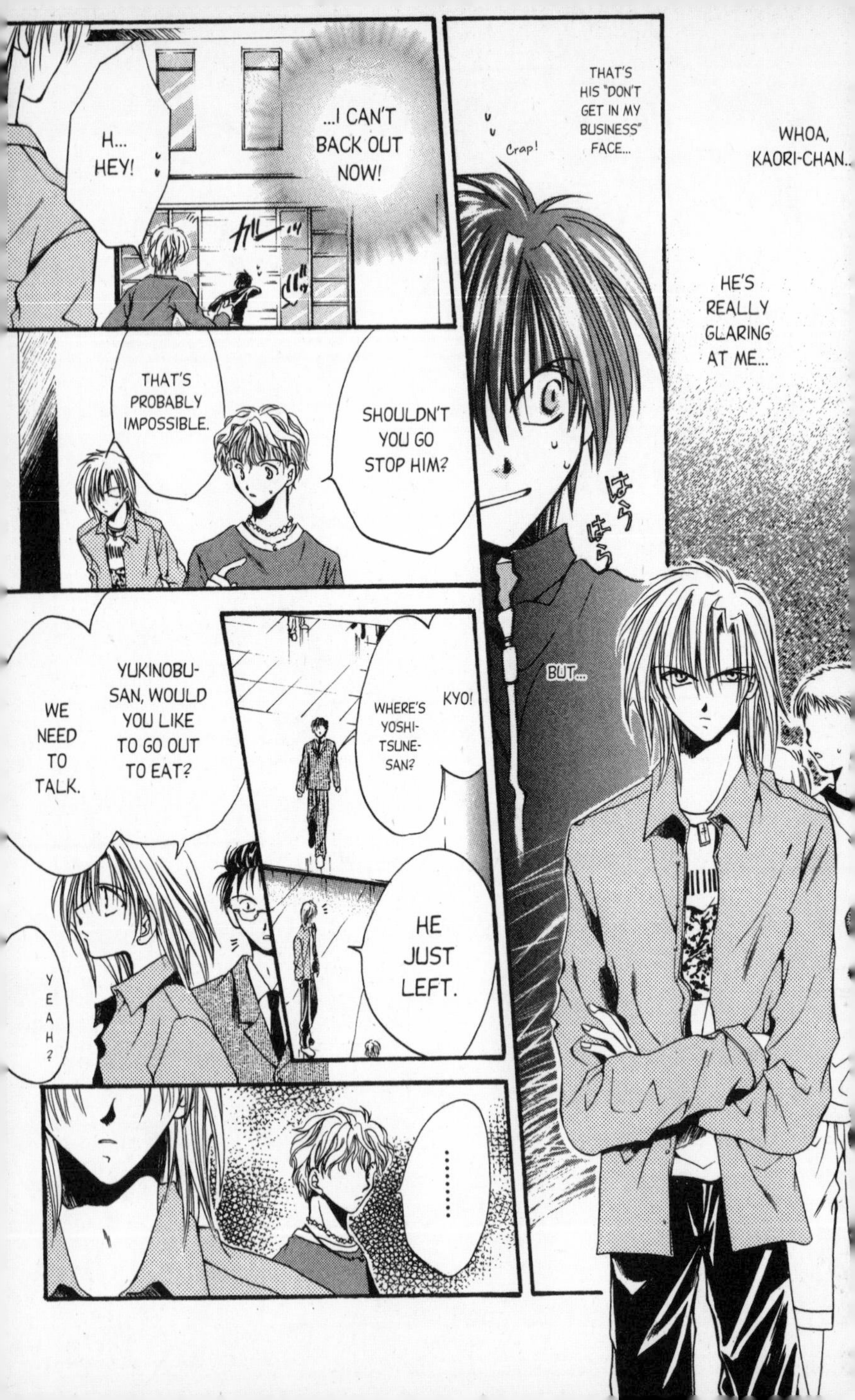
WHOA, KAORI-CHAN..
THAT'S HIS "DON'T GET IN MY BUSINESS" FACE...
Crap!
HE'S REALLY GLARING AT ME...
はらはら
BUT...
...I CAN'T BACK OUT NOW!
H... HEY!
SHOULDN'T YOU GO STOP HIM?
THAT'S PROBABLY IMPOSSIBLE.
KYO!
WHERE'S YOSHI-TSUNE-SAN?
HE JUST LEFT.
YUKINOBU-SAN, WOULD YOU LIKE TO GO OUT TO EAT?
WE NEED TO TALK.
YEAH?
....

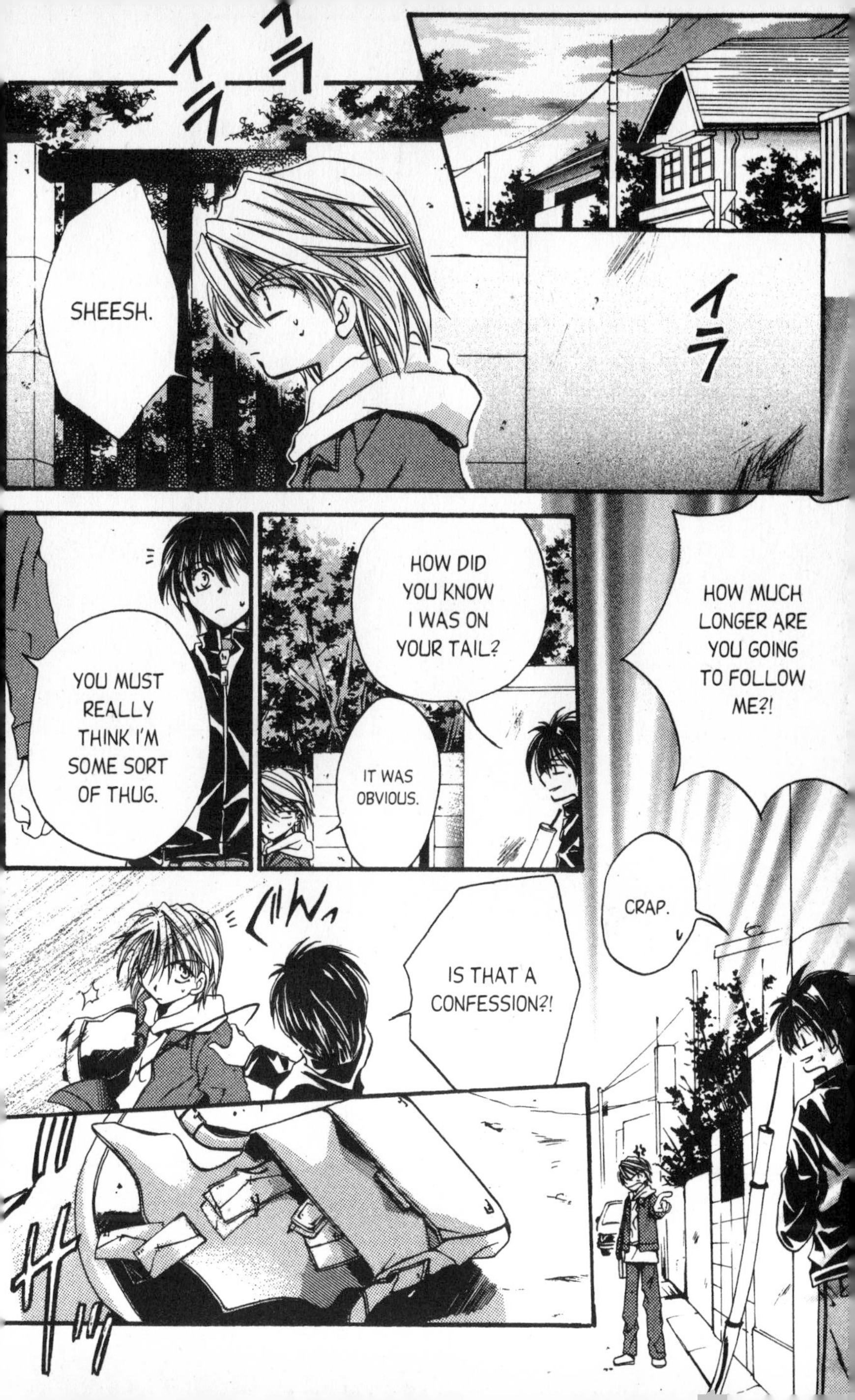

イライラ
イラ
SHEESH.
HOW MUCH LONGER ARE YOU GOING TO FOLLOW ME?!
CRAP.
HOW DID YOU KNOW I WAS ON YOUR TAIL?
IT WAS OBVIOUS.
YOU MUST REALLY THINK I'M SOME SORT OF THUG.
IS THAT A CONFESSION?!

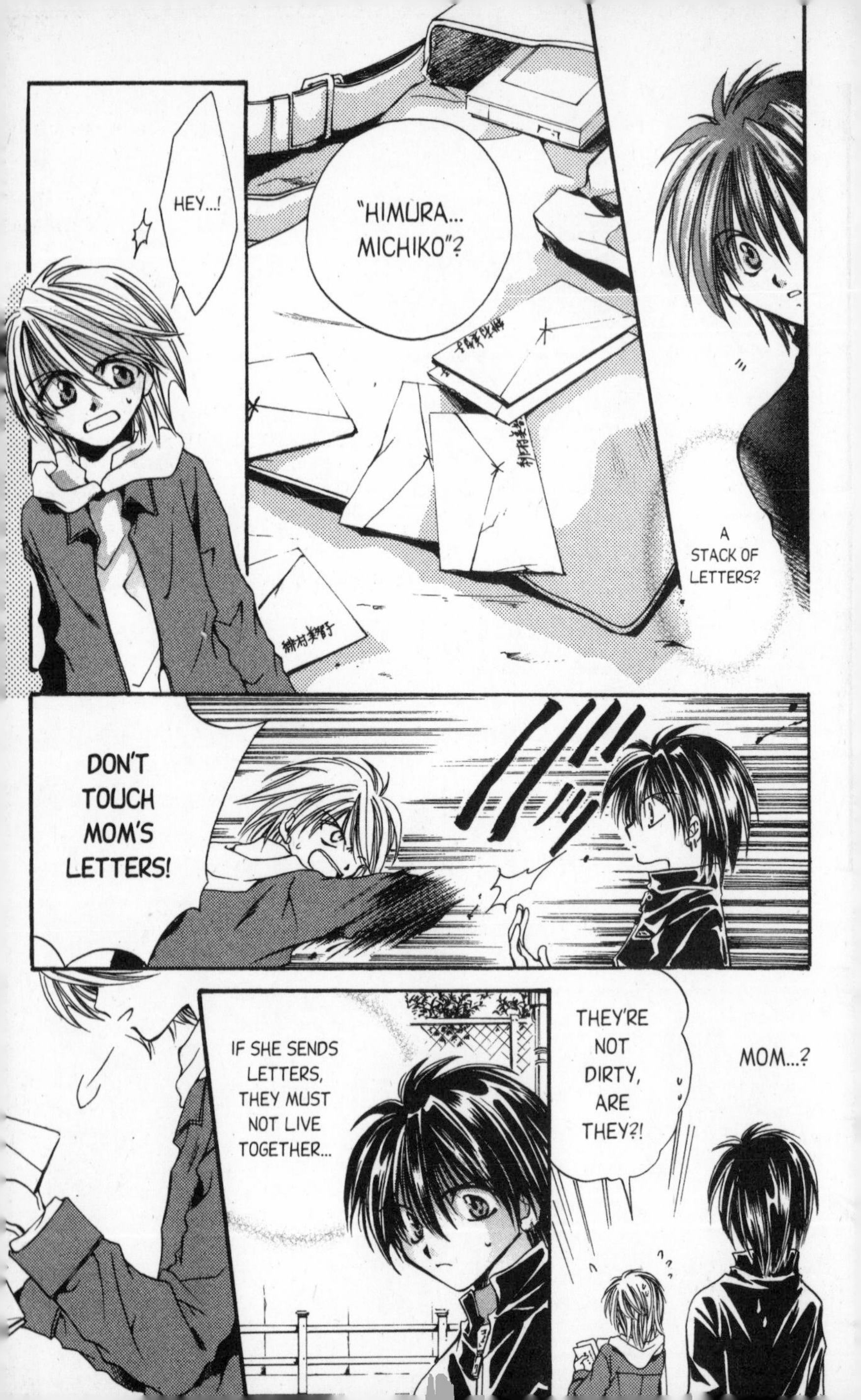
A STACK OF LETTERS?
"HIMURA... MICHIKO"?
HEY...!
DON'T TOUCH MOM'S LETTERS!
MOM...?
THEY'RE NOT DIRTY, ARE THEY?!
IF SHE SENDS LETTERS, THEY MUST NOT LIVE TOGETHER...

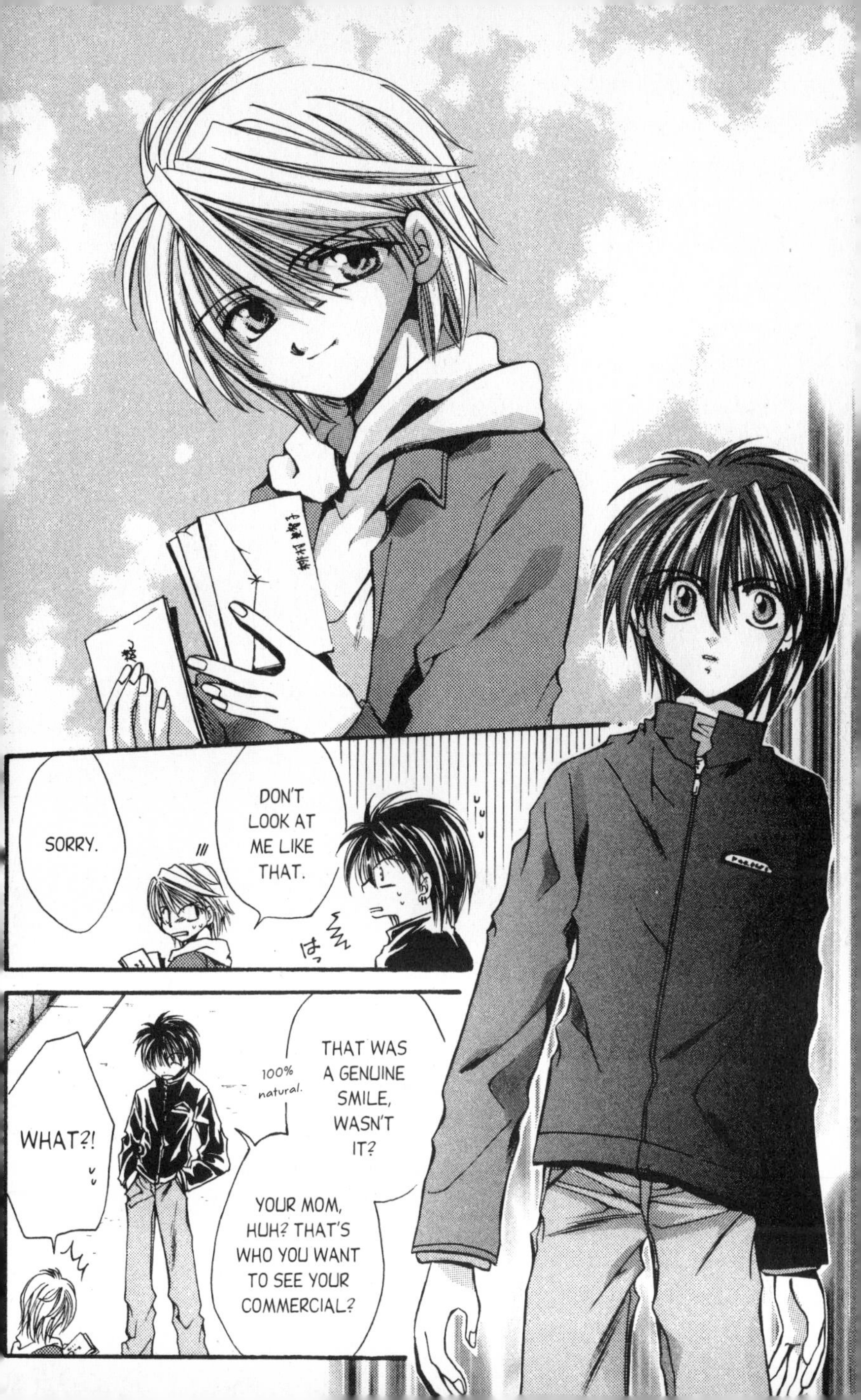
DON'T LOOK AT ME LIKE THAT.
SORRY.
THAT WAS A GENUINE SMILE, WASN'T IT?
100% natural.
WHAT?!
YOUR MOM, HUH? THAT'S WHO YOU WANT TO SEE YOUR COMMERCIAL?

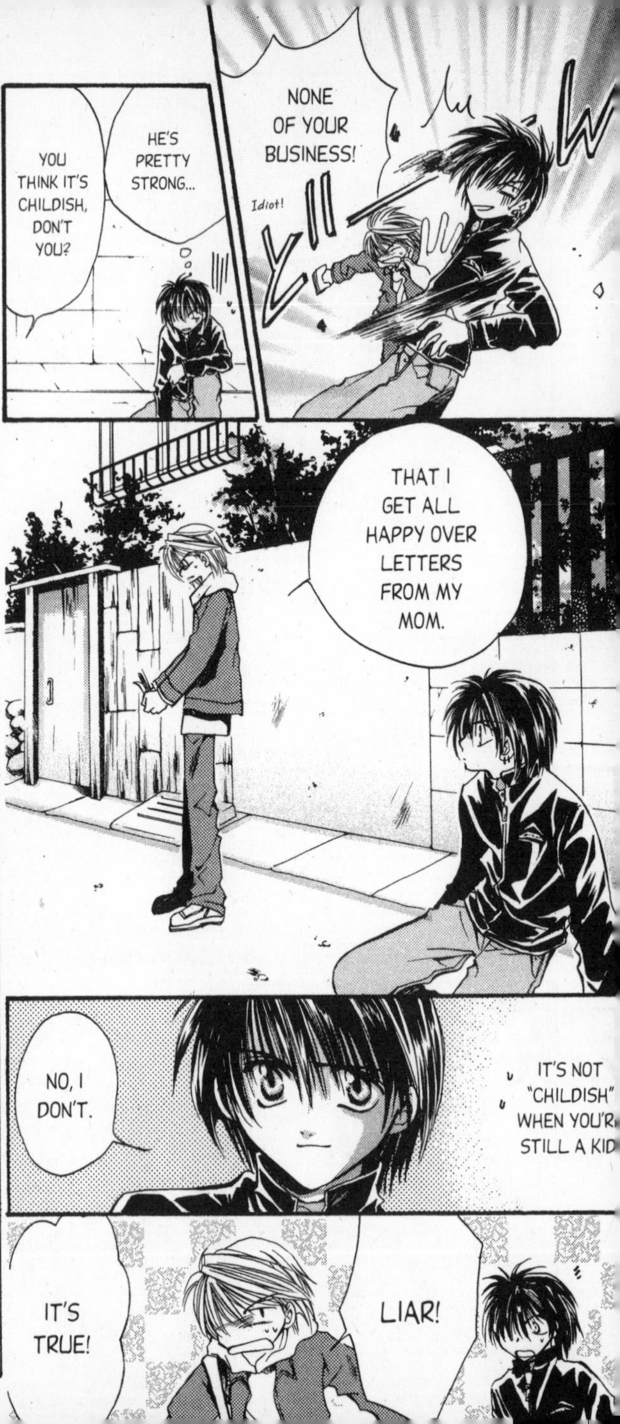
NONE OF YOUR BUSINESS!
Idiot!
HE'S PRETTY STRONG...
YOU THINK IT'S CHILDISH, DON'T YOU?
THAT I GET ALL HAPPY OVER LETTERS FROM MY MOM.
IT'S NOT "CHILDISH" WHEN YOU'R STILL A KID
NO, I DON'T.
LIAR!
IT'S TRUE!

Shinku was fun to draw, both as a bad boy and a goody-goody. He has a pretty wacky personality. For Shinku's name, I wanted to use the Chinese character 緋 which is the character for the color red. I ended up using another red word 深紅 --Shinku, or "deep red." Shinku's dad's name, Enji, is another red-type word, 臙脂. Shinku's mom, Michiko, was borrowed from friend of mine, so it has nothing to do with anything.

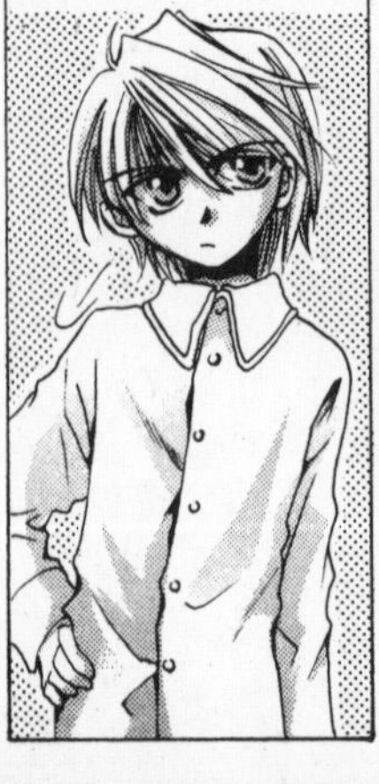

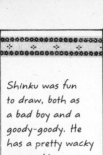

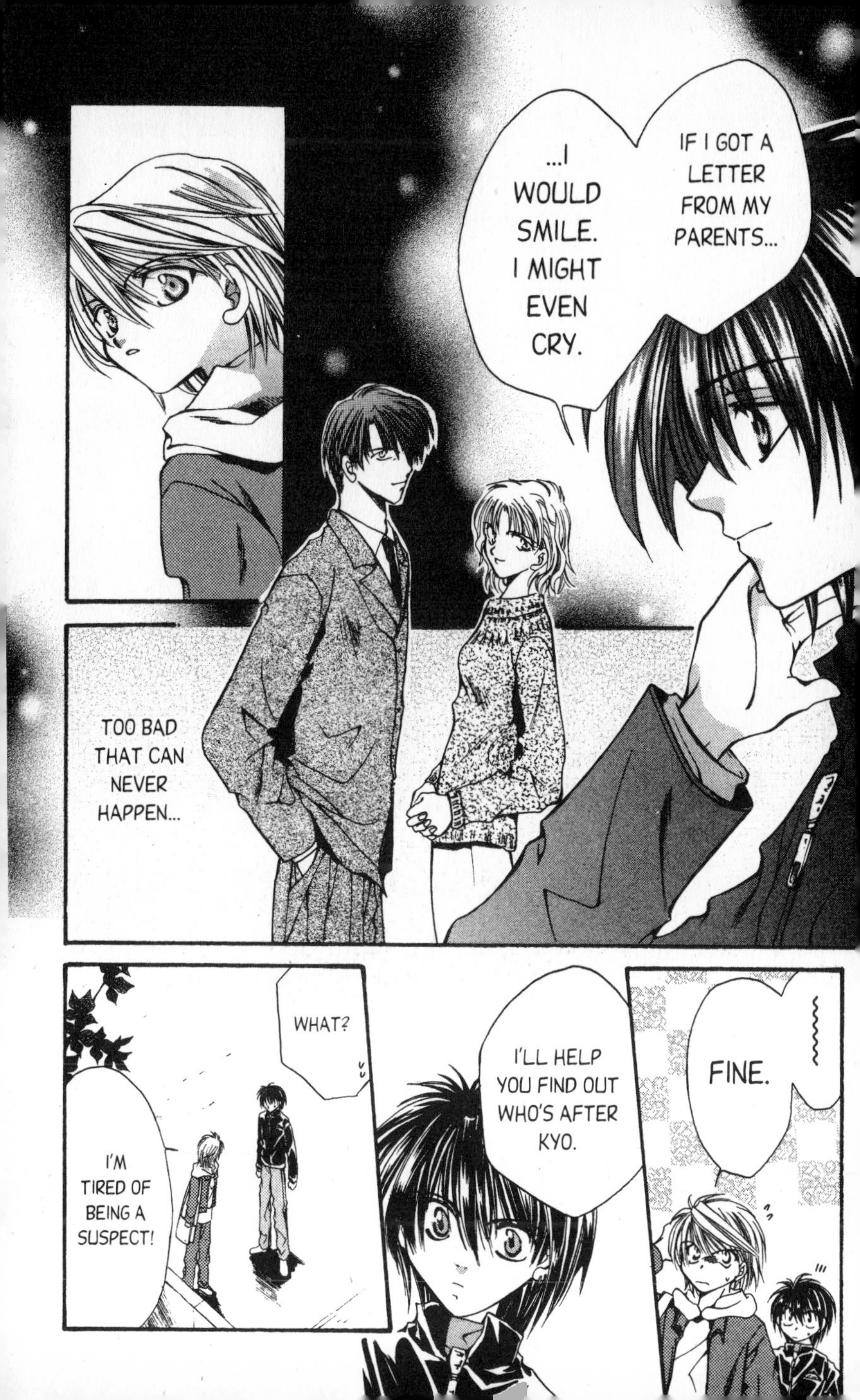
IF I GOT A LETTER FROM MY PARENTS...
...I WOULD SMILE. I MIGHT EVEN CRY.
TOO BAD THAT CAN NEVER HAPPEN...
FINE.
I'LL HELP YOU FIND OUT WHO'S AFTER KYO.
WHAT?
I'M TIRED OF BEING A SUSPECT!

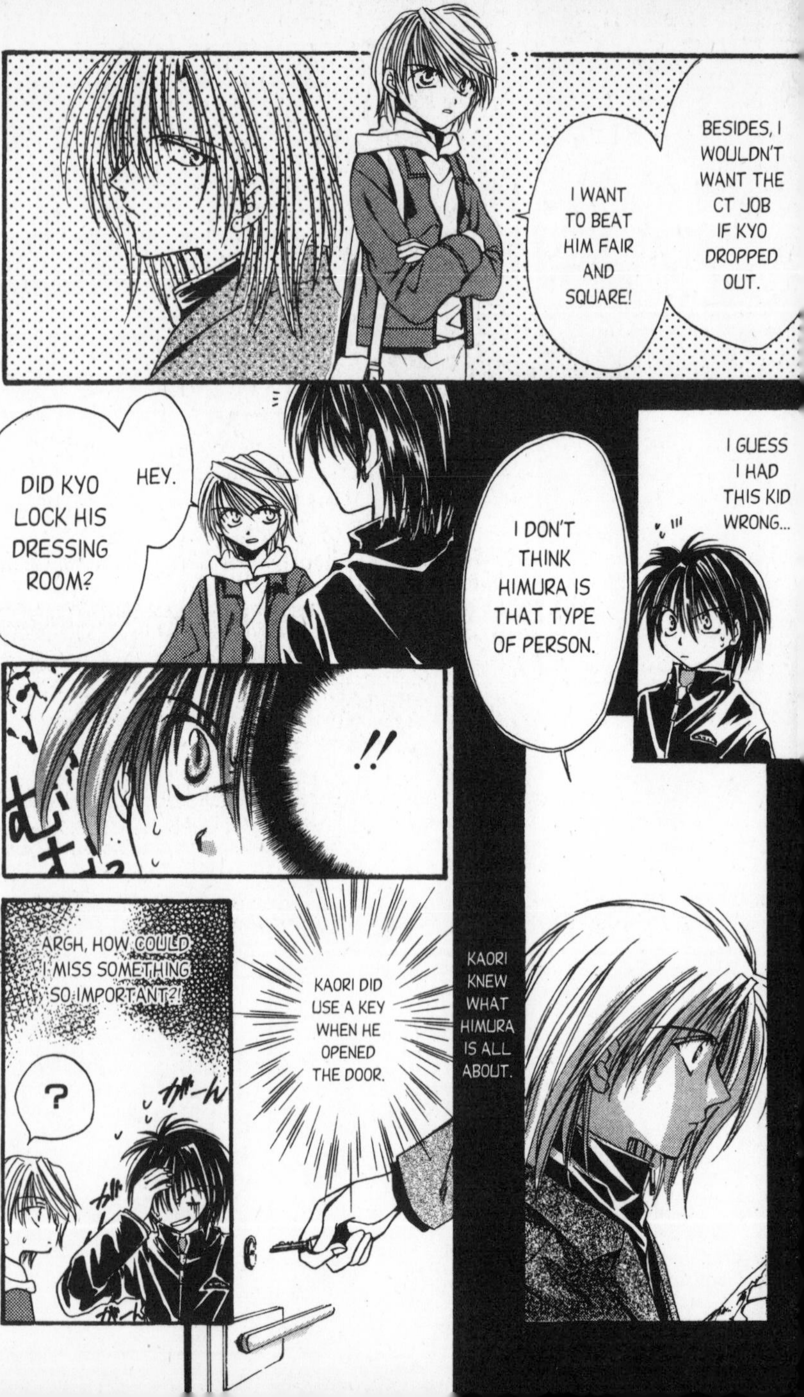
BESIDES, I WOULDN'T WANT THE CT JOB IF KYO DROPPED OUT.
I WANT TO BEAT HIM FAIR AND SQUARE!
I GUESS I HAD THIS KID WRONG...
I DON'T THINK HIMURA IS THAT TYPE OF PERSON.
KAORI KNEW WHAT HIMURA IS ALL ABOUT.
HEY.
DID KYO LOCK HIS DRESSING ROOM?
!!
KAORI DID USE A KEY WHEN HE OPENED THE DOOR.
ARGH, HOW COULD I MISS SOMETHING SO IMPORTANT?!
?

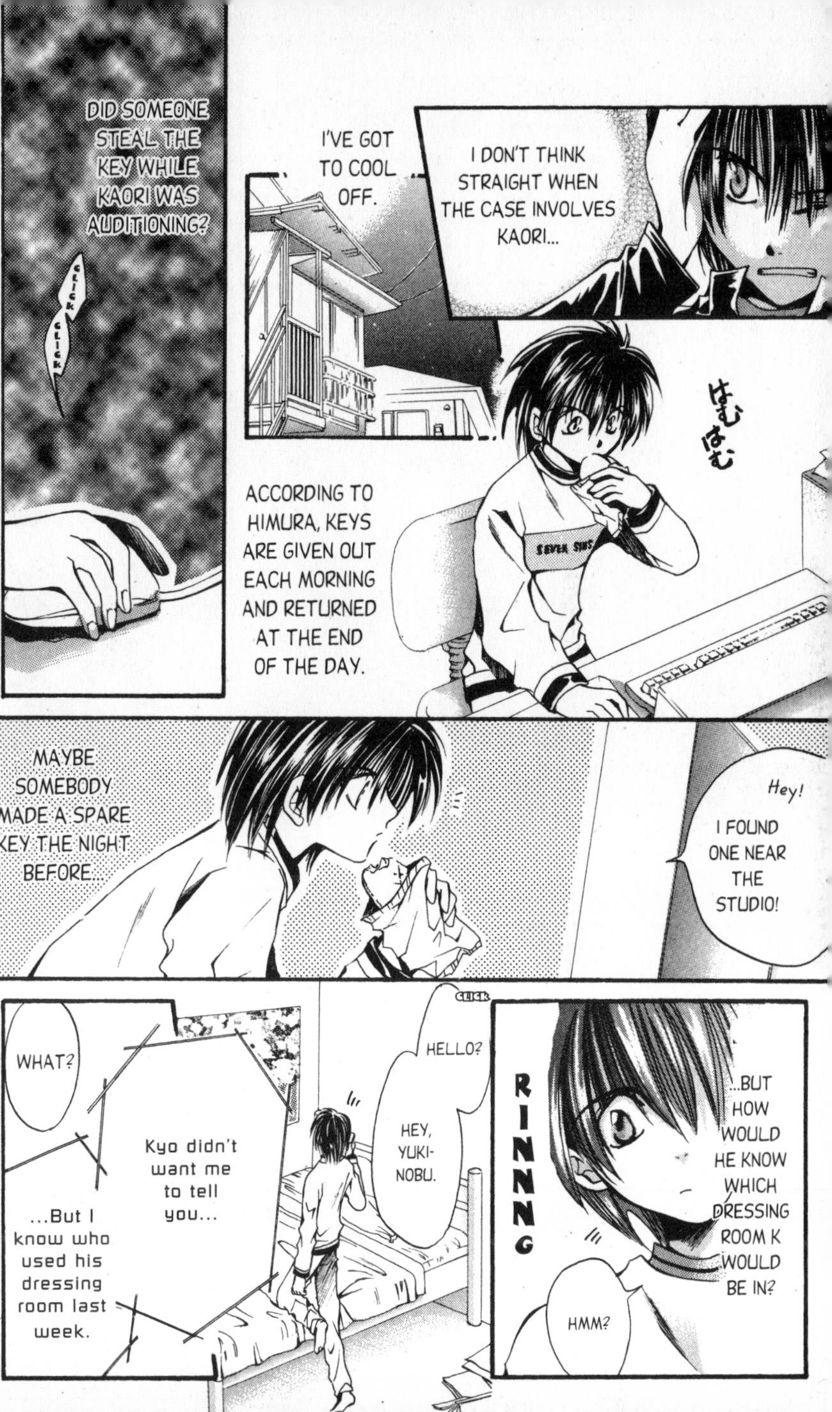
I DON'T THINK STRAIGHT WHEN THE CASE INVOLVES KAORI...
I'VE GOT TO COOL OFF.
はむはむ
ACCORDING TO HIMURA, KEYS ARE GIVEN OUT EACH MORNING AND RETURNED AT THE END OF THE DAY.
SEVEN SINS
DID SOMEONE STEAL THE KEY WHILE KAORI WAS AUDITIONING?
CLICK
CLICK
Hey!
I FOUND ONE NEAR THE STUDIO!
MAYBE SOMEBODY MADE A SPARE KEY THE NIGHT BEFORE...
...BUT HOW WOULD HE KNOW WHICH DRESSING ROOM K WOULD BE IN?
RINNNG
HMM?
CLICK
HELLO?
HEY, YUKI-NOBU.
WHAT?
Kyo didn't want me to tell you...
...But I know who used his dressing room last week.

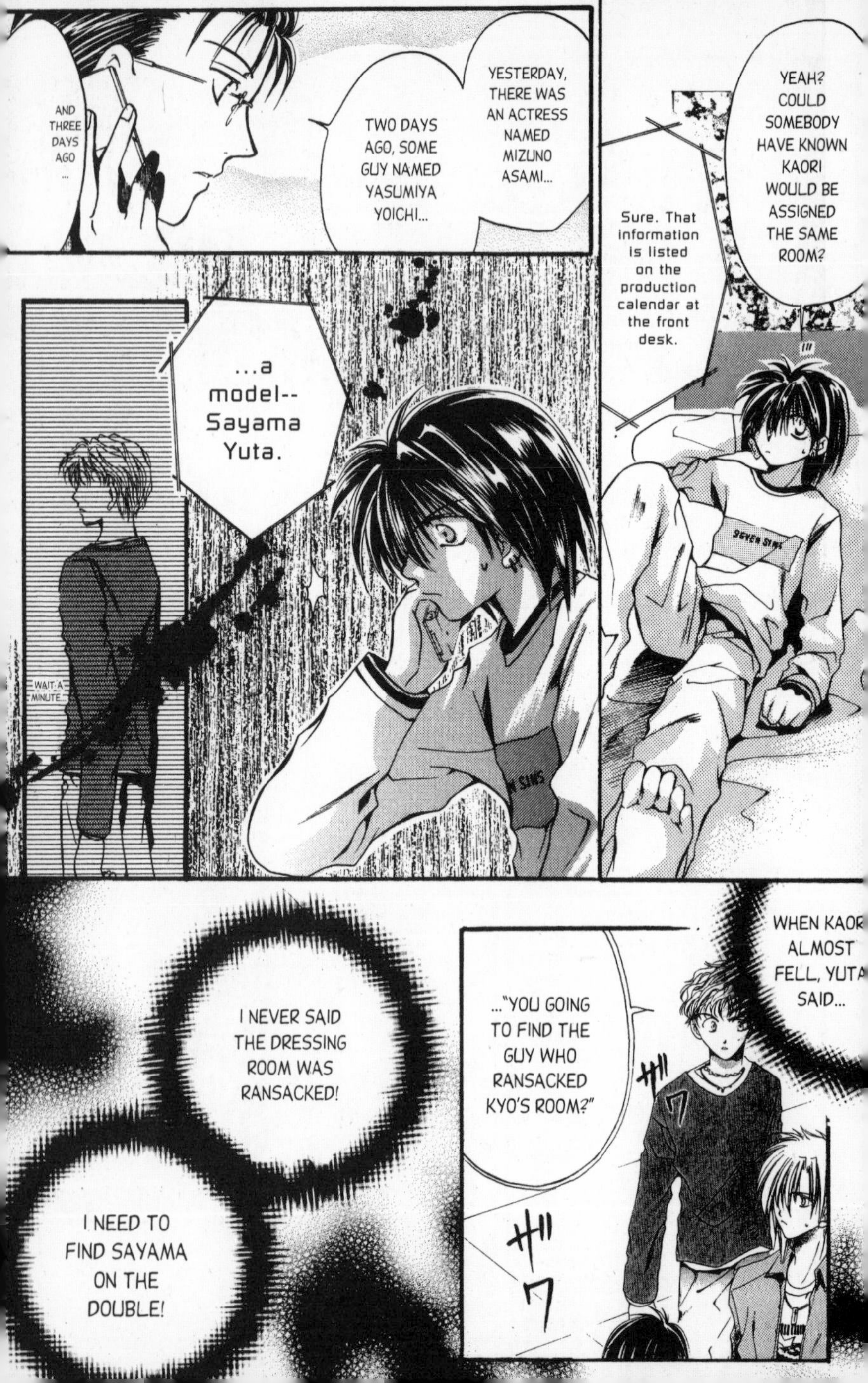
YEAH? COULD SOMEBODY HAVE KNOWN KAORI WOULD BE ASSIGNED THE SAME ROOM?
Sure. That information is listed on the production calendar at the front desk.
!!!
YESTERDAY, THERE WAS AN ACTRESS NAMED MIZUNO ASAMI...
TWO DAYS AGO, SOME GUY NAMED YASUMIYA YOICHI...
AND THREE DAYS AGO ...
...a model-- Sayama Yuta.
WAIT A MINUTE...
WHEN KAOR ALMOST FELL, YUTA SAID...
..."YOU GOING TO FIND THE GUY WHO RANSACKED KYO'S ROOM?"
ザワ
ザワ
I NEVER SAID THE DRESSING ROOM WAS RANSACKED!
I NEED TO FIND SAYAMA ON THE DOUBLE!

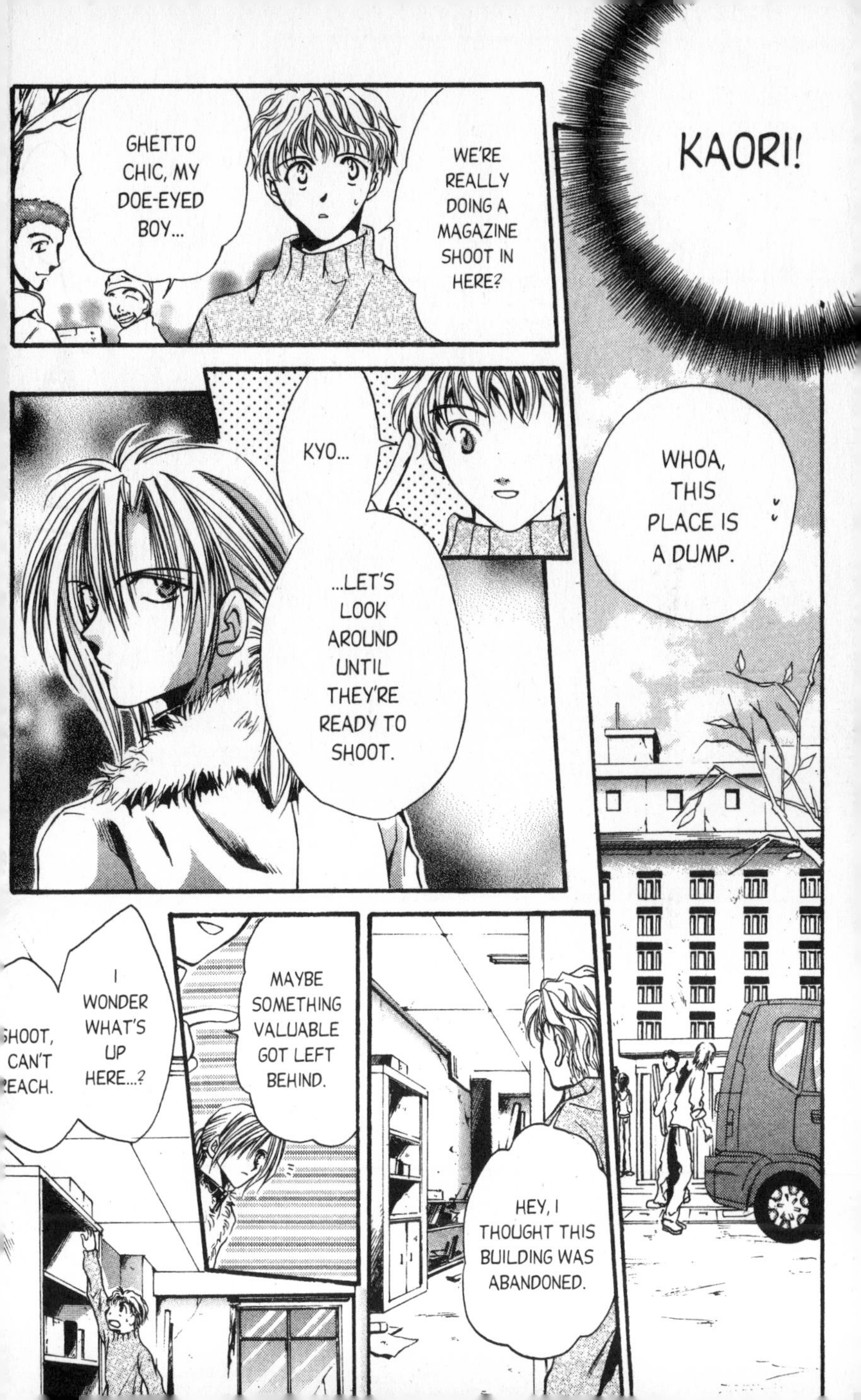
KAORI!
WHOA, THIS PLACE IS A DUMP.
WE'RE REALLY DOING A MAGAZINE SHOOT IN HERE?
GHETTO CHIC, MY DOE-EYED BOY...
KYO...
...LET'S LOOK AROUND UNTIL THEY'RE READY TO SHOOT.
HEY, I THOUGHT THIS BUILDING WAS ABANDONED.
MAYBE SOMETHING VALUABLE GOT LEFT BEHIND.
I WONDER WHAT'S UP HERE...?
HOOT, CAN'T EACH.

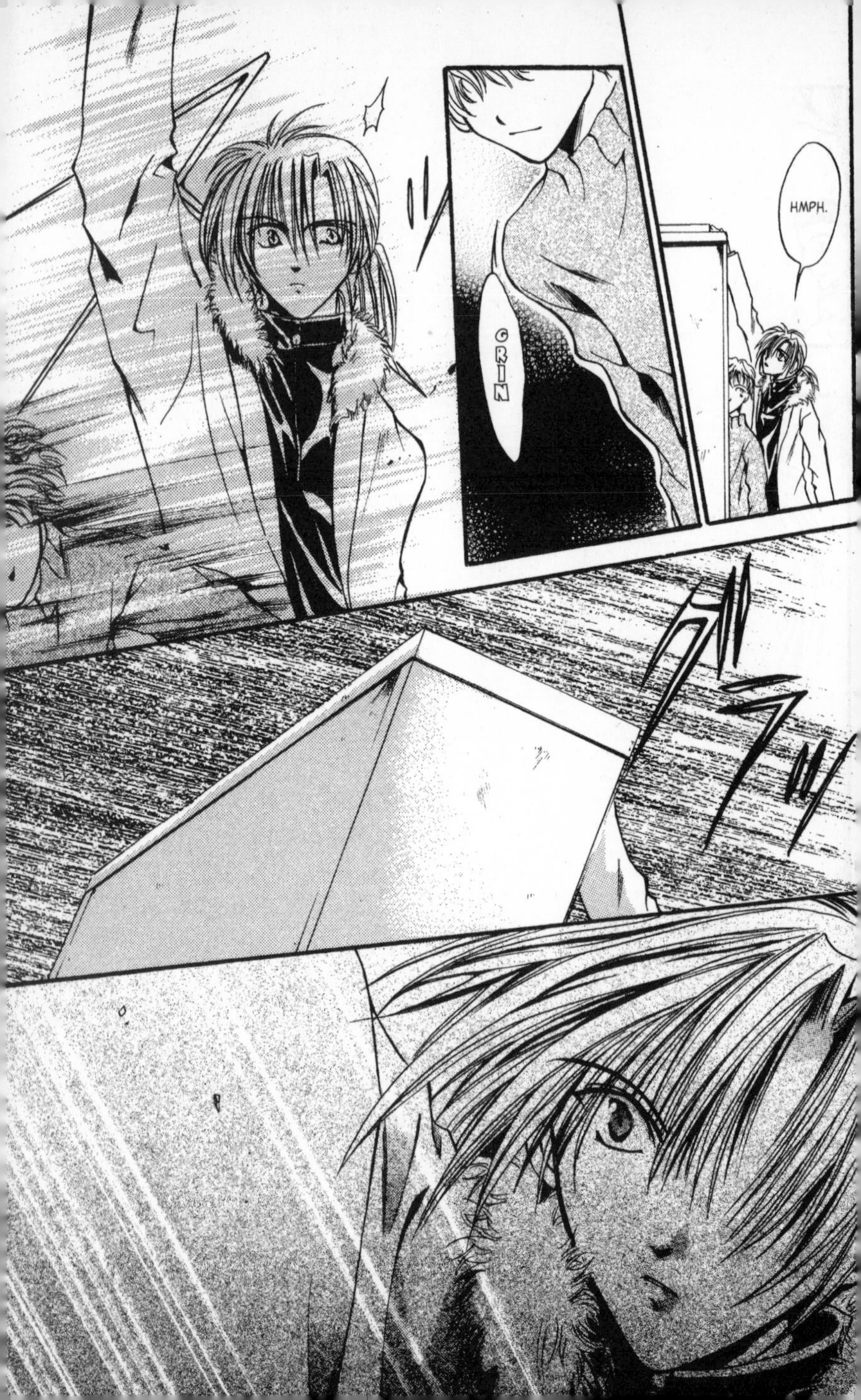
HMPH.
GRIN

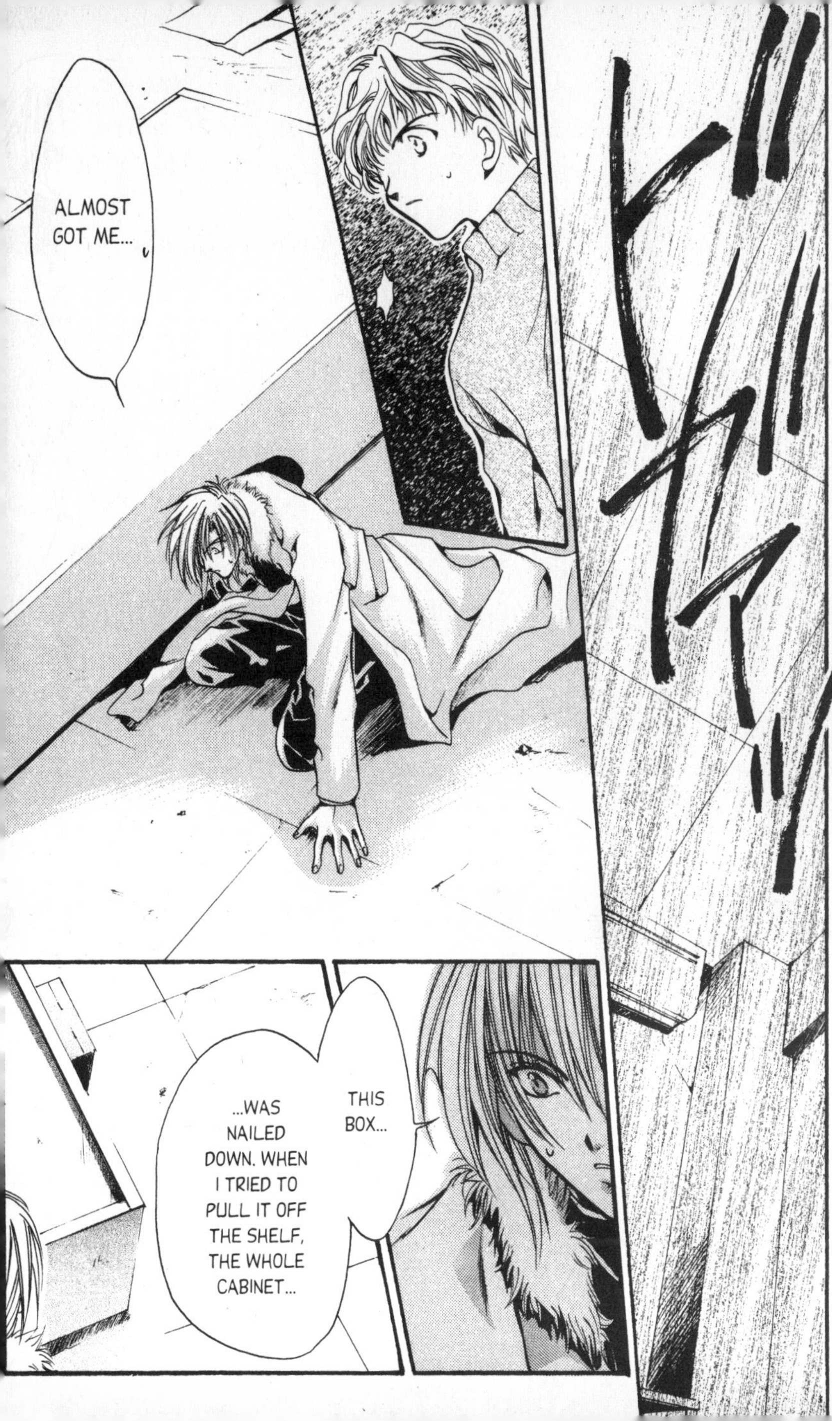
ALMOST GOT ME...
THIS BOX...
...WAS NAILED DOWN. WHEN I TRIED TO PULL IT OFF THE SHELF, THE WHOLE CABINET...

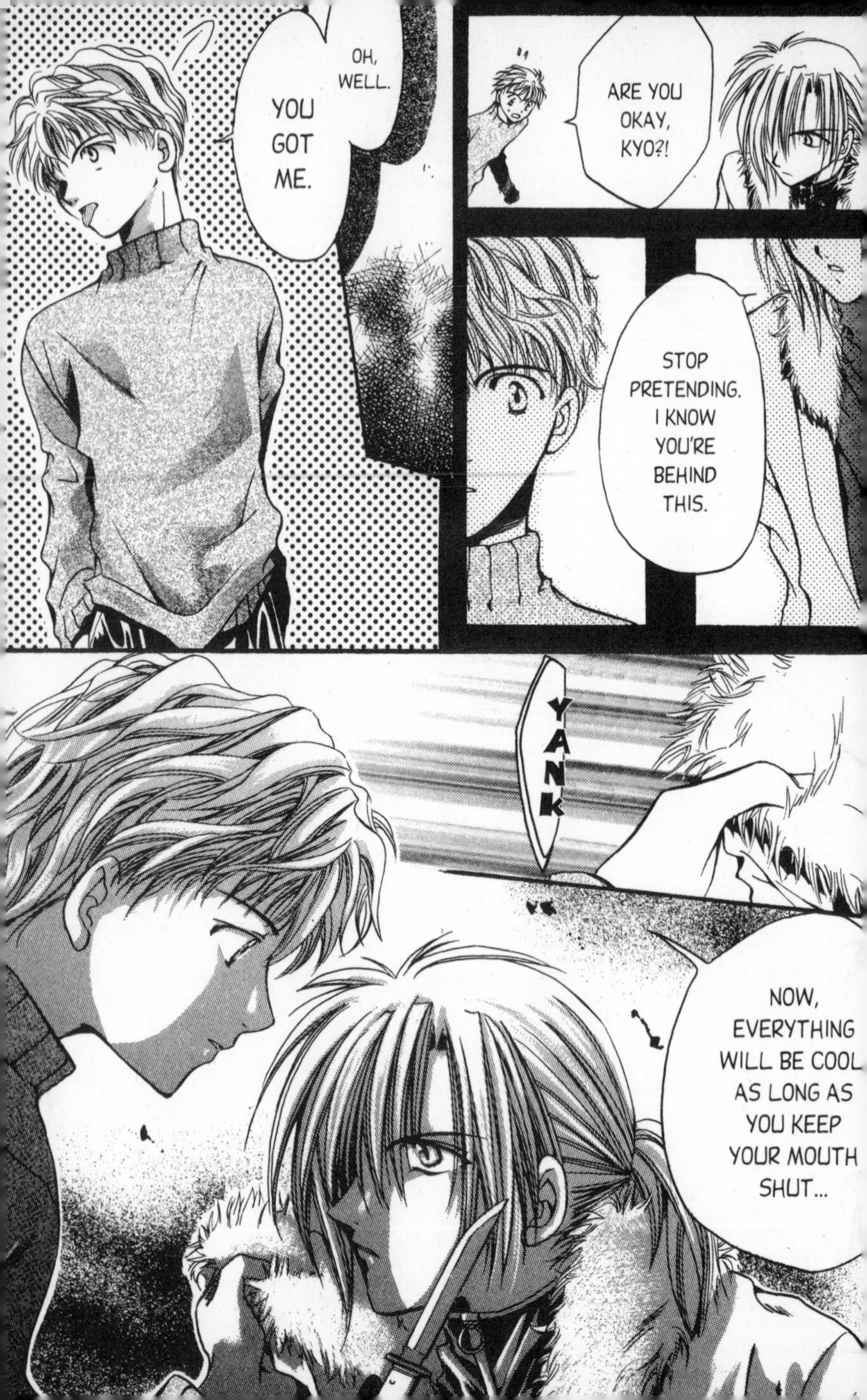

ARE YOU OKAY, KYO?!
STOP PRETENDING. I KNOW YOU'RE BEHIND THIS.
OH, WELL. YOU GOT ME.
YANK
NOW, EVERYTHING WILL BE COOL AS LONG AS YOU KEEP YOUR MOUTH SHUT...

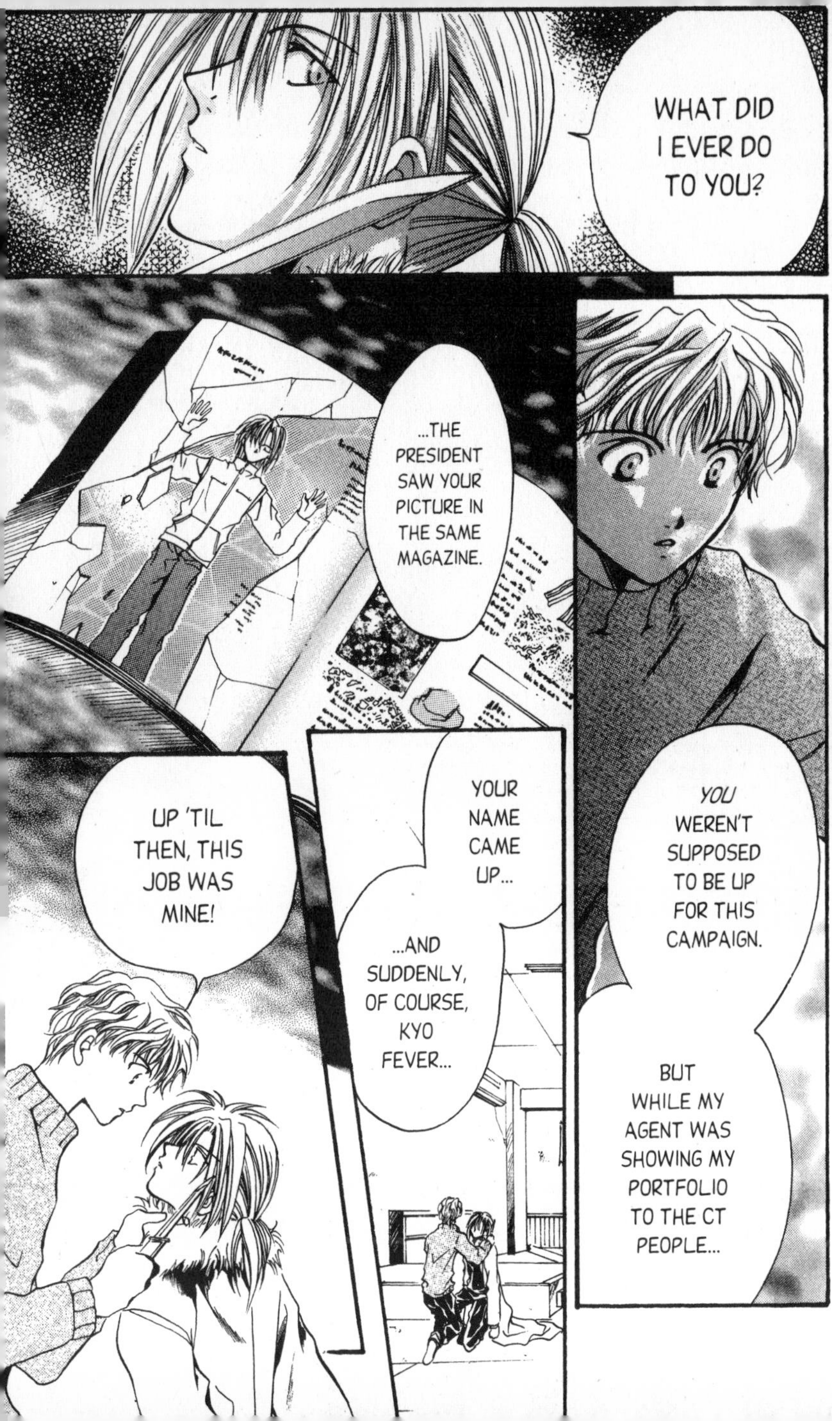
WHAT DID I EVER DO TO YOU?
YOU WEREN'T SUPPOSED TO BE UP FOR THIS CAMPAIGN.
BUT WHILE MY AGENT WAS SHOWING MY PORTFOLIO TO THE CT PEOPLE...
...THE PRESIDENT SAW YOUR PICTURE IN THE SAME MAGAZINE.
YOUR NAME CAME UP...
...AND SUDDENLY, OF COURSE, KYO FEVER...
UP 'TIL THEN, THIS JOB WAS MINE!

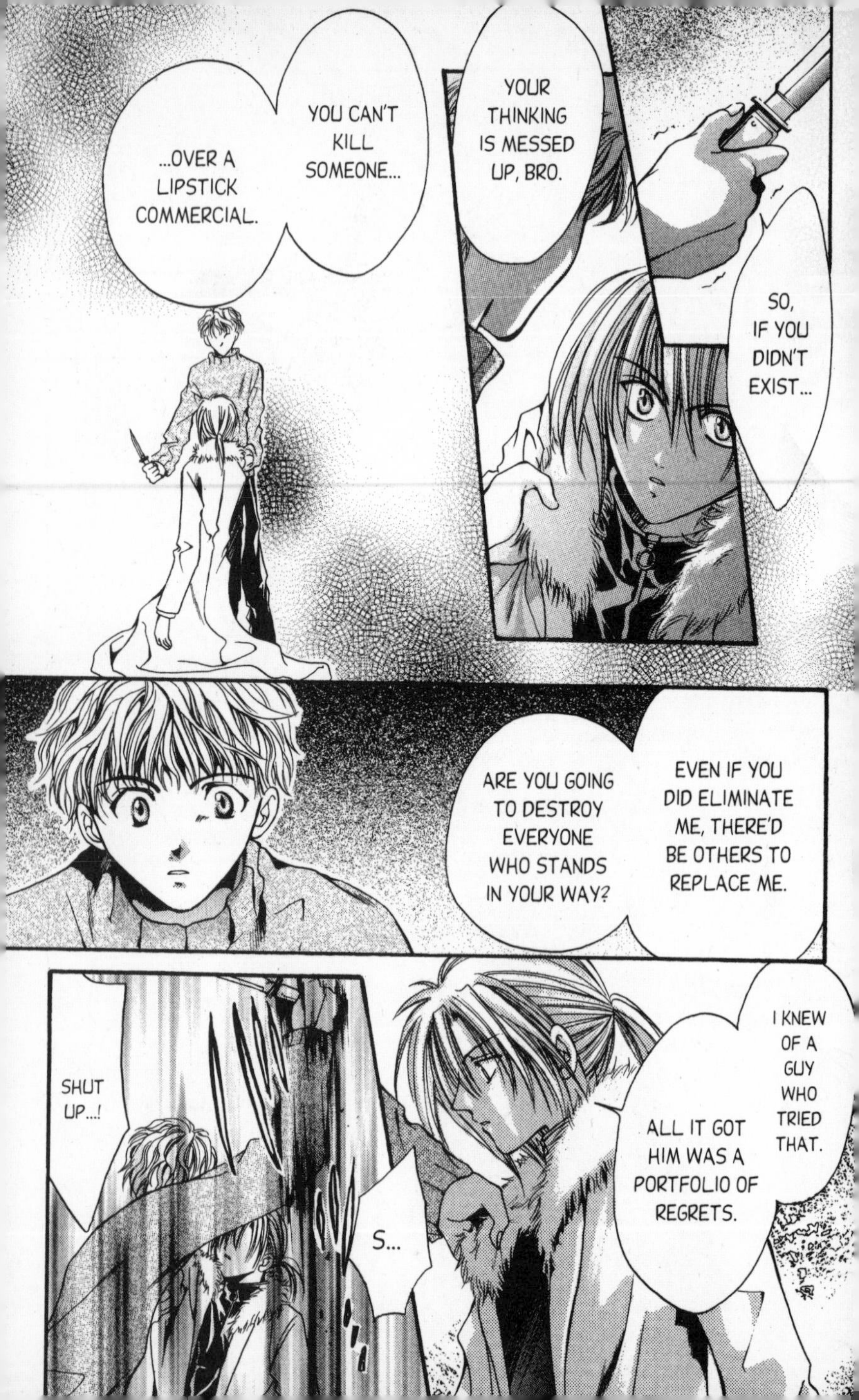
SO, IF YOU DIDN'T EXIST...
YOUR THINKING IS MESSED UP, BRO.
YOU CAN'T KILL SOMEONE...
...OVER A LIPSTICK COMMERCIAL.
EVEN IF YOU DID ELIMINATE ME, THERE'D BE OTHERS TO REPLACE ME.
ARE YOU GOING TO DESTROY EVERYONE WHO STANDS IN YOUR WAY?
I KNEW OF A GUY WHO TRIED THAT.
ALL IT GOT HIM WAS A PORTFOLIO OF REGRETS.
S...
SHUT UP...!

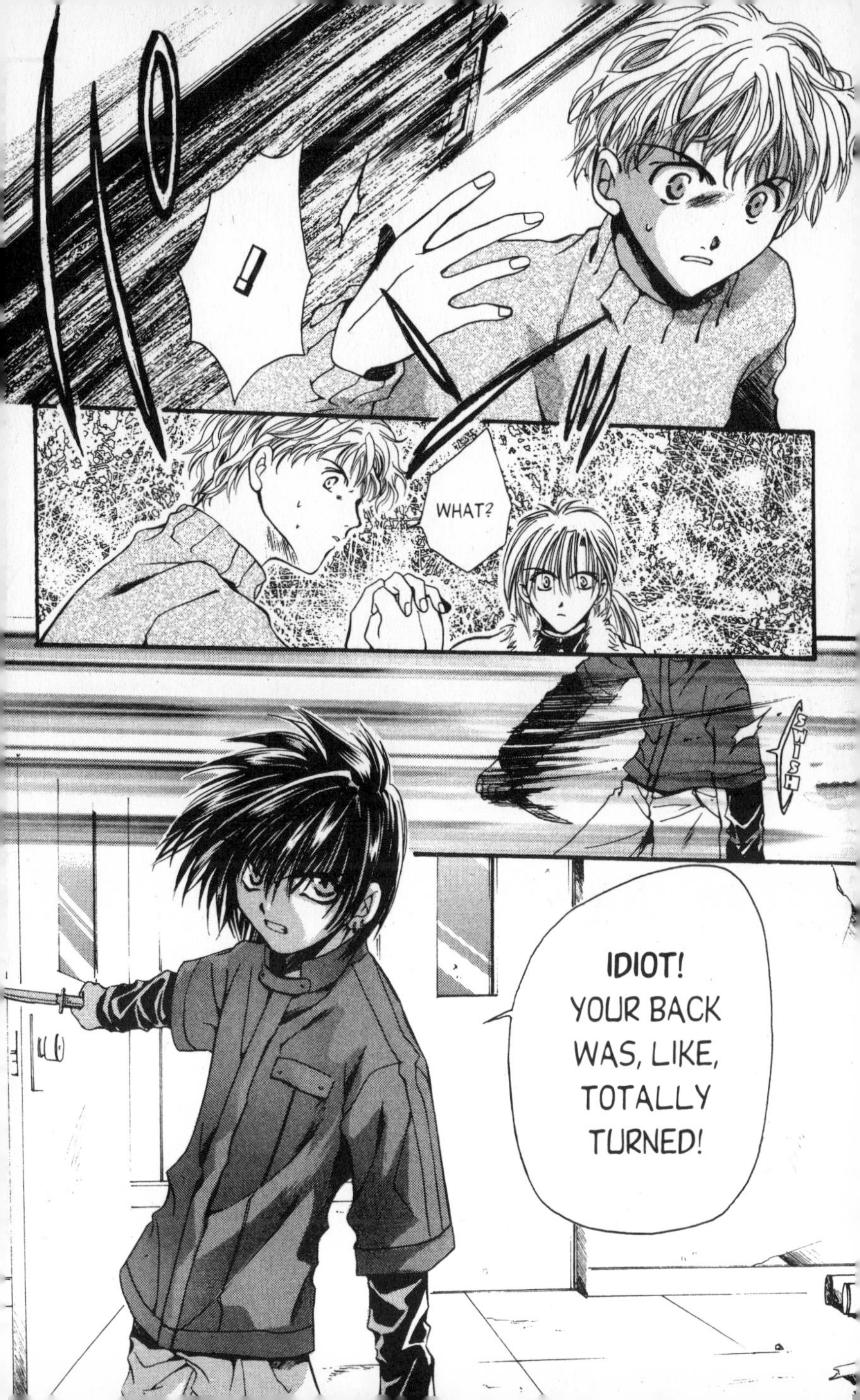
!
WHAT?
SWISH
IDIOT! YOUR BACK WAS, LIKE, TOTALLY TURNED!

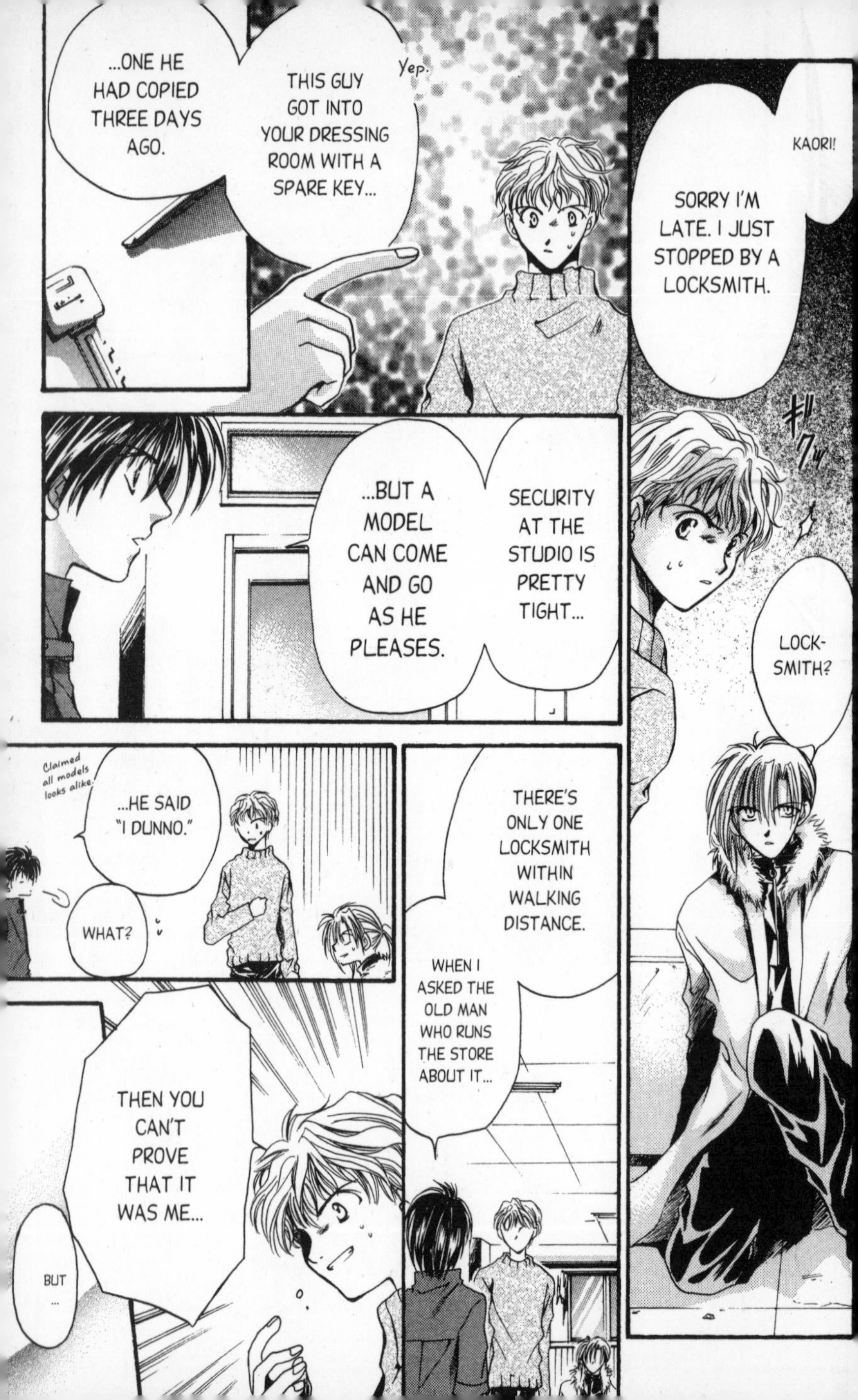
KAORI!
SORRY I'M LATE. I JUST STOPPED BY A LOCKSMITH.
LOCK-SMITH?
THIS GUY GOT INTO YOUR DRESSING ROOM WITH A SPARE KEY...
...ONE HE HAD COPIED THREE DAYS AGO.
Yep.
SECURITY AT THE STUDIO IS PRETTY TIGHT...
...BUT A MODEL CAN COME AND GO AS HE PLEASES.
THERE'S ONLY ONE LOCKSMITH WITHIN WALKING DISTANCE.
WHEN I ASKED THE OLD MAN WHO RUNS THE STORE ABOUT IT...
...HE SAID "I DUNNO."
Claimed all models looks alike.
WHAT?
THEN YOU CAN'T PROVE THAT IT WAS ME...
BUT ...

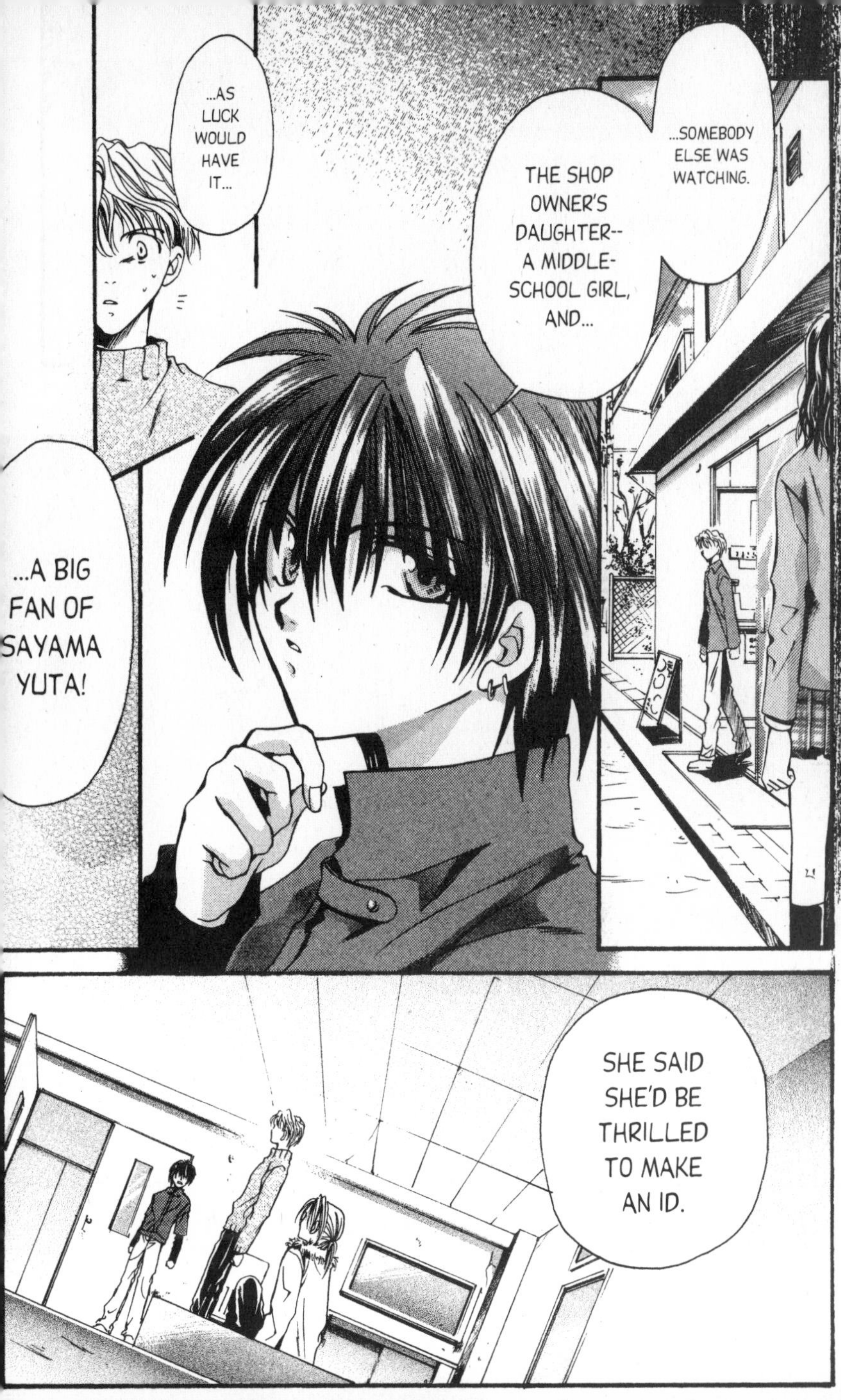
...SOMEBODY ELSE WAS WATCHING.
...AS LUCK WOULD HAVE IT...
THE SHOP OWNER'S DAUGHTER-- A MIDDLE-SCHOOL GIRL, AND...
...A BIG FAN OF SAYAMA YUTA!
SHE SAID SHE'D BE THRILLED TO MAKE AN ID.

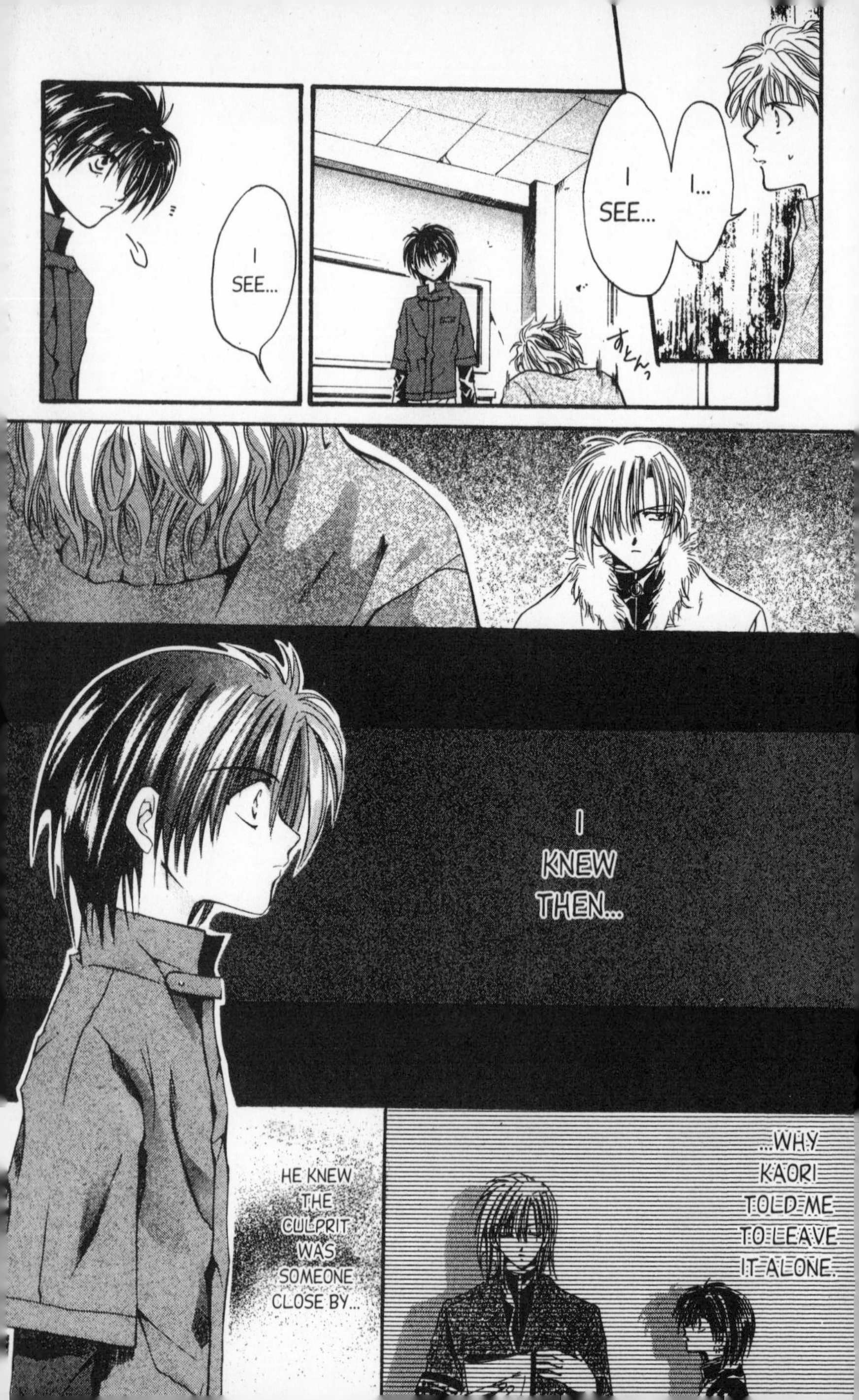
I...
I SEE...
すとんっ
I SEE...
I KNEW THEN...
...WHY KAORI TOLD ME TO LEAVE IT ALONE.
HE KNEW THE CULPRIT WAS SOMEONE CLOSE BY...

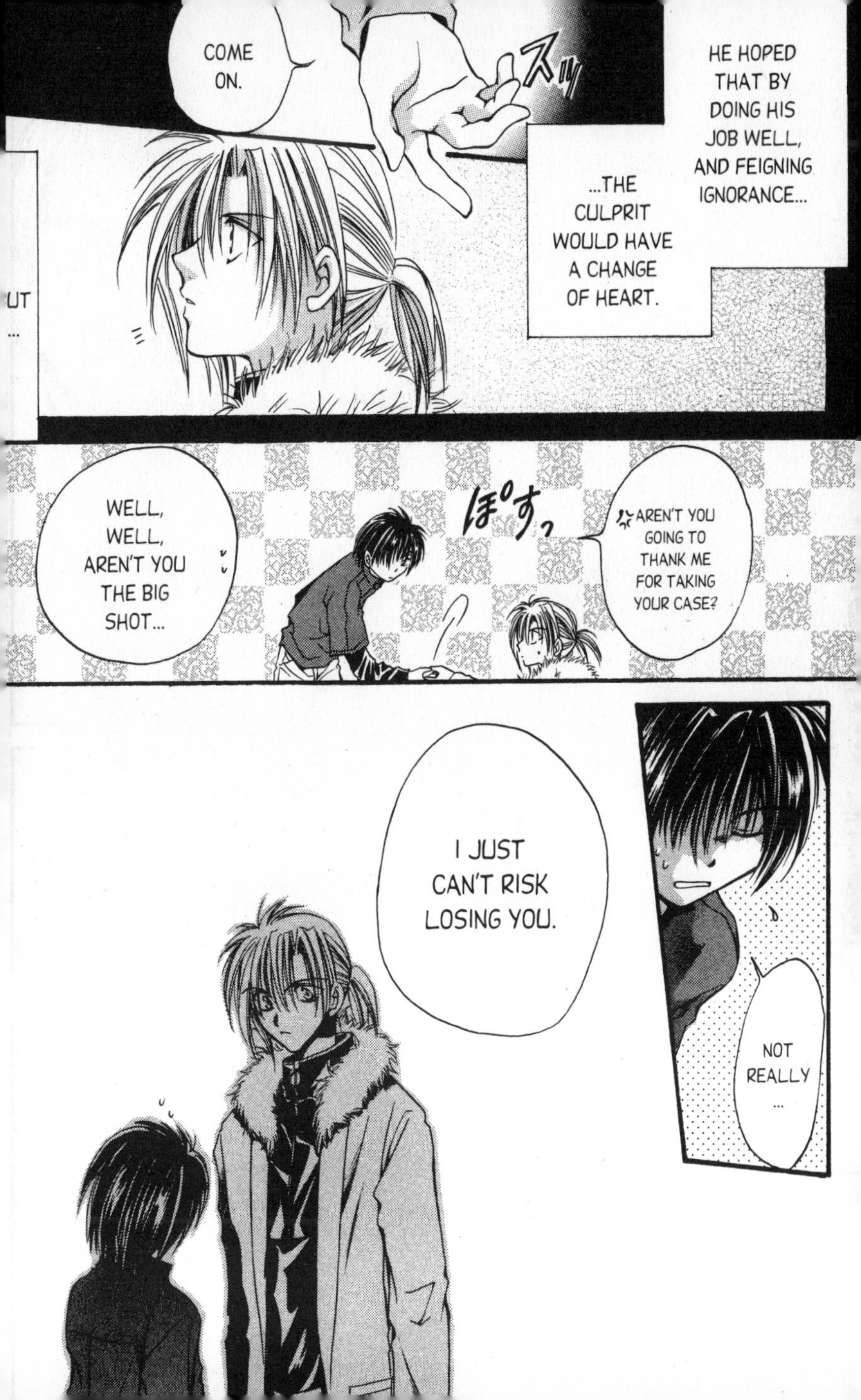
HE HOPED THAT BY DOING HIS JOB WELL, AND FEIGNING IGNORANCE...
...THE CULPRIT WOULD HAVE A CHANGE OF HEART.
スッ
COME ON.
AREN'T YOU GOING TO THANK ME FOR TAKING YOUR CASE?
ぽすっ
WELL, WELL, AREN'T YOU THE BIG SHOT...
NOT REALLY ...
I JUST CAN'T RISK LOSING YOU.

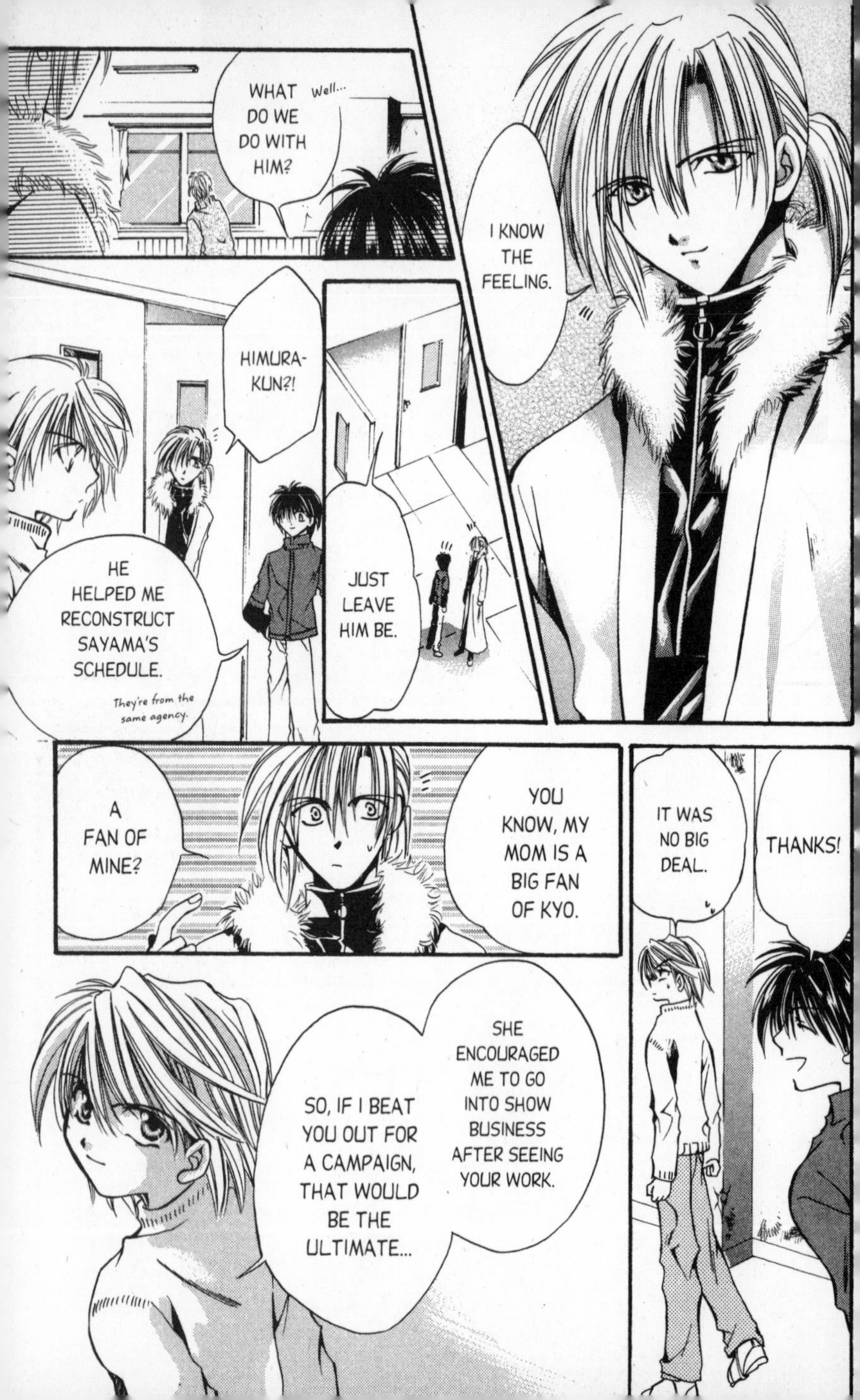
I KNOW THE FEELING.
WHAT DO WE DO WITH HIM?
Well...
JUST LEAVE HIM BE.
HIMURA-KUN?!
HE HELPED ME RECONSTRUCT SAYAMA'S SCHEDULE.
They're from the same agency.
THANKS!
IT WAS NO BIG DEAL.
YOU KNOW, MY MOM IS A BIG FAN OF KYO.
A FAN OF MINE?
SHE ENCOURAGED ME TO GO INTO SHOW BUSINESS AFTER SEEING YOUR WORK.
SO, IF I BEAT YOU OUT FOR A CAMPAIGN, THAT WOULD BE THE ULTIMATE...

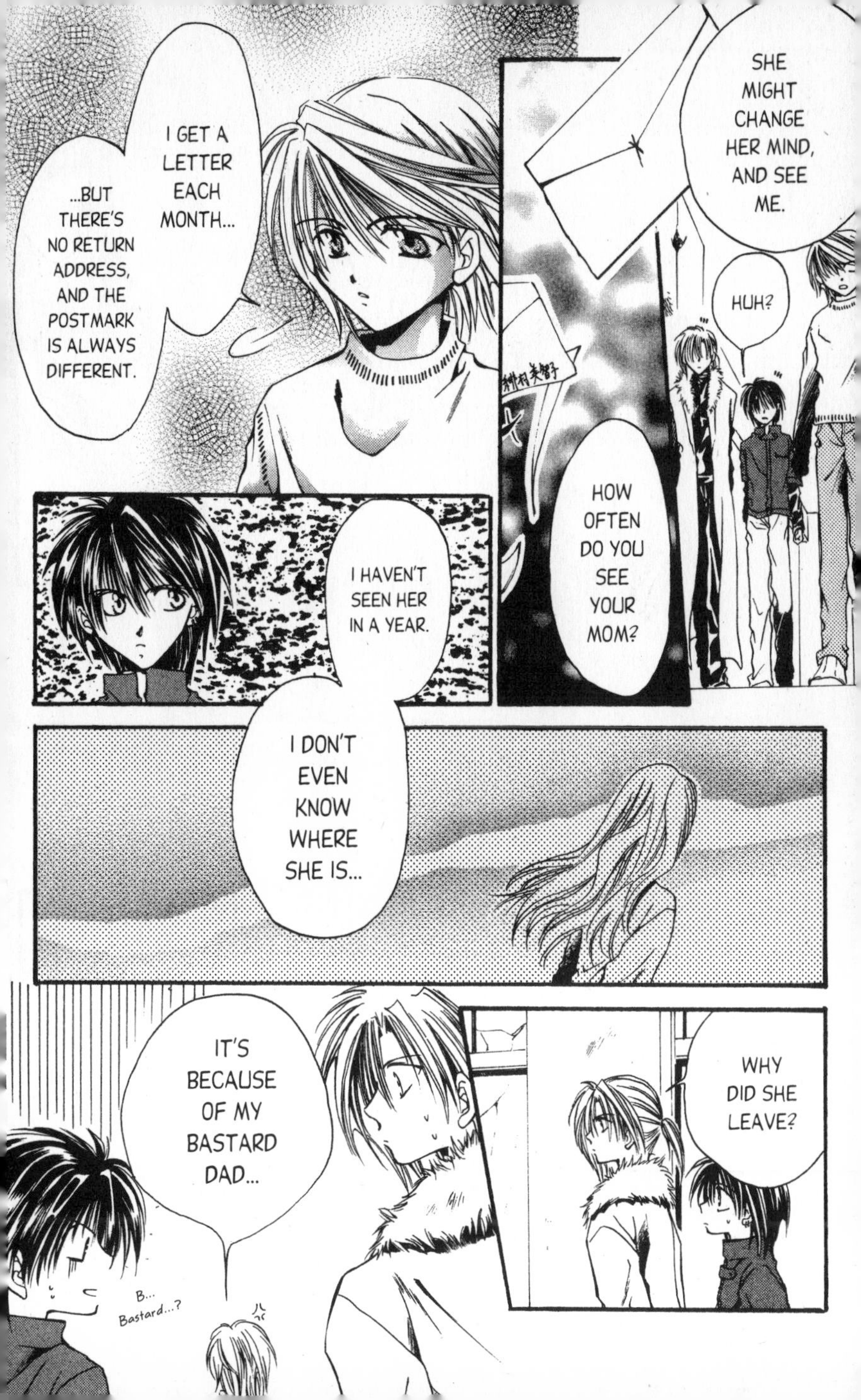
SHE MIGHT CHANGE HER MIND, AND SEE ME.
HUH?
HOW OFTEN DO YOU SEE YOUR MOM?
I GET A LETTER EACH MONTH...
...BUT THERE'S NO RETURN ADDRESS, AND THE POSTMARK IS ALWAYS DIFFERENT.
I HAVEN'T SEEN HER IN A YEAR.
I DON'T EVEN KNOW WHERE SHE IS...
WHY DID SHE LEAVE?
IT'S BECAUSE OF MY BASTARD DAD...
B... Bastard...?

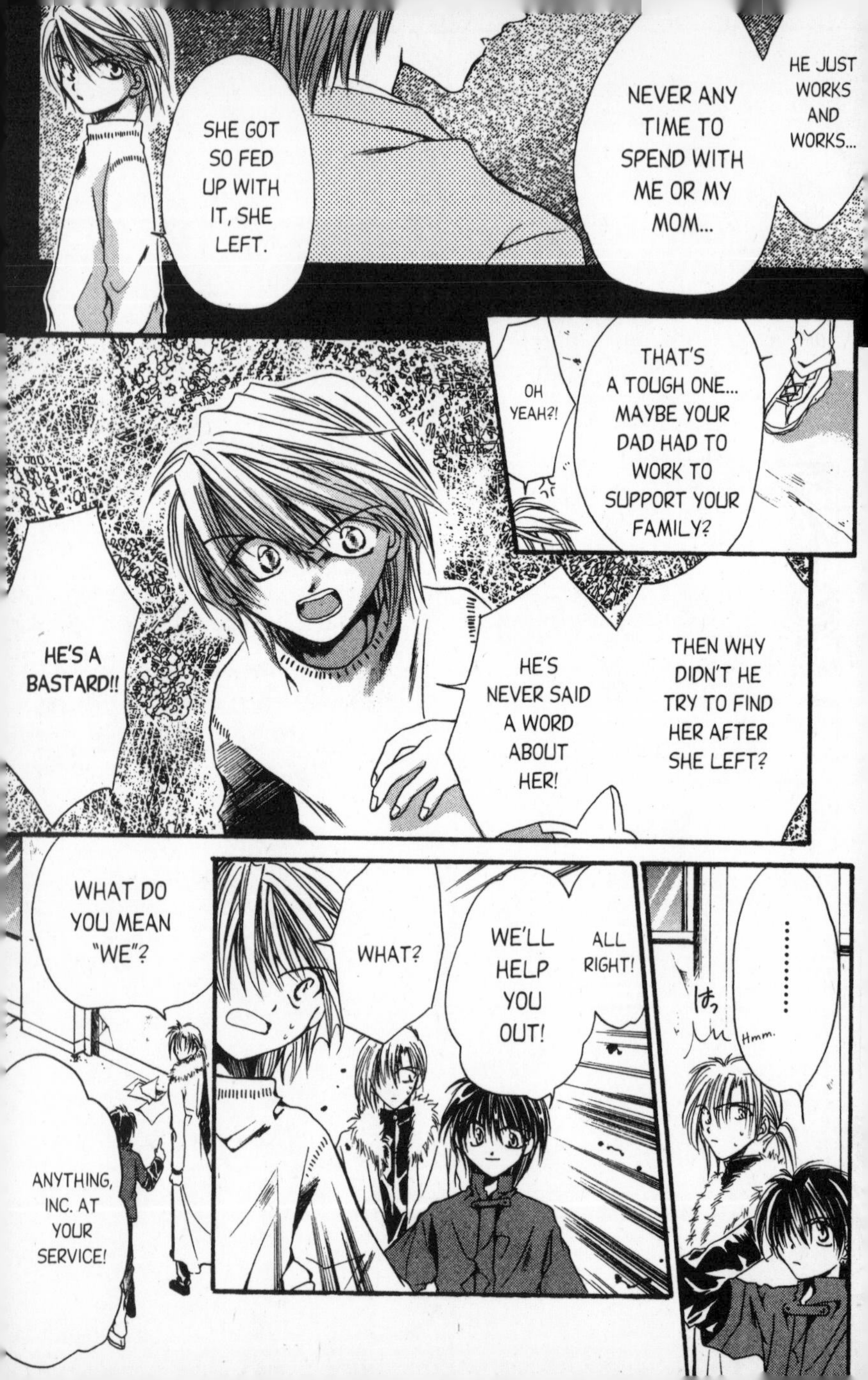
HE JUST WORKS AND WORKS...
NEVER ANY TIME TO SPEND WITH ME OR MY MOM...
SHE GOT SO FED UP WITH IT, SHE LEFT.
THAT'S A TOUGH ONE... MAYBE YOUR DAD HAD TO WORK TO SUPPORT YOUR FAMILY?
OH YEAH?!
THEN WHY DIDN'T HE TRY TO FIND HER AFTER SHE LEFT?
HE'S NEVER SAID A WORD ABOUT HER!
HE'S A BASTARD!!
......
はっ
Hmm.
ALL RIGHT!
WE'LL HELP YOU OUT!
WHAT?
WHAT DO YOU MEAN "WE"?
ANYTHING, INC. AT YOUR SERVICE!

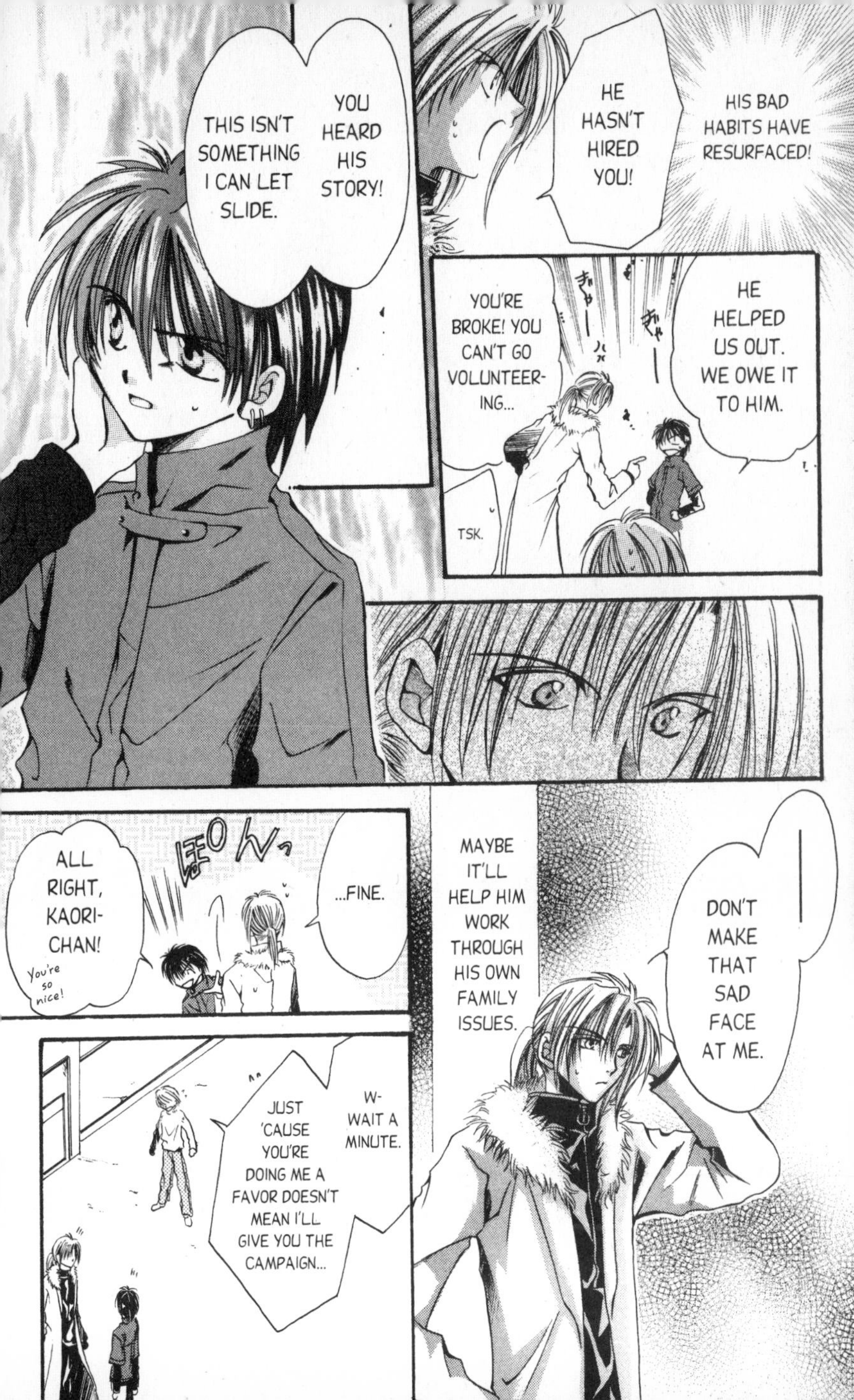
HE HASN'T HIRED YOU!
HIS BAD HABITS HAVE RESURFACED!
HE HELPED US OUT. WE OWE IT TO HIM.
YOU'RE BROKE! YOU CAN'T GO VOLUNTEERING...
TSK.
YOU HEARD HIS STORY!
THIS ISN'T SOMETHING I CAN LET SLIDE.
DON'T MAKE THAT SAD FACE AT ME.
MAYBE IT'LL HELP HIM WORK THROUGH HIS OWN FAMILY ISSUES.
...FINE.
ALL RIGHT, KAORI-CHAN!
You're so nice!
W-WAIT A MINUTE.
JUST 'CAUSE YOU'RE DOING ME A FAVOR DOESN'T MEAN I'LL GIVE YOU THE CAMPAIGN...

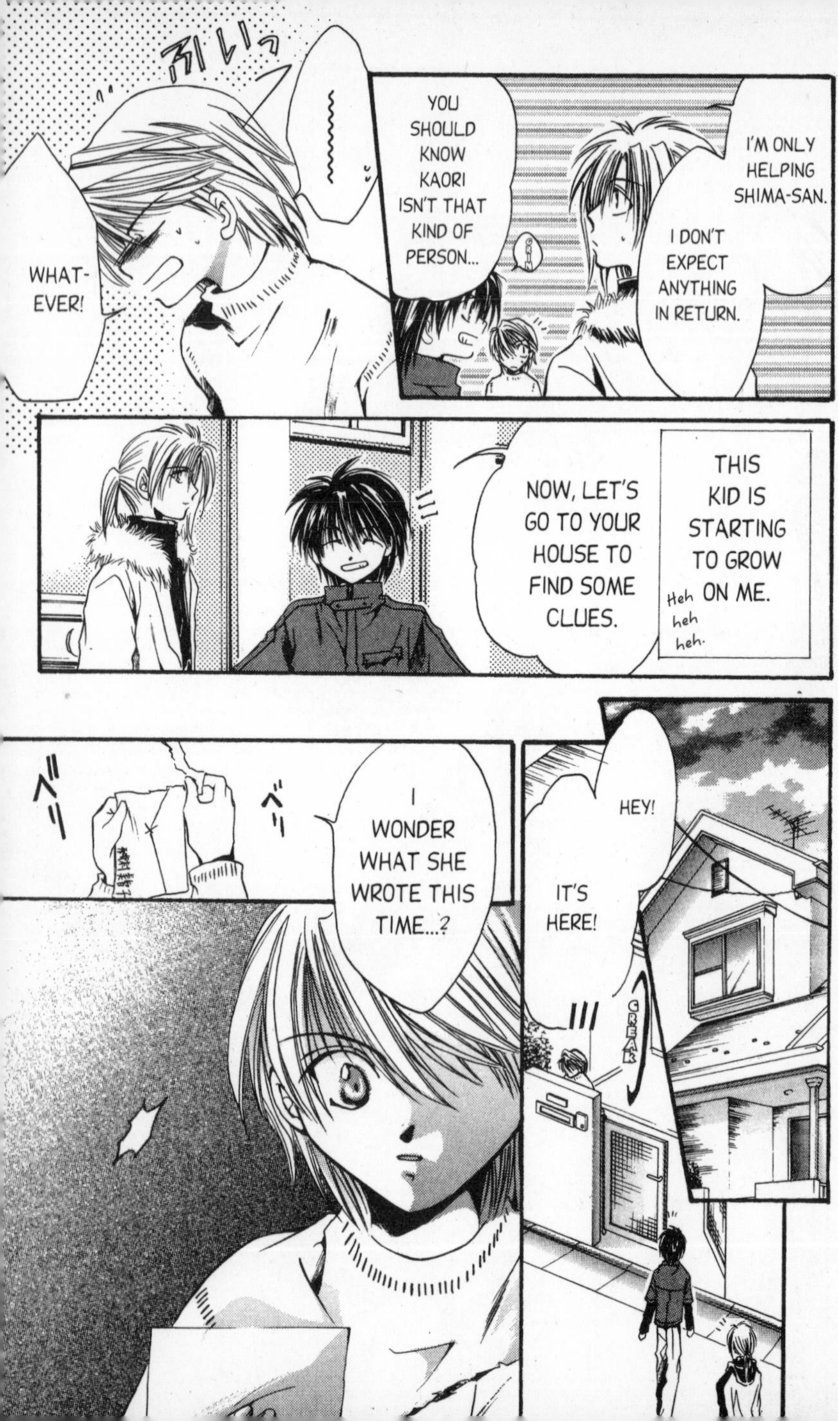
I'M ONLY HELPING SHIMA-SAN.
I DON'T EXPECT ANYTHING IN RETURN.
GRIN
YOU SHOULD KNOW KAORI ISN'T THAT KIND OF PERSON...
WHAT-EVER!
THIS KID IS STARTING TO GROW ON ME.
Heh heh heh.
NOW, LET'S GO TO YOUR HOUSE TO FIND SOME CLUES.
HEY!
IT'S HERE!
CREAK
I WONDER WHAT SHE WROTE THIS TIME...?
べり
べり

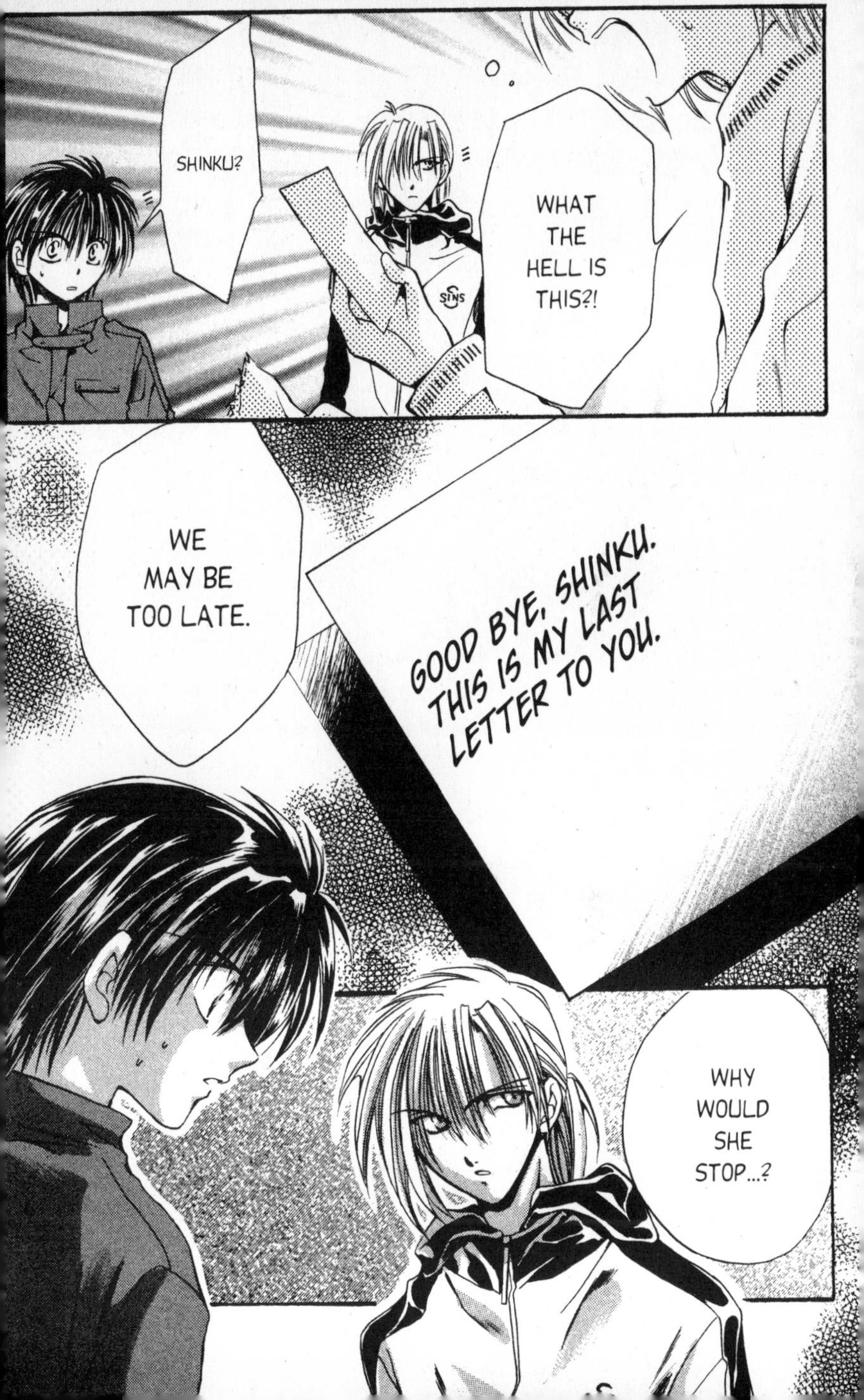
WHAT THE HELL IS THIS?!
SHINKU?
GOOD BYE, SHINKU. THIS IS MY LAST LETTER TO YOU.
WE MAY BE TOO LATE.
WHY WOULD SHE STOP...?

BROKEN MEMORIES

SATISFACTION GUARANTEED

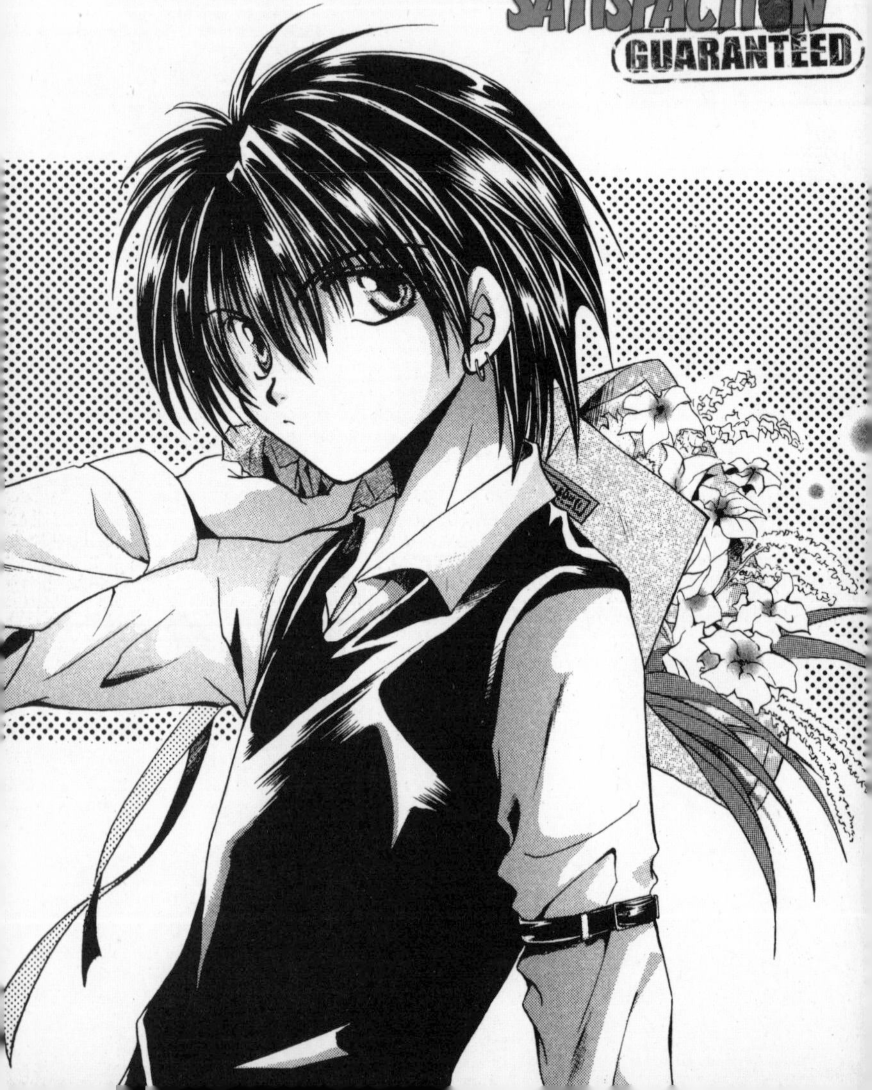

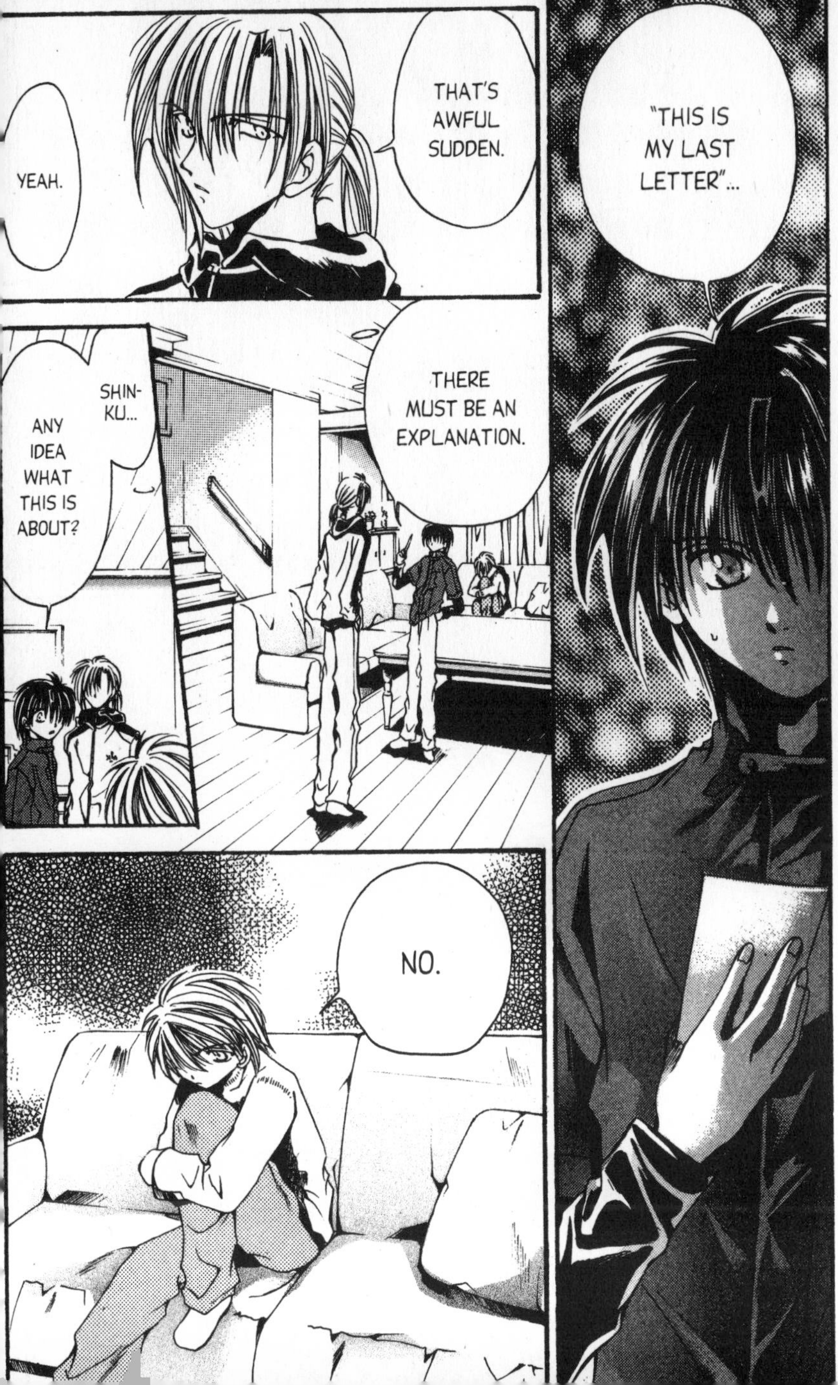
"THIS IS MY LAST LETTER"...
THAT'S AWFUL SUDDEN.
YEAH.
THERE MUST BE AN EXPLANATION.
SHIN-KU...
ANY IDEA WHAT THIS IS ABOUT?
NO.

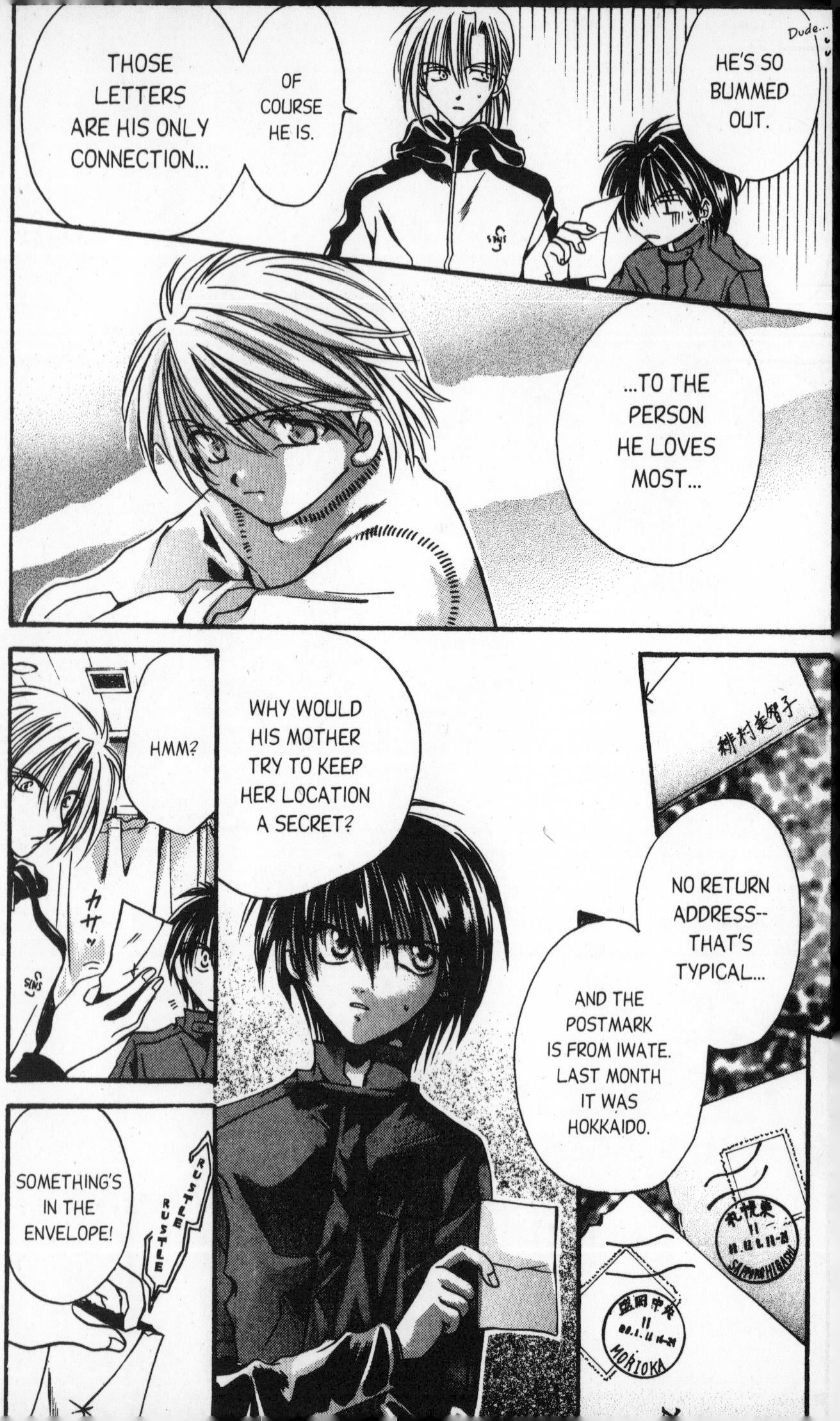

Dude...
HE'S SO BUMMED OUT.
OF COURSE HE IS.
THOSE LETTERS ARE HIS ONLY CONNECTION...
...TO THE PERSON HE LOVES MOST...
NO RETURN ADDRESS-- THAT'S TYPICAL...
AND THE POSTMARK IS FROM IWATE. LAST MONTH IT WAS HOKKAIDO.
MORIOKA
WHY WOULD HIS MOTHER TRY TO KEEP HER LOCATION A SECRET?
HMM?
カサ
SOMETHING'S IN THE ENVELOPE!
RUSTLE
RUSTLE

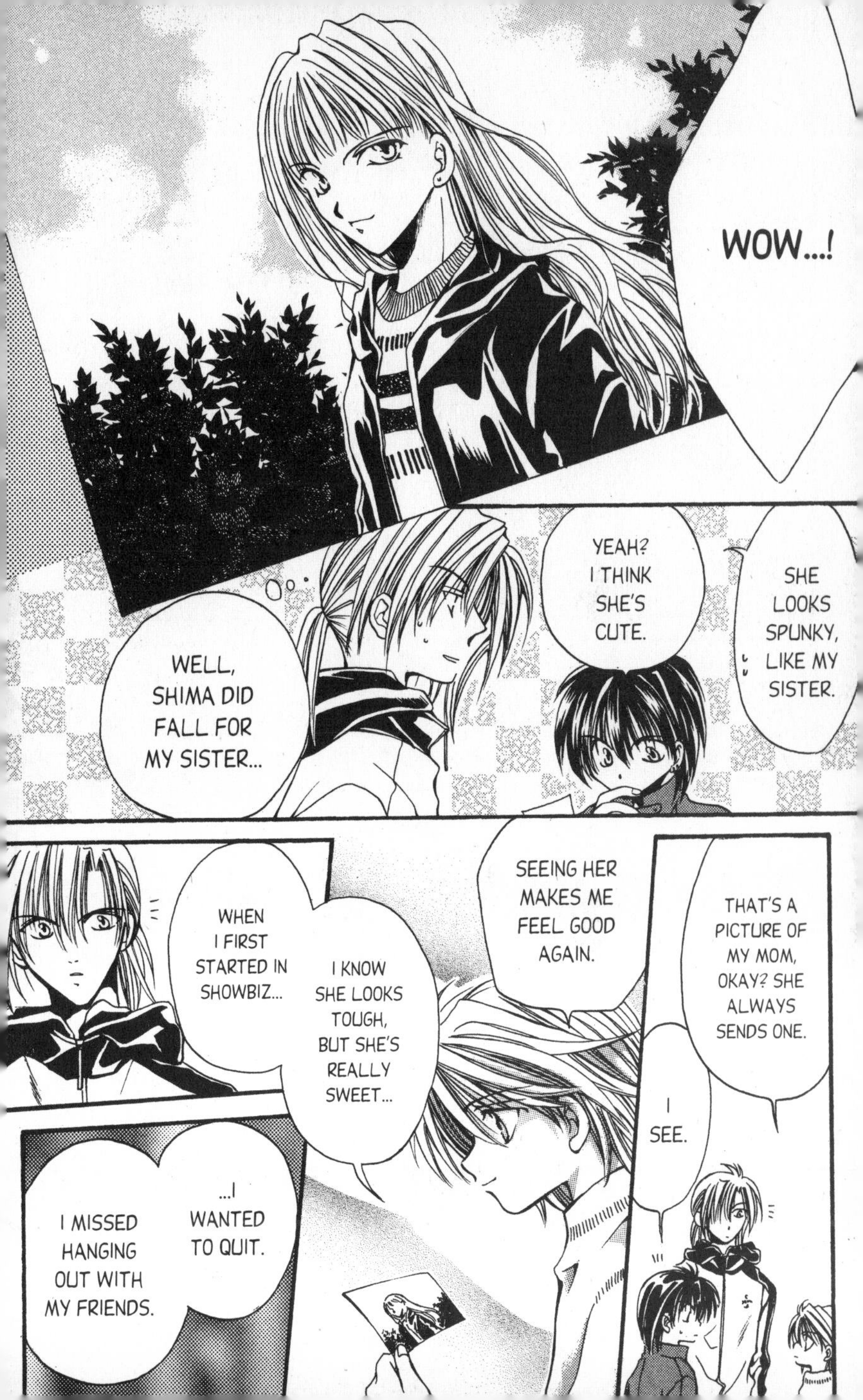
WOW...!
SHE LOOKS SPUNKY, LIKE MY SISTER.
YEAH? I THINK SHE'S CUTE.
WELL, SHIMA DID FALL FOR MY SISTER...
THAT'S A PICTURE OF MY MOM, OKAY? SHE ALWAYS SENDS ONE.
I SEE.
SEEING HER MAKES ME FEEL GOOD AGAIN.
I KNOW SHE LOOKS TOUGH, BUT SHE'S REALLY SWEET...
WHEN I FIRST STARTED IN SHOWBIZ...
...I WANTED TO QUIT.
I MISSED HANGING OUT WITH MY FRIENDS.

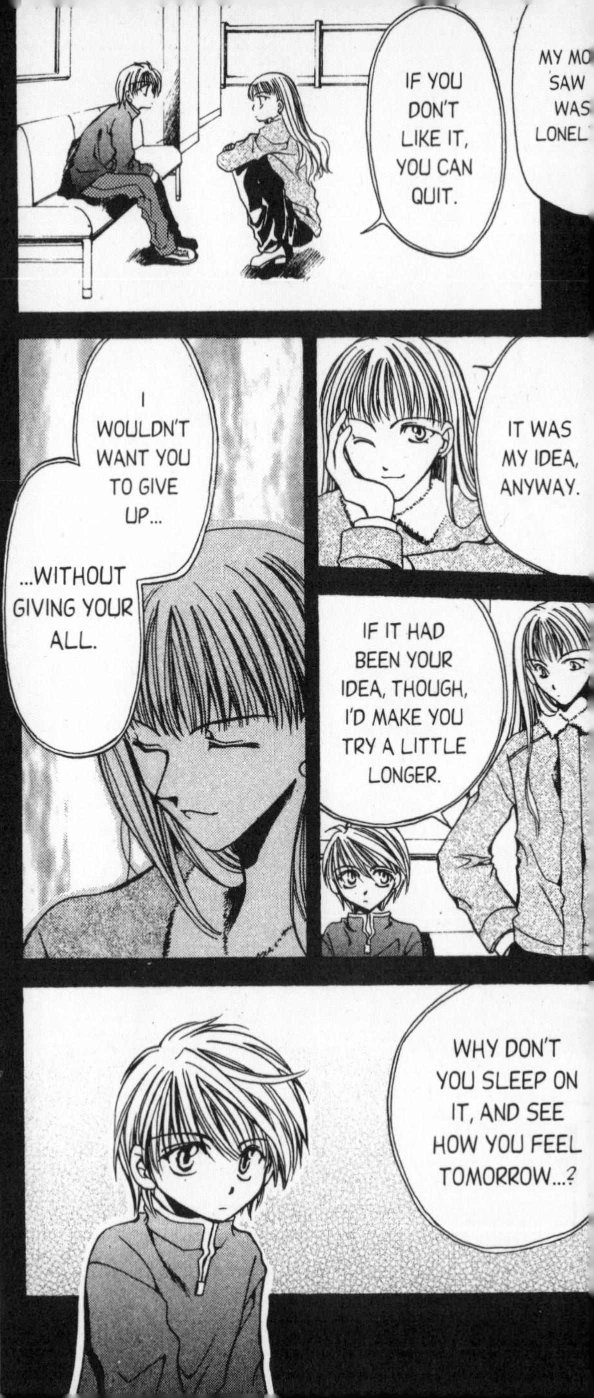
MY MO
SAW
WAS
LONEL
IF YOU DON'T LIKE IT, YOU CAN QUIT.
IT WAS MY IDEA, ANYWAY.
IF IT HAD BEEN YOUR IDEA, THOUGH, I'D MAKE YOU TRY A LITTLE LONGER.
I WOULDN'T WANT YOU TO GIVE UP...
...WITHOUT GIVING YOUR ALL.
WHY DON'T YOU SLEEP ON IT, AND SEE HOW YOU FEEL TOMORROW...?

In Kaori and Shinku's commercial, I make Kaori play a vampire. I'm kind of goth-obsessed. Angels, devils, vampires... I don't know why I love that stuff so much. I submitted a vampire manga to "Hana to Yume" comics.

Oh! By the way, I bought a picture book about human organs the other day. It's a little gross and wonderful at the same time. Hee hee hee... (I know I'm a little scary.)

I knew from the very beginning that Kaori was going to play a vampire! I knew he'd look hot in the outfit! Kaori is definitely the best-looking normal guy in this manga. The best-looking weirdo is, of course, APP. (Ha ha!)

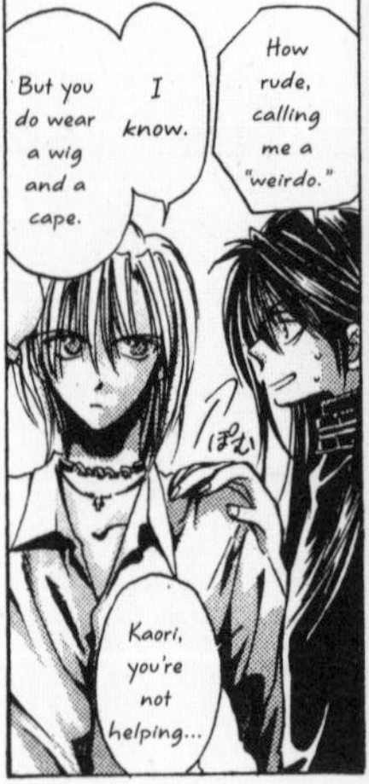
How rude, calling me a "weirdo."
I know.
But you do wear a wig and a cape.
ぽむ
Kaori, you're not helping...

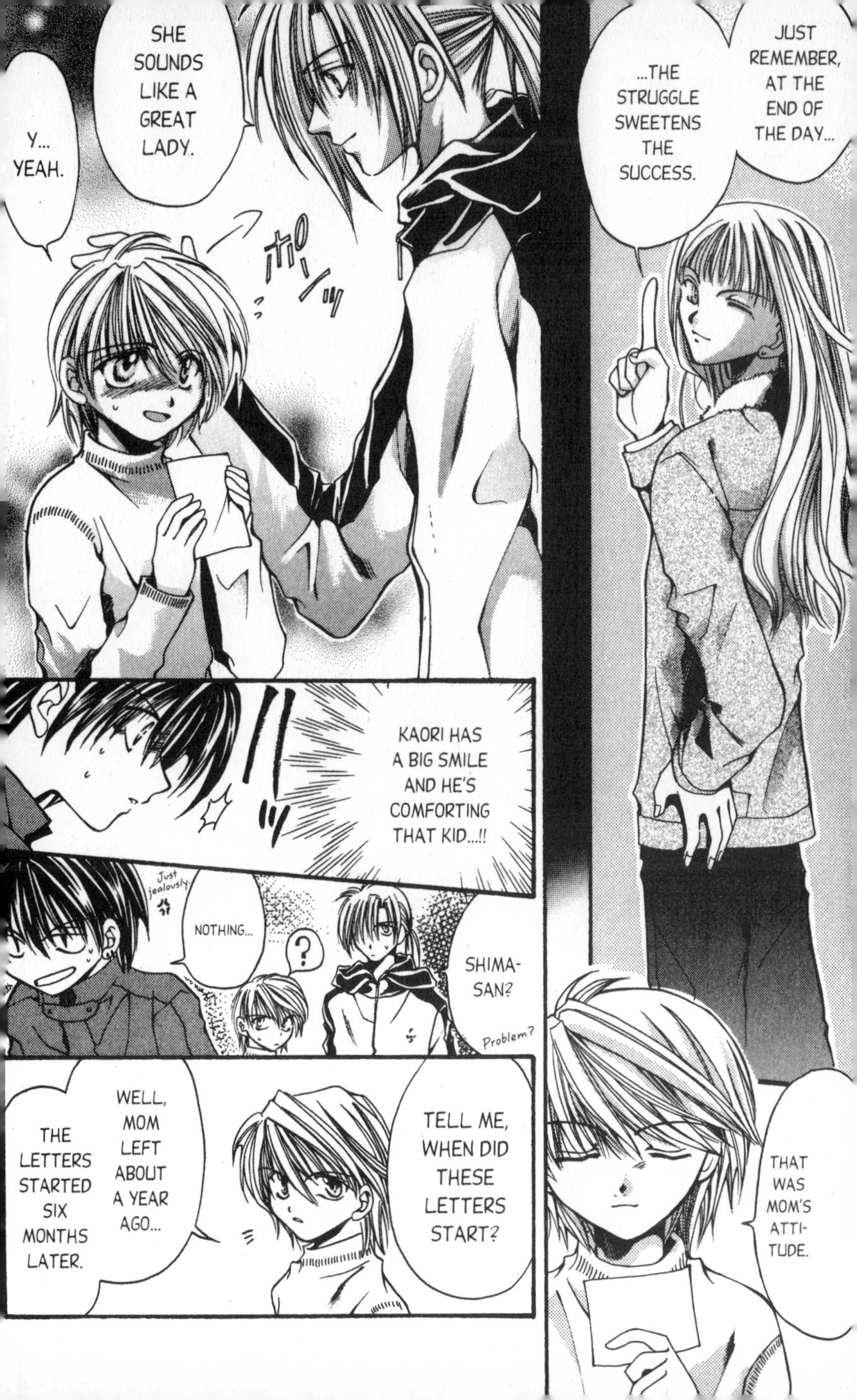
JUST REMEMBER, AT THE END OF THE DAY...
...THE STRUGGLE SWEETENS THE SUCCESS.
THAT WAS MOM'S ATTI-TUDE.
SHE SOUNDS LIKE A GREAT LADY.
Y... YEAH.
KAORI HAS A BIG SMILE AND HE'S COMFORTING THAT KID...!!
SHIMA-SAN?
Problem?
NOTHING...
Just jealously.
TELL ME, WHEN DID THESE LETTERS START?
WELL, MOM LEFT ABOUT A YEAR AGO...
THE LETTERS STARTED SIX MONTHS LATER.

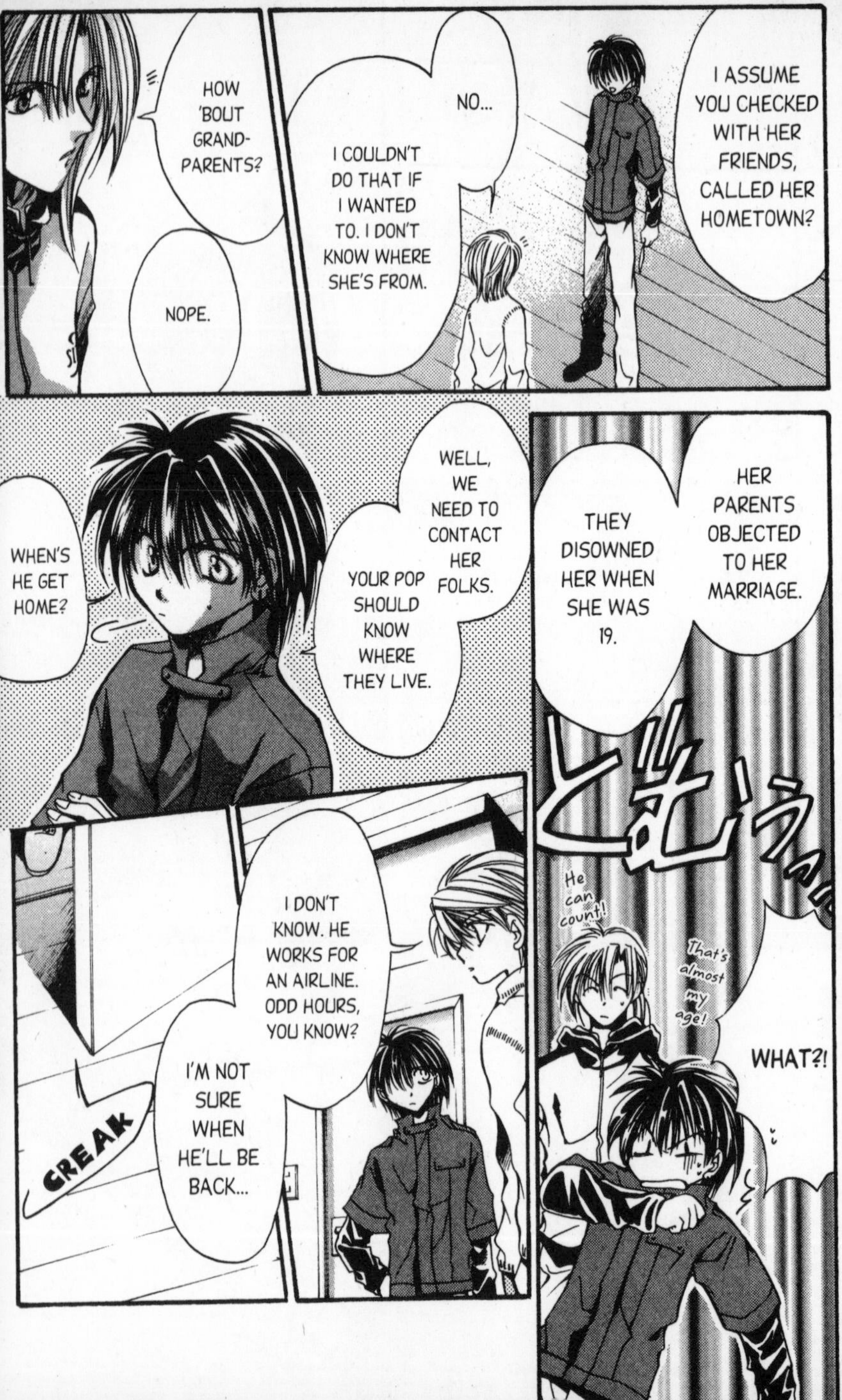
I ASSUME YOU CHECKED WITH HER FRIENDS, CALLED HER HOMETOWN?
NO...
I COULDN'T DO THAT IF I WANTED TO. I DON'T KNOW WHERE SHE'S FROM.
HOW 'BOUT GRAND-PARENTS?
NOPE.
HER PARENTS OBJECTED TO HER MARRIAGE.
THEY DISOWNED HER WHEN SHE WAS 19.
WHAT?!
That's almost my age!
He can count!
WELL, WE NEED TO CONTACT HER FOLKS.
YOUR POP SHOULD KNOW WHERE THEY LIVE.
WHEN'S HE GET HOME?
I DON'T KNOW. HE WORKS FOR AN AIRLINE. ODD HOURS, YOU KNOW?
I'M NOT SURE WHEN HE'LL BE BACK...
CREAK

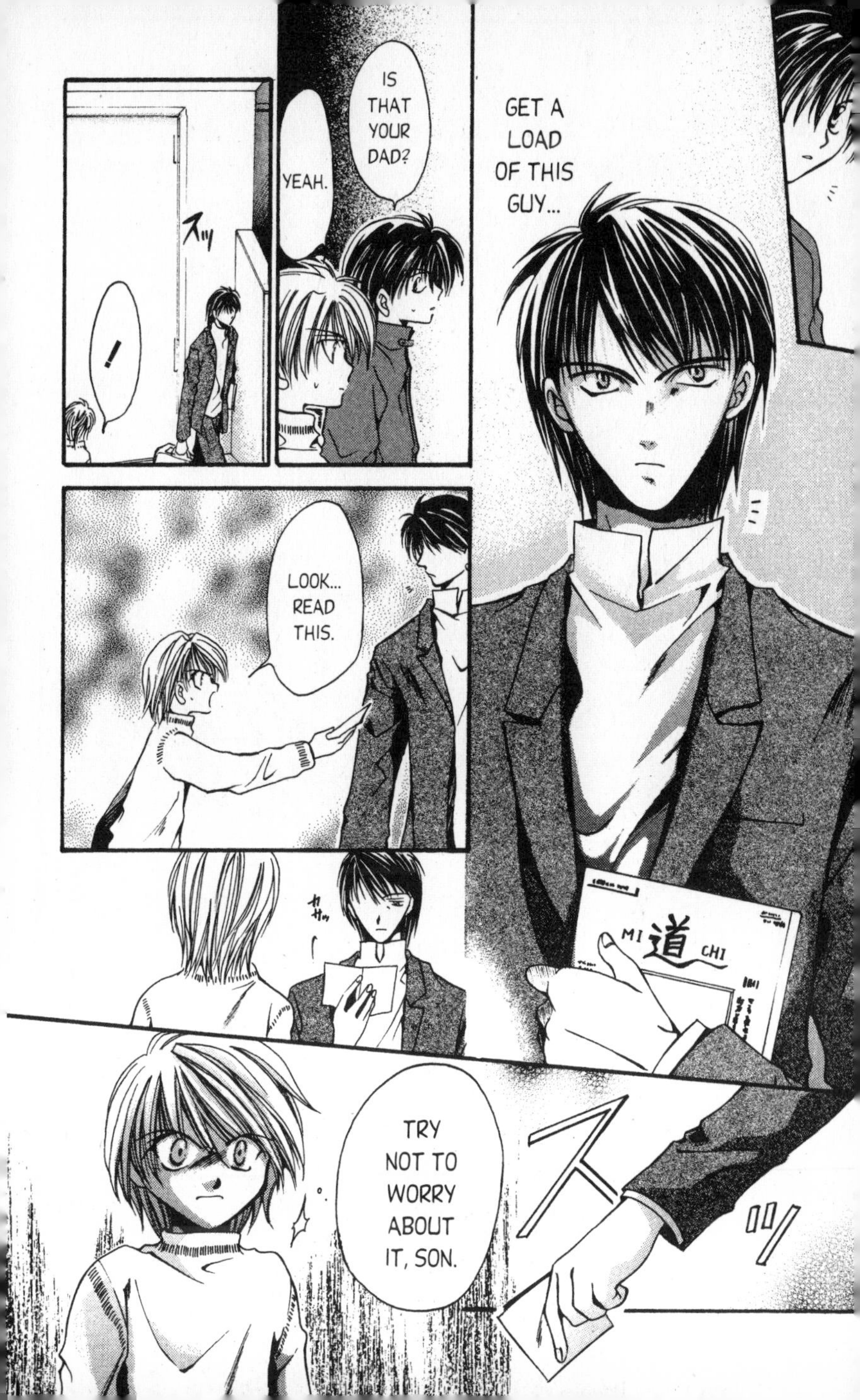

GET A LOAD OF THIS GUY...
MI 道 CHI
IS THAT YOUR DAD?
YEAH.
ズッ
!
LOOK... READ THIS.
TRY NOT TO WORRY ABOUT IT, SON.

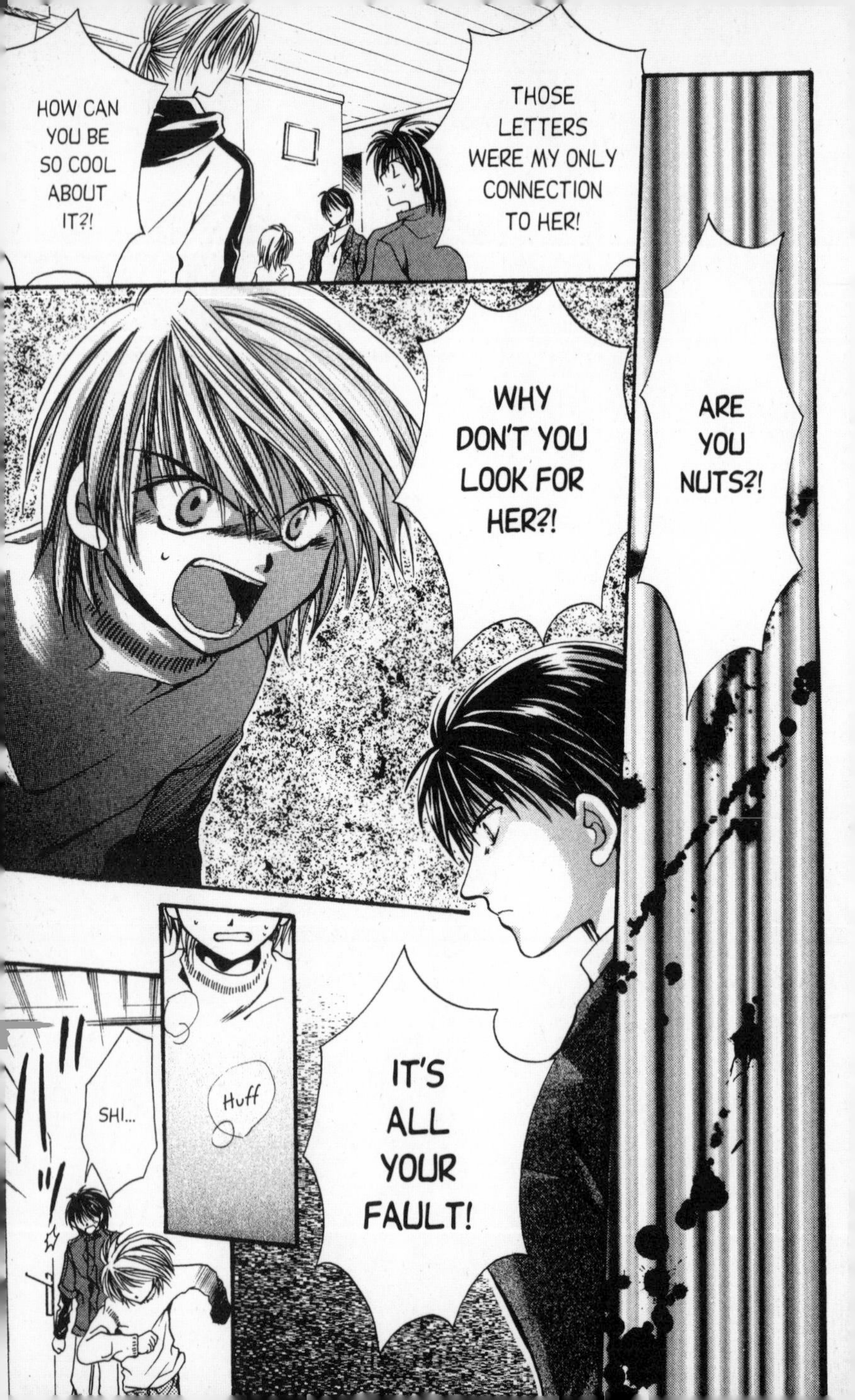
THOSE LETTERS WERE MY ONLY CONNECTION TO HER!
HOW CAN YOU BE SO COOL ABOUT IT?!
ARE YOU NUTS?!
WHY DON'T YOU LOOK FOR HER?!
IT'S ALL YOUR FAULT!
Huff
SHI...

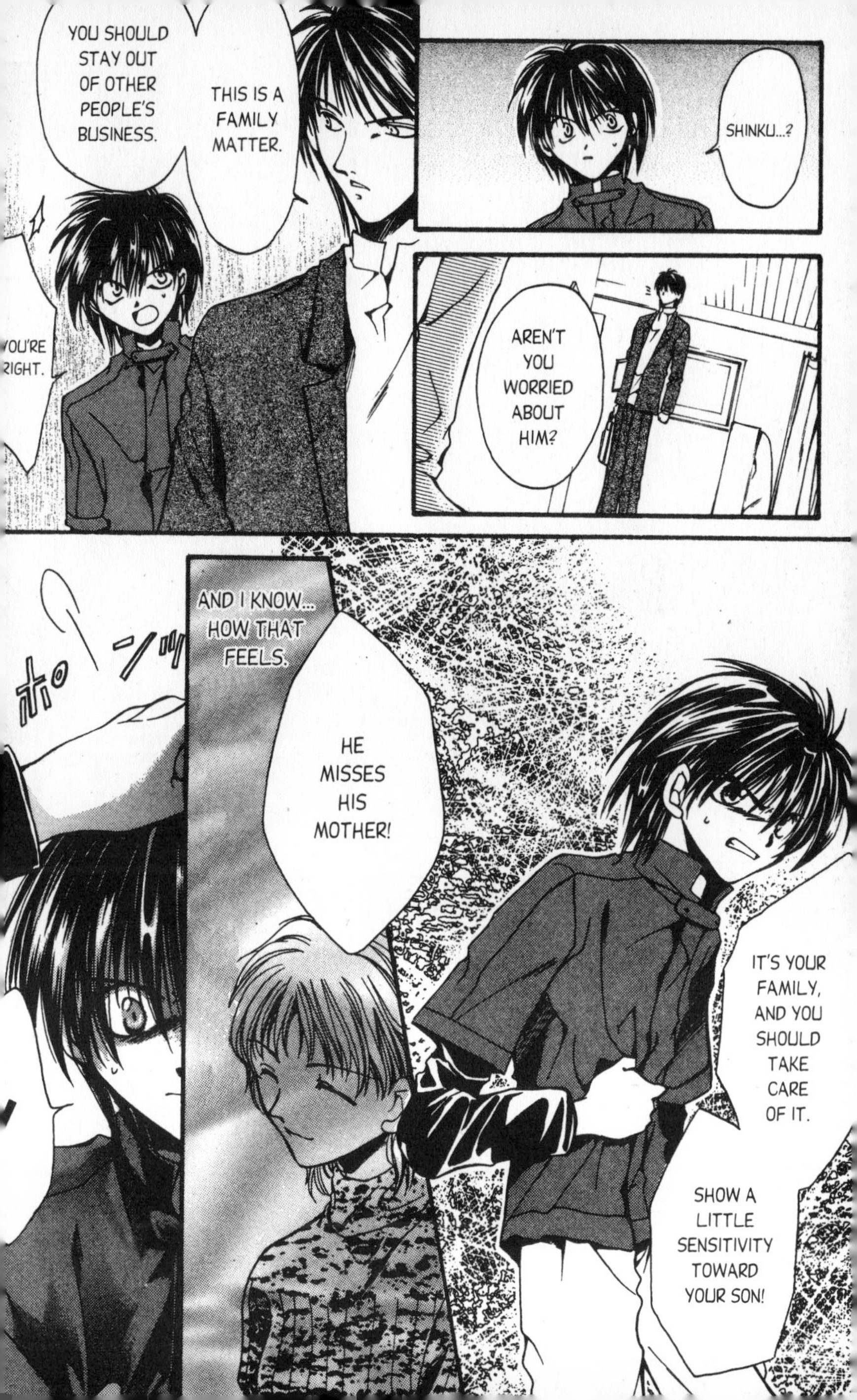
SHINKU...?
AREN'T YOU WORRIED ABOUT HIM?
THIS IS A FAMILY MATTER.
YOU SHOULD STAY OUT OF OTHER PEOPLE'S BUSINESS.
YOU'RE RIGHT.
IT'S YOUR FAMILY, AND YOU SHOULD TAKE CARE OF IT.
SHOW A LITTLE SENSITIVITY TOWARD YOUR SON!
HE MISSES HIS MOTHER!
AND I KNOW... HOW THAT FEELS.
ポンッ

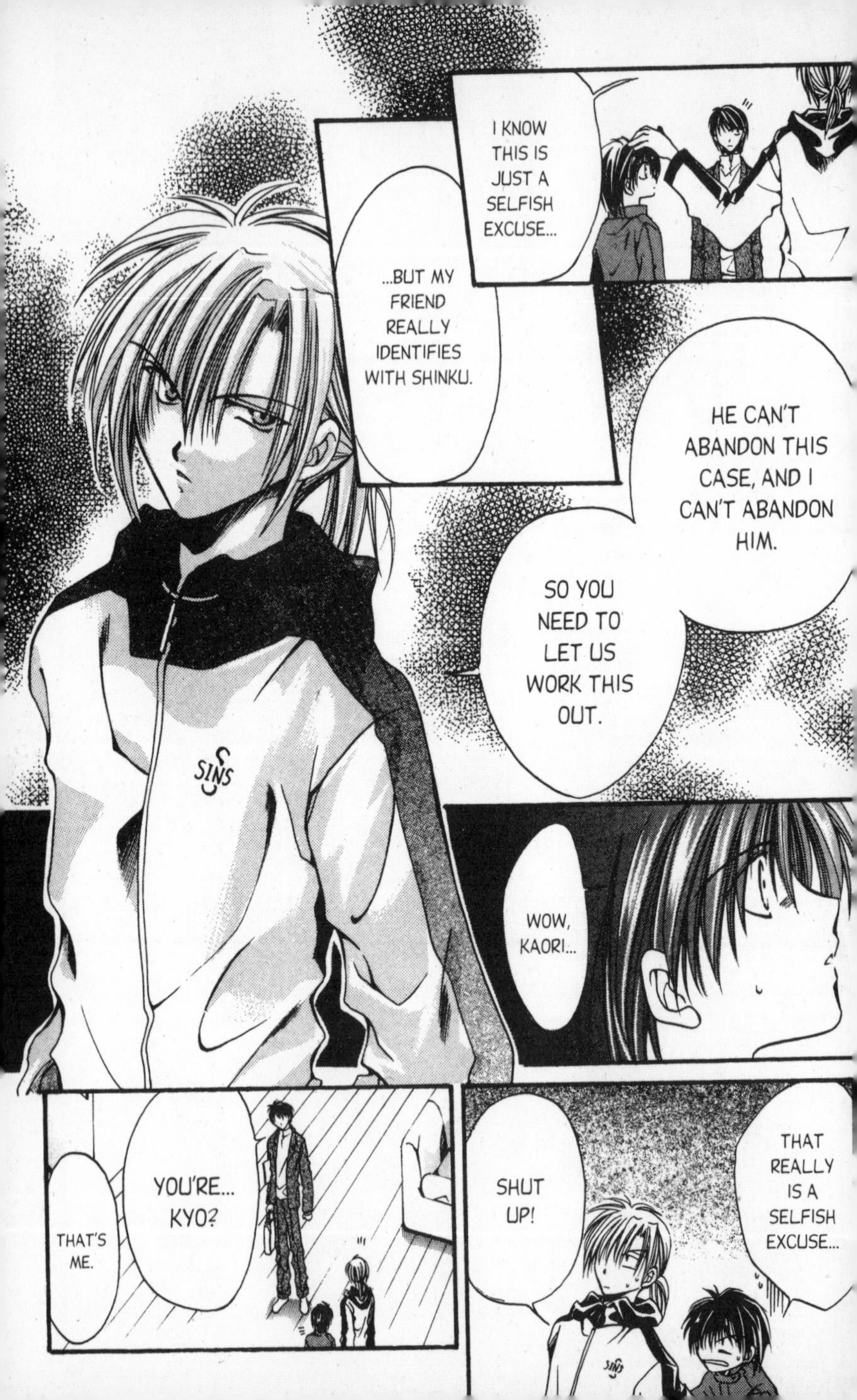
I KNOW THIS IS JUST A SELFISH EXCUSE...
...BUT MY FRIEND REALLY IDENTIFIES WITH SHINKU.
HE CAN'T ABANDON THIS CASE, AND I CAN'T ABANDON HIM.
SO YOU NEED TO LET US WORK THIS OUT.
SINS
WOW, KAORI...
THAT REALLY IS A SELFISH EXCUSE...
SHUT UP!
YOU'RE... KYO?
THAT'S ME.

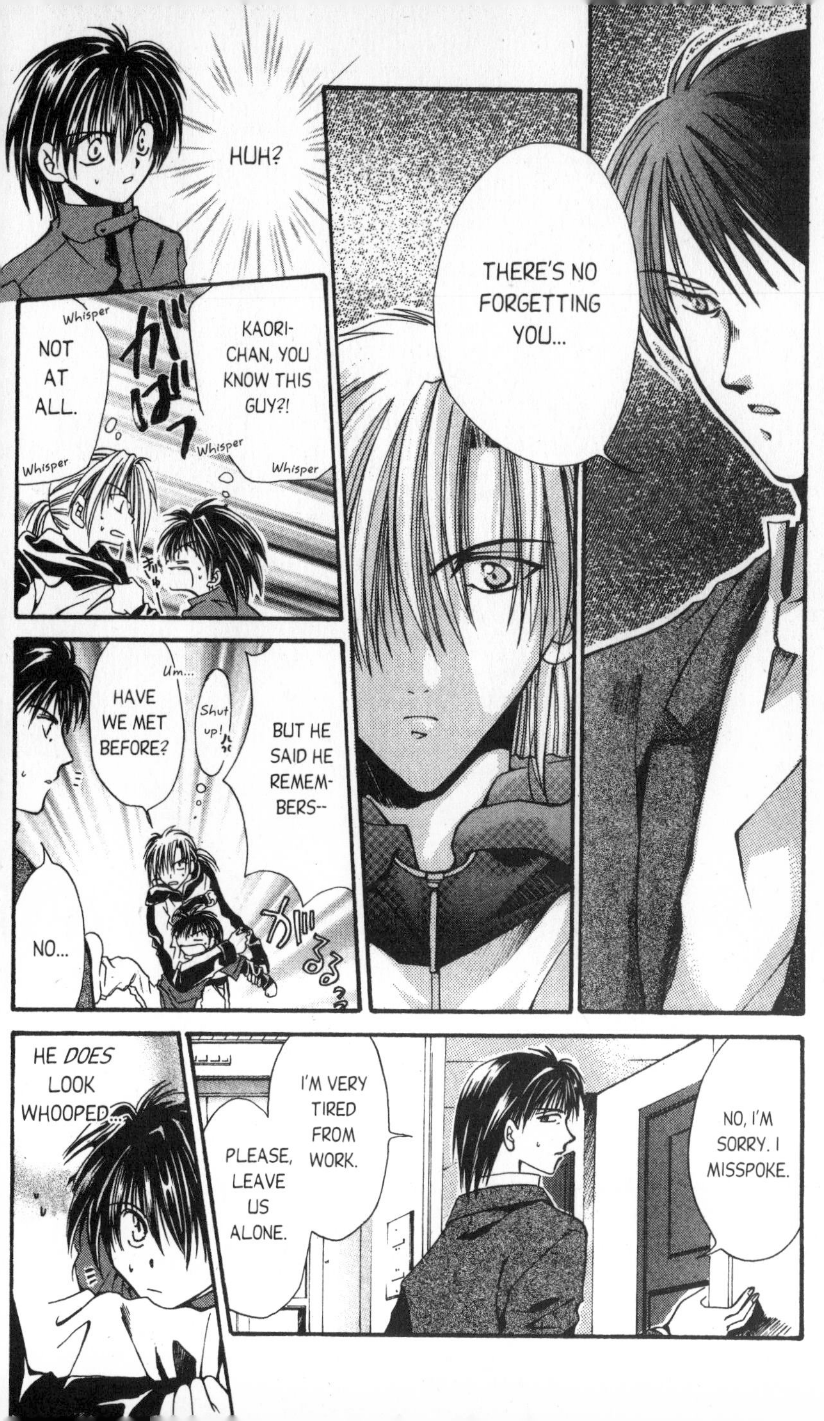

THERE'S NO FORGETTING YOU...
HUH?
Whisper
Whisper
Whisper
Whisper
KAORI-CHAN, YOU KNOW THIS GUY?!
がばっ
NOT AT ALL.
Um...
HAVE WE MET BEFORE?
BUT HE SAID HE REMEMBERS--
Shut up!
NO...
がるるる
NO, I'M SORRY. I MISSPOKE.
I'M VERY TIRED FROM WORK.
PLEASE, LEAVE US ALONE.
HE *DOES* LOOK WHOOPED...

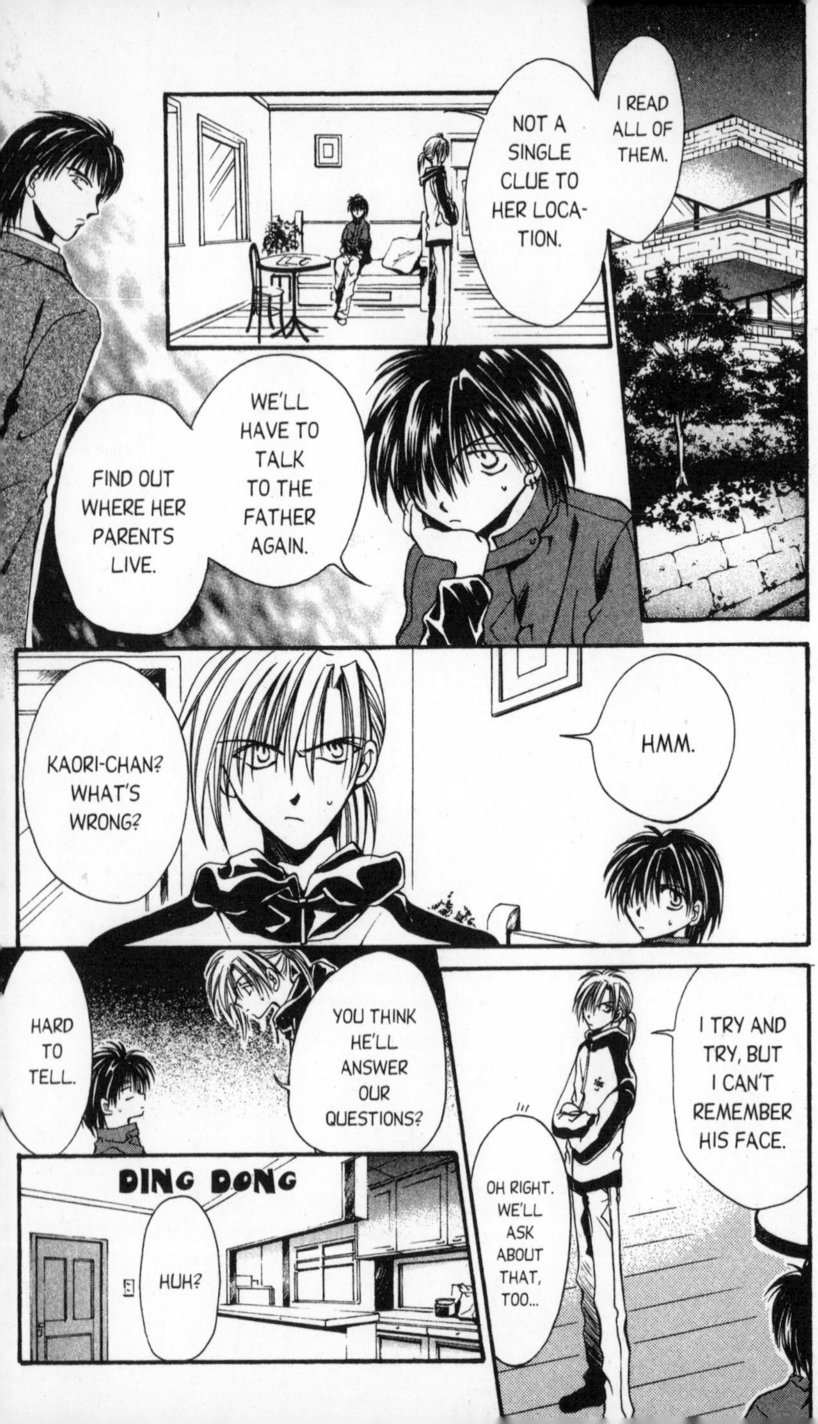
I READ ALL OF THEM.
NOT A SINGLE CLUE TO HER LOCATION.
WE'LL HAVE TO TALK TO THE FATHER AGAIN.
FIND OUT WHERE HER PARENTS LIVE.
HMM.
KAORI-CHAN? WHAT'S WRONG?
I TRY AND TRY, BUT I CAN'T REMEMBER HIS FACE.
OH RIGHT. WE'LL ASK ABOUT THAT, TOO...
YOU THINK HE'LL ANSWER OUR QUESTIONS?
HARD TO TELL.
DING DONG
HUH?

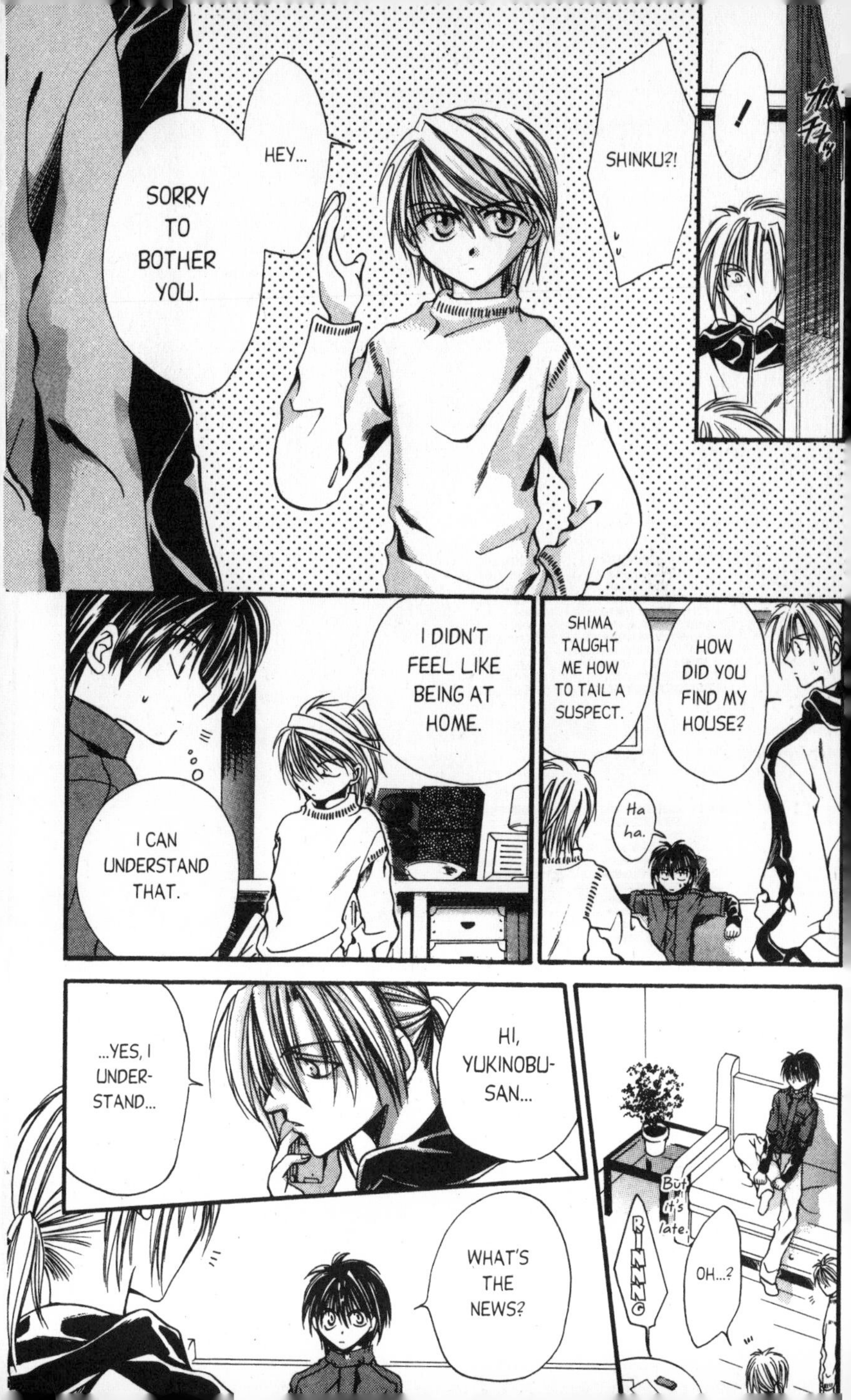
!
SHINKU?!
HEY...
SORRY TO BOTHER YOU.
HOW DID YOU FIND MY HOUSE?
SHIMA TAUGHT ME HOW TO TAIL A SUSPECT.
Ha ha.
I DIDN'T FEEL LIKE BEING AT HOME.
I CAN UNDERSTAND THAT.
But it's late.
RINNNG
OH...?
HI, YUKINOBU-SAN...
...YES, I UNDER-STAND...
WHAT'S THE NEWS?

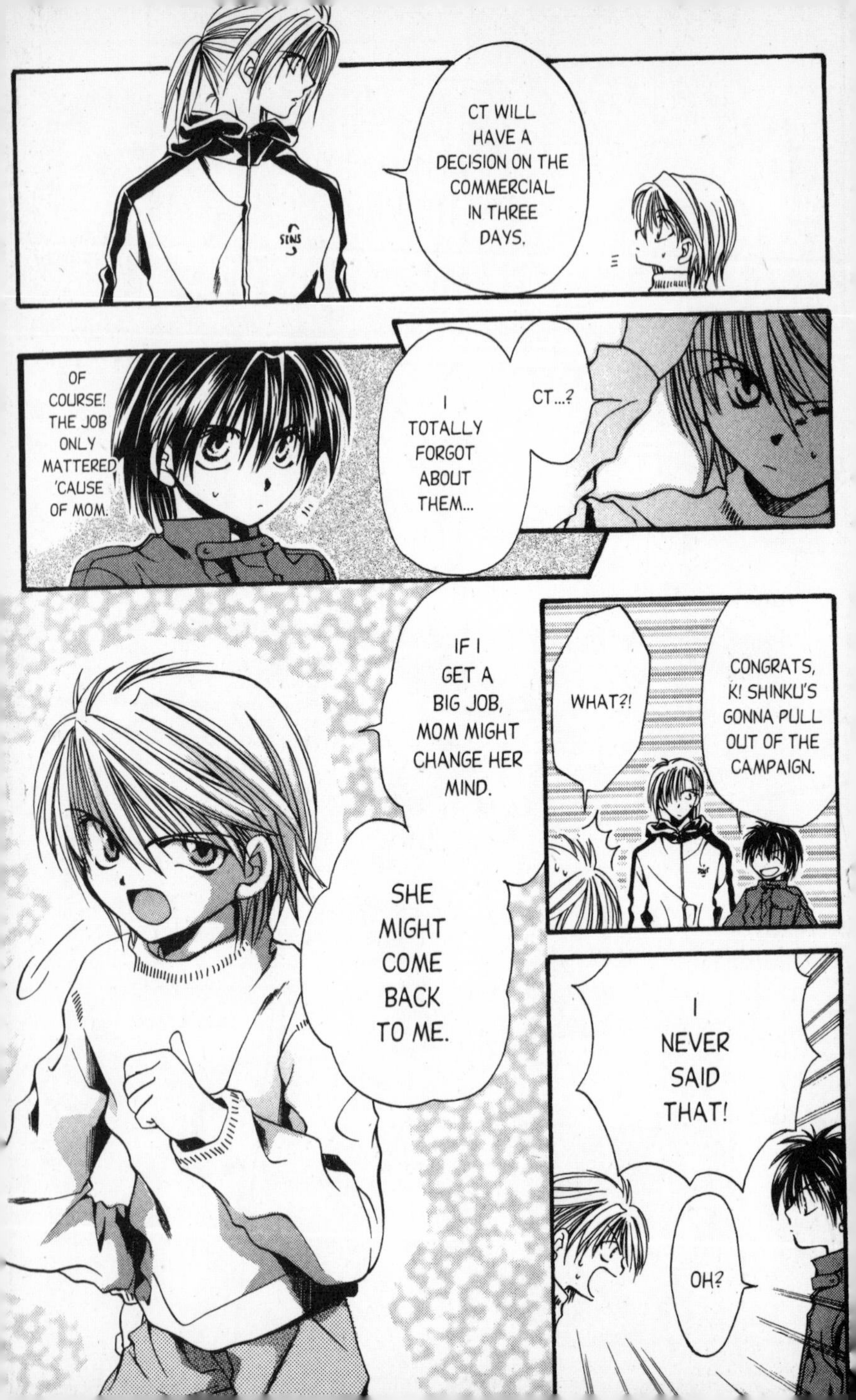
CT WILL HAVE A DECISION ON THE COMMERCIAL IN THREE DAYS.
CT...?
I TOTALLY FORGOT ABOUT THEM...
OF COURSE! THE JOB ONLY MATTERED 'CAUSE OF MOM.
CONGRATS, K! SHINKU'S GONNA PULL OUT OF THE CAMPAIGN.
WHAT?!
I NEVER SAID THAT!
OH?
IF I GET A BIG JOB, MOM MIGHT CHANGE HER MIND.
SHE MIGHT COME BACK TO ME.

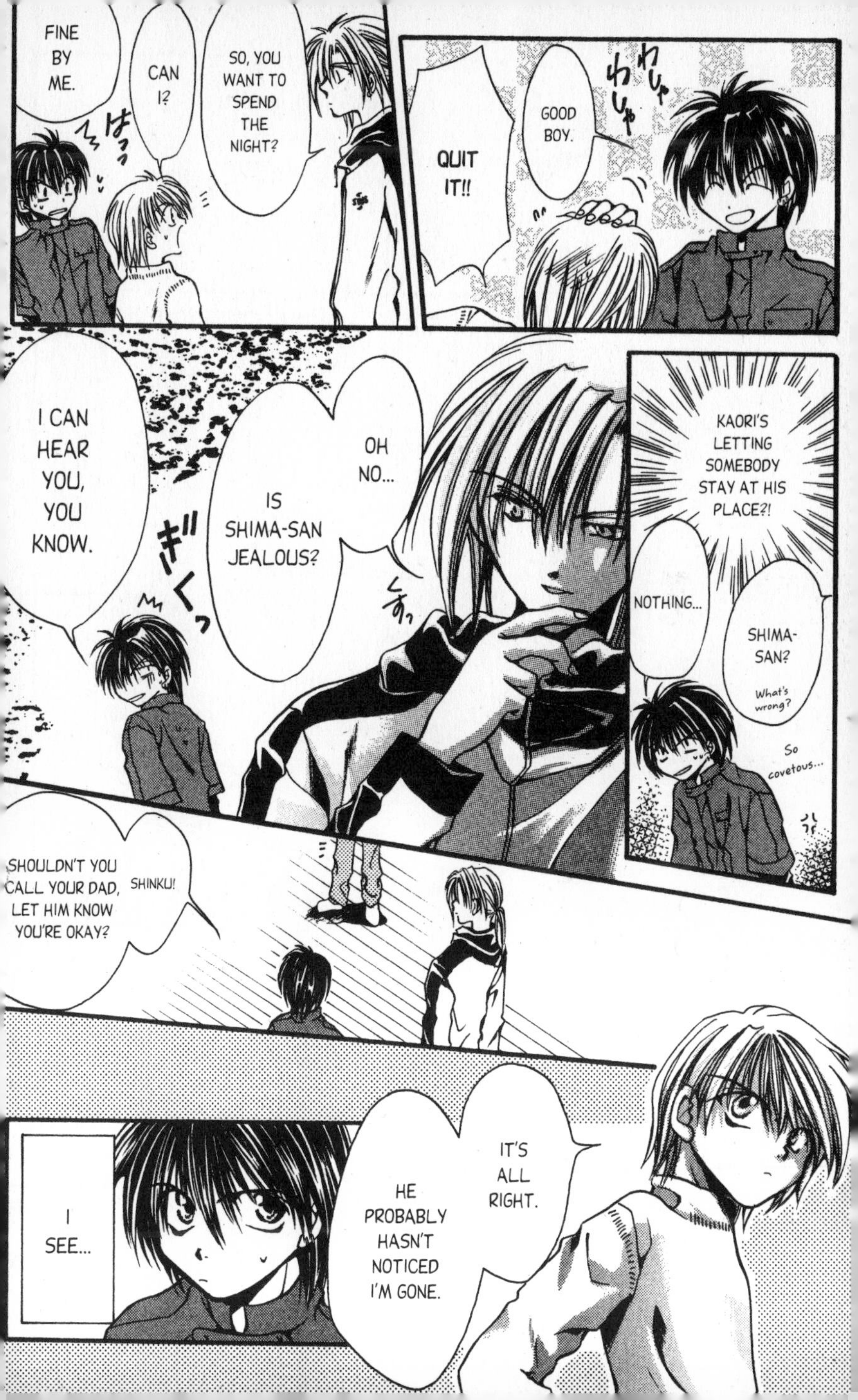
GOOD BOY.
わしゃわしゃ
QUIT IT!!
SO, YOU WANT TO SPEND THE NIGHT?
CAN I?
FINE BY ME.
KAORI'S LETTING SOMEBODY STAY AT HIS PLACE?!
SHIMA-SAN?
What's wrong?
NOTHING...
So covetous...
OH NO...
IS SHIMA-SAN JEALOUS?
くすっ
ぎくっ
I CAN HEAR YOU, YOU KNOW.
SHINKU!
SHOULDN'T YOU CALL YOUR DAD, LET HIM KNOW YOU'RE OKAY?
IT'S ALL RIGHT.
HE PROBABLY HASN'T NOTICED I'M GONE.
I SEE...

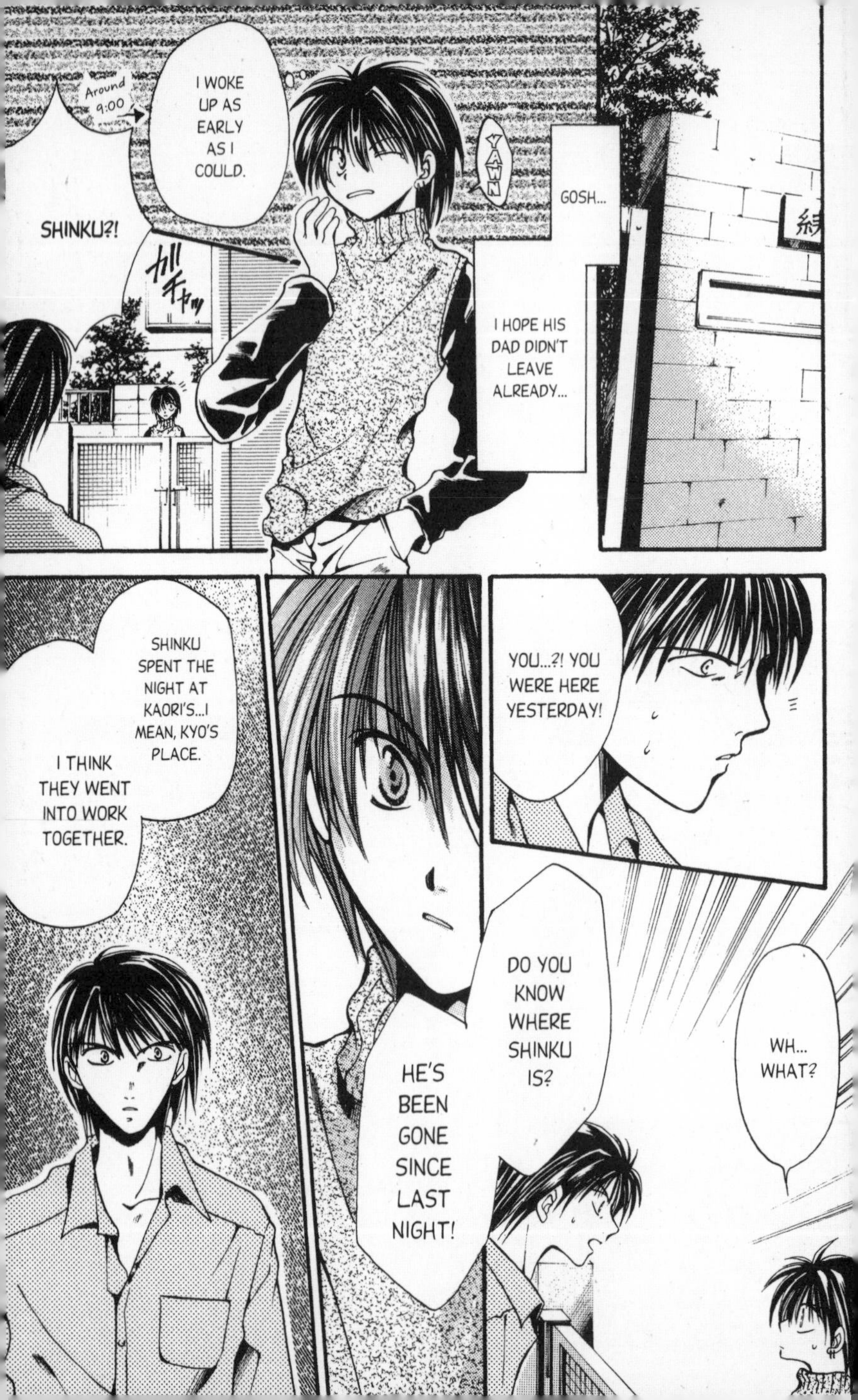
GOSH...
I HOPE HIS DAD DIDN'T LEAVE ALREADY...
YAWN
I WOKE UP AS EARLY AS I COULD.
Around 9:00
SHINKU?!
ガチャッ
YOU...?! YOU WERE HERE YESTERDAY!
WH... WHAT?
DO YOU KNOW WHERE SHINKU IS?
HE'S BEEN GONE SINCE LAST NIGHT!
SHINKU SPENT THE NIGHT AT KAORI'S...I MEAN, KYO'S PLACE.
I THINK THEY WENT INTO WORK TOGETHER.

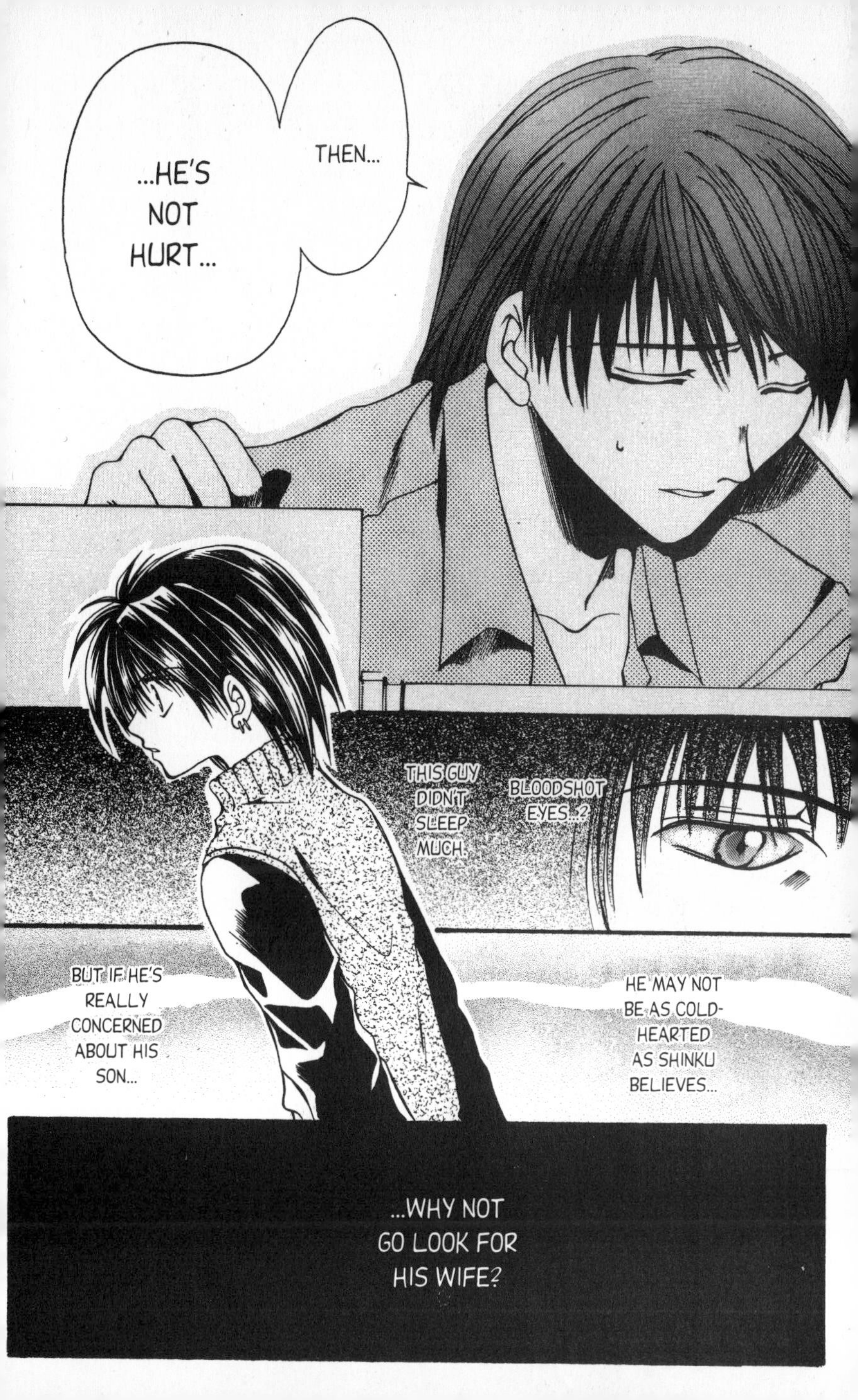
THEN...
...HE'S NOT HURT...
BLOODSHOT EYES...?
THIS GUY DIDN'T SLEEP MUCH.
HE MAY NOT BE AS COLD-HEARTED AS SHINKU BELIEVES...
BUT IF HE'S REALLY CONCERNED ABOUT HIS SON...
...WHY NOT GO LOOK FOR HIS WIFE?

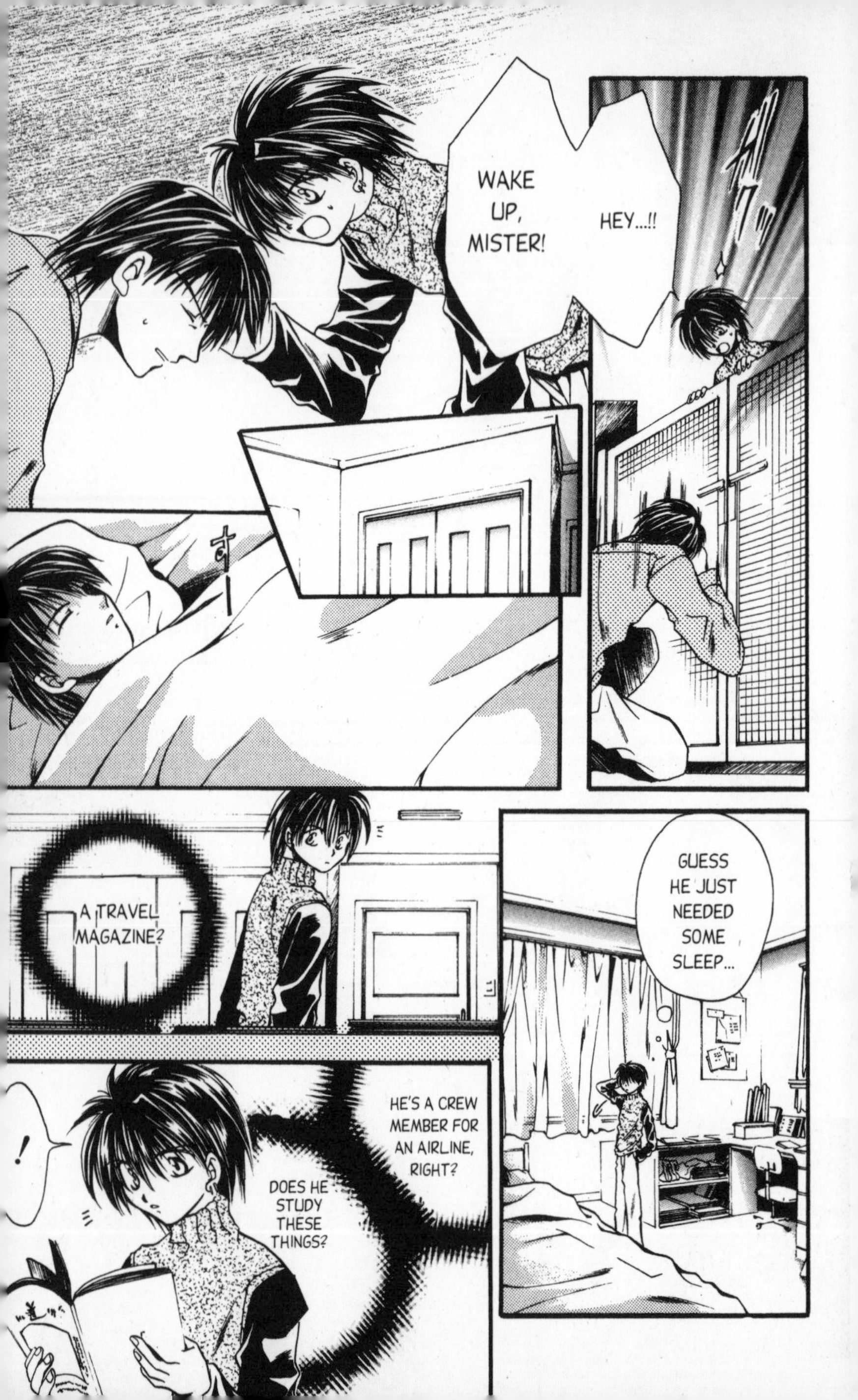
HEY...!!
WAKE UP, MISTER!
GUESS HE JUST NEEDED SOME SLEEP...
A TRAVEL MAGAZINE?
!
HE'S A CREW MEMBER FOR AN AIRLINE, RIGHT?
DOES HE STUDY THESE THINGS?

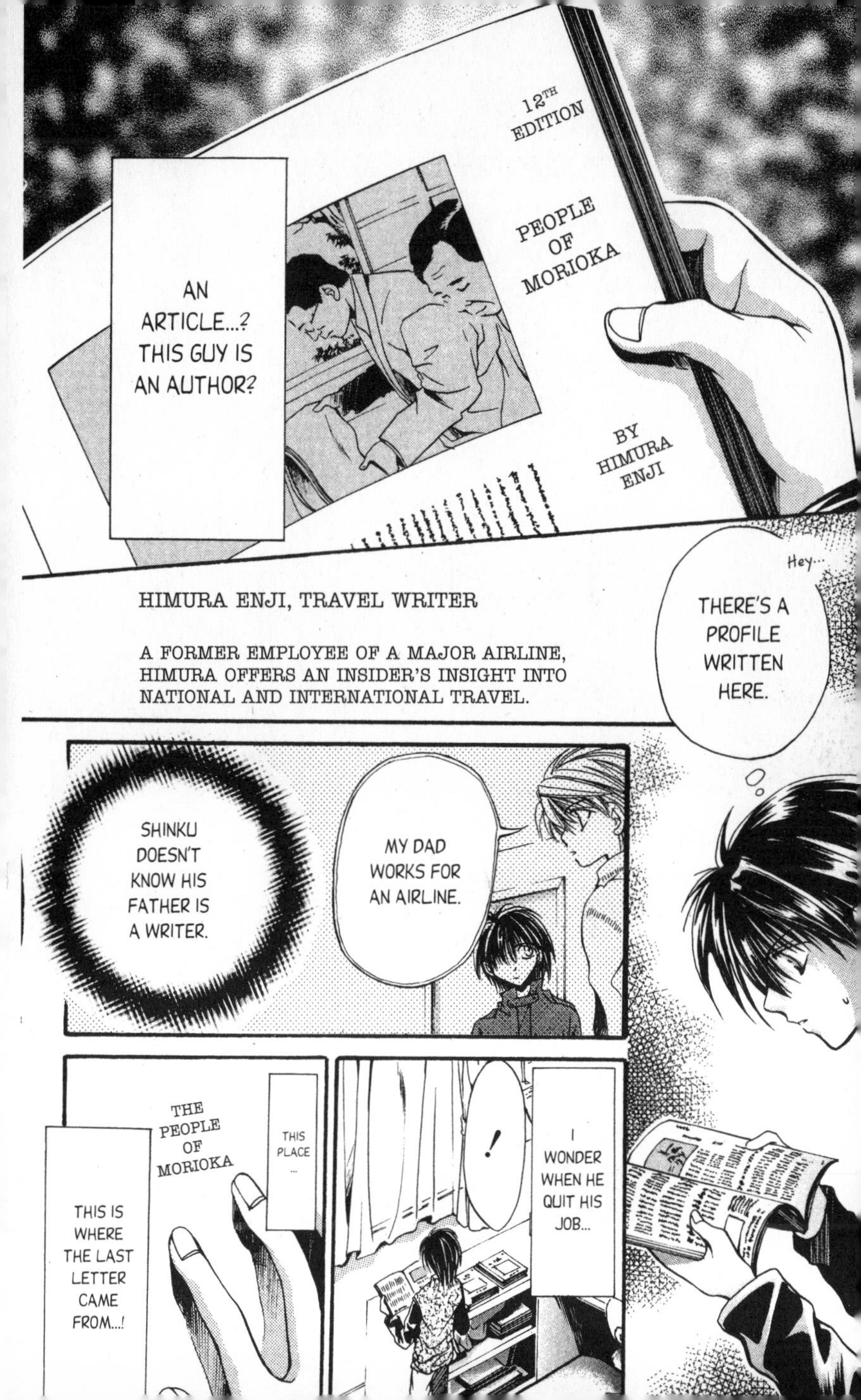
12TH EDITION
PEOPLE OF MORIOKA
BY HIMURA ENJI
AN ARTICLE...? THIS GUY IS AN AUTHOR?
Hey...
THERE'S A PROFILE WRITTEN HERE.
HIMURA ENJI, TRAVEL WRITER
A FORMER EMPLOYEE OF A MAJOR AIRLINE, HIMURA OFFERS AN INSIDER'S INSIGHT INTO NATIONAL AND INTERNATIONAL TRAVEL.
MY DAD WORKS FOR AN AIRLINE.
SHINKU DOESN'T KNOW HIS FATHER IS A WRITER.
I WONDER WHEN HE QUIT HIS JOB...
!
THIS PLACE ...
THE PEOPLE OF MORIOKA
THIS IS WHERE THE LAST LETTER CAME FROM...!

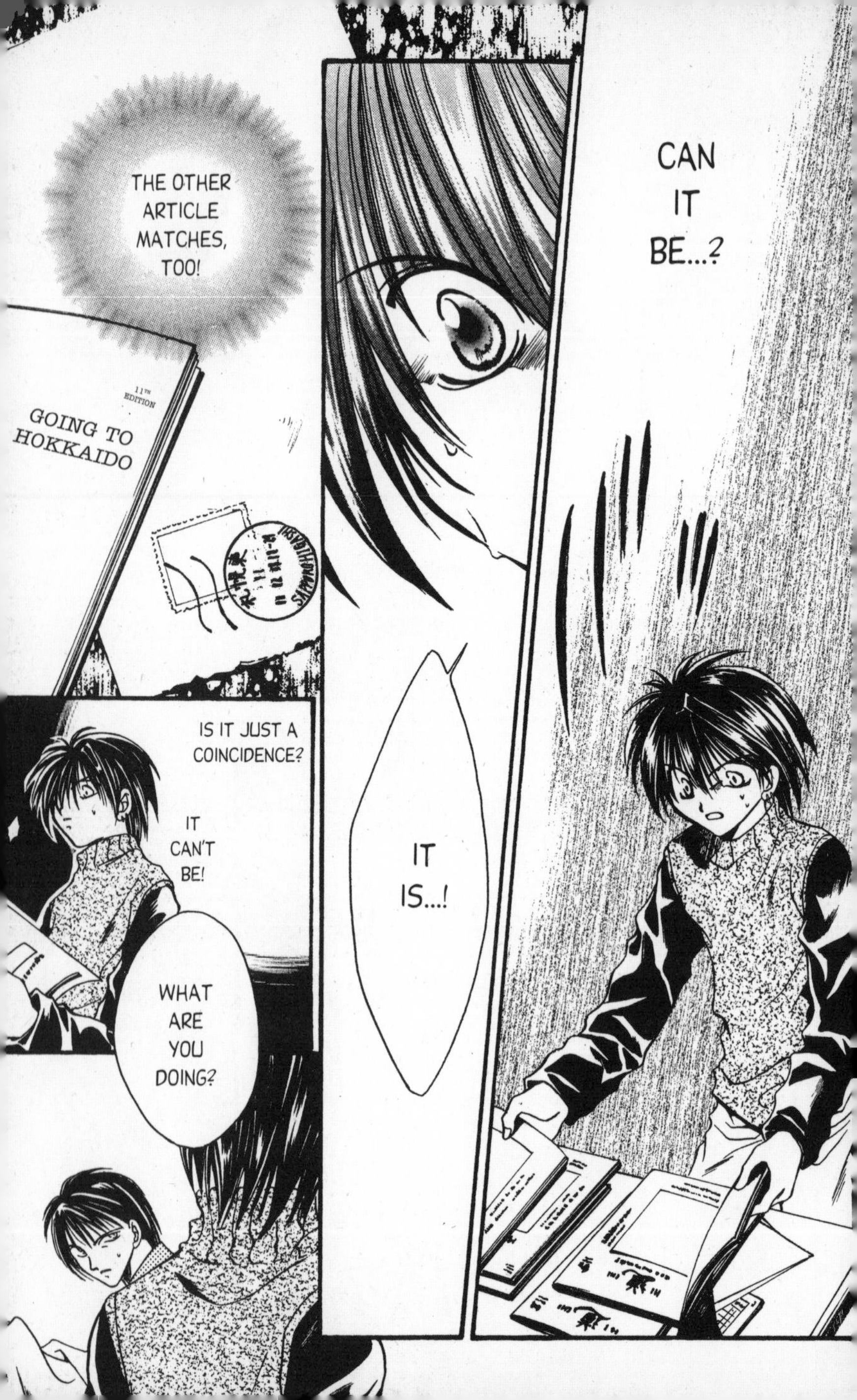
CAN IT BE...?
IT IS...!
THE OTHER ARTICLE MATCHES, TOO!
11TH EDITION
GOING TO HOKKAIDO
IS IT JUST A COINCIDENCE?
IT CAN'T BE!
WHAT ARE YOU DOING?

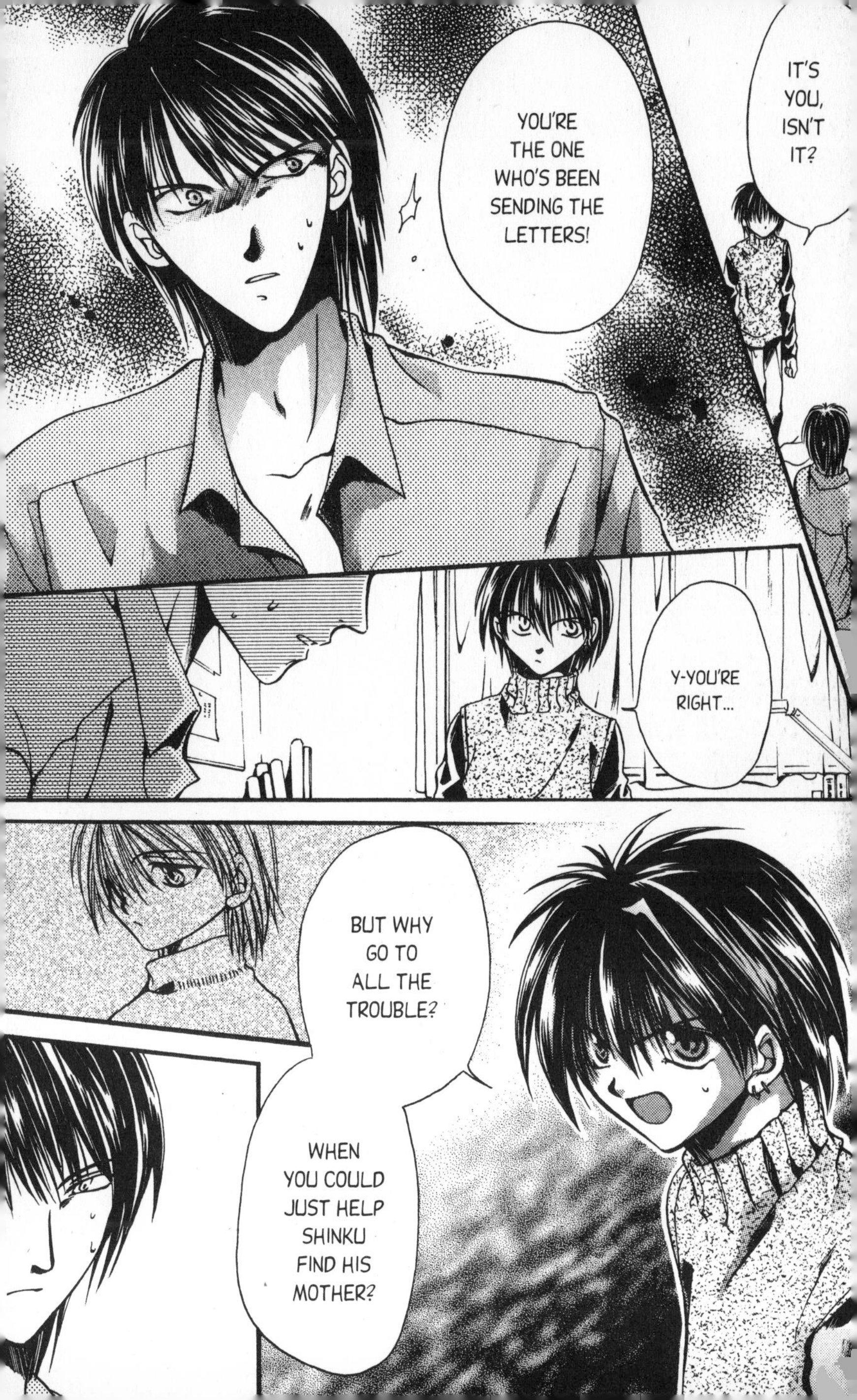
IT'S YOU, ISN'T IT?
YOU'RE THE ONE WHO'S BEEN SENDING THE LETTERS!
Y-YOU'RE RIGHT...
BUT WHY GO TO ALL THE TROUBLE?
WHEN YOU COULD JUST HELP SHINKU FIND HIS MOTHER?

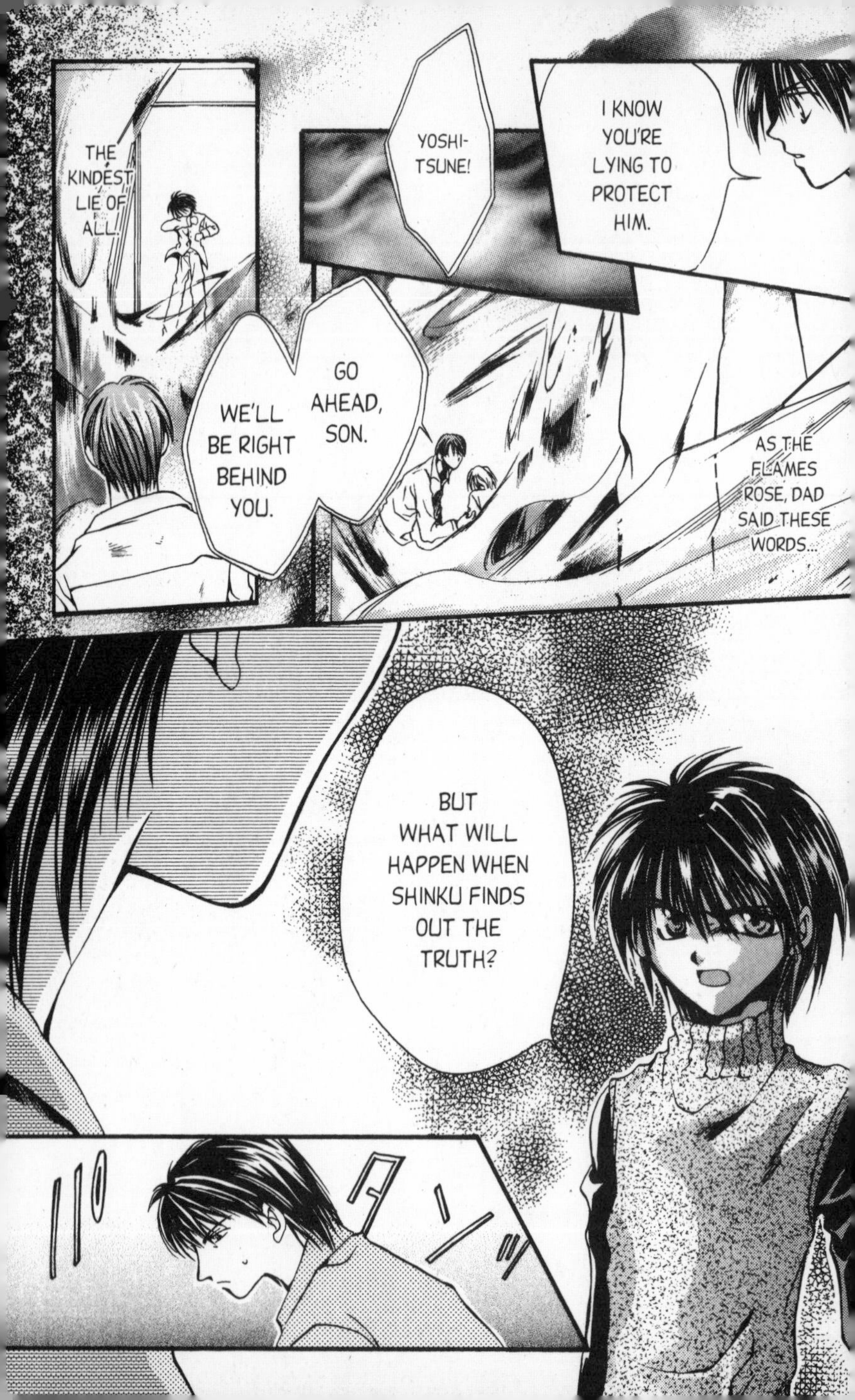
I KNOW YOU'RE LYING TO PROTECT HIM.
YOSHI-TSUNE!
AS THE FLAMES ROSE, DAD SAID THESE WORDS...
GO AHEAD, SON.
WE'LL BE RIGHT BEHIND YOU.
THE KINDEST LIE OF ALL.
BUT WHAT WILL HAPPEN WHEN SHINKU FINDS OUT THE TRUTH?

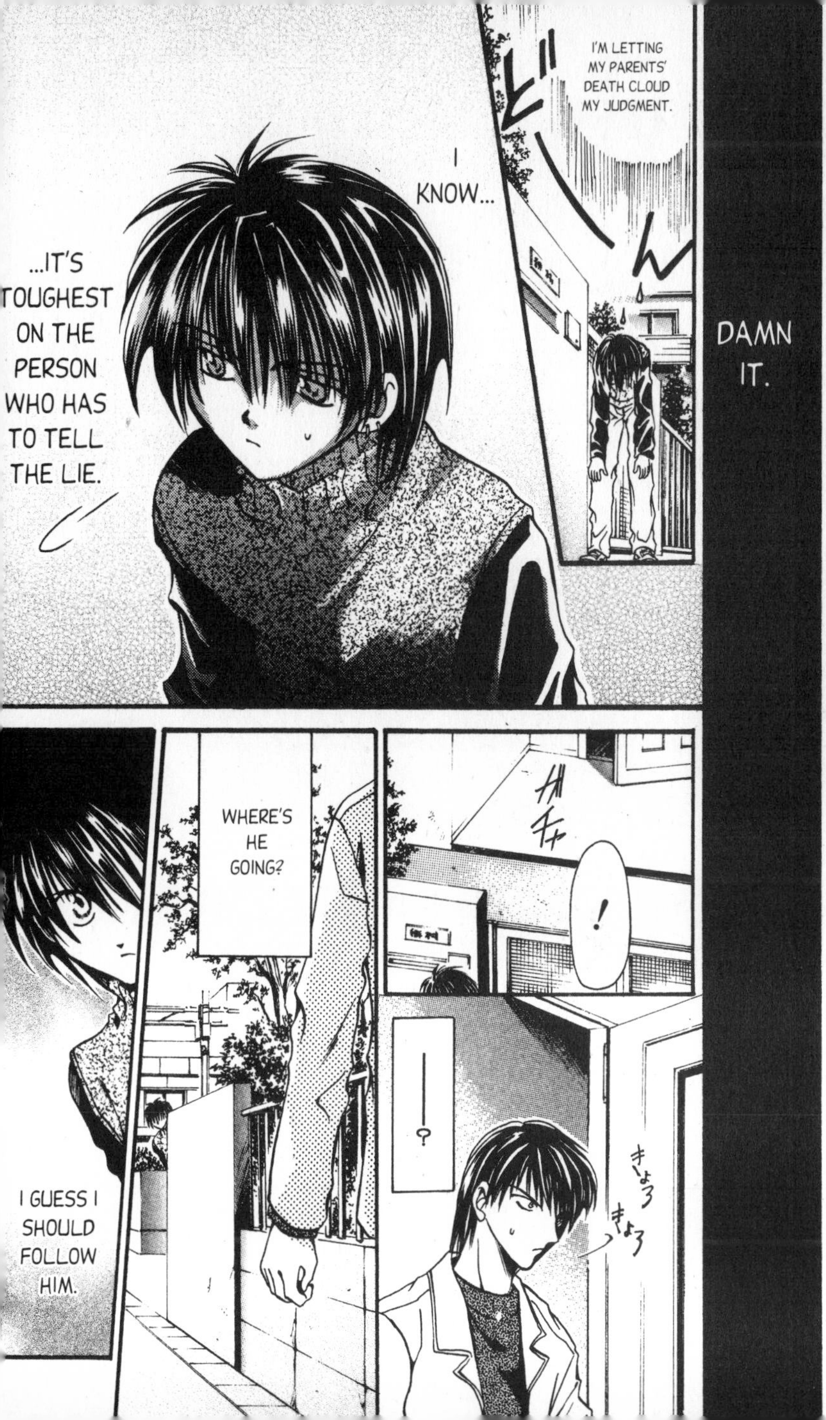
DAMN IT.
I'M LETTING MY PARENTS' DEATH CLOUD MY JUDGMENT.
どーん
I KNOW...
...IT'S TOUGHEST ON THE PERSON WHO HAS TO TELL THE LIE.
ガチャ
!
——?
きょろ
きょろ
WHERE'S HE GOING?
I GUESS I SHOULD FOLLOW HIM.

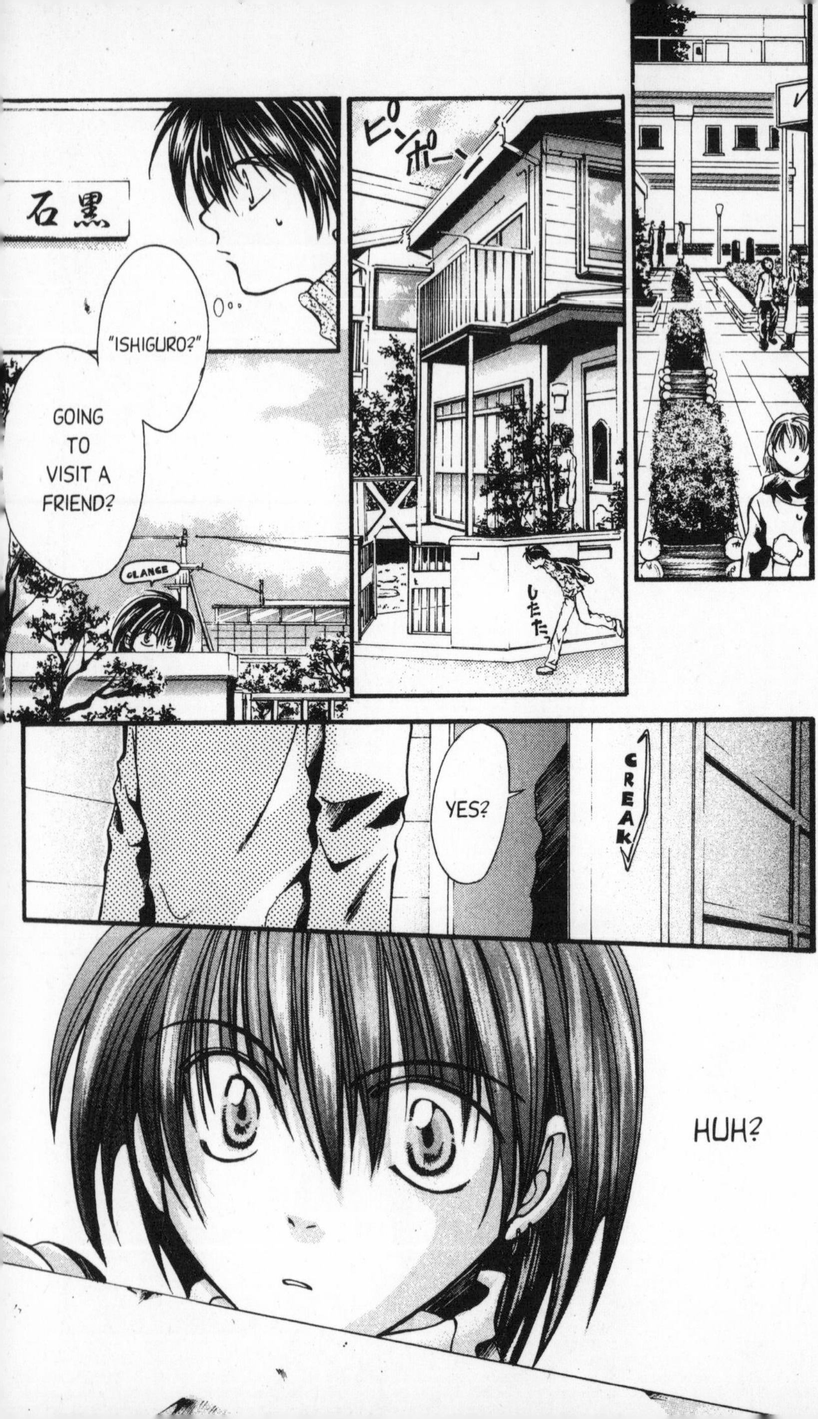

ピンポーン
したたっ
石黒
O..
"ISHIGURO?"
GOING TO VISIT A FRIEND?
GLANCE
CREAK
YES?
HUH?

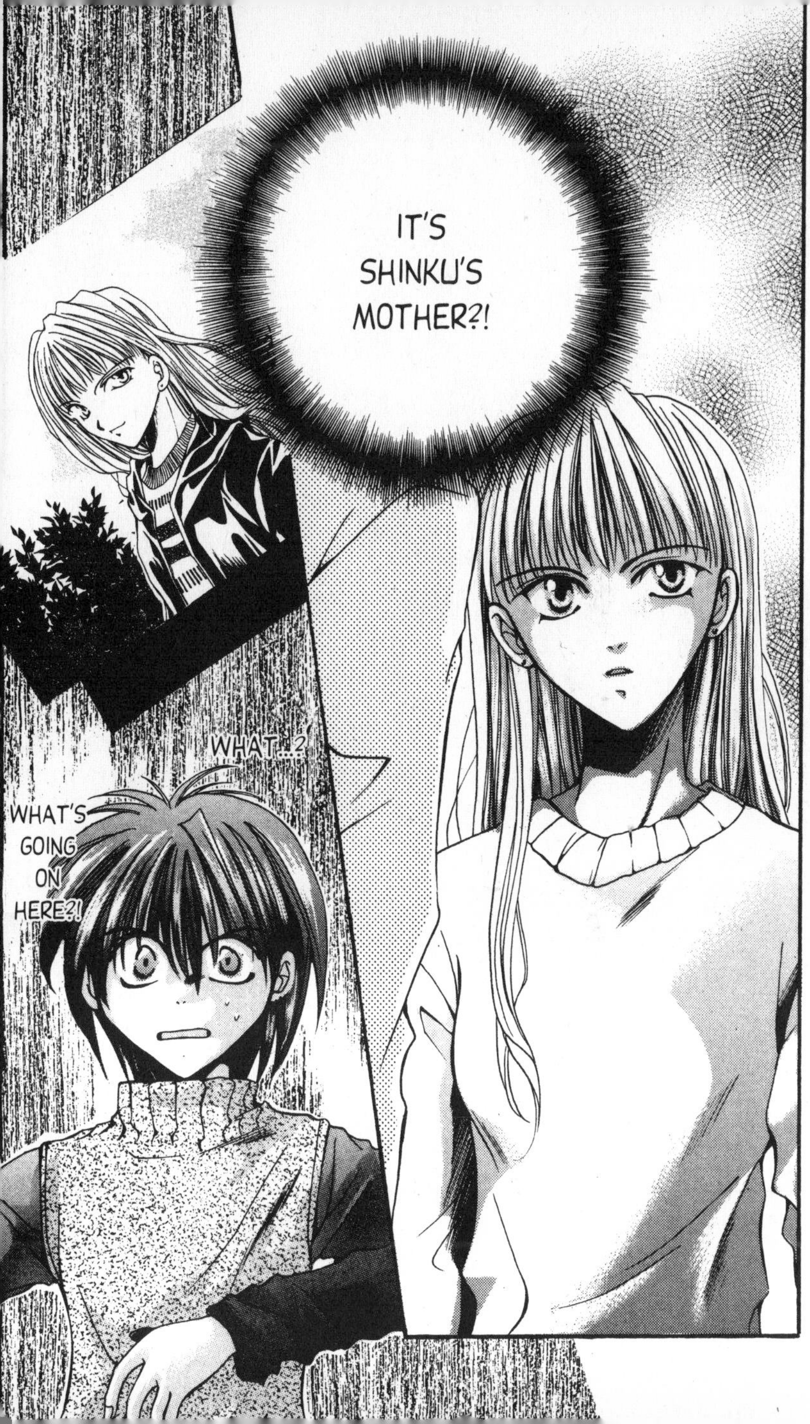
IT'S SHINKU'S MOTHER?!
WHAT...?
WHAT'S GOING ON HERE?!

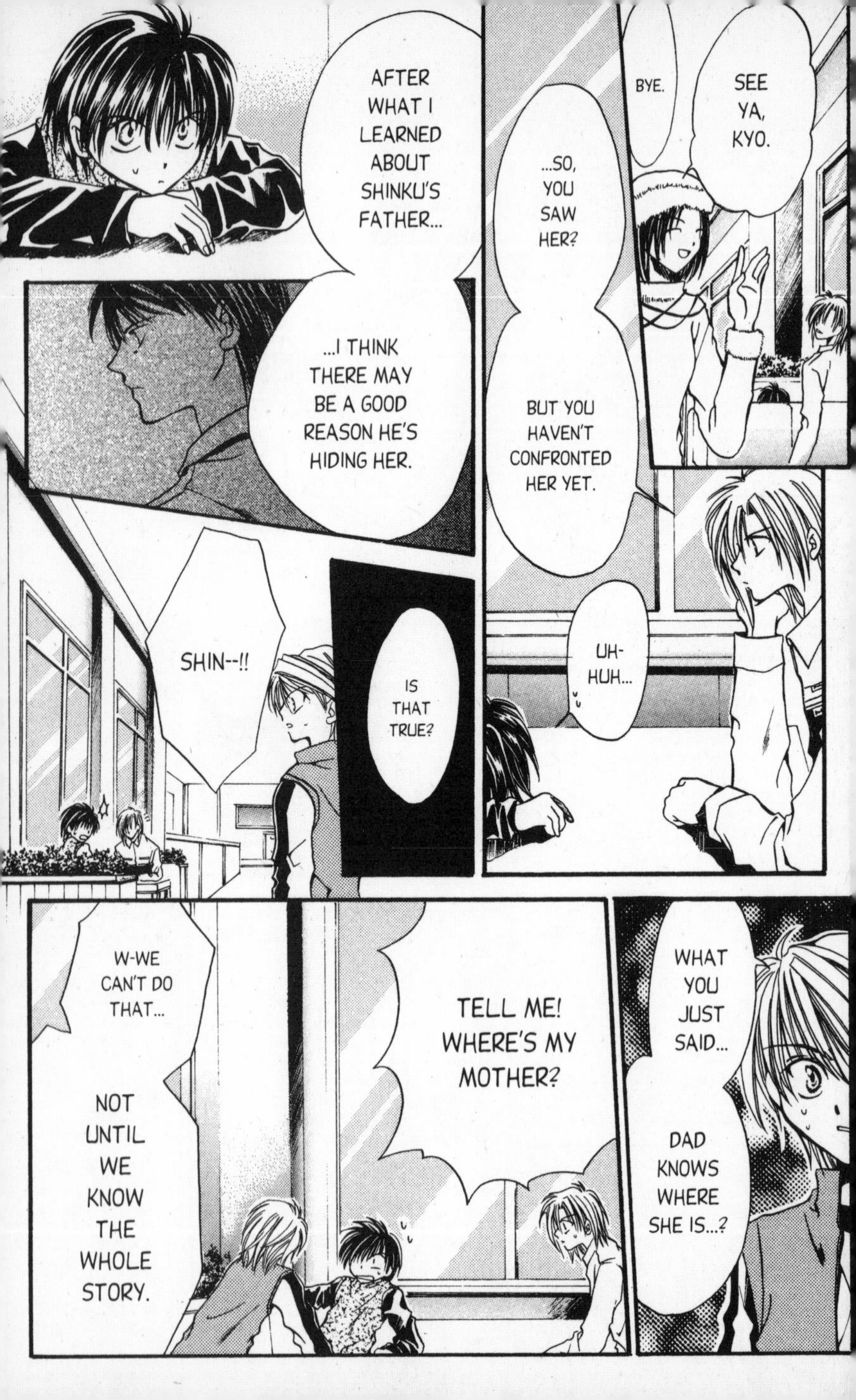

SEE YA, KYO.
BYE.
...SO, YOU SAW HER?
BUT YOU HAVEN'T CONFRONTED HER YET.
UH-HUH...
AFTER WHAT I LEARNED ABOUT SHINKU'S FATHER...
...I THINK THERE MAY BE A GOOD REASON HE'S HIDING HER.
IS THAT TRUE?
SHIN--!!
WHAT YOU JUST SAID...
DAD KNOWS WHERE SHE IS...?
TELL ME! WHERE'S MY MOTHER?
W-WE CAN'T DO THAT...
NOT UNTIL WE KNOW THE WHOLE STORY.

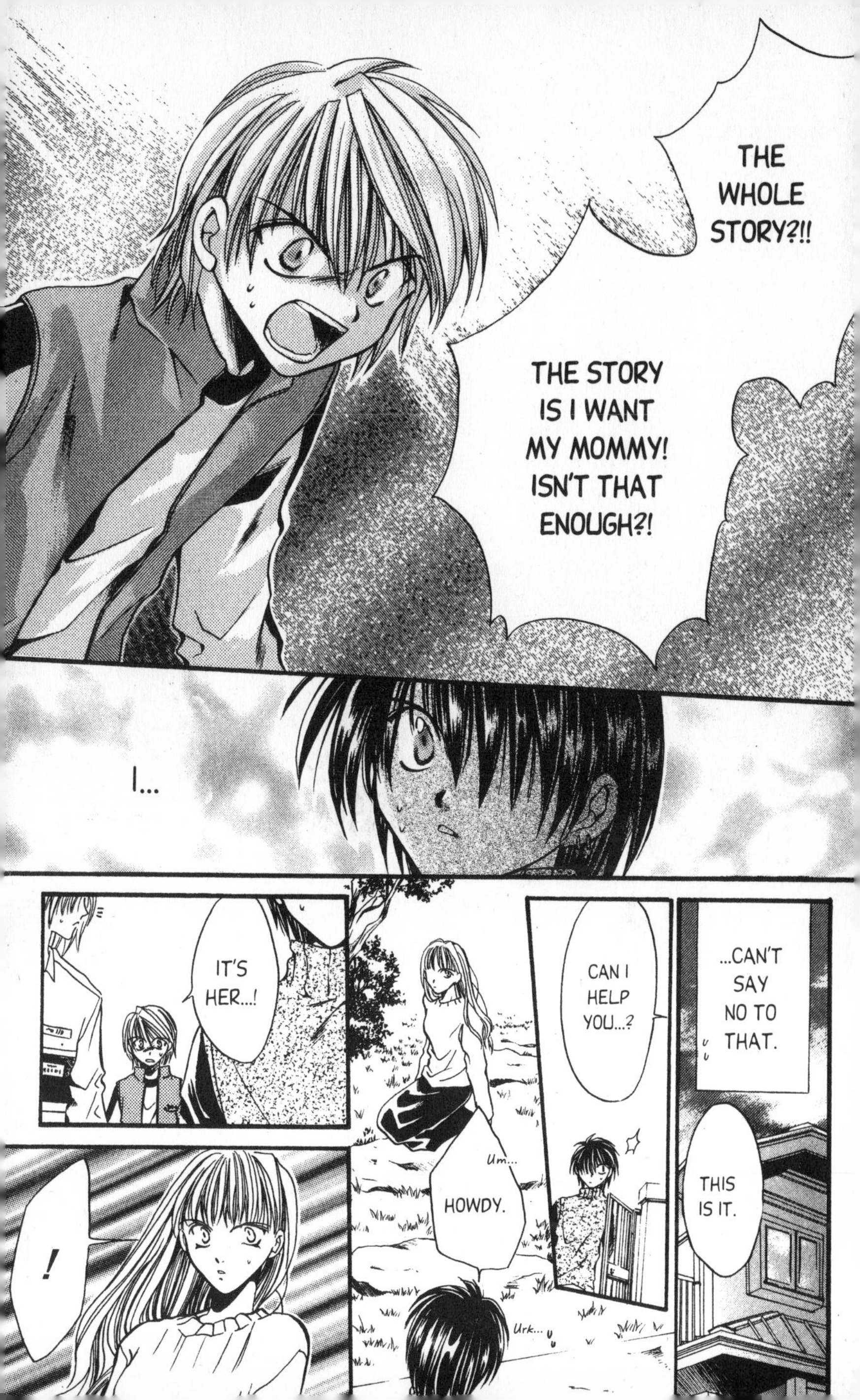
THE WHOLE STORY?!!
THE STORY IS I WANT MY MOMMY! ISN'T THAT ENOUGH?!
I...
...CAN'T SAY NO TO THAT.
THIS IS IT.
CAN I HELP YOU...?
Um...
HOWDY.
Urk...
IT'S HER...!
!

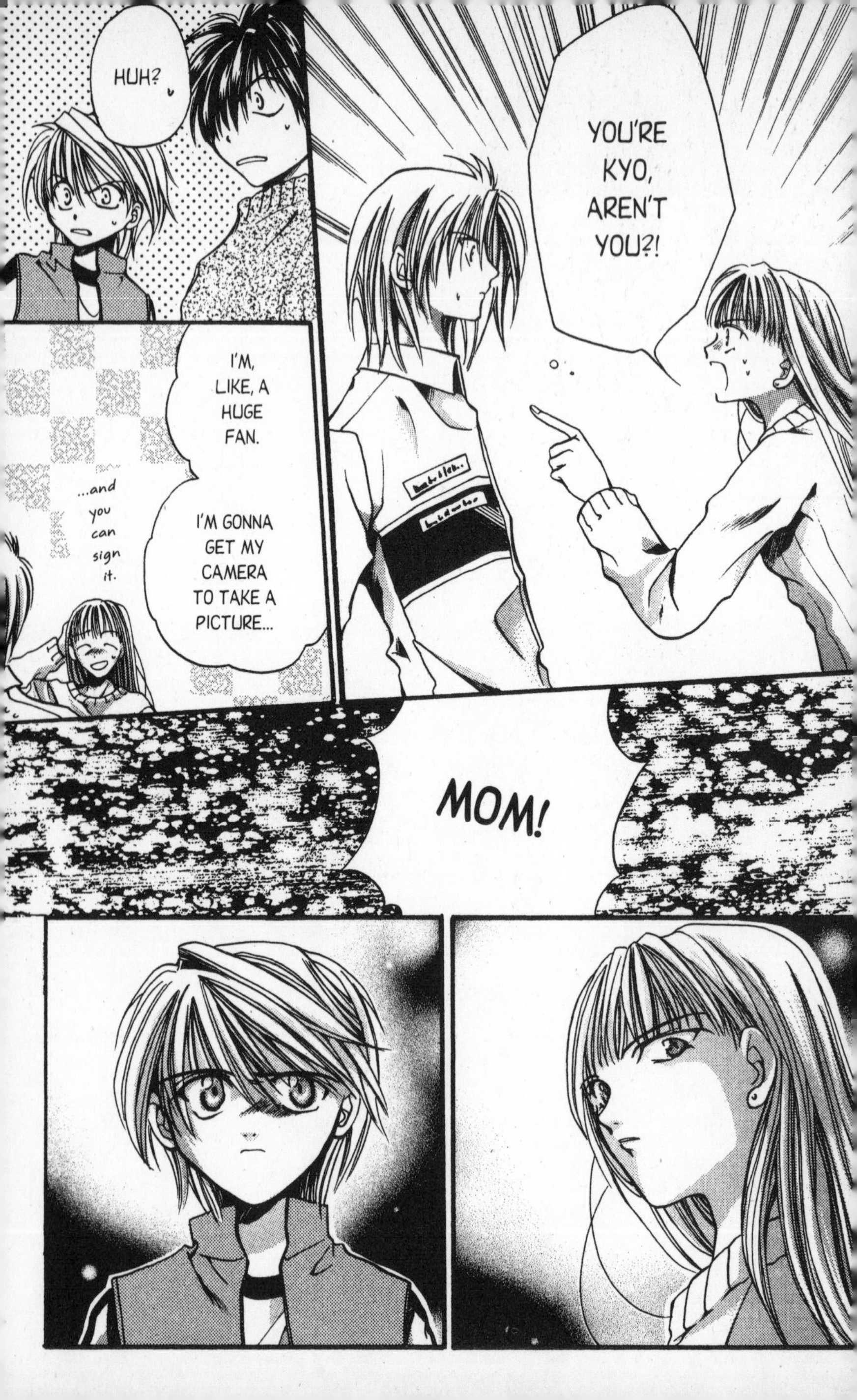
YOU'RE KYO, AREN'T YOU?!
HUH?
I'M, LIKE, A HUGE FAN.
I'M GONNA GET MY CAMERA TO TAKE A PICTURE...
...and you can sign it.
MOM!

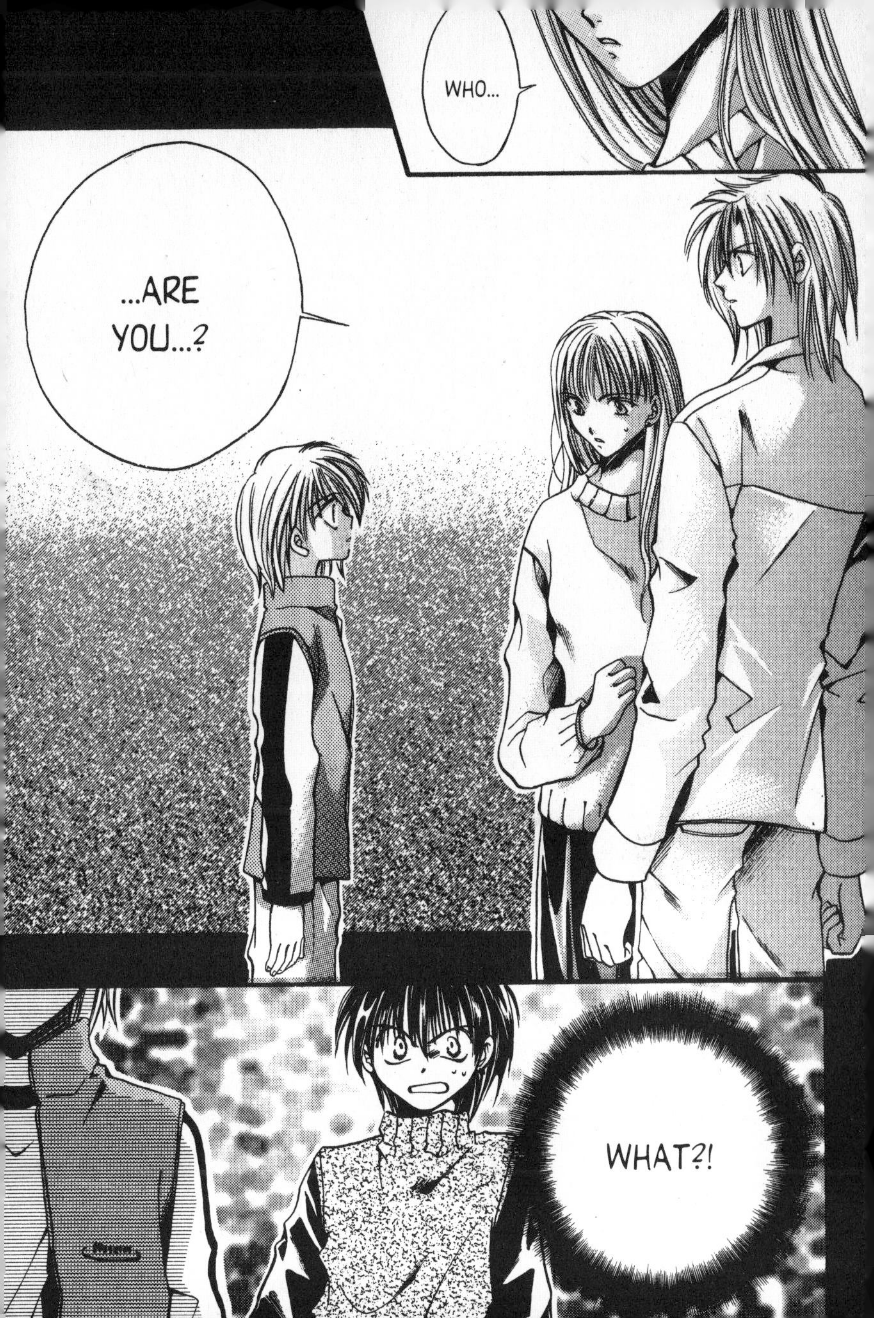
WHO...
...ARE YOU...?
WHAT?!

BROKEN MEMORIES

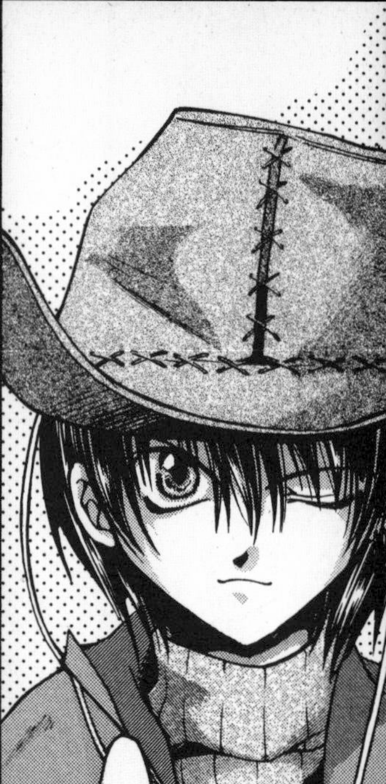

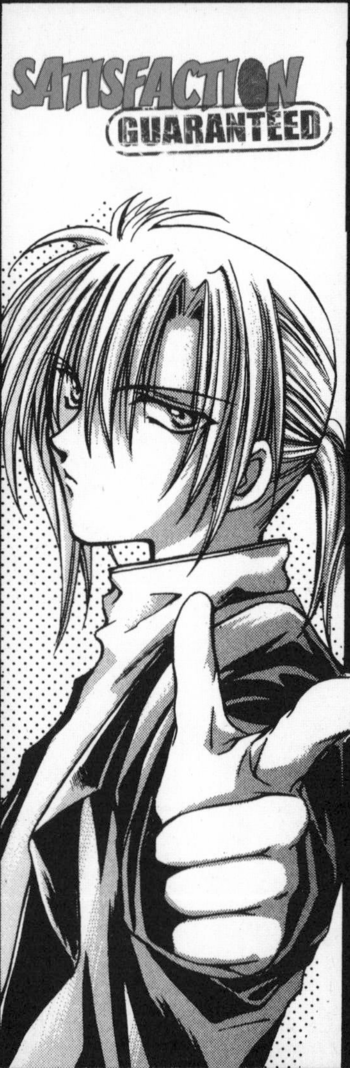
SATISFACTION
GUARANTEED

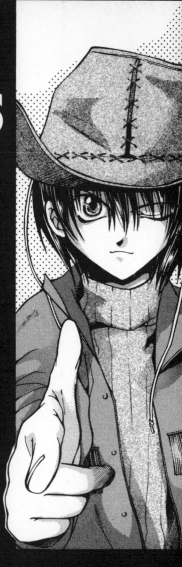

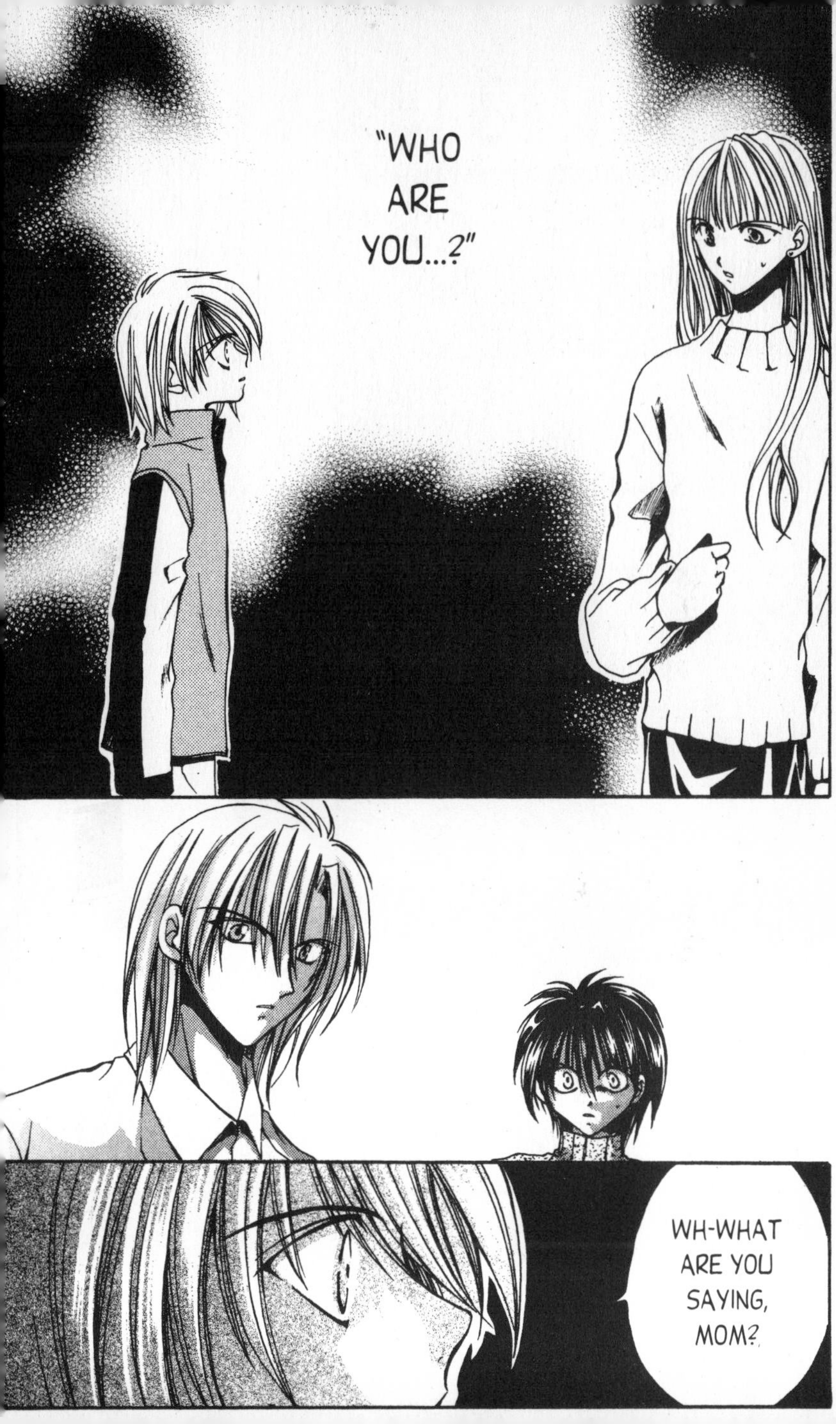
"WHO ARE YOU...?"
WH-WHAT ARE YOU SAYING, MOM?

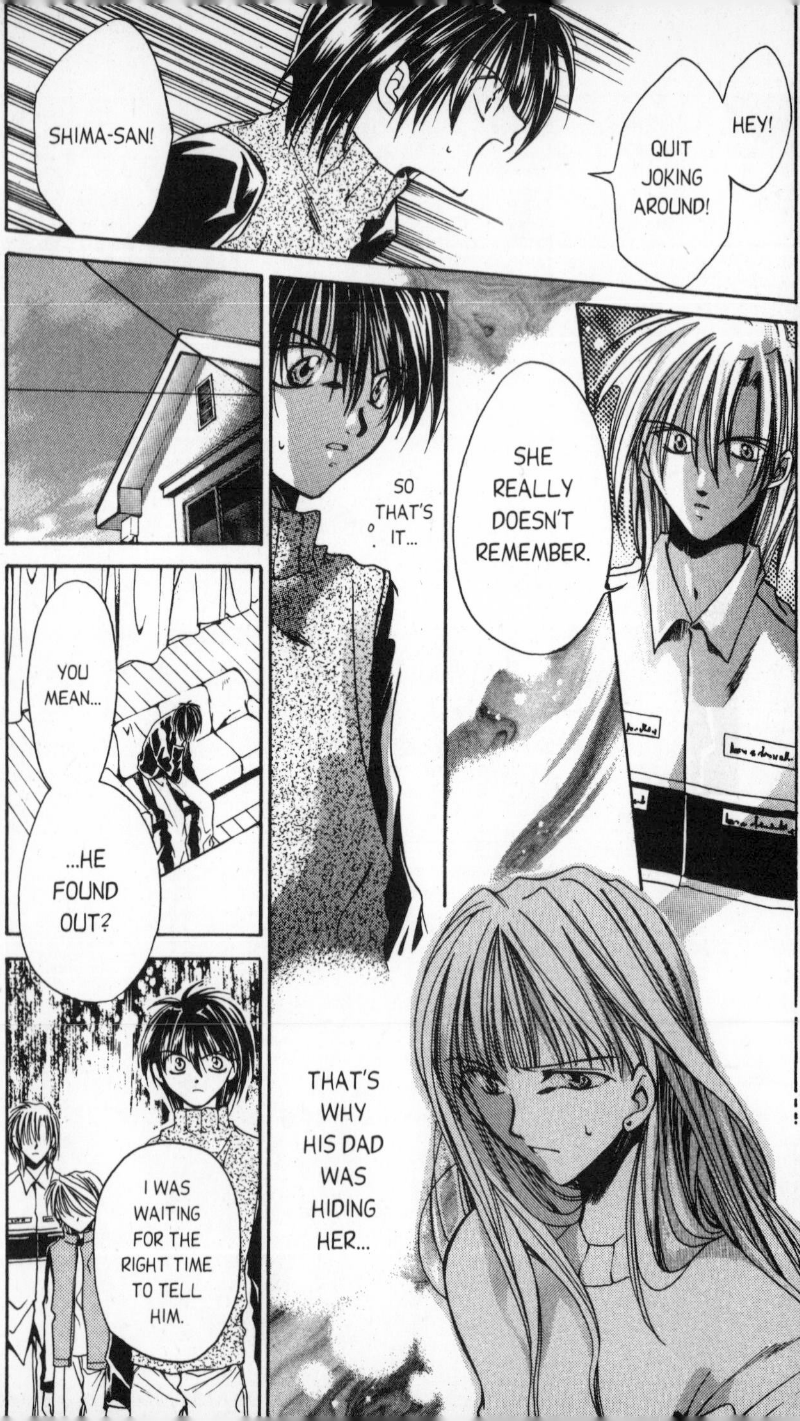
HEY! QUIT JOKING AROUND!
SHIMA-SAN!
SHE REALLY DOESN'T REMEMBER.
SO THAT'S IT...
YOU MEAN...
...HE FOUND OUT?
THAT'S WHY HIS DAD WAS HIDING HER...
I WAS WAITING FOR THE RIGHT TIME TO TELL HIM.

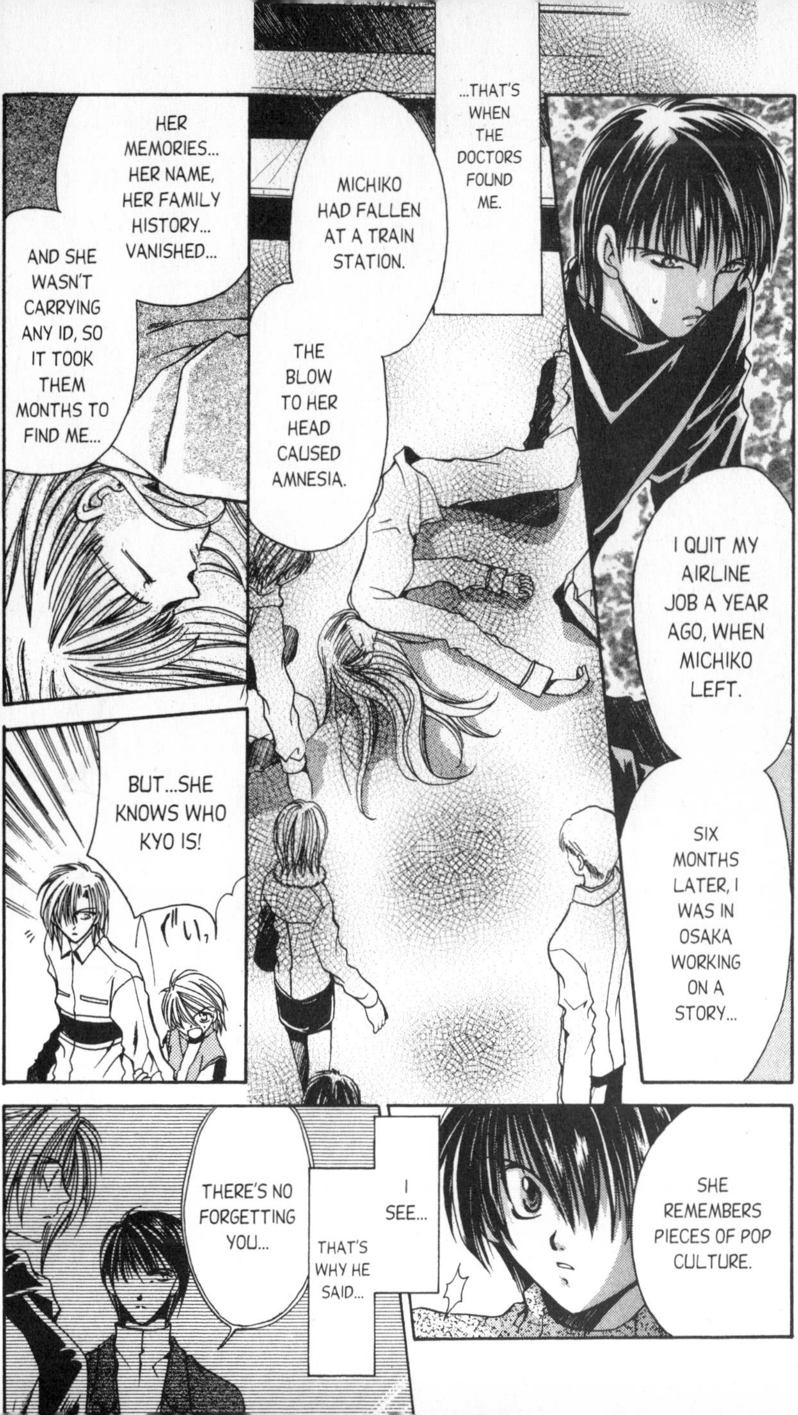
I QUIT MY AIRLINE JOB A YEAR AGO, WHEN MICHIKO LEFT.
SIX MONTHS LATER, I WAS IN OSAKA WORKING ON A STORY...
...THAT'S WHEN THE DOCTORS FOUND ME.
MICHIKO HAD FALLEN AT A TRAIN STATION.
THE BLOW TO HER HEAD CAUSED AMNESIA.
HER MEMORIES... HER NAME, HER FAMILY HISTORY... VANISHED...
AND SHE WASN'T CARRYING ANY ID, SO IT TOOK THEM MONTHS TO FIND ME...
BUT...SHE KNOWS WHO KYO IS!
SHE REMEMBERS PIECES OF POP CULTURE.
I SEE...
THAT'S WHY HE SAID...
THERE'S NO FORGETTING YOU...

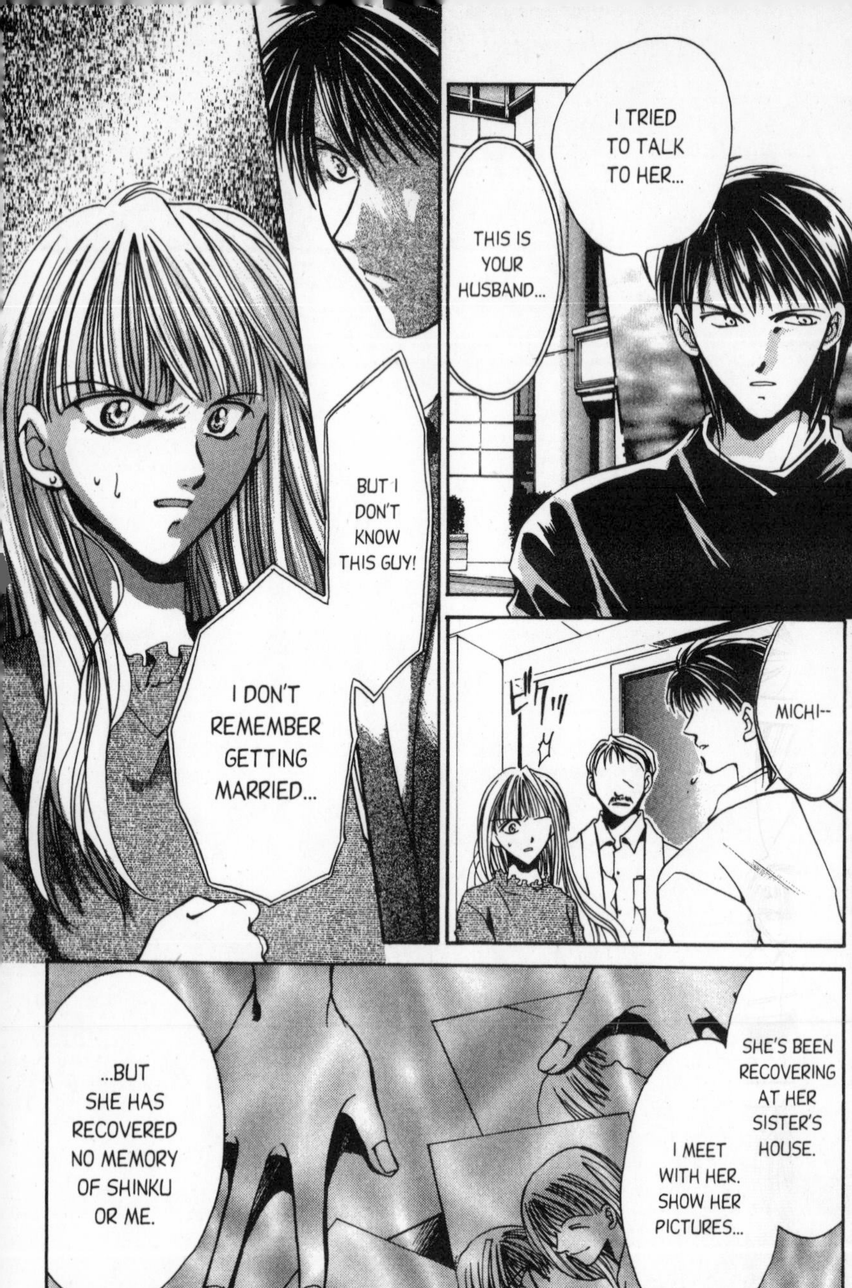
I TRIED TO TALK TO HER...
THIS IS YOUR HUSBAND...
ビクッ
MICHI--
BUT I DON'T KNOW THIS GUY!
I DON'T REMEMBER GETTING MARRIED...
SHE'S BEEN RECOVERING AT HER SISTER'S HOUSE.
I MEET WITH HER. SHOW HER PICTURES...
...BUT SHE HAS RECOVERED NO MEMORY OF SHINKU OR ME.

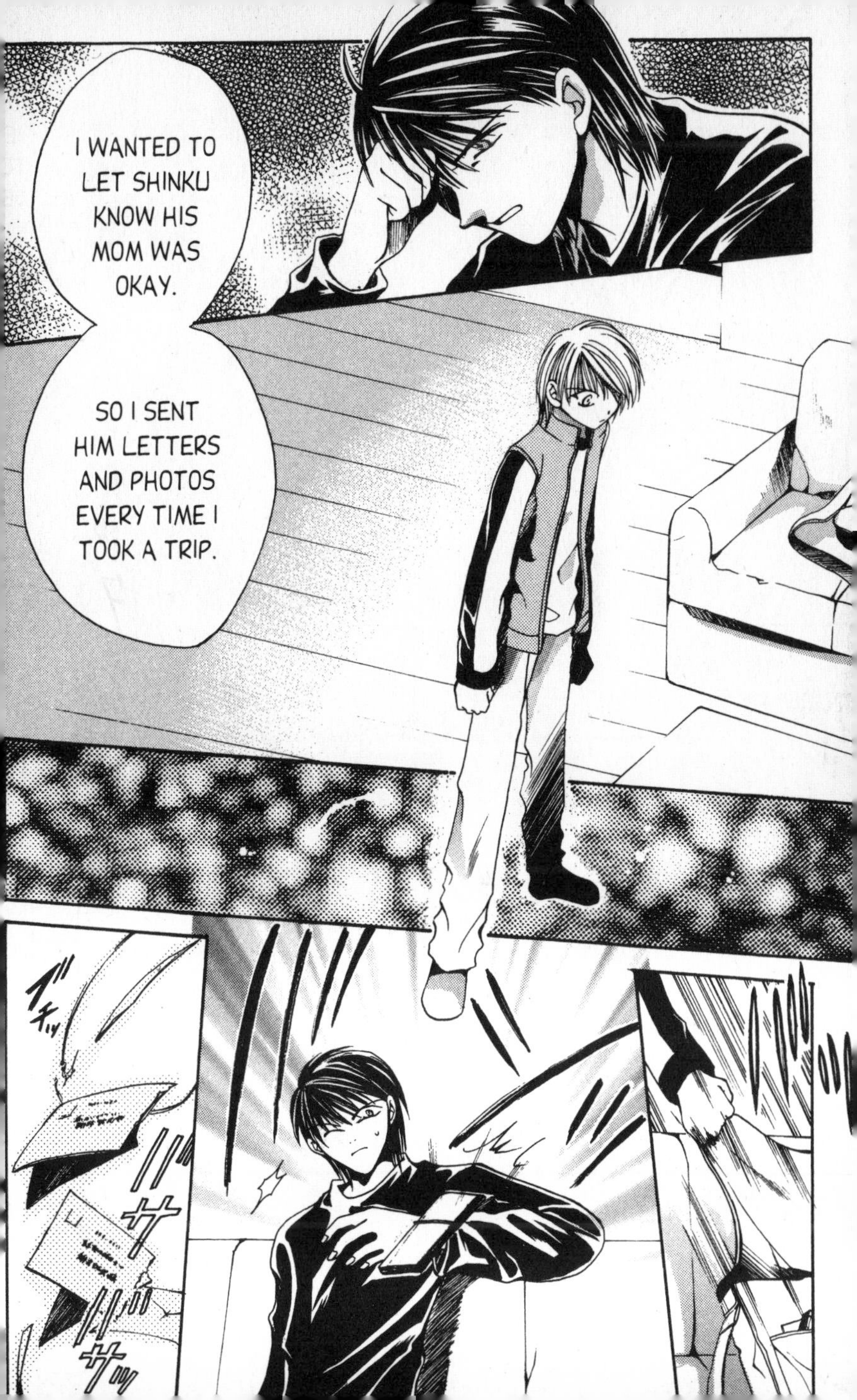
I WANTED TO LET SHINKU KNOW HIS MOM WAS OKAY.
SO I SENT HIM LETTERS AND PHOTOS EVERY TIME I TOOK A TRIP.

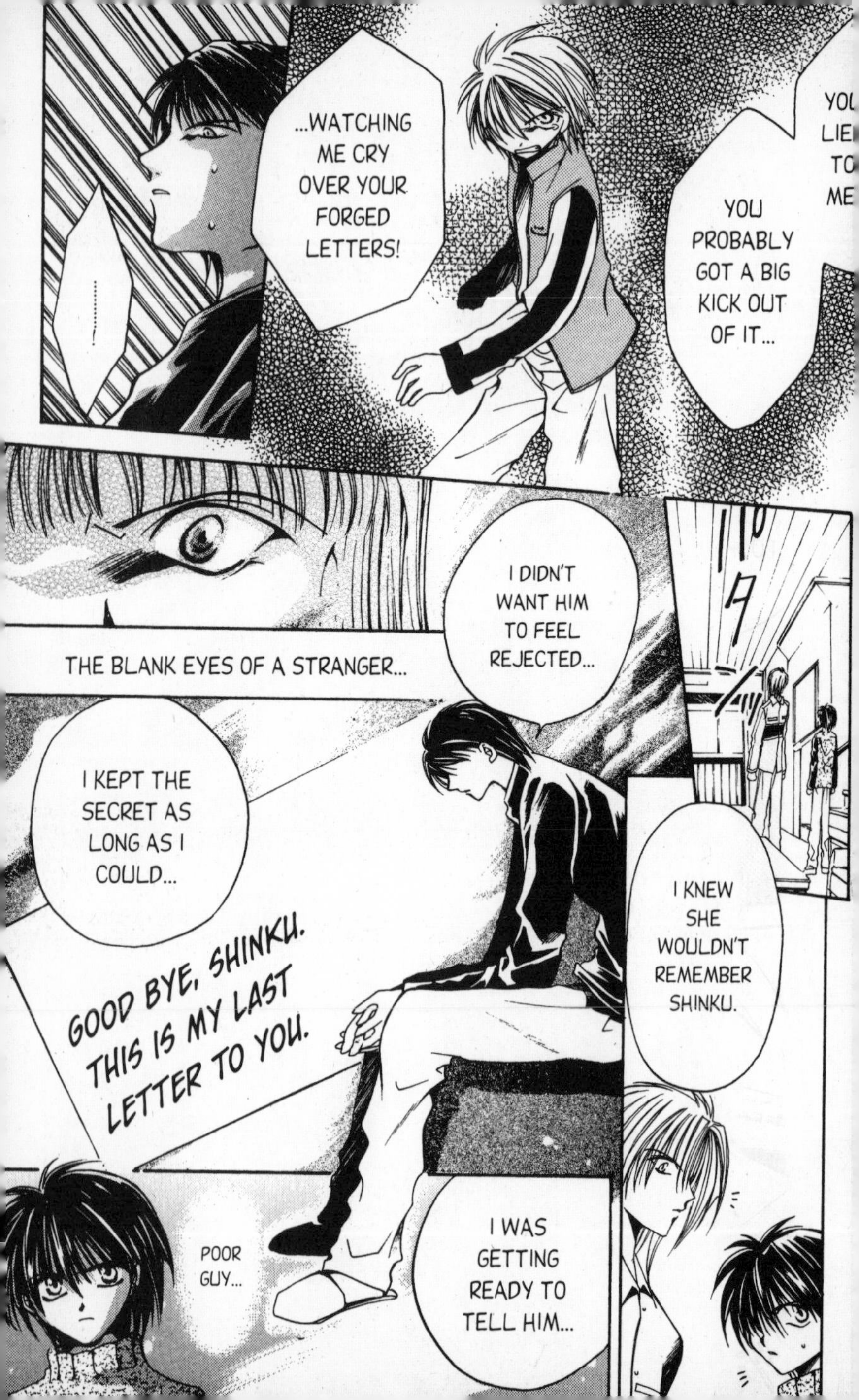
YOU LIE TO ME
YOU PROBABLY GOT A BIG KICK OUT OF IT...
...WATCHING ME CRY OVER YOUR FORGED LETTERS!
......!
パタ
I DIDN'T WANT HIM TO FEEL REJECTED...
THE BLANK EYES OF A STRANGER...
I KNEW SHE WOULDN'T REMEMBER SHINKU.
I KEPT THE SECRET AS LONG AS I COULD...
GOOD BYE, SHINKU. THIS IS MY LAST LETTER TO YOU.
I WAS GETTING READY TO TELL HIM...
POOR GUY...

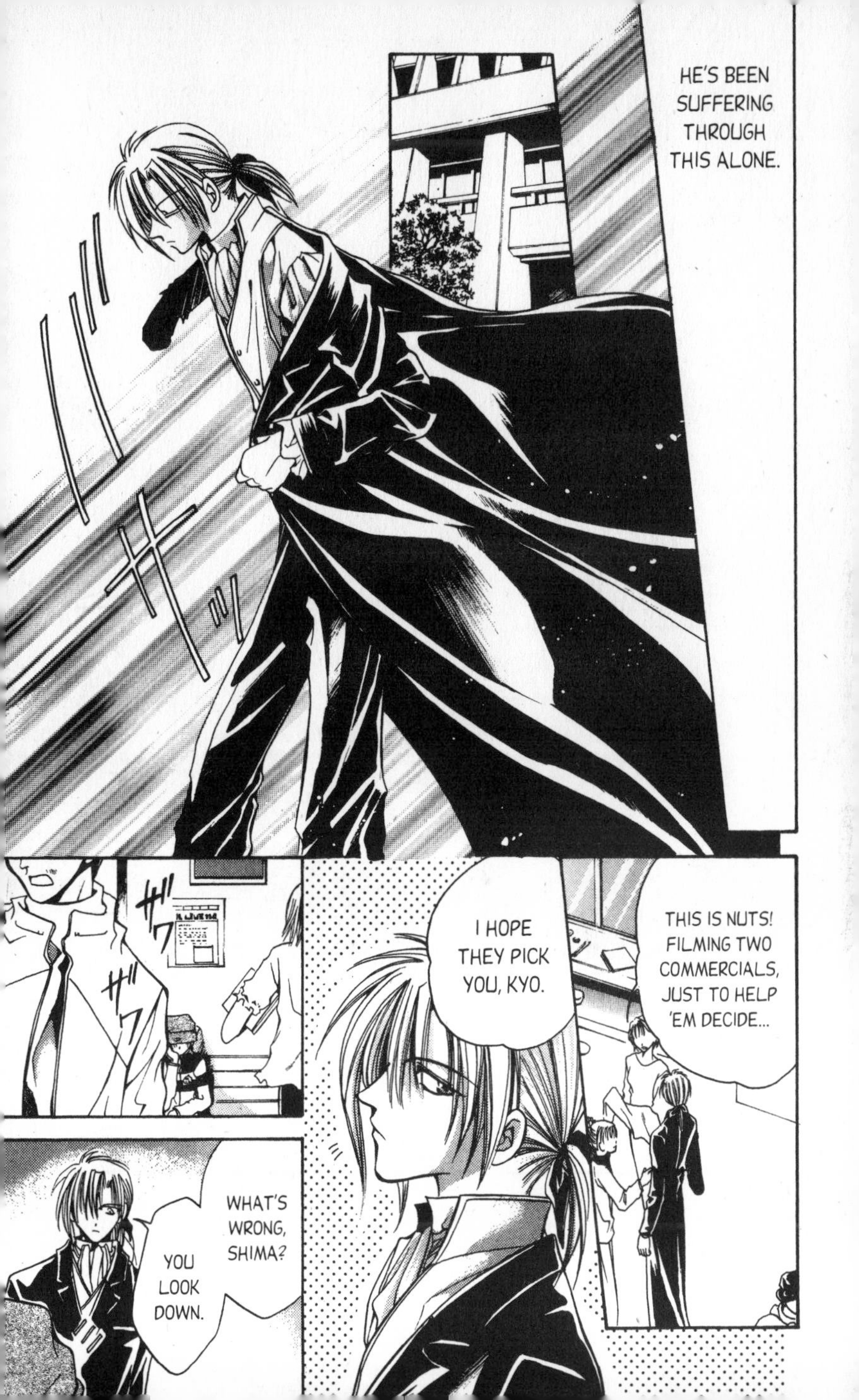
HE'S BEEN SUFFERING THROUGH THIS ALONE.
THIS IS NUTS! FILMING TWO COMMERCIALS, JUST TO HELP 'EM DECIDE...
I HOPE THEY PICK YOU, KYO.
ザワ
ザワ
WHAT'S WRONG, SHIMA?
YOU LOOK DOWN.

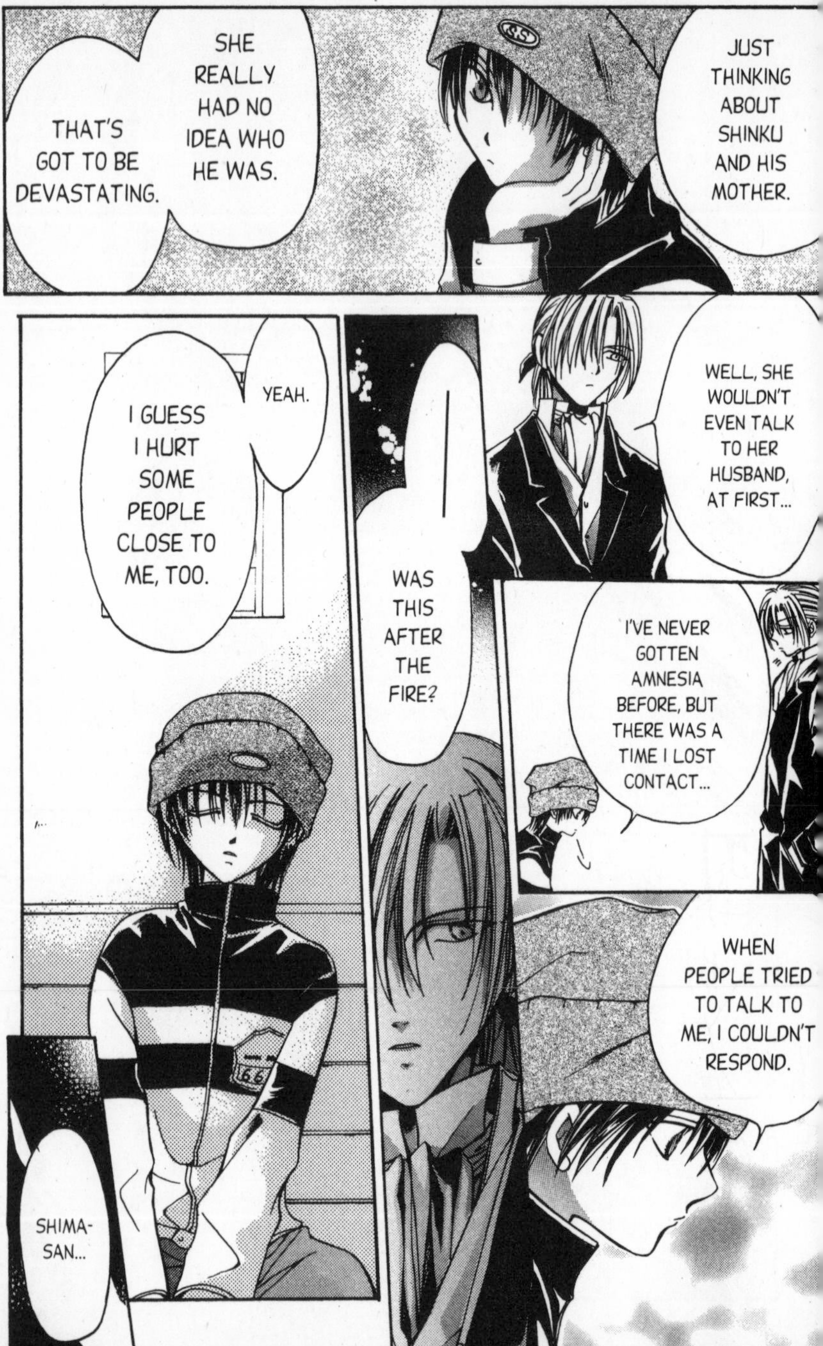
JUST THINKING ABOUT SHINKU AND HIS MOTHER.
SHE REALLY HAD NO IDEA WHO HE WAS.
THAT'S GOT TO BE DEVASTATING.
WELL, SHE WOULDN'T EVEN TALK TO HER HUSBAND, AT FIRST...
WAS THIS AFTER THE FIRE?
I'VE NEVER GOTTEN AMNESIA BEFORE, BUT THERE WAS A TIME I LOST CONTACT...
WHEN PEOPLE TRIED TO TALK TO ME, I COULDN'T RESPOND.
YEAH.
I GUESS I HURT SOME PEOPLE CLOSE TO ME, TOO.
SHIMA-SAN...

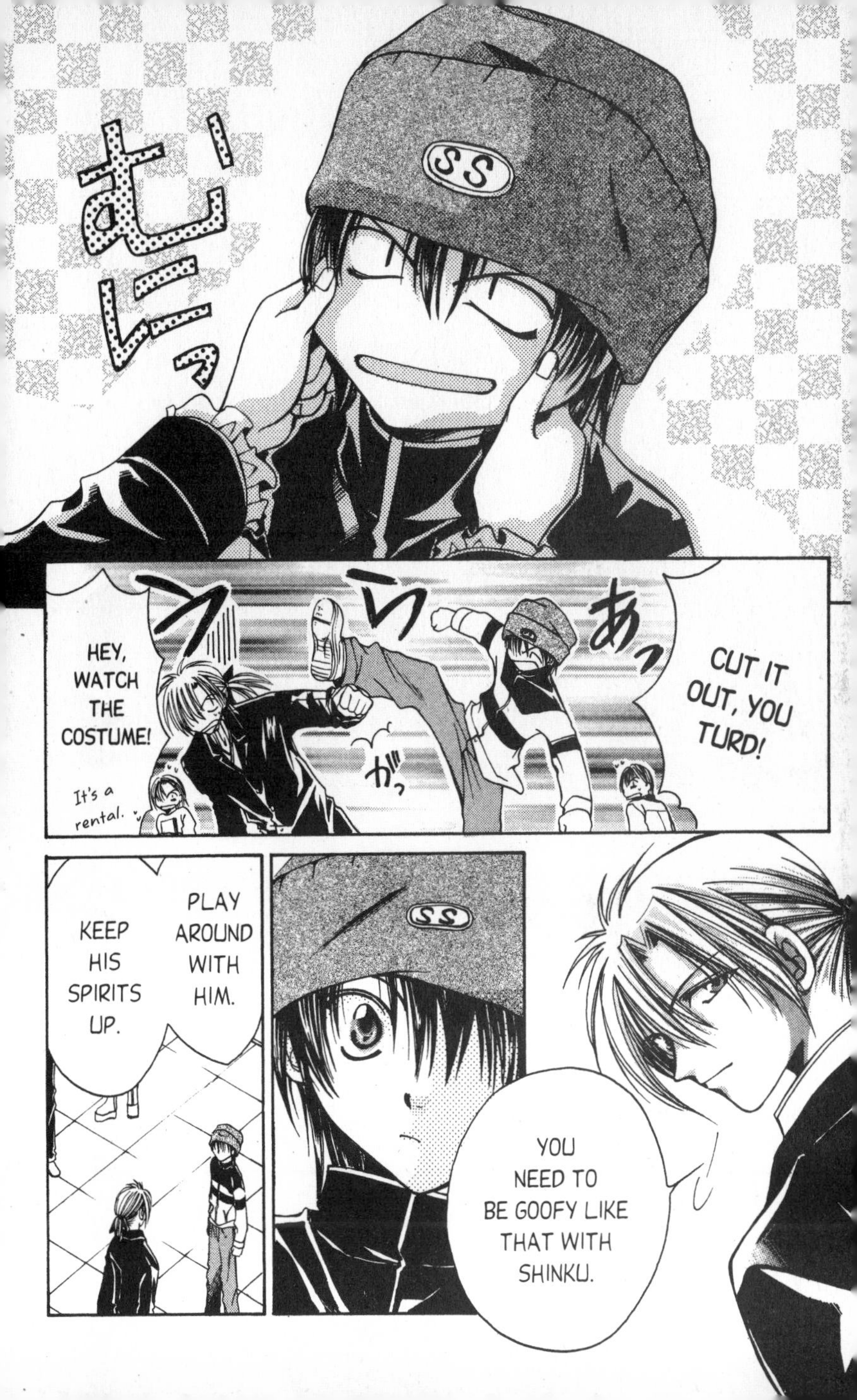
むにっ
CUT IT OUT, YOU TURD!
がっ
HEY, WATCH THE COSTUME!
It's a rental.
YOU NEED TO BE GOOFY LIKE THAT WITH SHINKU.
PLAY AROUND WITH HIM.
KEEP HIS SPIRITS UP.

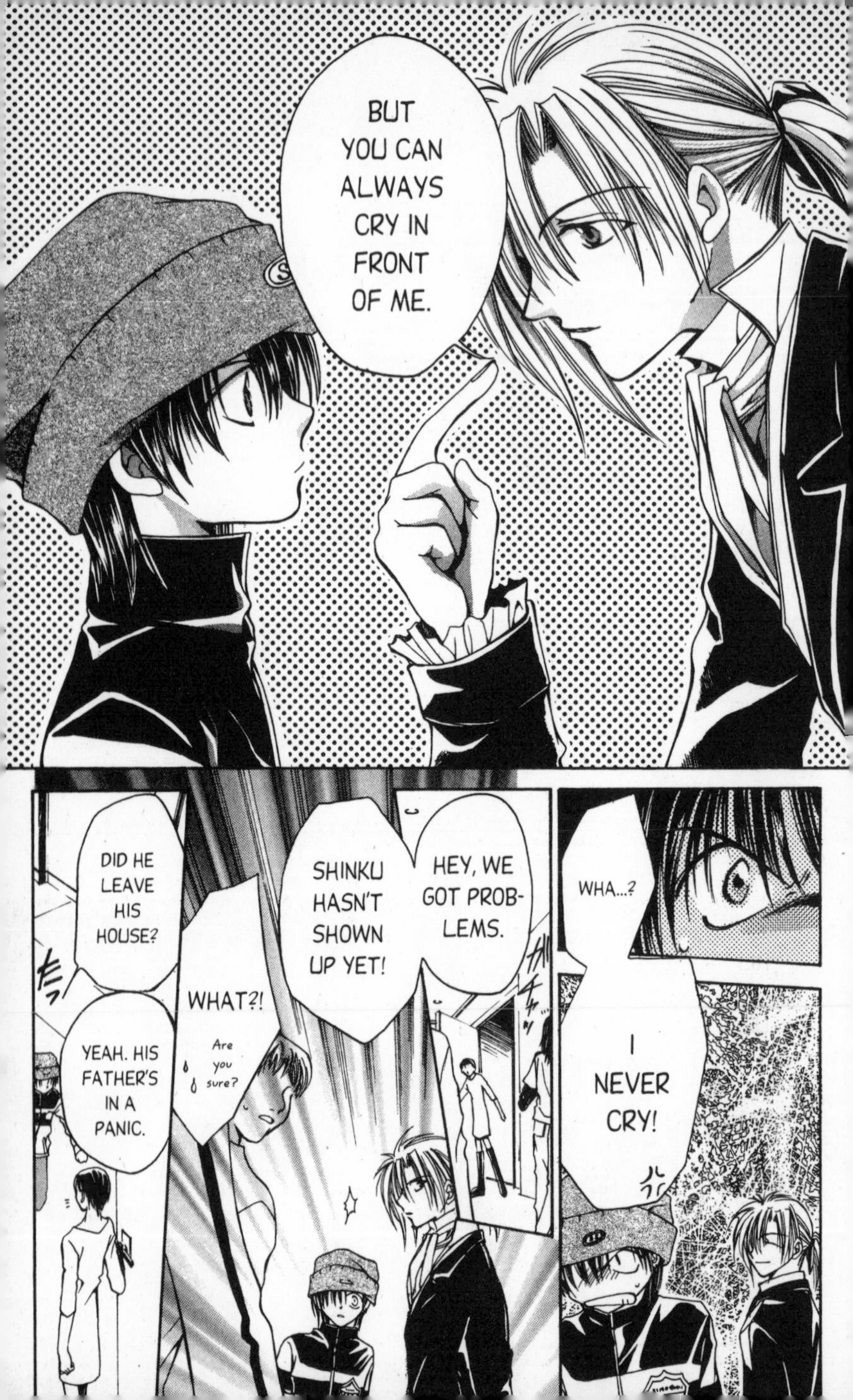
BUT YOU CAN ALWAYS CRY IN FRONT OF ME.
WHA...?
I NEVER CRY!
HEY, WE GOT PROB-LEMS.
SHINKU HASN'T SHOWN UP YET!
WHAT?!
Are you sure?
DID HE LEAVE HIS HOUSE?
YEAH. HIS FATHER'S IN A PANIC.

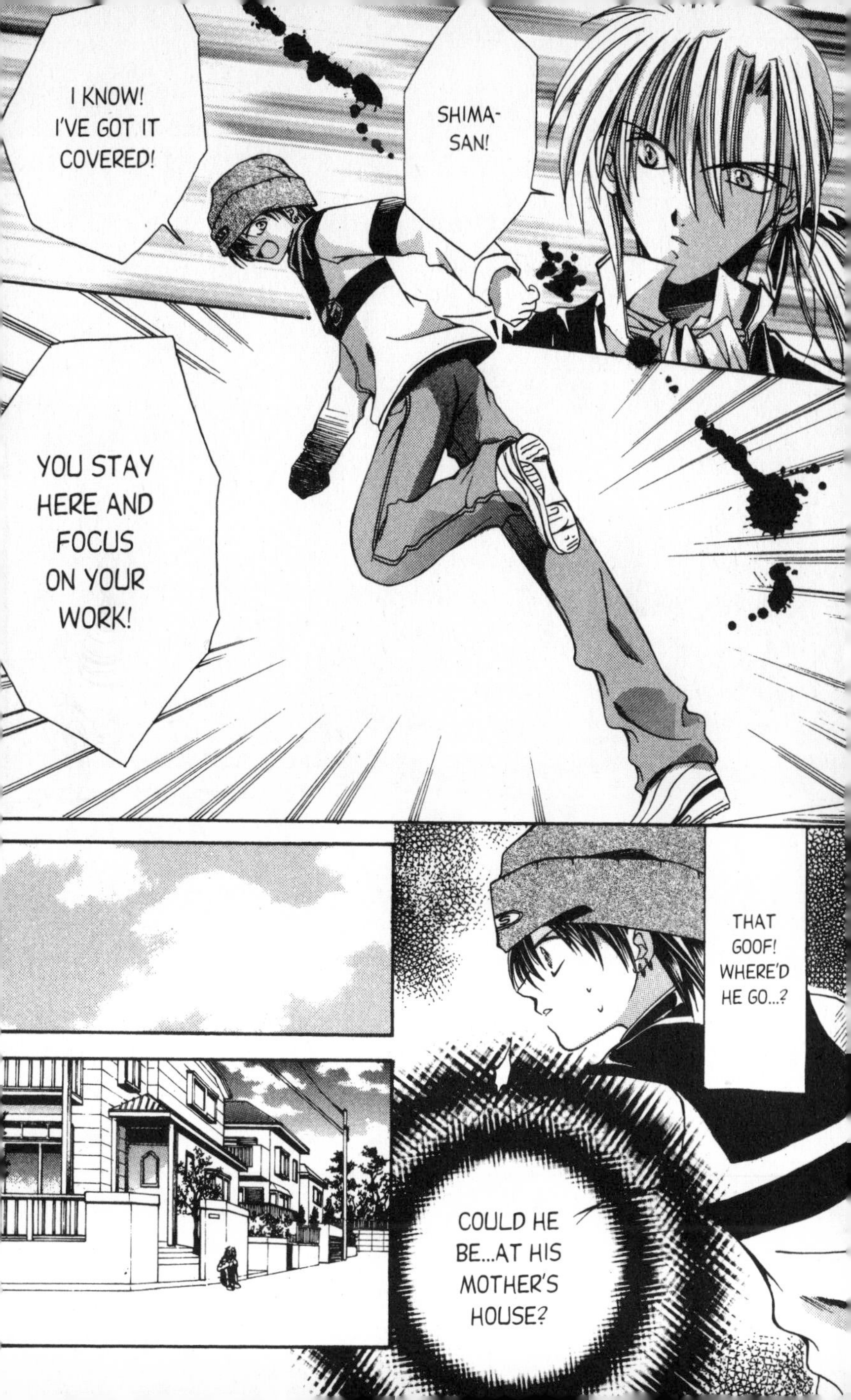
SHIMA-SAN!
I KNOW! I'VE GOT IT COVERED!
YOU STAY HERE AND FOCUS ON YOUR WORK!
THAT GOOF! WHERE'D HE GO...?
COULD HE BE...AT HIS MOTHER'S HOUSE?

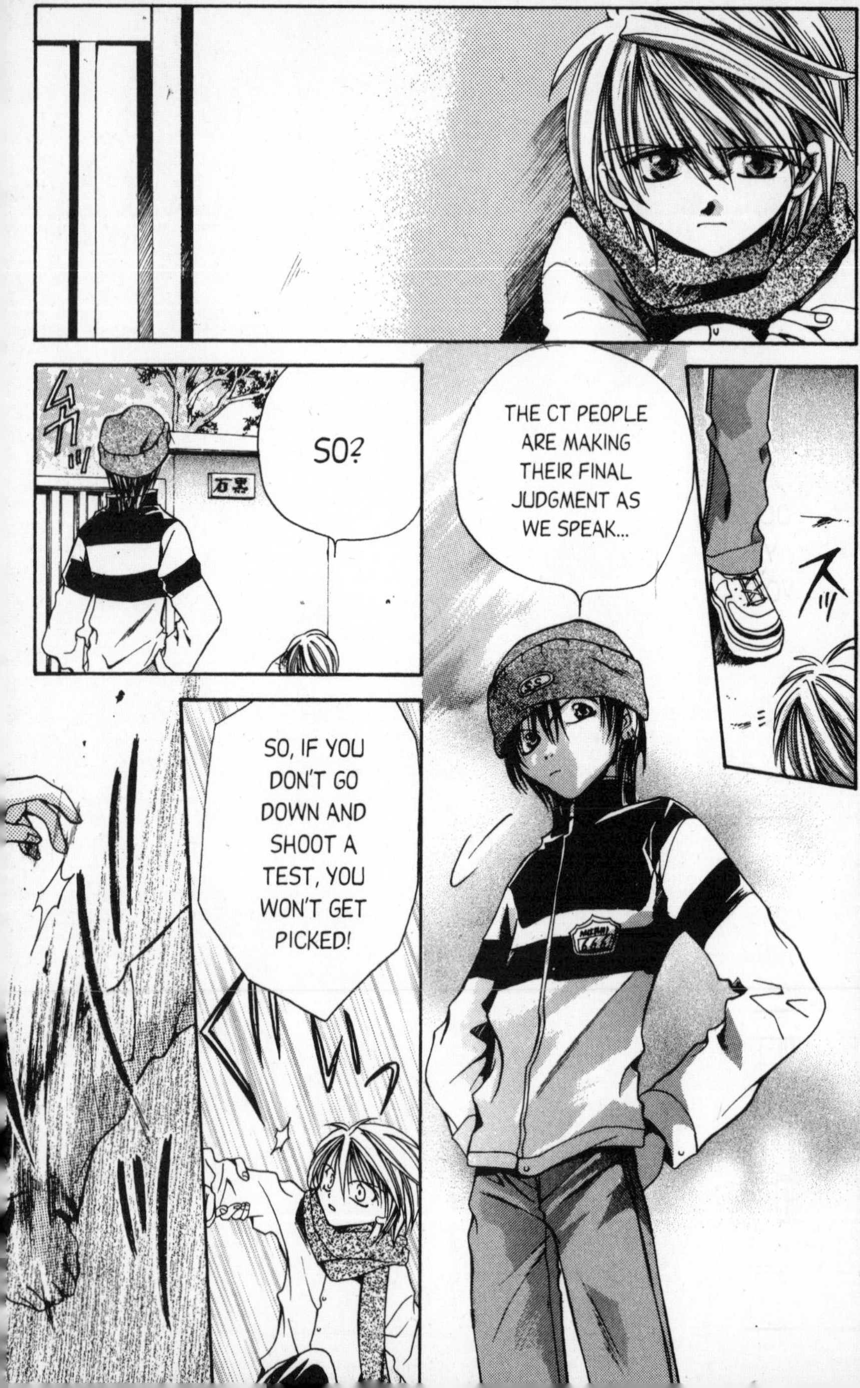
THE CT PEOPLE ARE MAKING THEIR FINAL JUDGMENT AS WE SPEAK...
SO?
SO, IF YOU DON'T GO DOWN AND SHOOT A TEST, YOU WON'T GET PICKED!

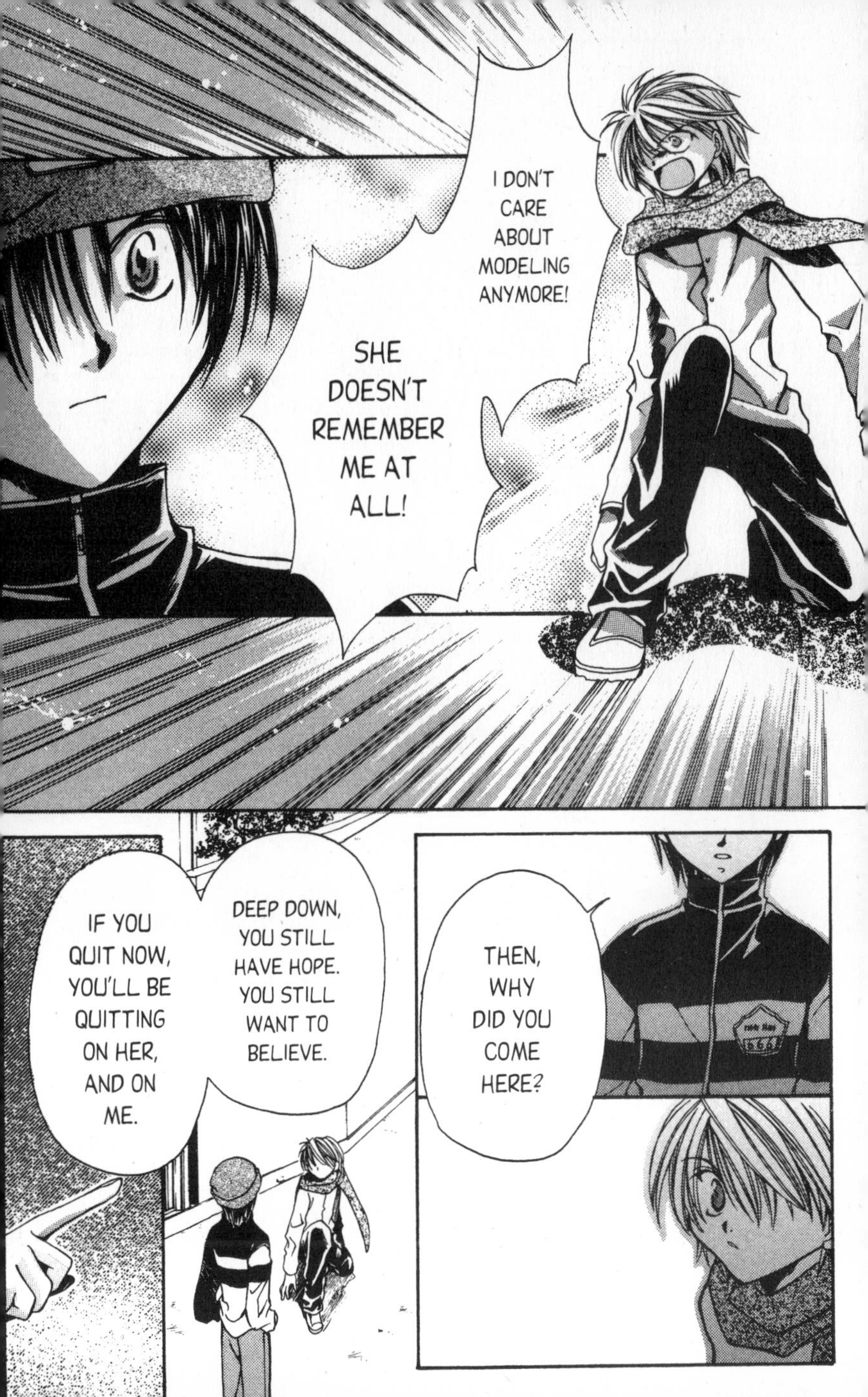
I DON'T CARE ABOUT MODELING ANYMORE!
SHE DOESN'T REMEMBER ME AT ALL!
THEN, WHY DID YOU COME HERE?
DEEP DOWN, YOU STILL HAVE HOPE. YOU STILL WANT TO BELIEVE.
IF YOU QUIT NOW, YOU'LL BE QUITTING ON HER, AND ON ME.

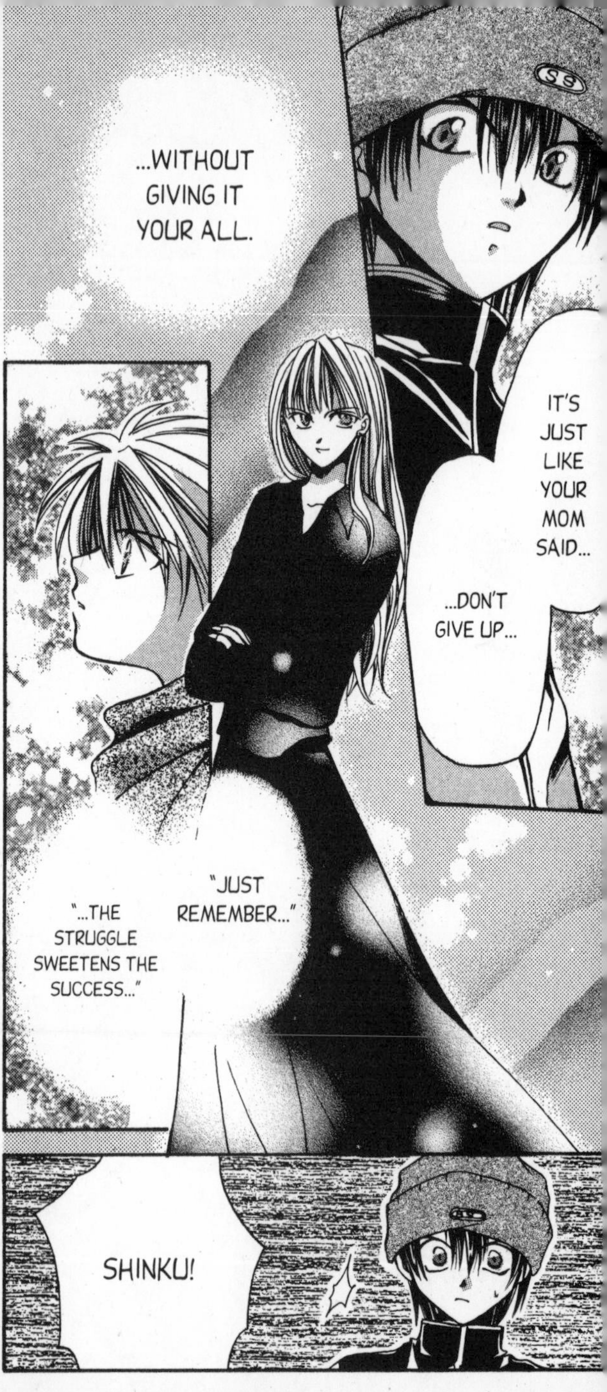
IT'S JUST LIKE YOUR MOM SAID...
...DON'T GIVE UP...
...WITHOUT GIVING IT YOUR ALL.
"JUST REMEMBER..."
"...THE STRUGGLE SWEETENS THE SUCCESS..."
SHINKU!

The other day when I was talking to Ms. Tanoma Yumu on the phone, the topic of "bugs" came up. I hate bugs. Especially cockroaches. Ms. T can kill bugs without a second glance. I'm jealous. In the summer, I spend an hour a day battling roaches.

Speaking of summer, my apartment is near the river, and one summer a typhoon hit our area and the river started to rise. I live on the first floor, and I was afraid I might get flooded, all my drafts and drawings floating away on the tide! But I got lucky. The river held its banks.

When I was a kid, and a typhoon hit, I would get really wild. I screamed at every clap of thunder. I'm not scared of thunder now, but it is distracting when you're trying to work.

Children and nature are a lethal combination.

...that's a random statement...

...I need to find better ways to end these notes.

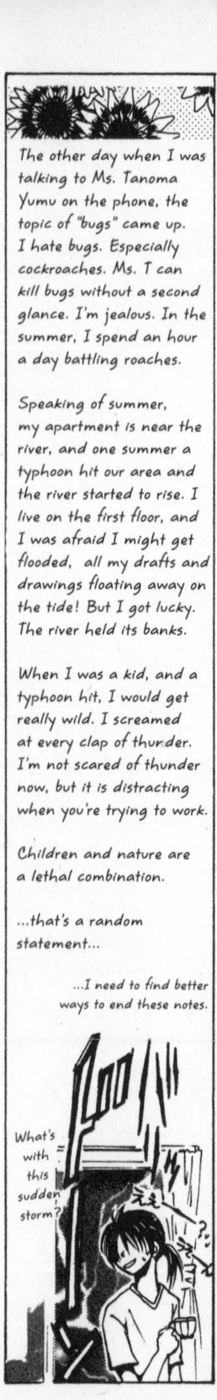
What's with this sudden storm?

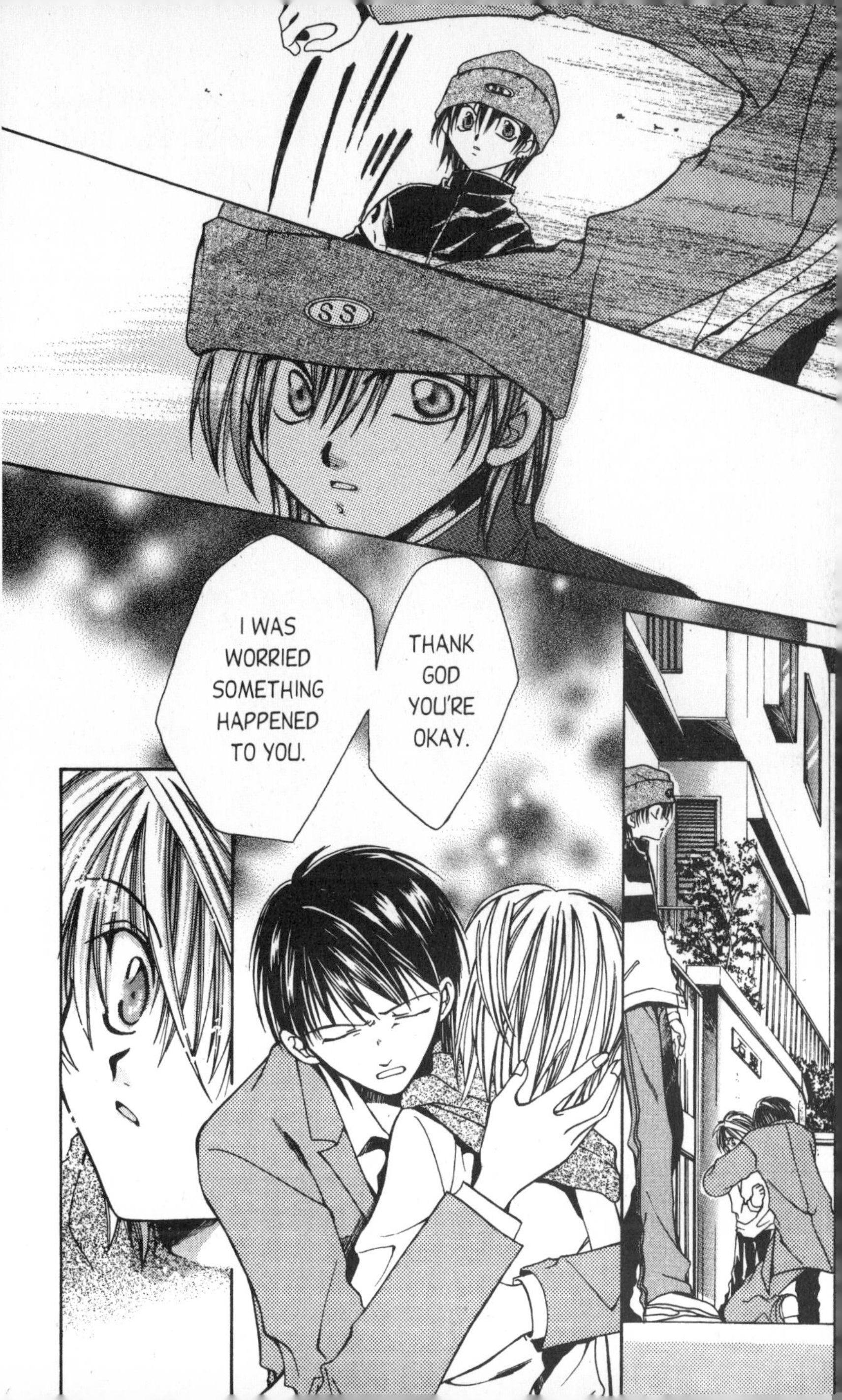
I WAS WORRIED SOMETHING HAPPENED TO YOU.
THANK GOD YOU'RE OKAY.

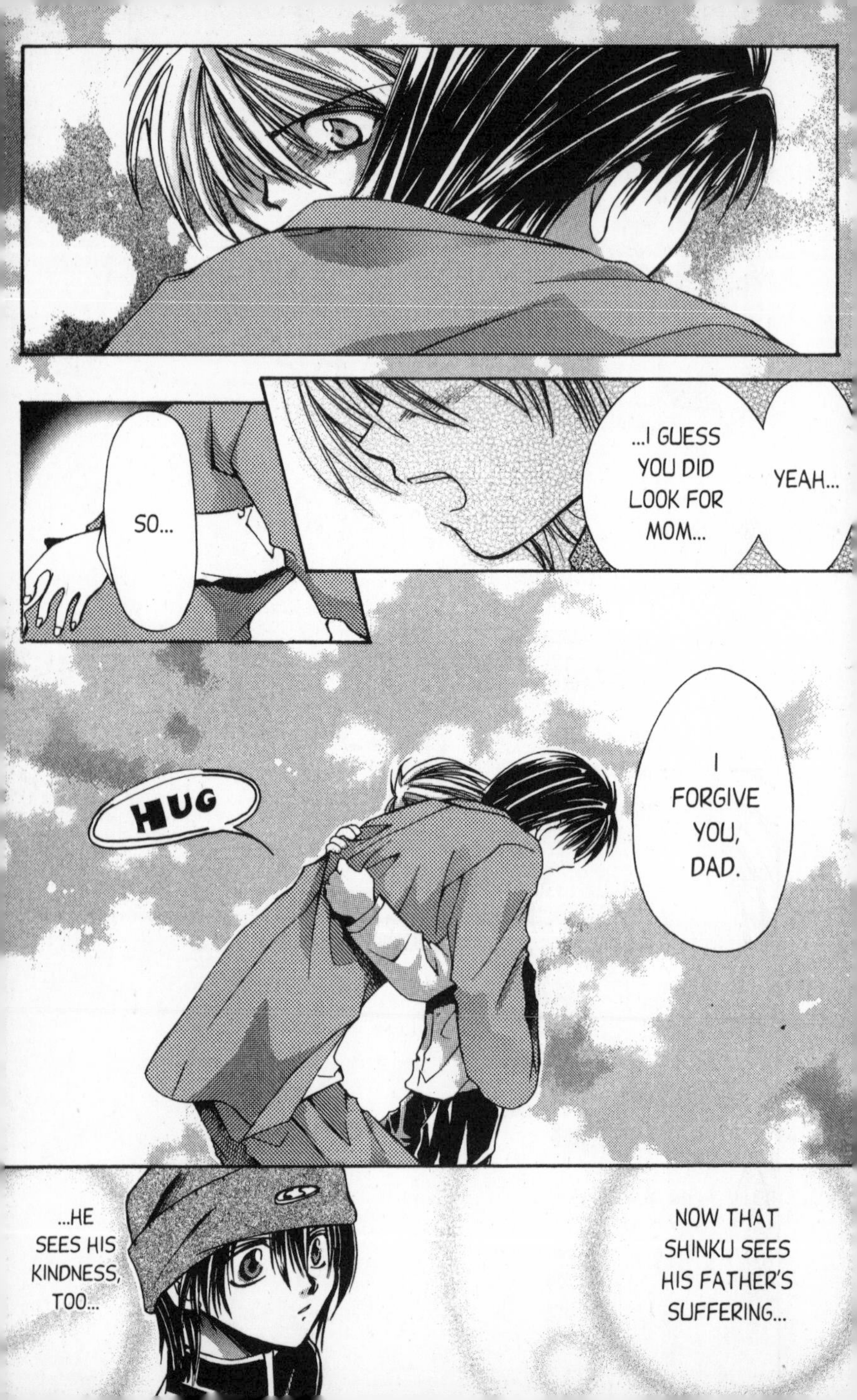
YEAH...
...I GUESS YOU DID LOOK FOR MOM...
SO...
I FORGIVE YOU, DAD.
HUG
NOW THAT SHINKU SEES HIS FATHER'S SUFFERING...
...HE SEES HIS KINDNESS, TOO...

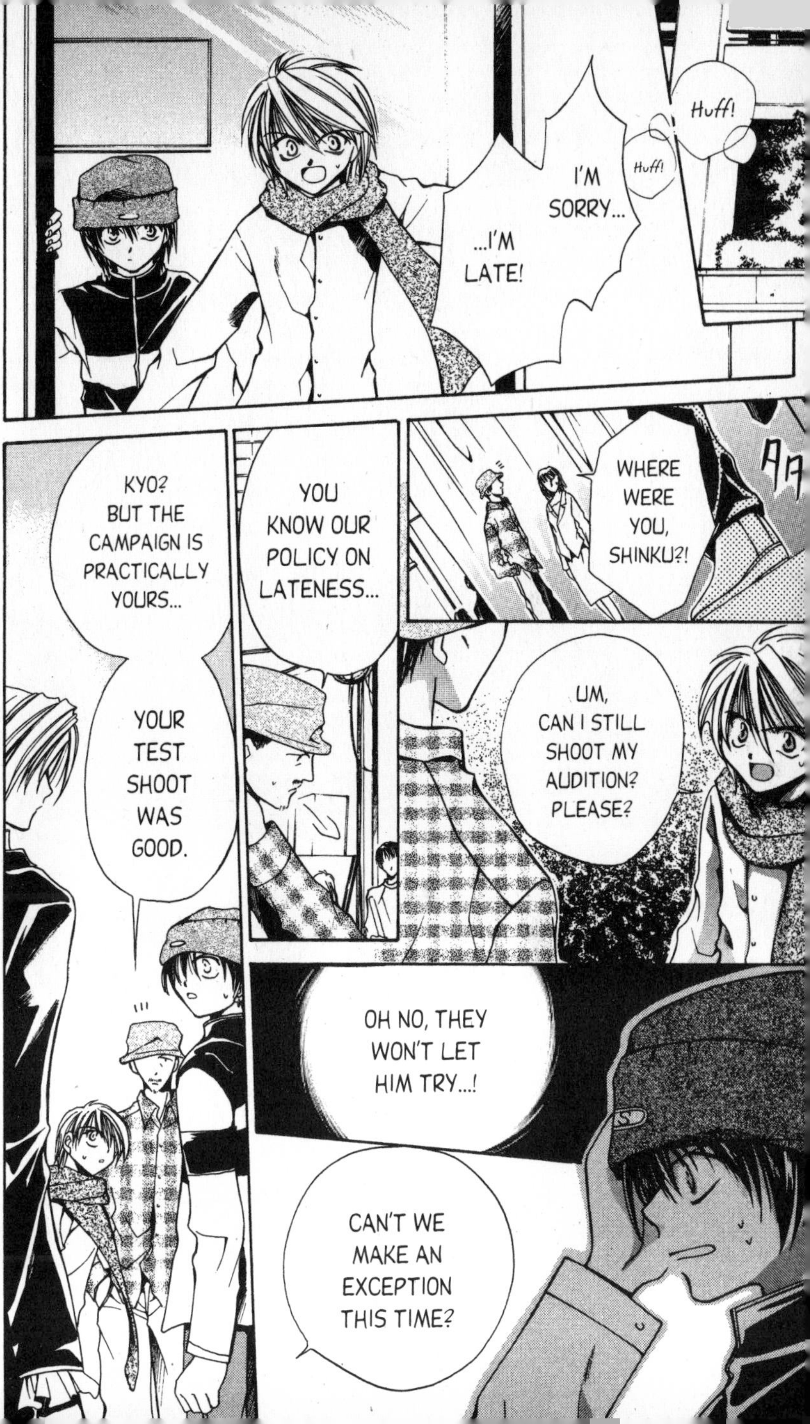
Huff!
Huff!
I'M SORRY...
...I'M LATE!
WHERE WERE YOU, SHINKU?!
UM, CAN I STILL SHOOT MY AUDITION? PLEASE?
YOU KNOW OUR POLICY ON LATENESS...
OH NO, THEY WON'T LET HIM TRY...!
CAN'T WE MAKE AN EXCEPTION THIS TIME?
KYO? BUT THE CAMPAIGN IS PRACTICALLY YOURS...
YOUR TEST SHOOT WAS GOOD.

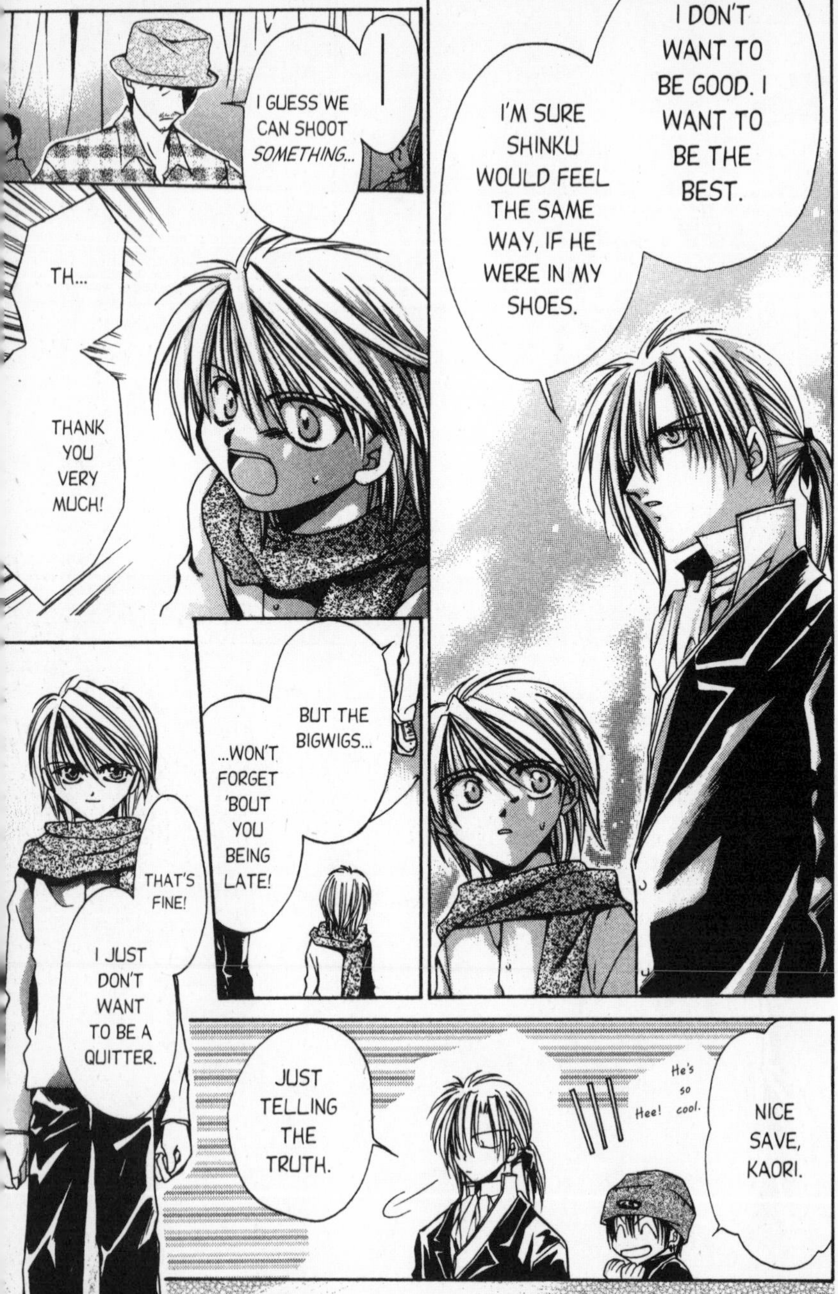
I DON'T WANT TO BE GOOD. I WANT TO BE THE BEST.
I'M SURE SHINKU WOULD FEEL THE SAME WAY, IF HE WERE IN MY SHOES.
I GUESS WE CAN SHOOT *SOMETHING...*
TH...
THANK YOU VERY MUCH!
BUT THE BIGWIGS...
...WON'T FORGET 'BOUT YOU BEING LATE!
THAT'S FINE!
I JUST DON'T WANT TO BE A QUITTER.
NICE SAVE, KAORI.
He's so cool.
Hee!
JUST TELLING THE TRUTH.

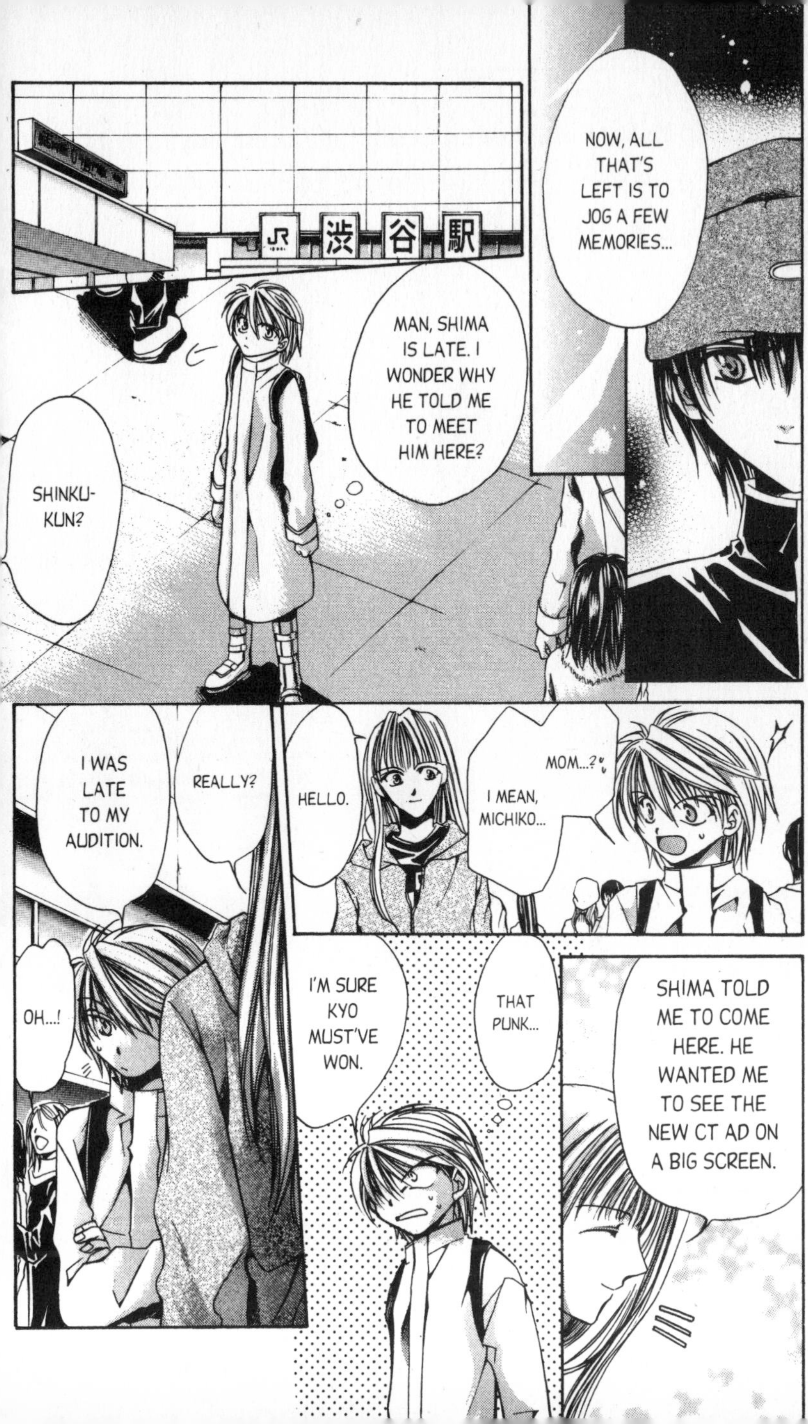
NOW, ALL THAT'S LEFT IS TO JOG A FEW MEMORIES...
渋谷駅
MAN, SHIMA IS LATE. I WONDER WHY HE TOLD ME TO MEET HIM HERE?
SHINKU-KUN?
MOM...?
I MEAN, MICHIKO...
HELLO.
REALLY?
I WAS LATE TO MY AUDITION.
SHIMA TOLD ME TO COME HERE. HE WANTED ME TO SEE THE NEW CT AD ON A BIG SCREEN.
THAT PUNK...
I'M SURE KYO MUST'VE WON.
OH...!

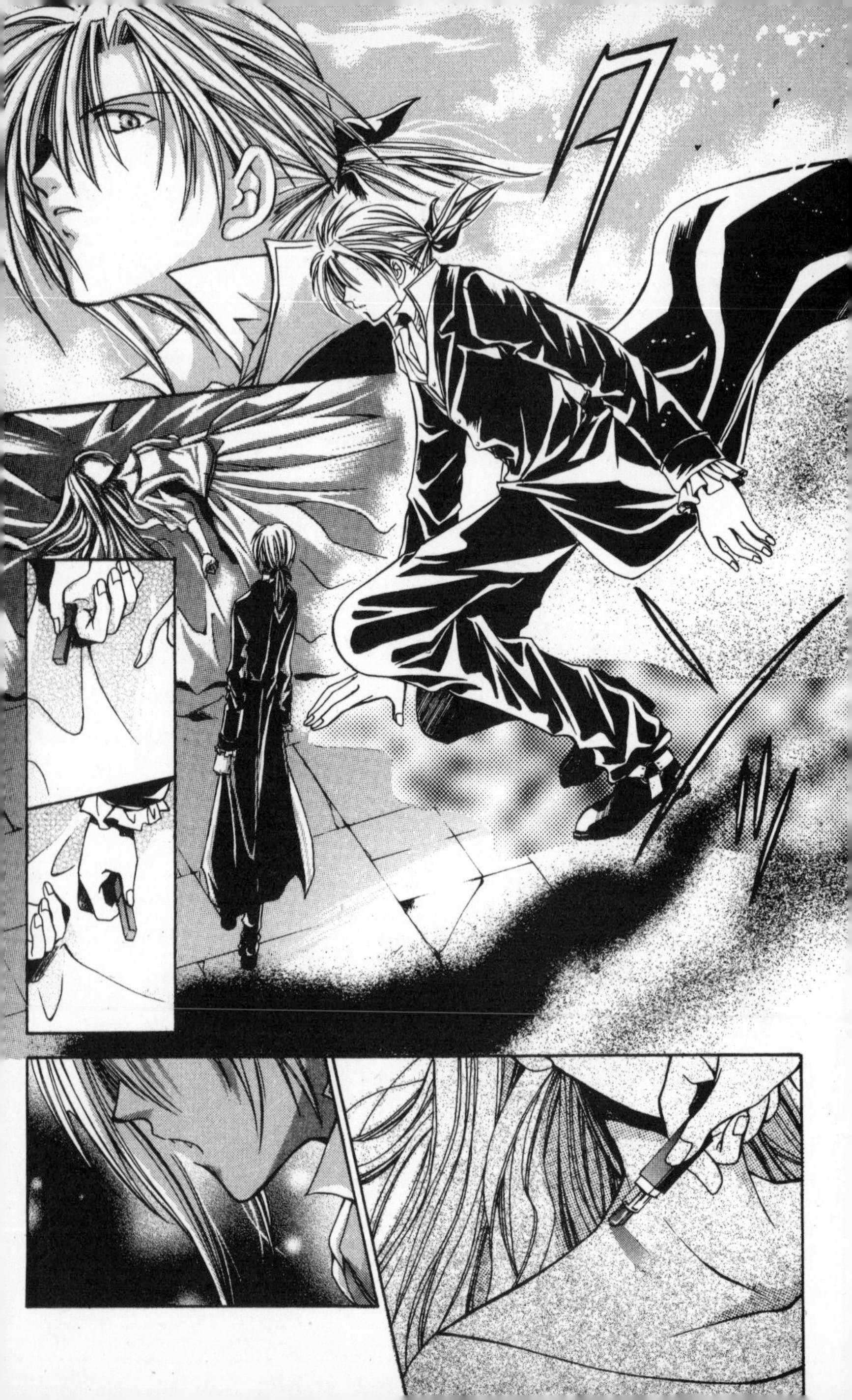

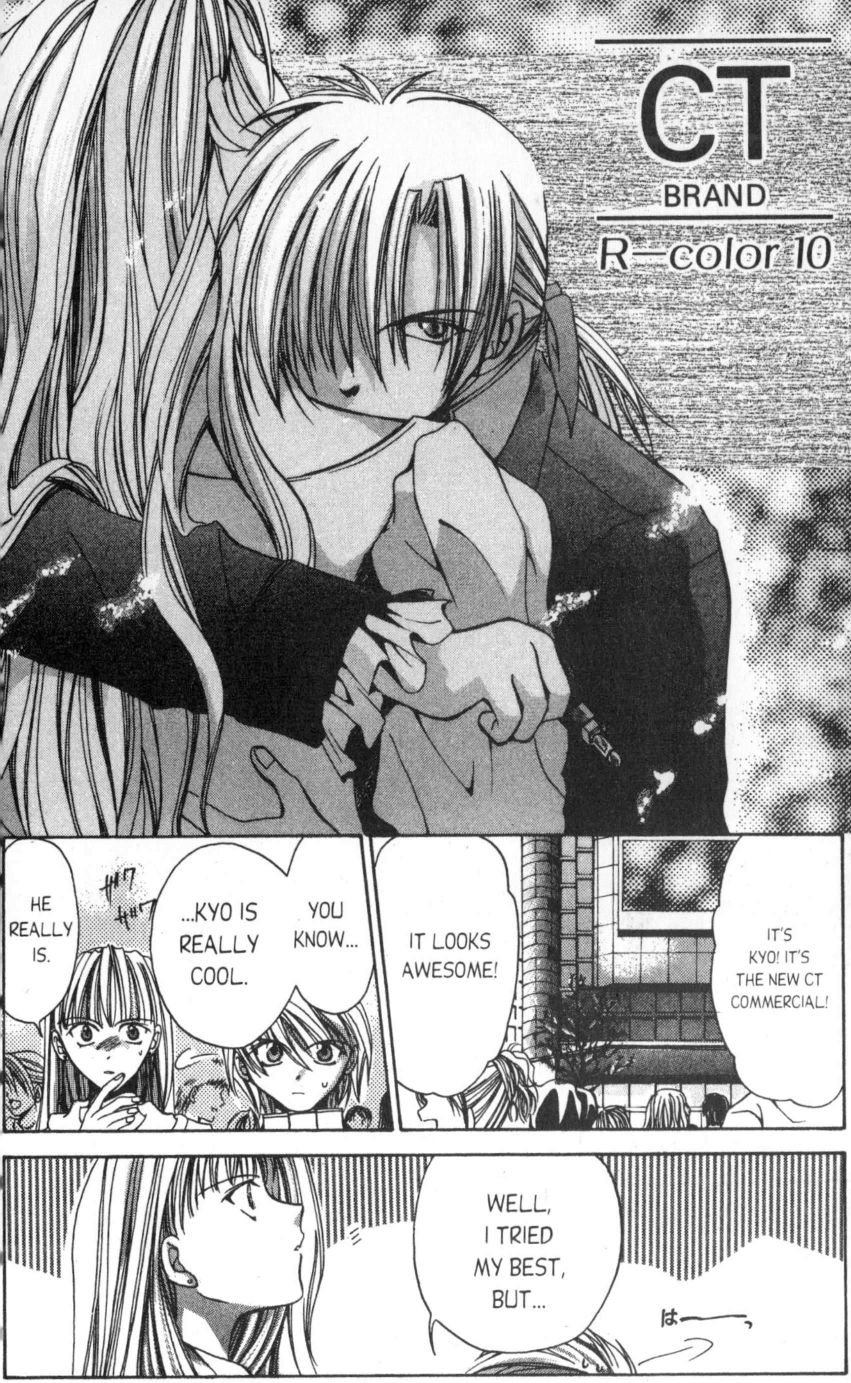
CT
BRAND
R—color 10
IT'S KYO! IT'S THE NEW CT COMMERCIAL!
IT LOOKS AWESOME!
YOU KNOW...
...KYO IS REALLY COOL.
HE REALLY IS.
WELL, I TRIED MY BEST, BUT...
は――っ

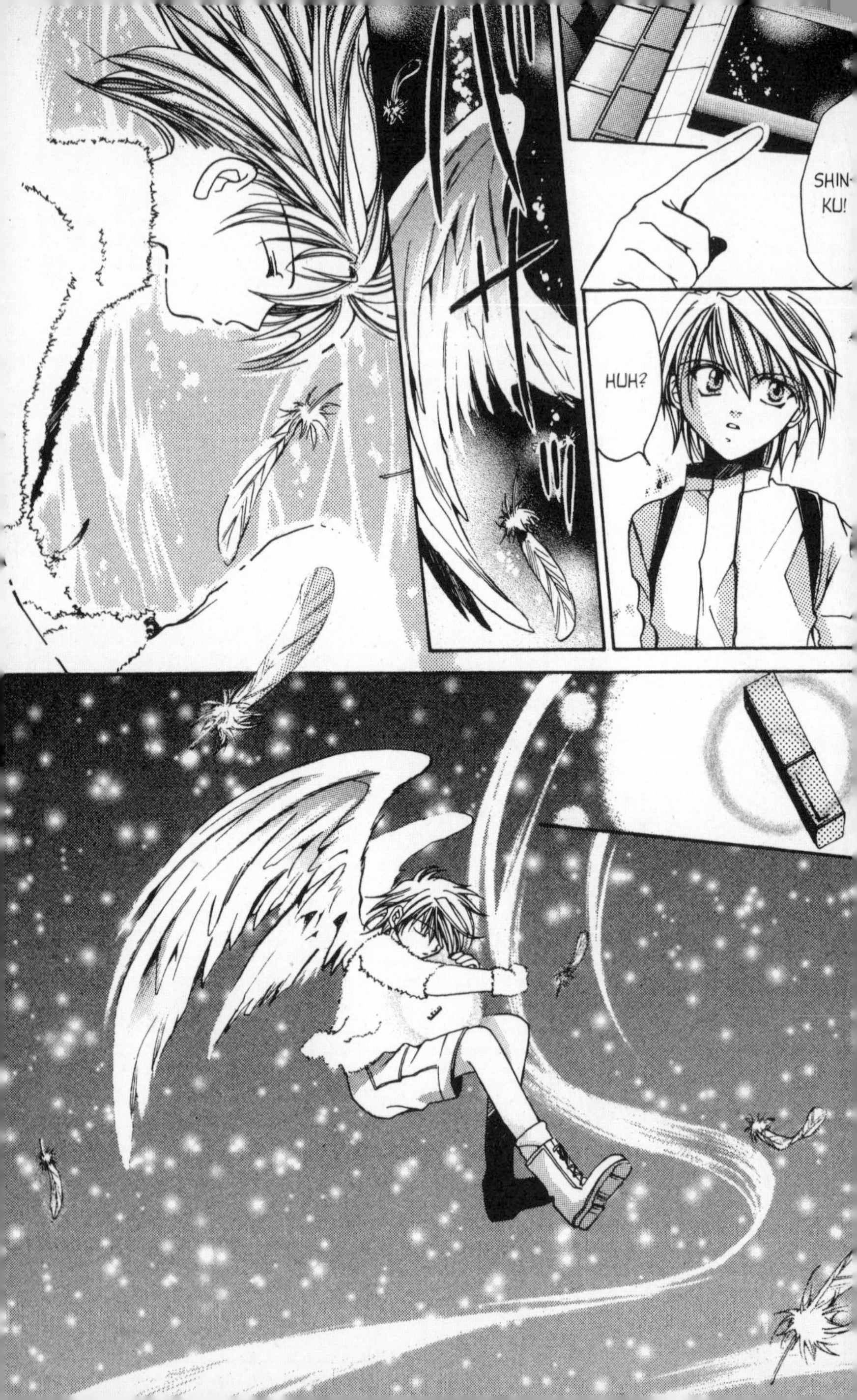
SHIN-
KU!
HUH?

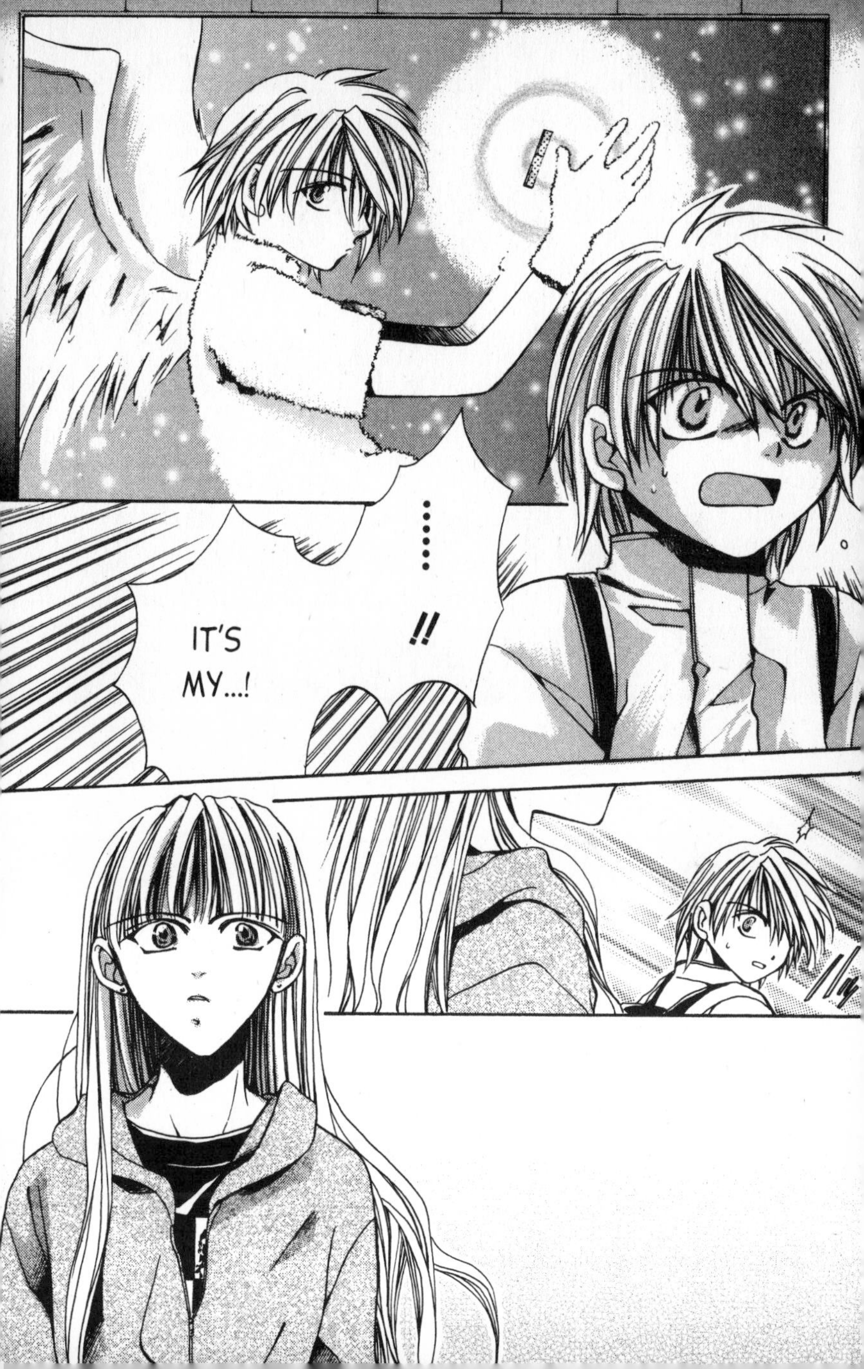
......!!
IT'S MY...!

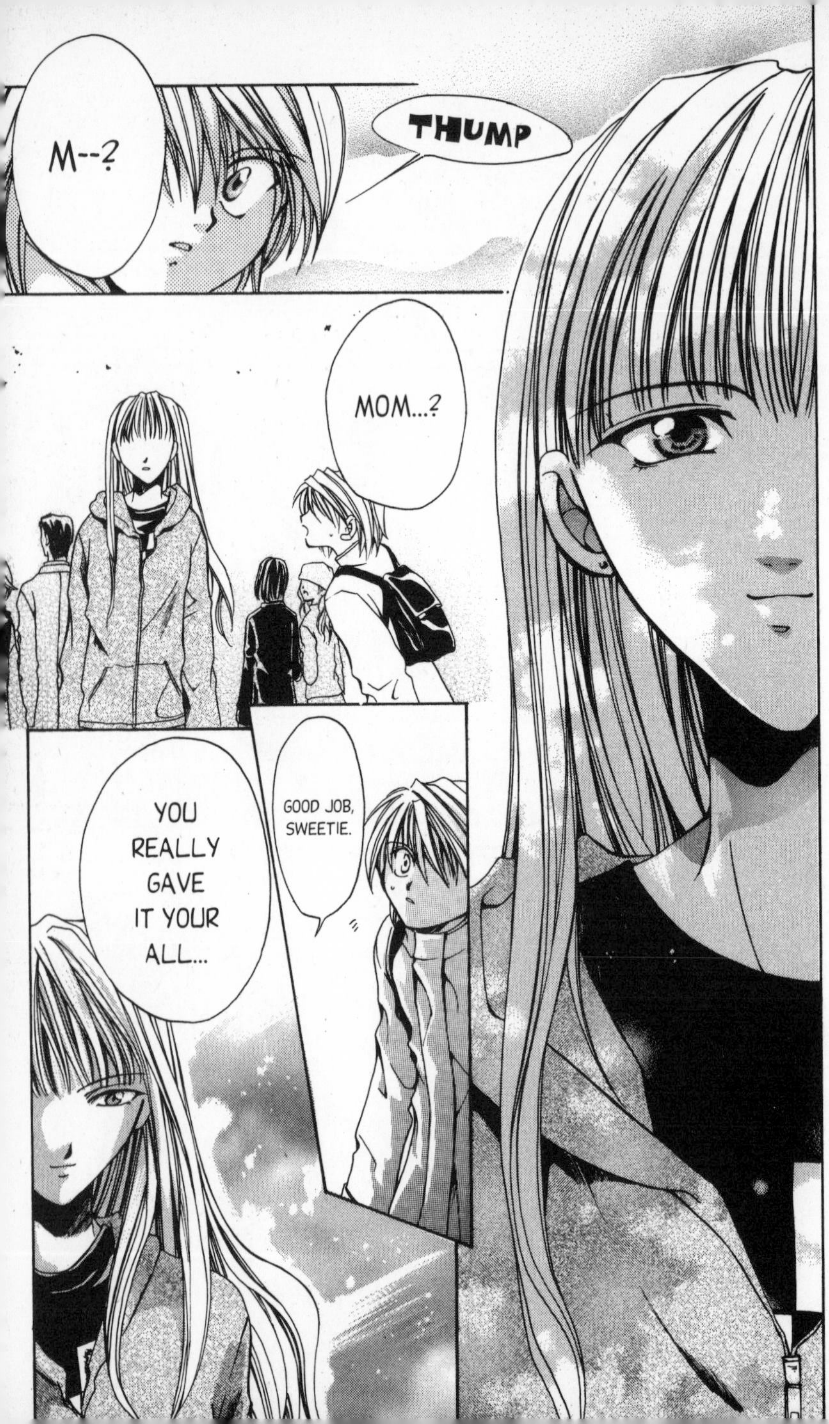
THUMP
M--?
MOM...?
GOOD JOB, SWEETIE.
YOU REALLY GAVE IT YOUR ALL...

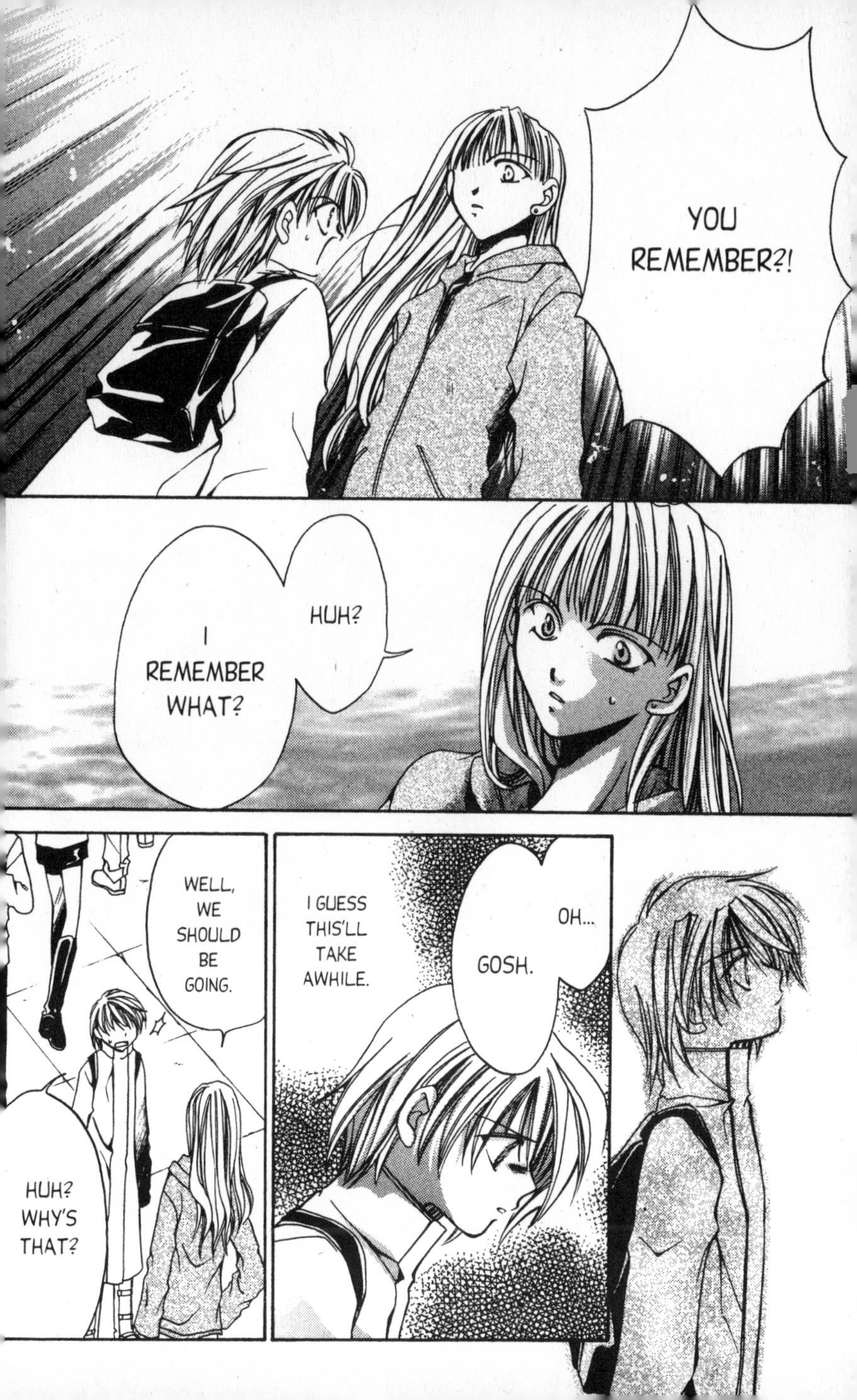
YOU REMEMBER?!
HUH?
I REMEMBER WHAT?
OH...
GOSH.
I GUESS THIS'LL TAKE AWHILE.
WELL, WE SHOULD BE GOING.
HUH? WHY'S THAT?

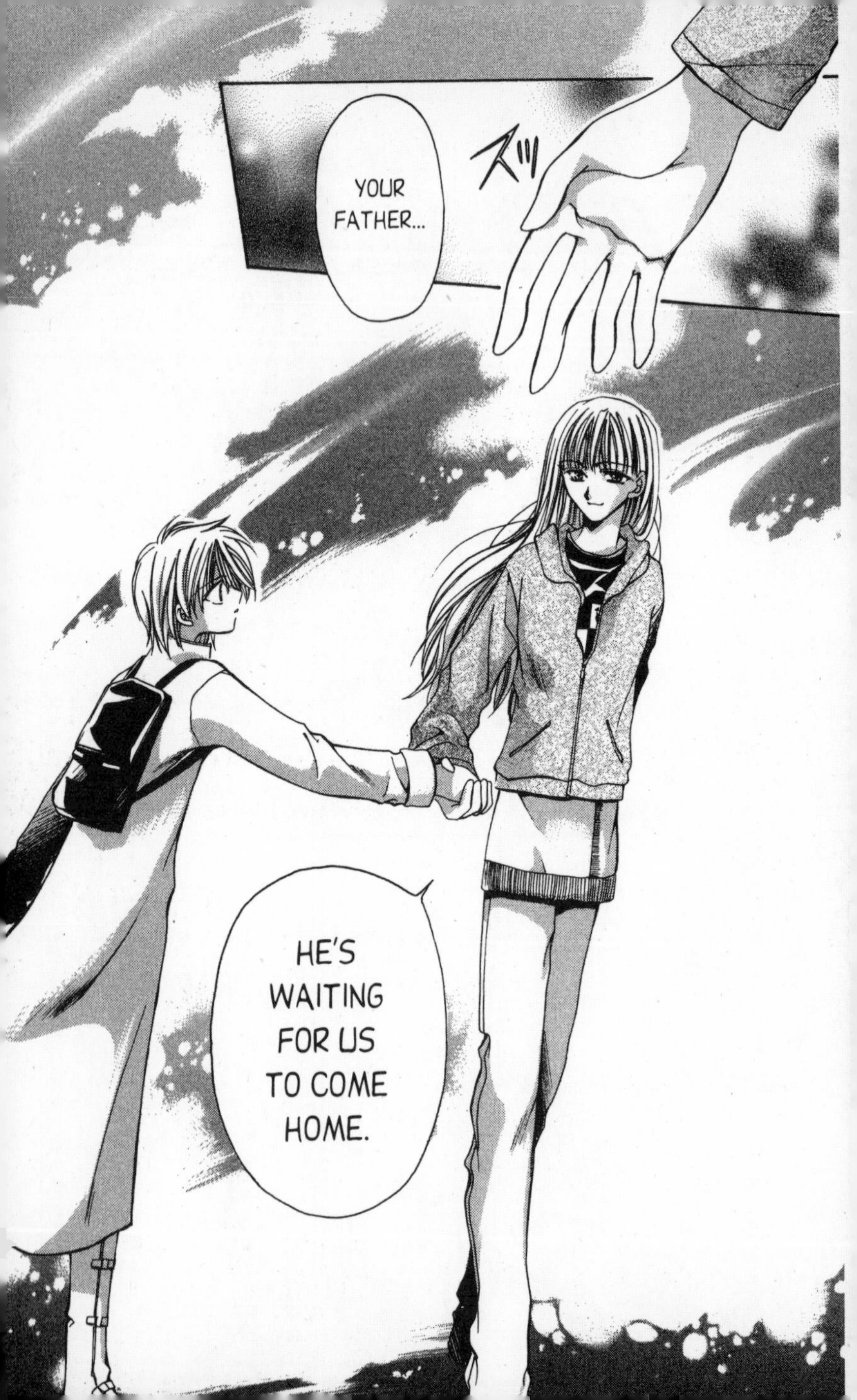
ズッ
YOUR FATHER...
HE'S WAITING FOR US TO COME HOME.

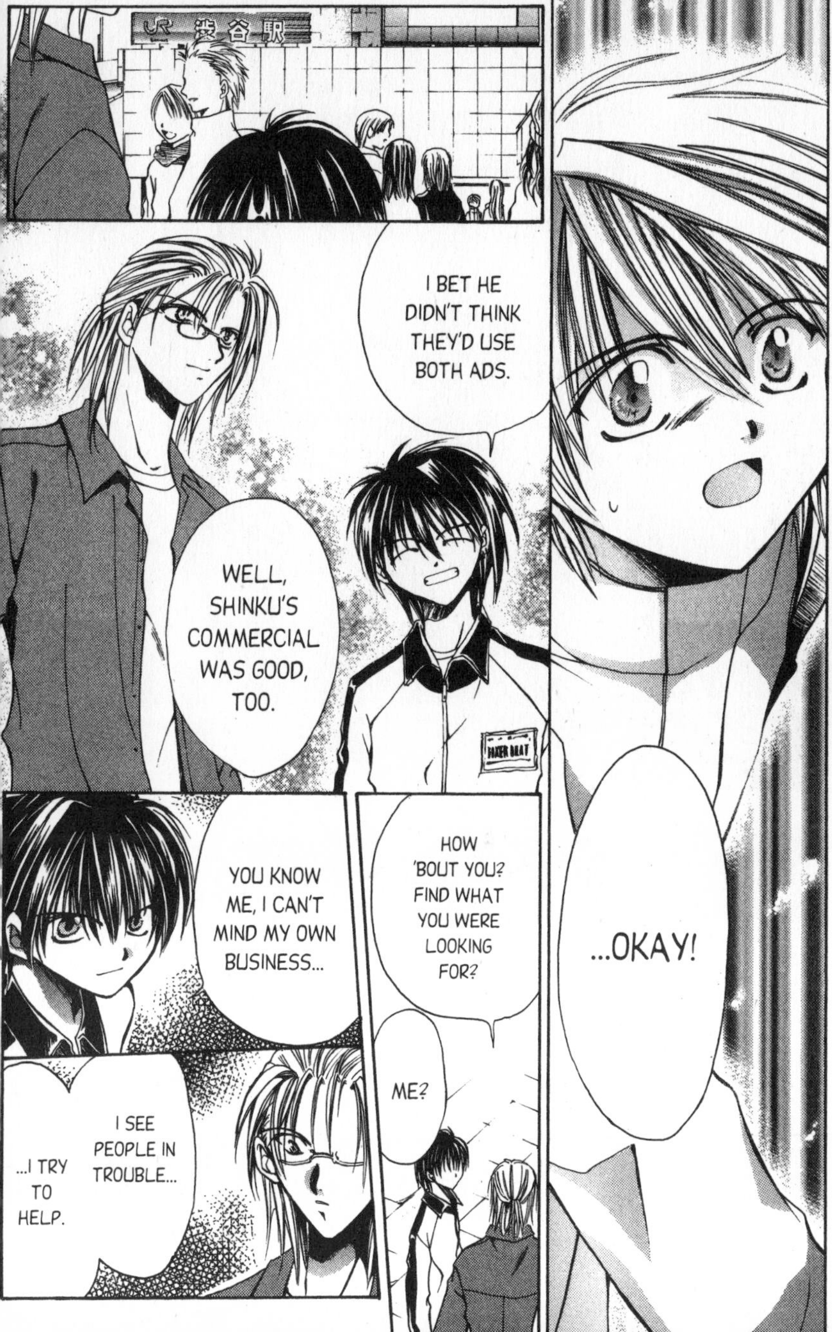
...OKAY!
JR 渋谷駅
I BET HE DIDN'T THINK THEY'D USE BOTH ADS.
WELL, SHINKU'S COMMERCIAL WAS GOOD, TOO.
HOW 'BOUT YOU? FIND WHAT YOU WERE LOOKING FOR?
ME?
YOU KNOW ME, I CAN'T MIND MY OWN BUSINESS...
I SEE PEOPLE IN TROUBLE...
...I TRY TO HELP.

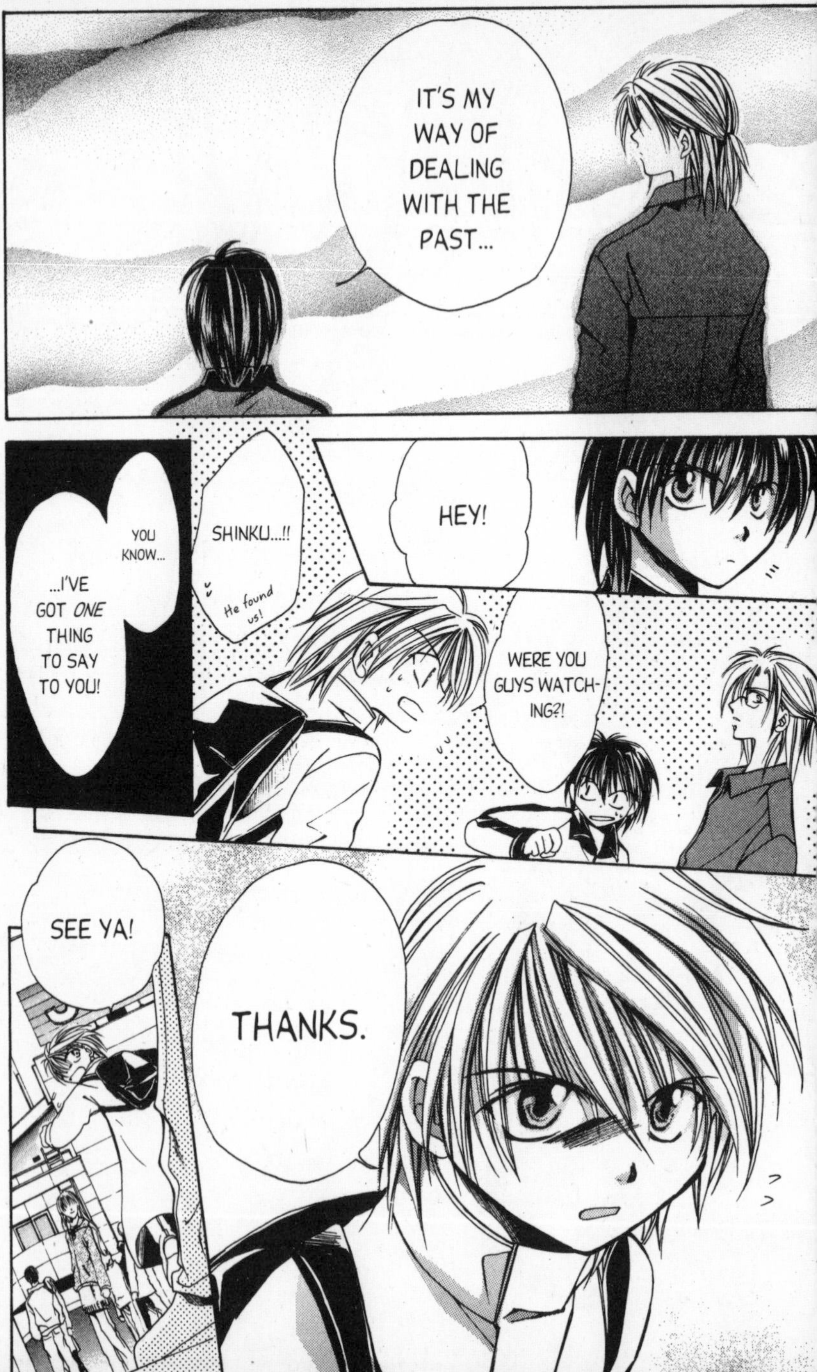
IT'S MY WAY OF DEALING WITH THE PAST...
HEY!
WERE YOU GUYS WATCHING?!
SHINKU...!!
He found us!
YOU KNOW...
...I'VE GOT *ONE* THING TO SAY TO YOU!
THANKS.
SEE YA!

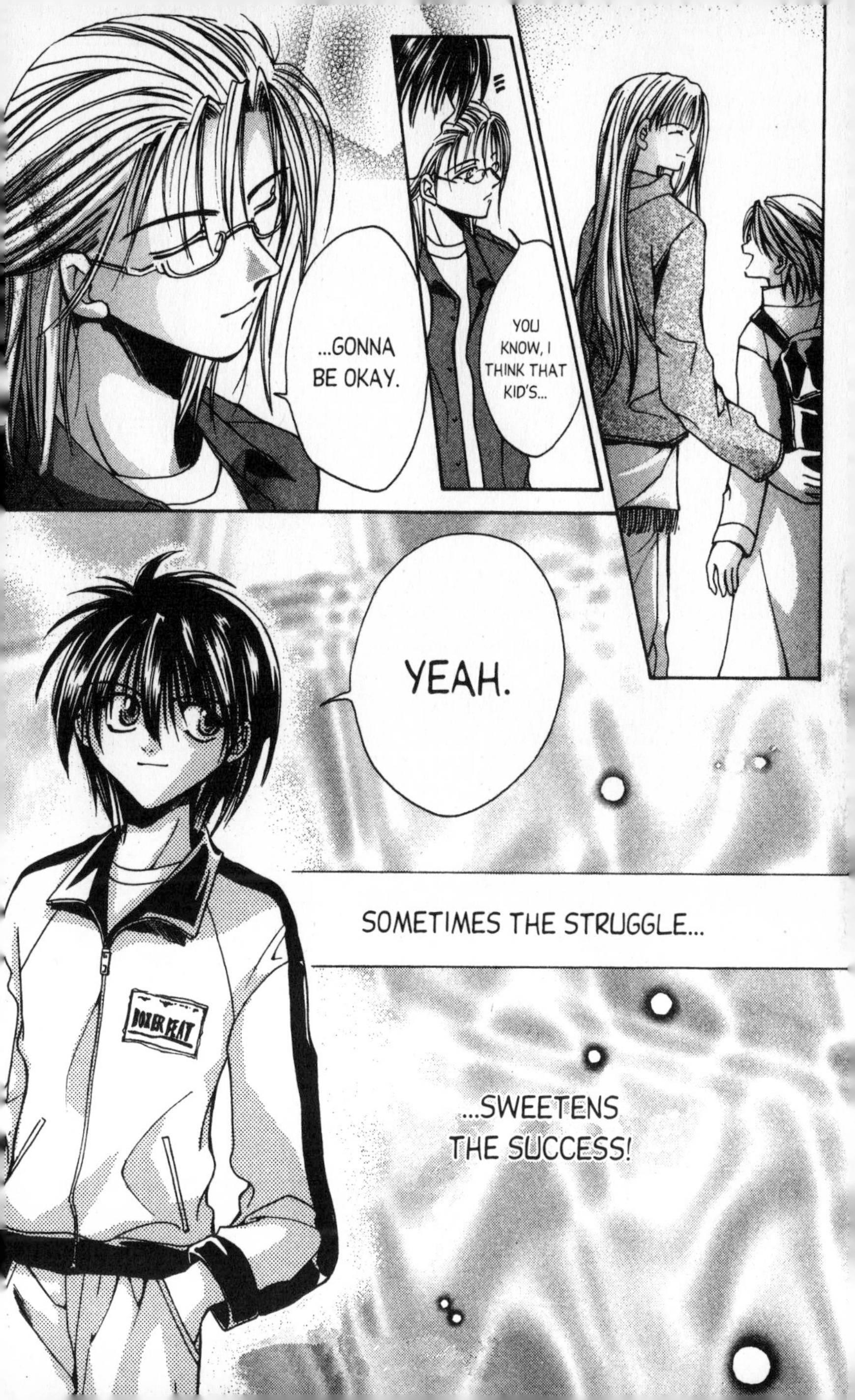
YOU KNOW, I THINK THAT KID'S...
...GONNA BE OKAY.
YEAH.
SOMETIMES THE STRUGGLE...
...SWEETENS THE SUCCESS!
BOXER BEAT

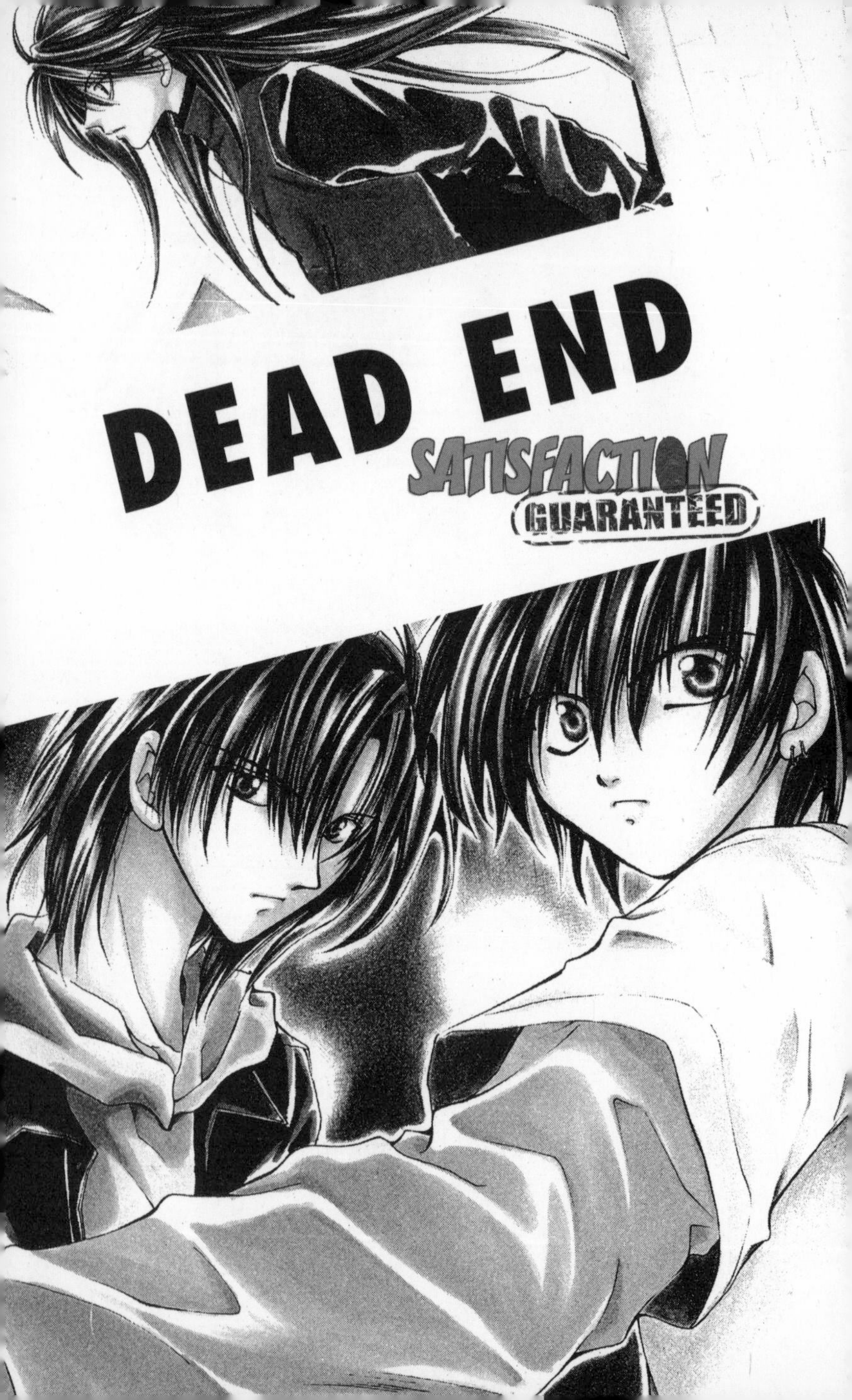
DEAD END
SATISFACTION
GUARANTEED

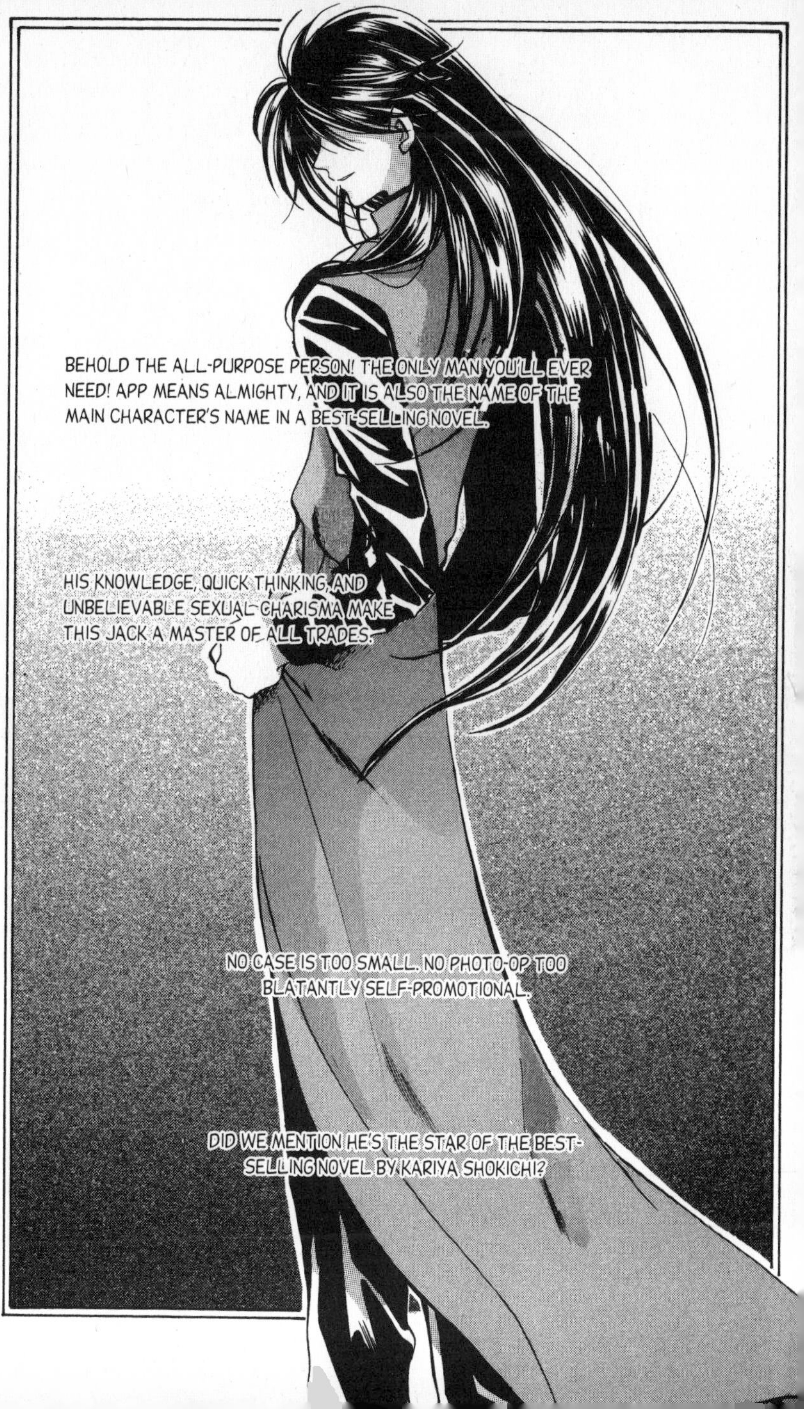
BEHOLD THE ALL-PURPOSE PERSON! THE ONLY MAN YOU'LL EVER NEED! APP MEANS ALMIGHTY, AND IT IS ALSO THE NAME OF THE MAIN CHARACTER'S NAME IN A BEST-SELLING NOVEL.
HIS KNOWLEDGE, QUICK THINKING, AND UNBELIEVABLE SEXUAL CHARISMA MAKE THIS JACK A MASTER OF ALL TRADES.
NO CASE IS TOO SMALL, NO PHOTO-OP TOO BLATANTLY SELF-PROMOTIONAL.
DID WE MENTION HE'S THE STAR OF THE BEST-SELLING NOVEL BY KARIYA SHOKICHI?

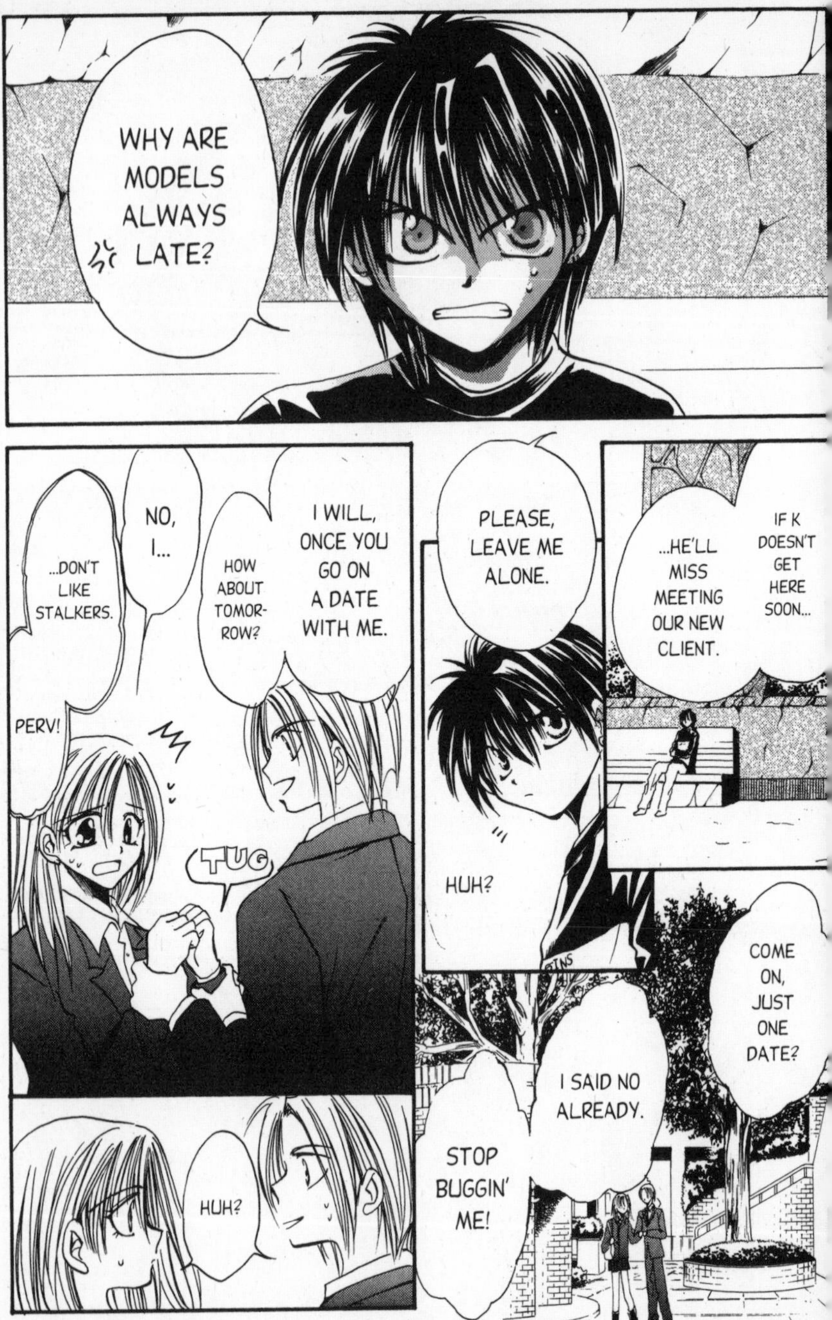
WHY ARE MODELS ALWAYS LATE?
IF K DOESN'T GET HERE SOON...
...HE'LL MISS MEETING OUR NEW CLIENT.
PLEASE, LEAVE ME ALONE.
HUH?
COME ON, JUST ONE DATE?
I SAID NO ALREADY.
STOP BUGGIN' ME!
I WILL, ONCE YOU GO ON A DATE WITH ME.
HOW ABOUT TOMOR-ROW?
NO, I...
...DON'T LIKE STALKERS.
PERV!
TUG
HUH?

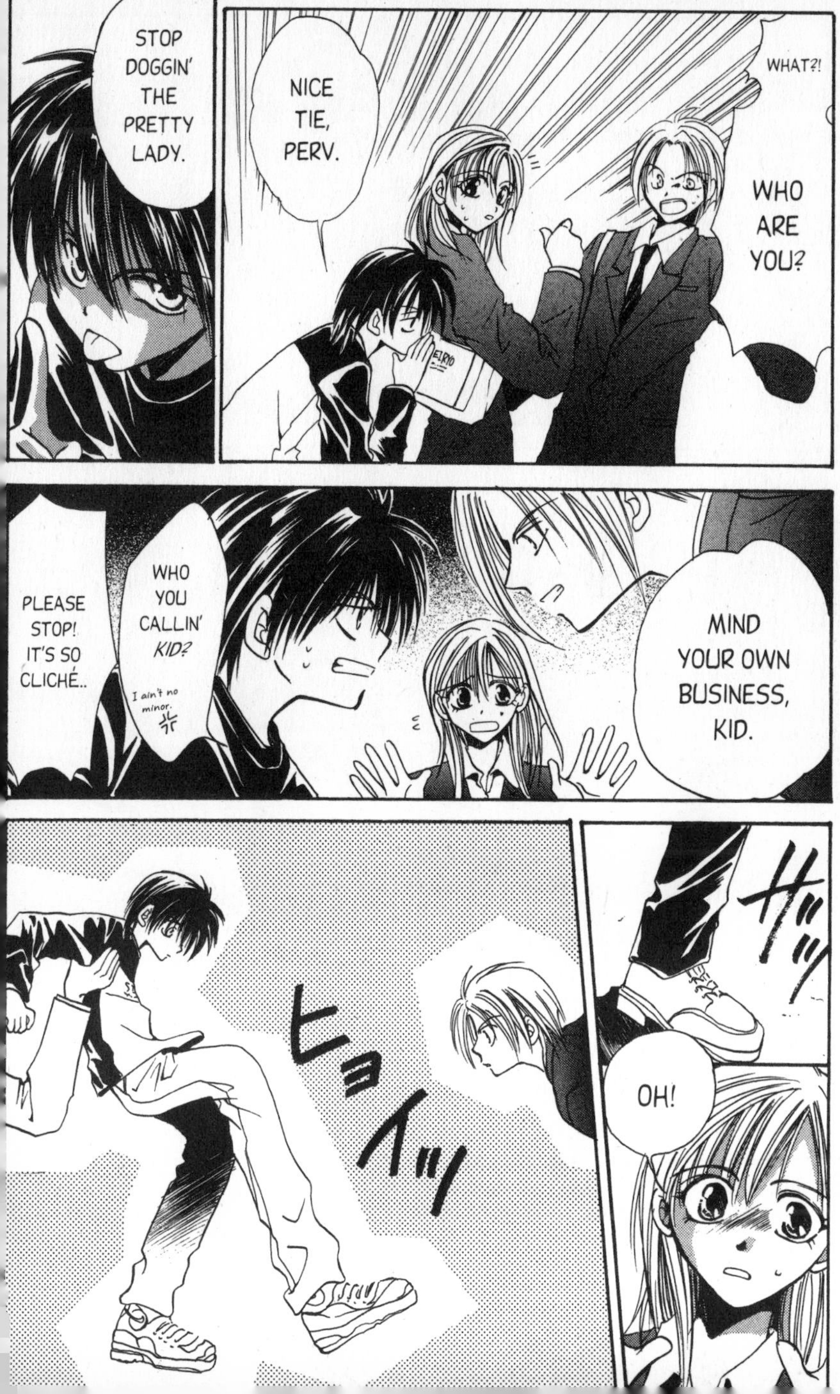
WHAT?!
WHO ARE YOU?
NICE TIE, PERV.
STOP DOGGIN' THE PRETTY LADY.
MIND YOUR OWN BUSINESS, KID.
WHO YOU CALLIN' *KID?*
I ain't no minor.
PLEASE STOP! IT'S SO CLICHÉ..
ザッ
OH!
ヒョイッ

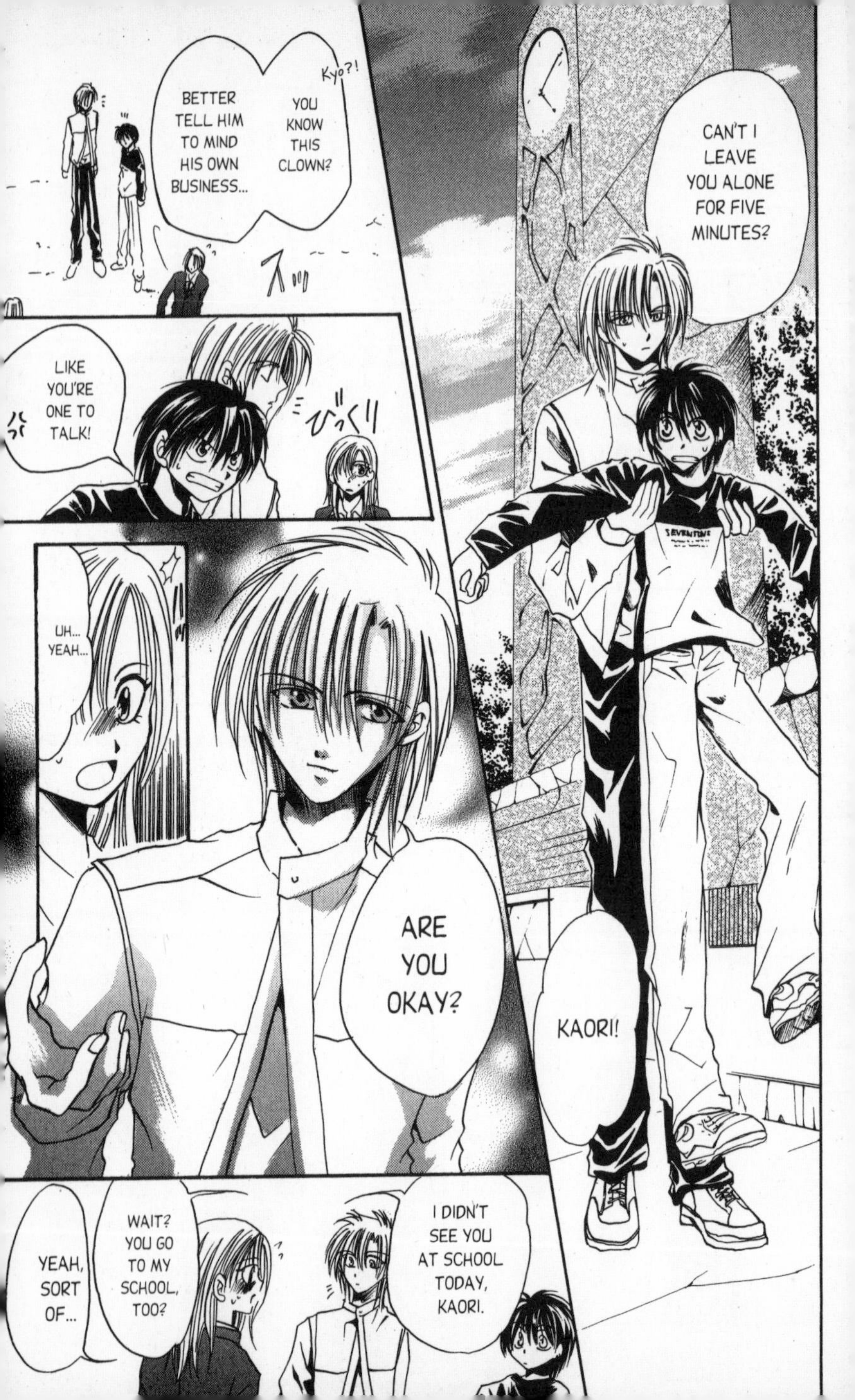
CAN'T I LEAVE YOU ALONE FOR FIVE MINUTES?
KAORI!
Kyo?!
YOU KNOW THIS CLOWN?
BETTER TELL HIM TO MIND HIS OWN BUSINESS...
スッ
びっくり
LIKE YOU'RE ONE TO TALK!
ARE YOU OKAY?
UH... YEAH...
I DIDN'T SEE YOU AT SCHOOL TODAY, KAORI.
WAIT? YOU GO TO MY SCHOOL, TOO?
YEAH, SORT OF...

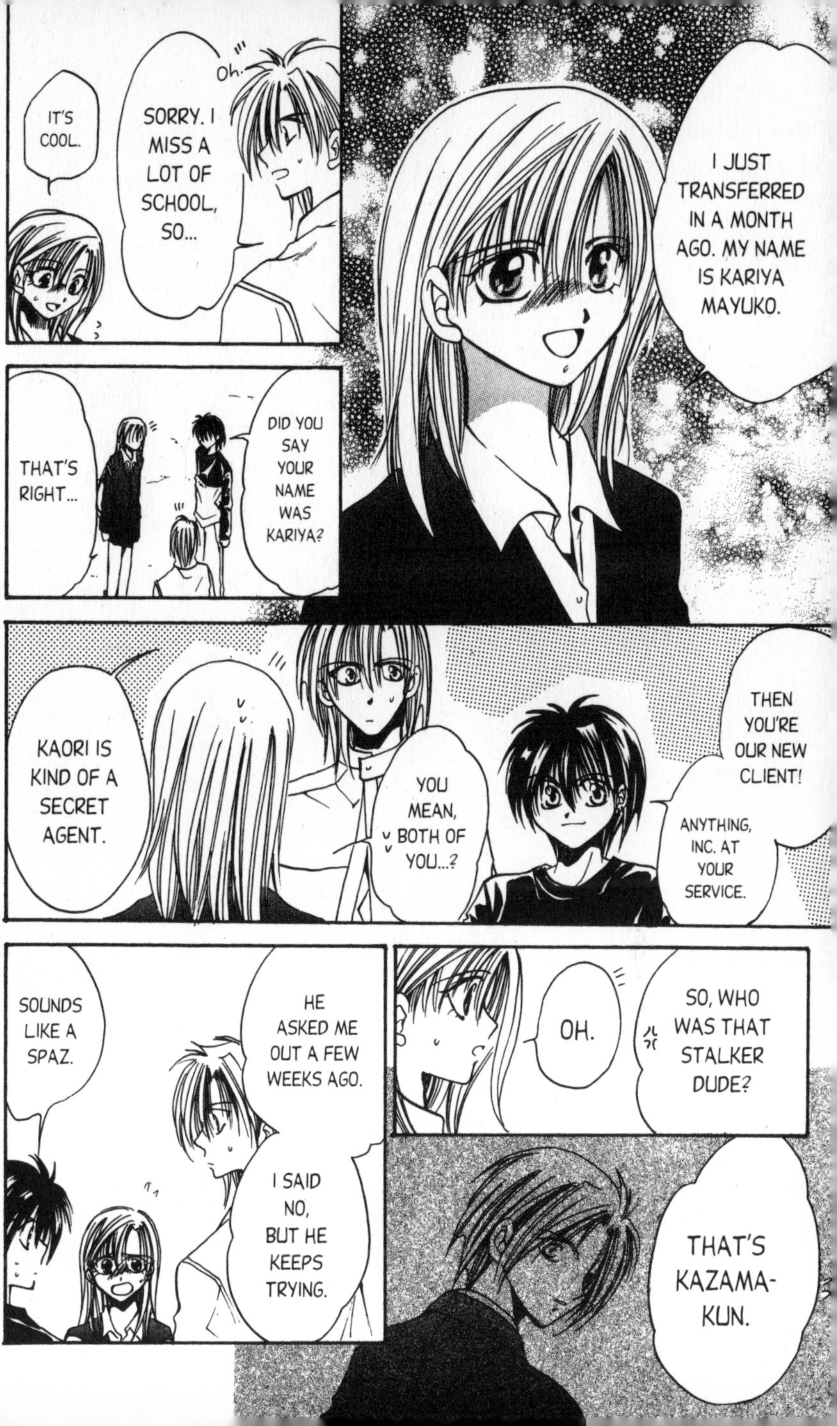
I JUST TRANSFERRED IN A MONTH AGO. MY NAME IS KARIYA MAYUKO.
Oh.
SORRY. I MISS A LOT OF SCHOOL, SO...
IT'S COOL.
DID YOU SAY YOUR NAME WAS KARIYA?
THAT'S RIGHT...
THEN YOU'RE OUR NEW CLIENT!
ANYTHING, INC. AT YOUR SERVICE.
YOU MEAN, BOTH OF YOU...?
KAORI IS KIND OF A SECRET AGENT.
SO, WHO WAS THAT STALKER DUDE?
OH.
THAT'S KAZAMA-KUN.
HE ASKED ME OUT A FEW WEEKS AGO.
I SAID NO, BUT HE KEEPS TRYING.
SOUNDS LIKE A SPAZ.

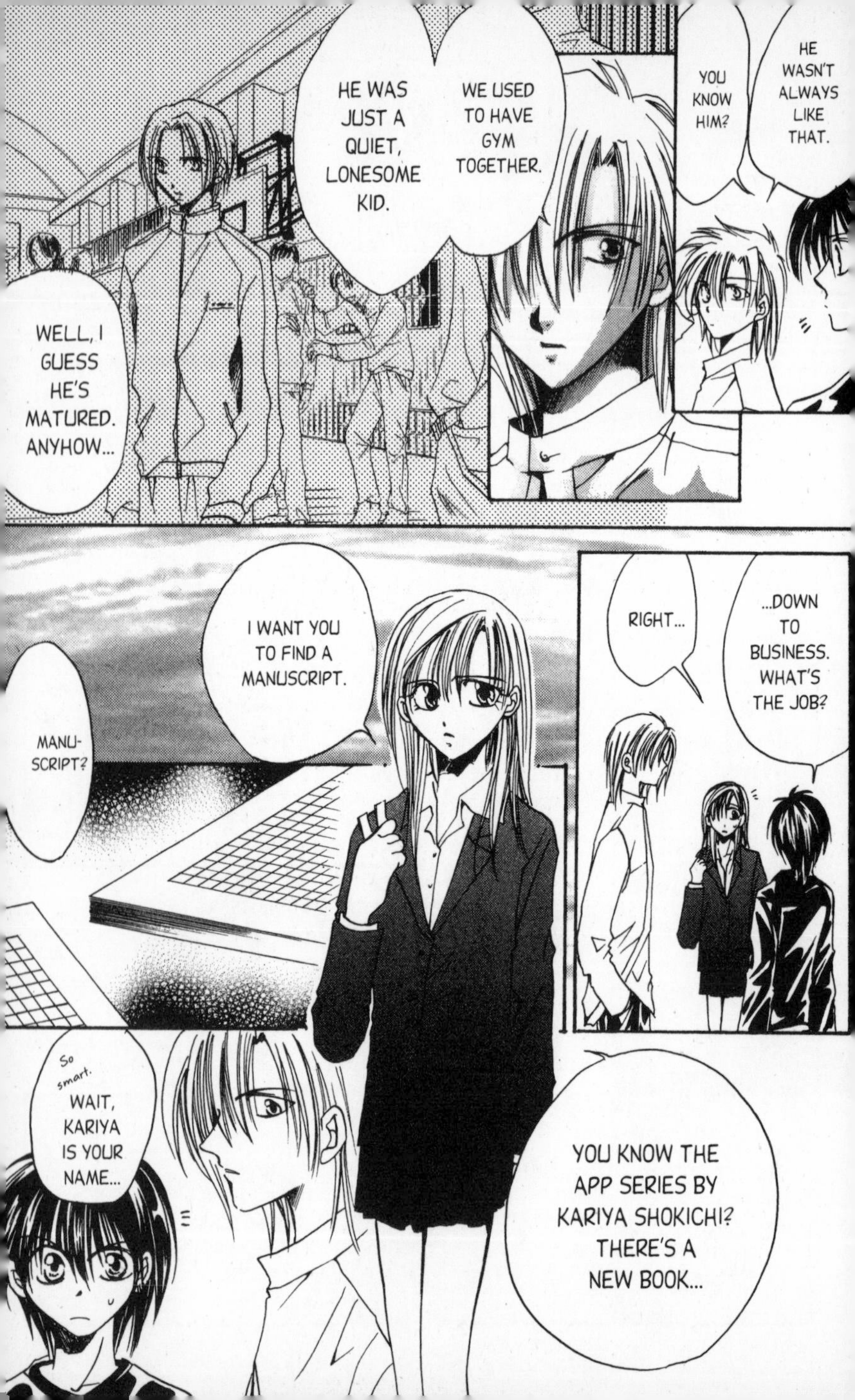
HE WASN'T ALWAYS LIKE THAT.
YOU KNOW HIM?
WE USED TO HAVE GYM TOGETHER.
HE WAS JUST A QUIET, LONESOME KID.
WELL, I GUESS HE'S MATURED. ANYHOW...
...DOWN TO BUSINESS. WHAT'S THE JOB?
RIGHT...
I WANT YOU TO FIND A MANUSCRIPT.
MANU-SCRIPT?
YOU KNOW THE APP SERIES BY KARIYA SHOKICHI? THERE'S A NEW BOOK...
So smart.
WAIT, KARIYA IS YOUR NAME...

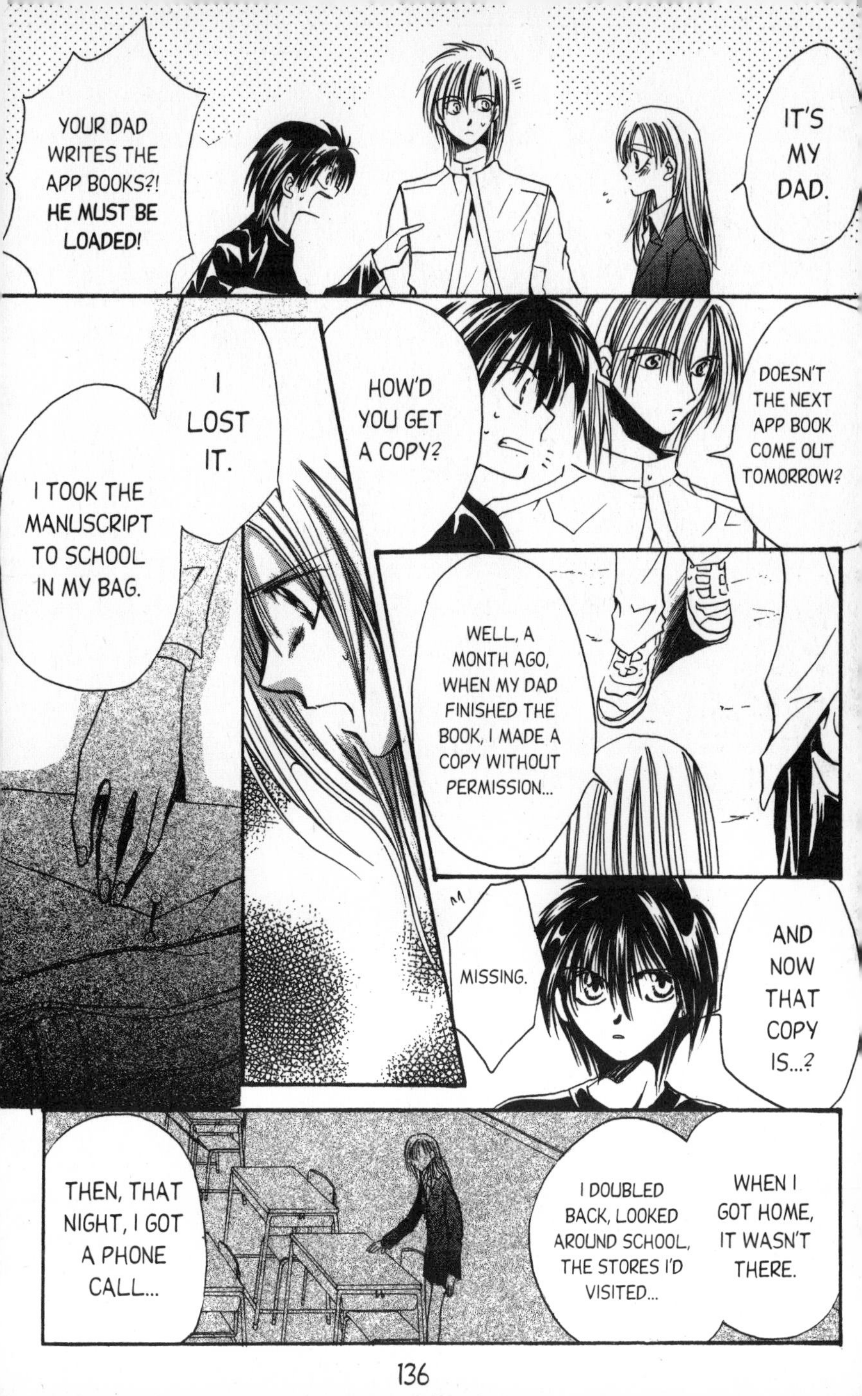
IT'S MY DAD.
YOUR DAD WRITES THE APP BOOKS?! HE MUST BE LOADED!
DOESN'T THE NEXT APP BOOK COME OUT TOMORROW?
HOW'D YOU GET A COPY?
WELL, A MONTH AGO, WHEN MY DAD FINISHED THE BOOK, I MADE A COPY WITHOUT PERMISSION...
AND NOW THAT COPY IS...?
MISSING.
I LOST IT.
I TOOK THE MANUSCRIPT TO SCHOOL IN MY BAG.
WHEN I GOT HOME, IT WASN'T THERE.
I DOUBLED BACK, LOOKED AROUND SCHOOL, THE STORES I'D VISITED...
THEN, THAT NIGHT, I GOT A PHONE CALL...

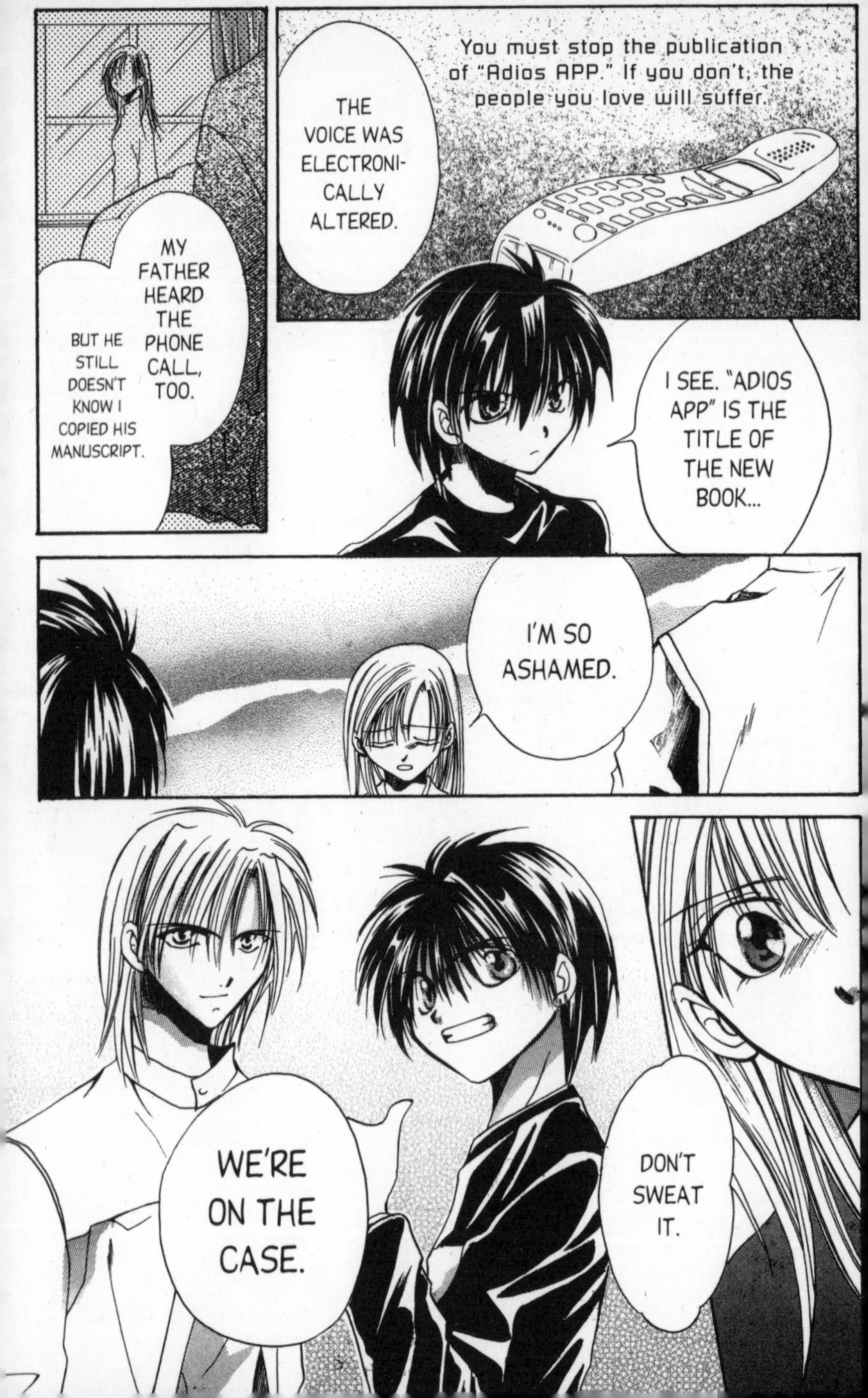
You must stop the publication of "Adios APP." If you don't, the people you love will suffer.
THE VOICE WAS ELECTRONICALLY ALTERED.
I SEE. "ADIOS APP" IS THE TITLE OF THE NEW BOOK...
MY FATHER HEARD THE PHONE CALL, TOO.
BUT HE STILL DOESN'T KNOW I COPIED HIS MANUSCRIPT.
I'M SO ASHAMED.
DON'T SWEAT IT.
WE'RE ON THE CASE.

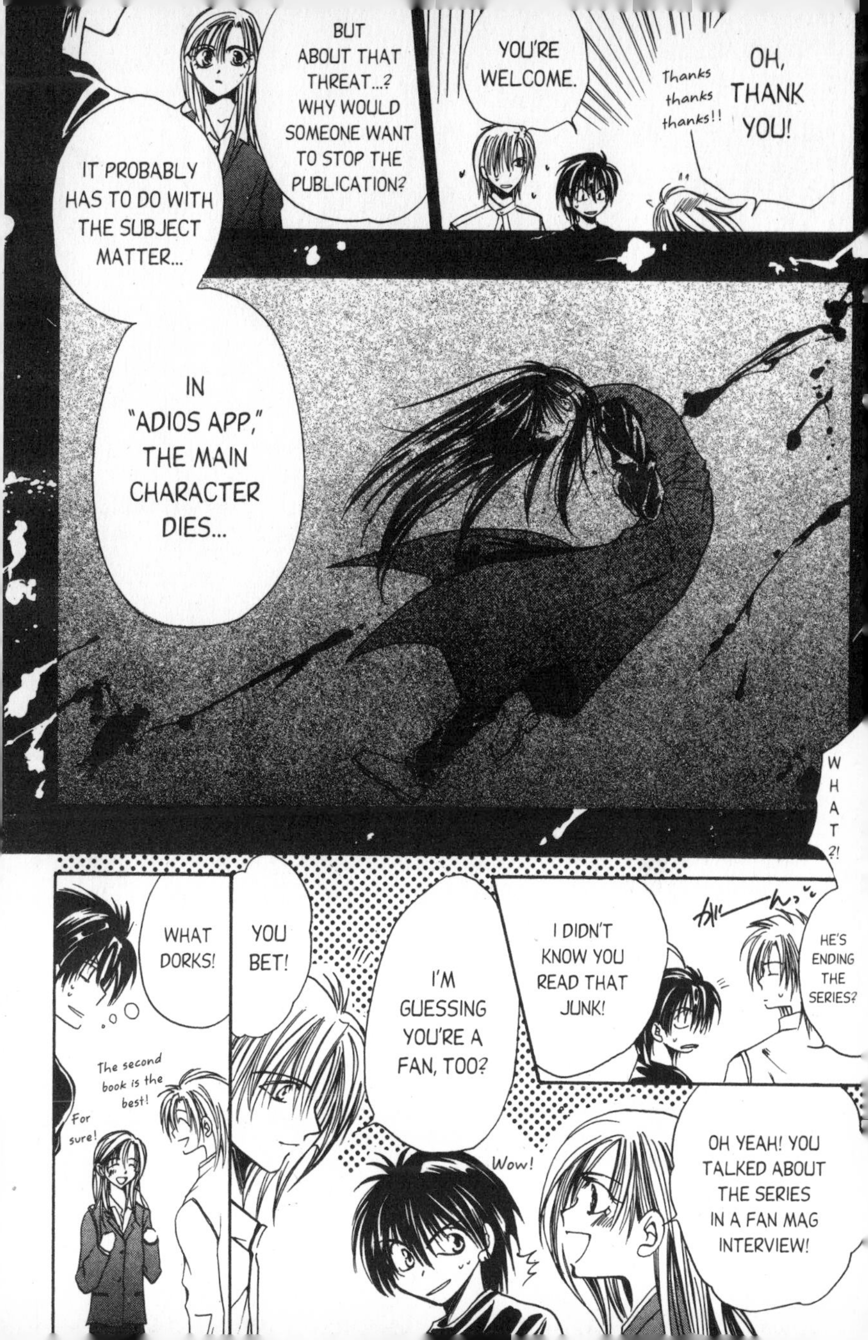
OH, THANK YOU!
Thanks thanks thanks!!
YOU'RE WELCOME.
BUT ABOUT THAT THREAT...? WHY WOULD SOMEONE WANT TO STOP THE PUBLICATION?
IT PROBABLY HAS TO DO WITH THE SUBJECT MATTER...
IN "ADIOS APP," THE MAIN CHARACTER DIES...
WHAT?!
HE'S ENDING THE SERIES?
I DIDN'T KNOW YOU READ THAT JUNK!
I'M GUESSING YOU'RE A FAN, TOO?
YOU BET!
WHAT DORKS!
The second book is the best!
For sure!
OH YEAH! YOU TALKED ABOUT THE SERIES IN A FAN MAG INTERVIEW!
Wow!

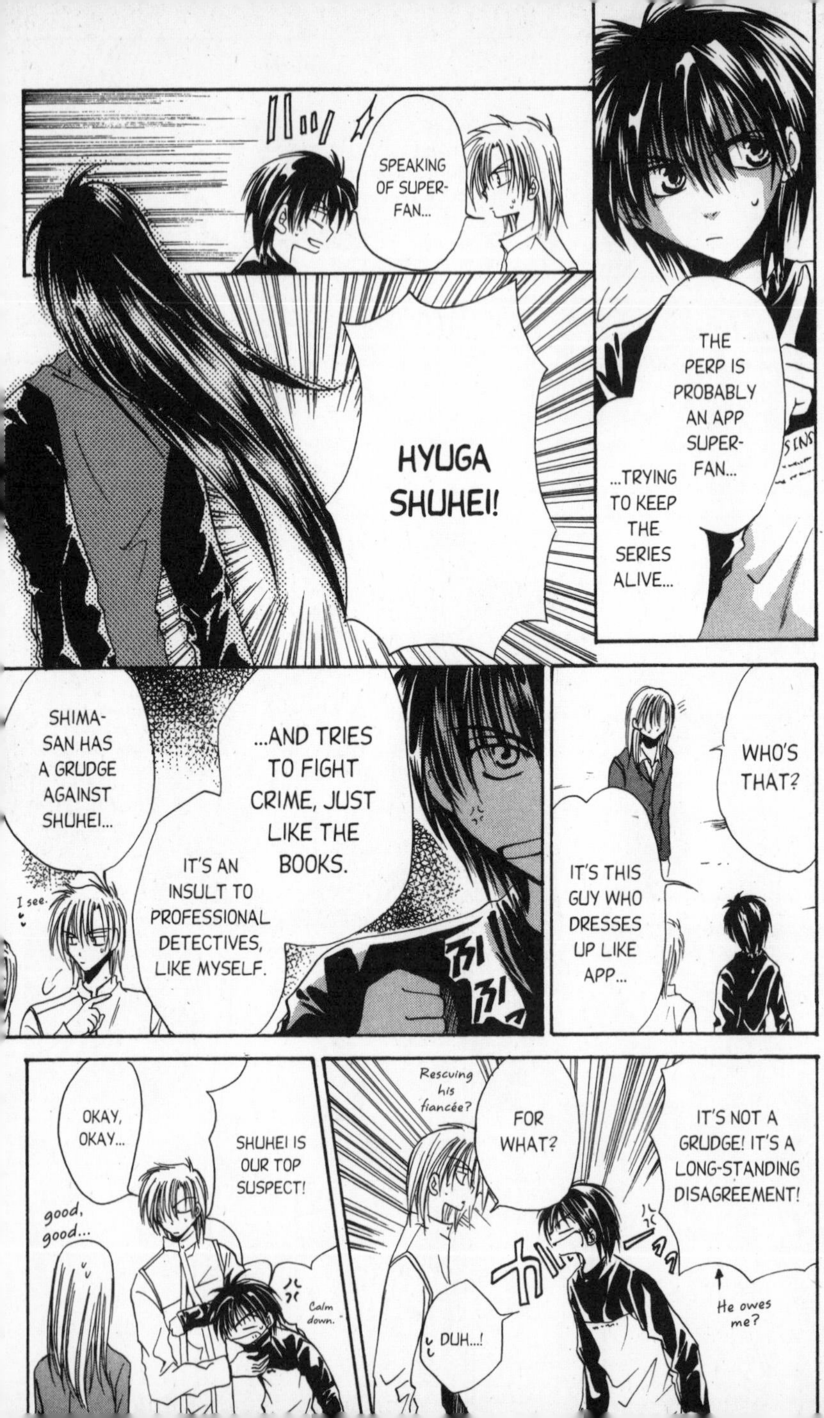
THE PERP IS PROBABLY AN APP SUPER-FAN...
...TRYING TO KEEP THE SERIES ALIVE...
SPEAKING OF SUPER-FAN...
HYUGA SHUHEI!
WHO'S THAT?
IT'S THIS GUY WHO DRESSES UP LIKE APP...
...AND TRIES TO FIGHT CRIME, JUST LIKE THE BOOKS.
IT'S AN INSULT TO PROFESSIONAL DETECTIVES, LIKE MYSELF.
SHIMA-SAN HAS A GRUDGE AGAINST SHUHEI...
I see.
IT'S NOT A GRUDGE! IT'S A LONG-STANDING DISAGREEMENT!
He owes me?
FOR WHAT?
Rescuing his fiancée?
DUH...!
SHUHEI IS OUR TOP SUSPECT!
OKAY, OKAY...
Calm down.
good, good...

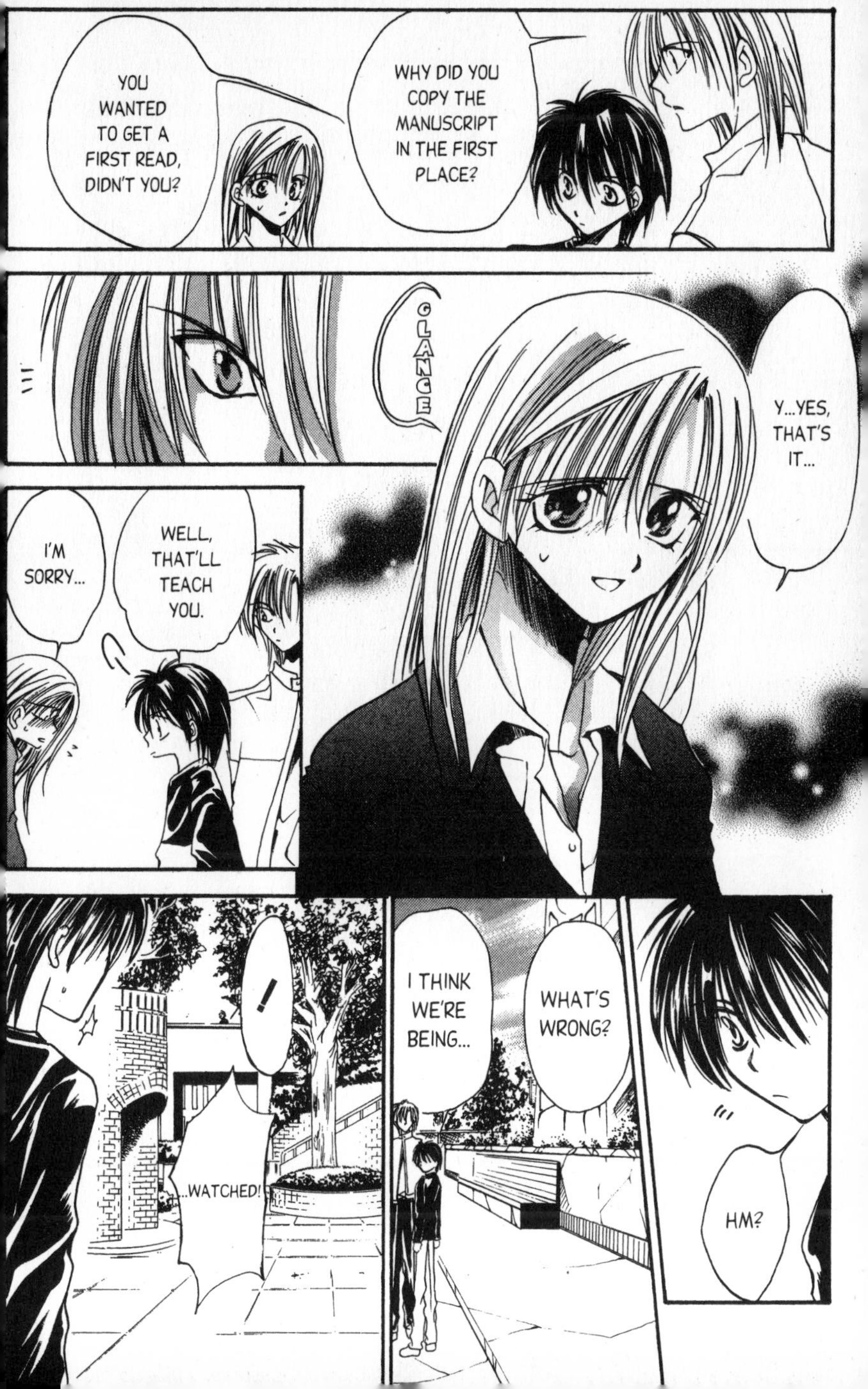
WHY DID YOU COPY THE MANUSCRIPT IN THE FIRST PLACE?
YOU WANTED TO GET A FIRST READ, DIDN'T YOU?
Y...YES, THAT'S IT...
GLANCE
WELL, THAT'LL TEACH YOU.
I'M SORRY...
HM?
WHAT'S WRONG?
I THINK WE'RE BEING...
!
...WATCHED!

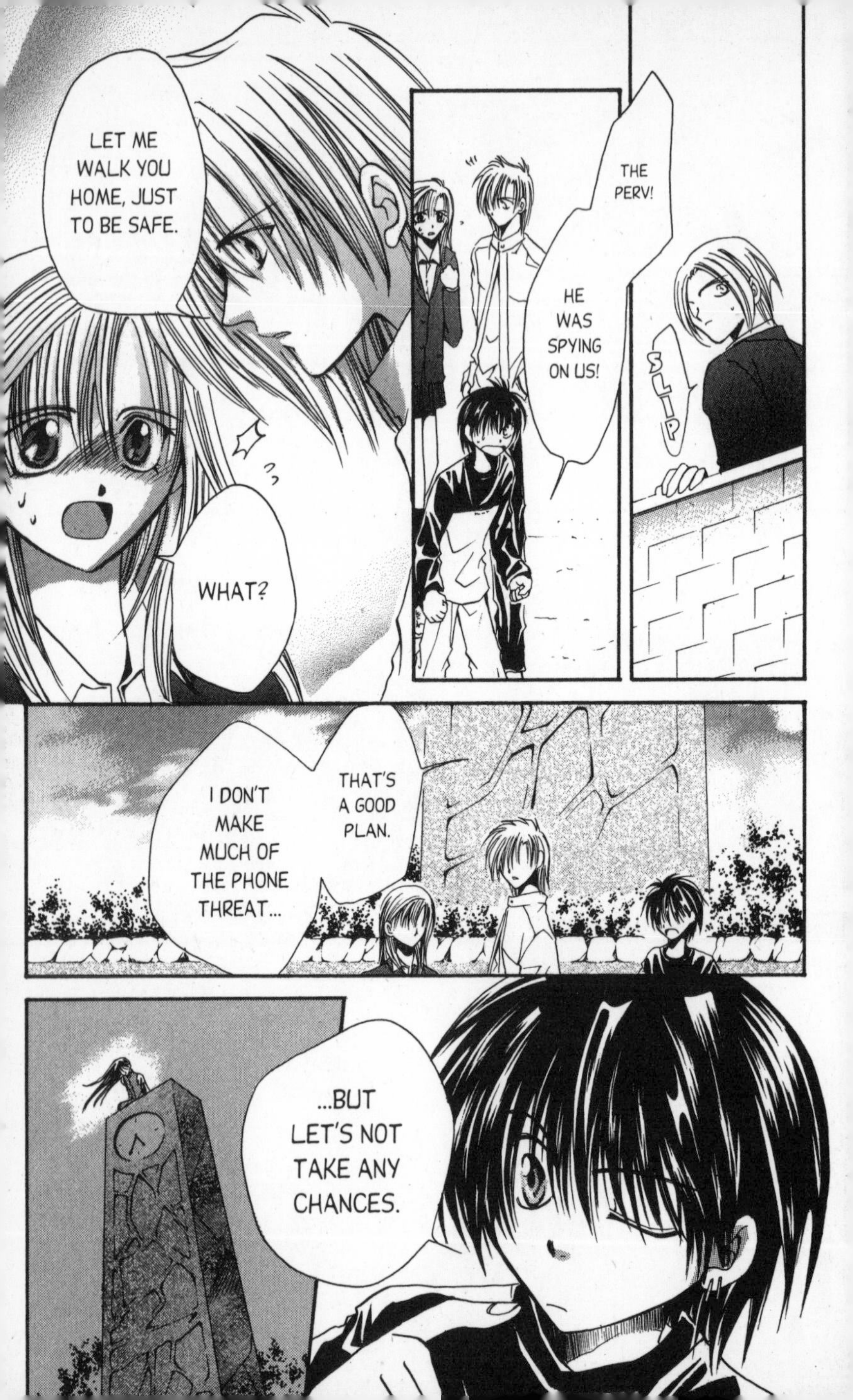
SLIP
THE PERV!
HE WAS SPYING ON US!
LET ME WALK YOU HOME, JUST TO BE SAFE.
WHAT?
THAT'S A GOOD PLAN.
I DON'T MAKE MUCH OF THE PHONE THREAT...
...BUT LET'S NOT TAKE ANY CHANCES.

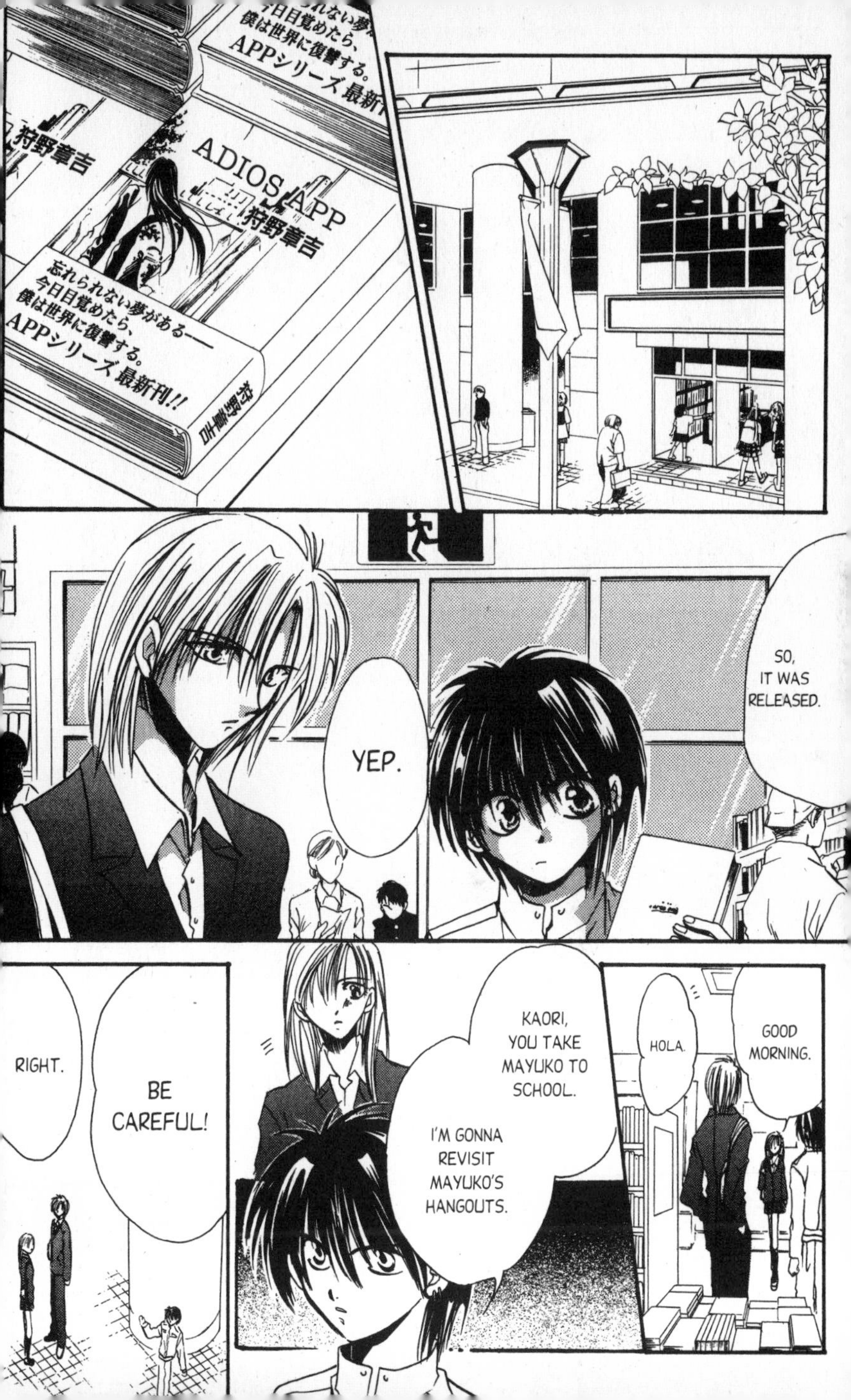
ADIOS APP
狩野章吉
忘れられない夢がある——
今日目覚めたら、
僕は世界に復讐する。
APPシリーズ 最新刊!!
SO, IT WAS RELEASED.
YEP.
GOOD MORNING.
HOLA.
KAORI, YOU TAKE MAYUKO TO SCHOOL.
I'M GONNA REVISIT MAYUKO'S HANGOUTS.
BE CAREFUL!
RIGHT.

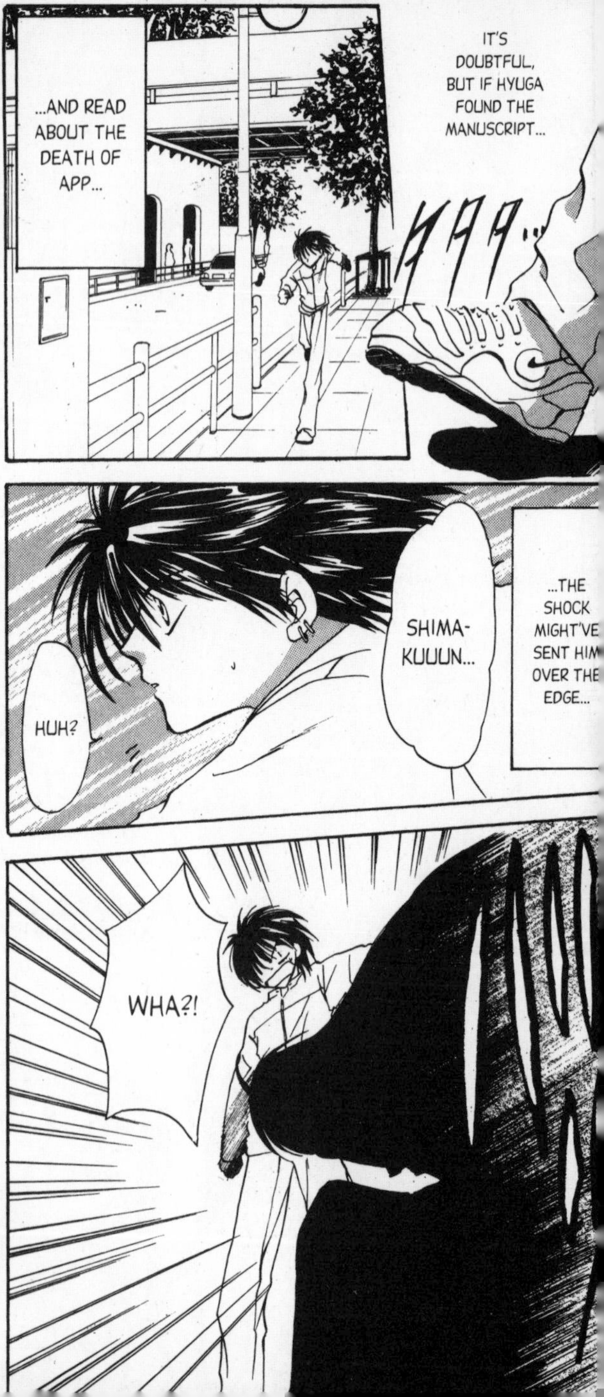
IT'S DOUBTFUL, BUT IF HYUGA FOUND THE MANUSCRIPT...
...AND READ ABOUT THE DEATH OF APP...
...THE SHOCK MIGHT'VE SENT HIM OVER THE EDGE...
SHIMA-KUUUN...
HUH?
WHA?!

I held my first autograph session the day after volume 2 was released. I was so nervous. I kept wondering, is anyone going to come? Then, when I got there, and saw people waiting in line, my hands were shaking so much I couldn't sign!

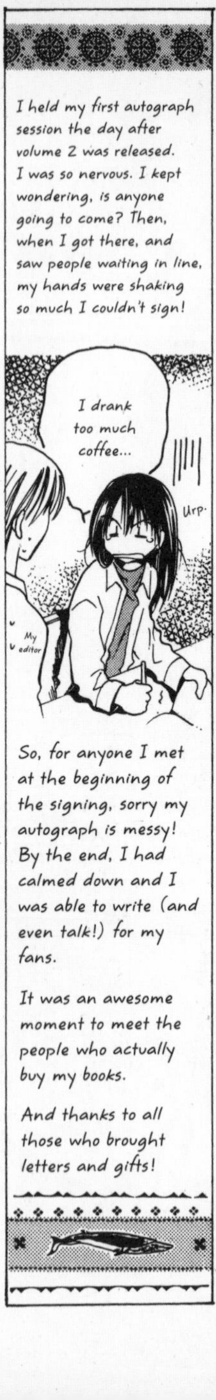
I drank too much coffee...
Urp.
My editor

So, for anyone I met at the beginning of the signing, sorry my autograph is messy! By the end, I had calmed down and I was able to write (and even talk!) for my fans.

It was an awesome moment to meet the people who actually buy my books.

And thanks to all those who brought letters and gifts!

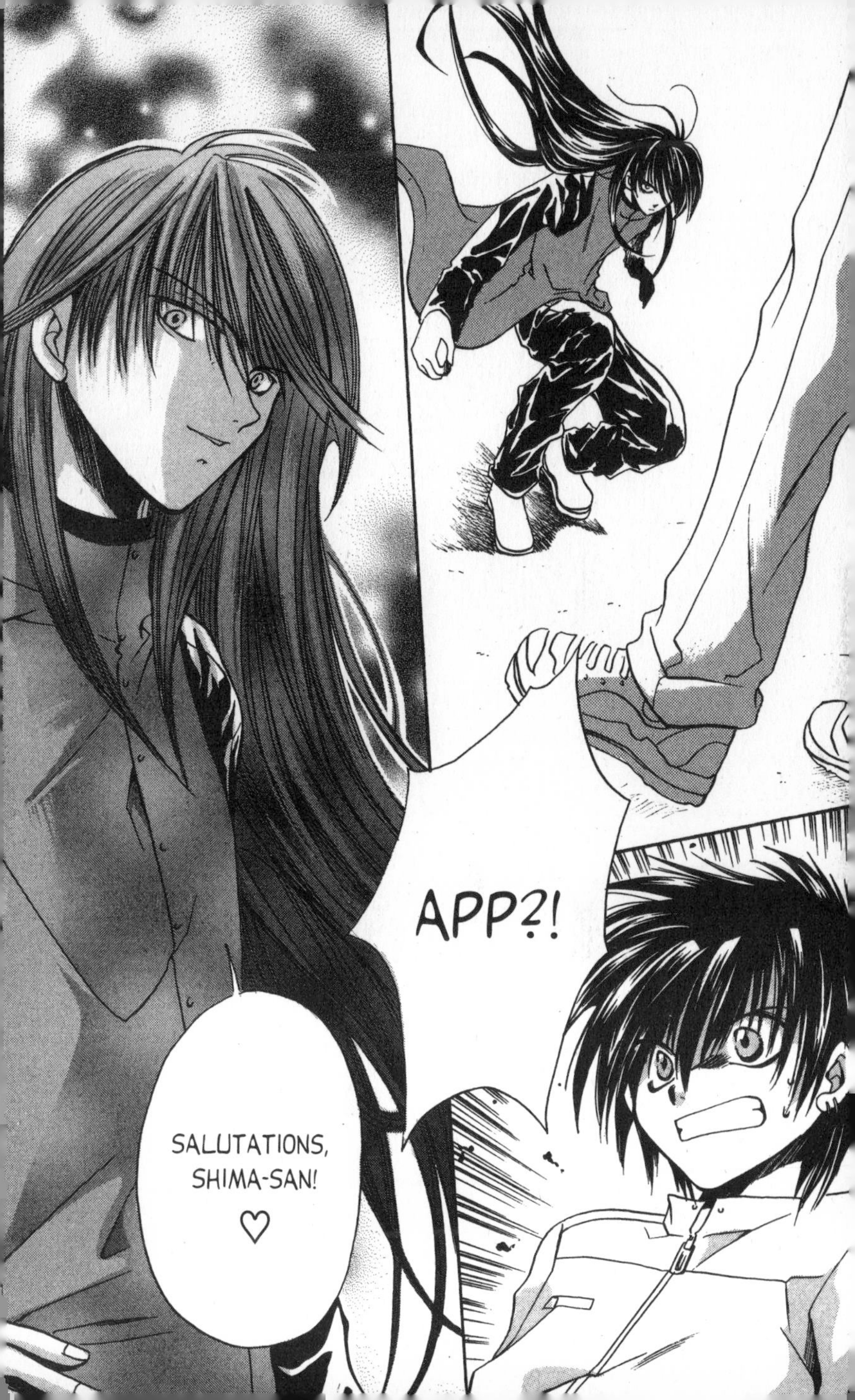
APP?!
SALUTATIONS, SHIMA-SAN! ♡

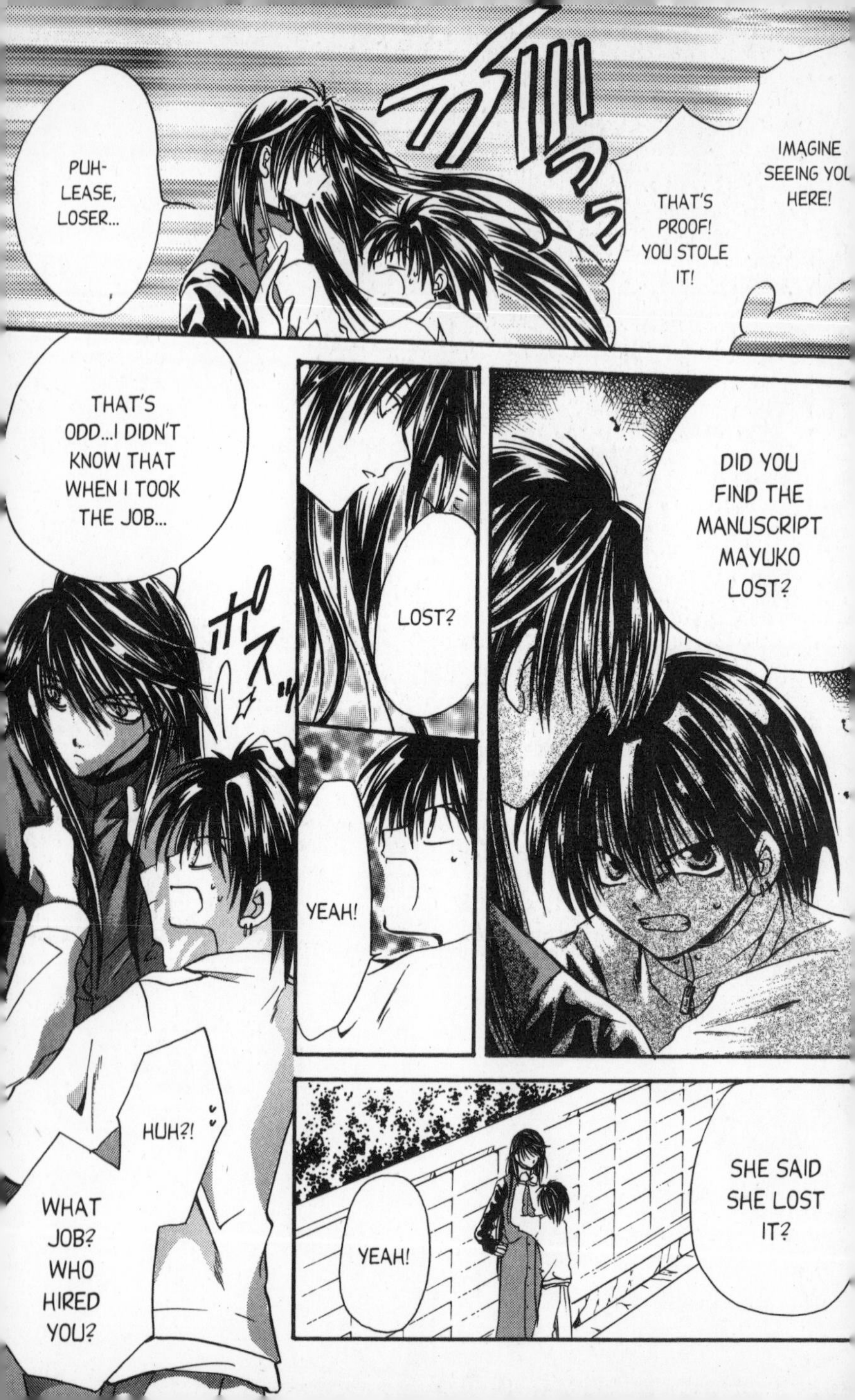
IMAGINE SEEING YOU HERE!
THAT'S PROOF! YOU STOLE IT!
PUH-LEASE, LOSER...
DID YOU FIND THE MANUSCRIPT MAYUKO LOST?
LOST?
YEAH!
SHE SAID SHE LOST IT?
YEAH!
THAT'S ODD...I DIDN'T KNOW THAT WHEN I TOOK THE JOB...
ポスッ
HUH?!
WHAT JOB? WHO HIRED YOU?

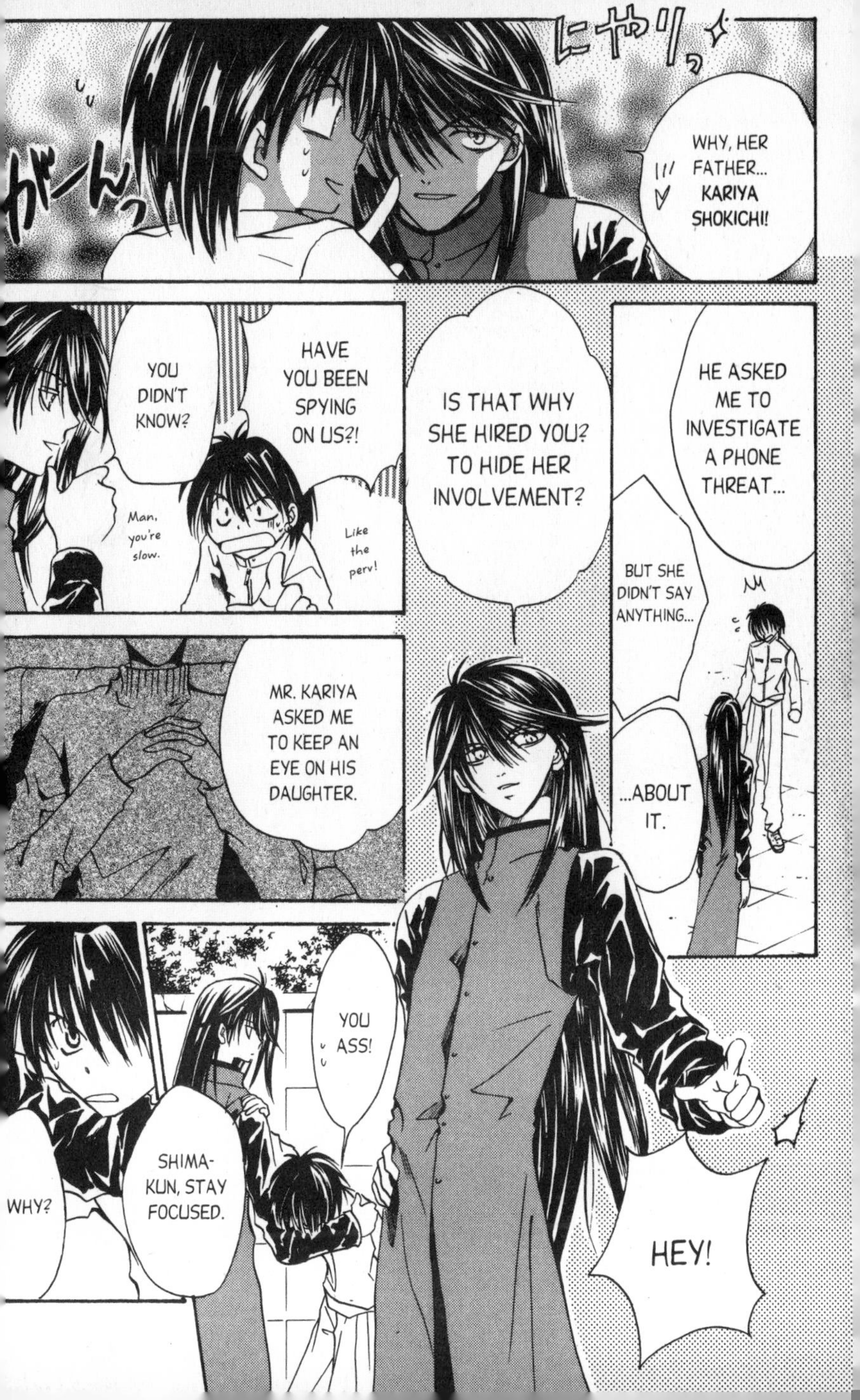

にやりっ
WHY, HER FATHER... KARIYA SHOKICHI!
がーんっ
HE ASKED ME TO INVESTIGATE A PHONE THREAT...
BUT SHE DIDN'T SAY ANYTHING...
...ABOUT IT.
IS THAT WHY SHE HIRED YOU? TO HIDE HER INVOLVEMENT?
HAVE YOU BEEN SPYING ON US?!
Like the perv!
YOU DIDN'T KNOW?
Man, you're slow.
MR. KARIYA ASKED ME TO KEEP AN EYE ON HIS DAUGHTER.
HEY!
YOU ASS!
SHIMA-KUN, STAY FOCUSED.
WHY?

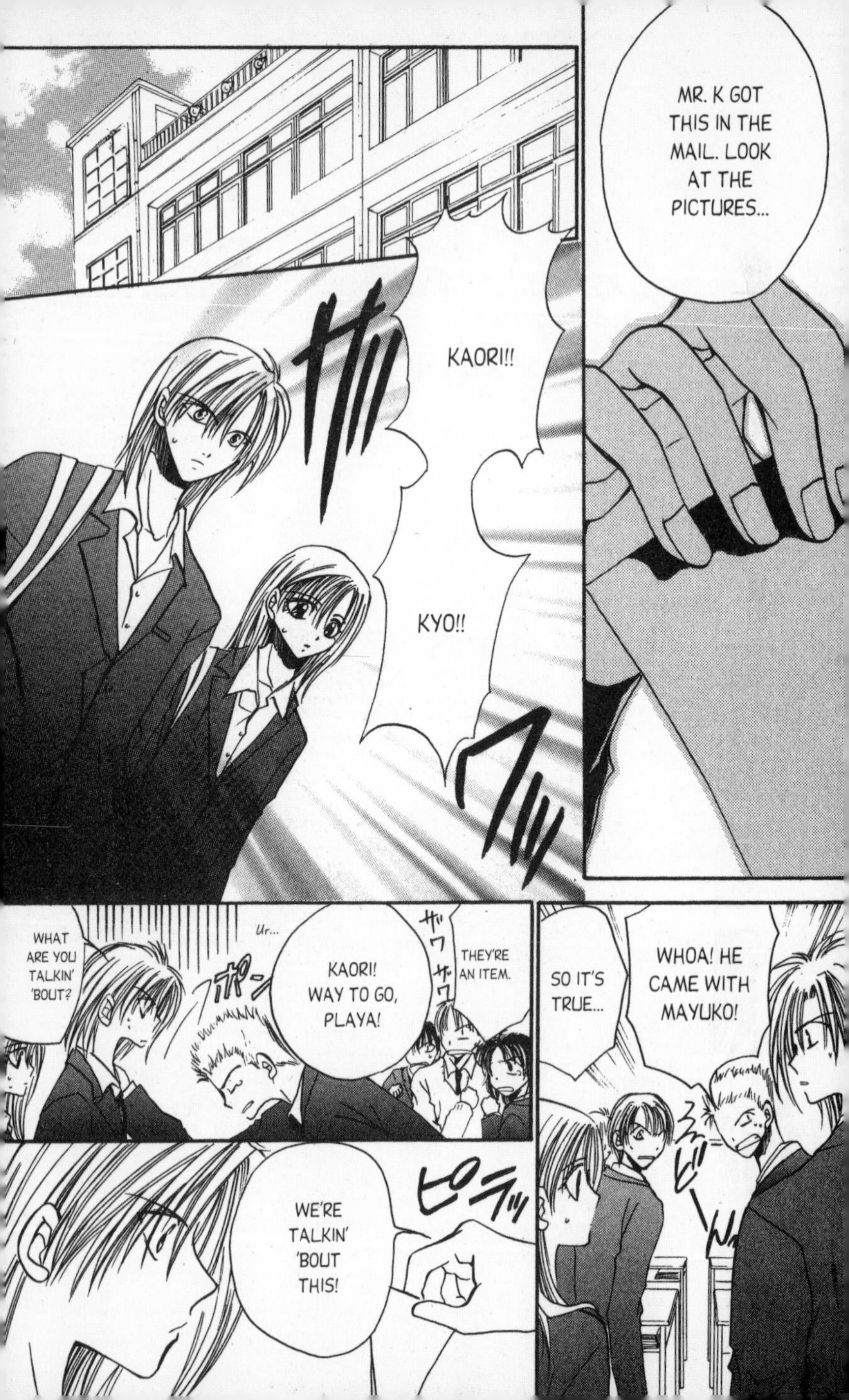
MR. K GOT THIS IN THE MAIL. LOOK AT THE PICTURES...
KAORI!!
KYO!!
WHOA! HE CAME WITH MAYUKO!
SO IT'S TRUE...
THEY'RE AN ITEM.
KAORI! WAY TO GO, PLAYA!
Ur...
WHAT ARE YOU TALKIN' 'BOUT?
WE'RE TALKIN' 'BOUT THIS!

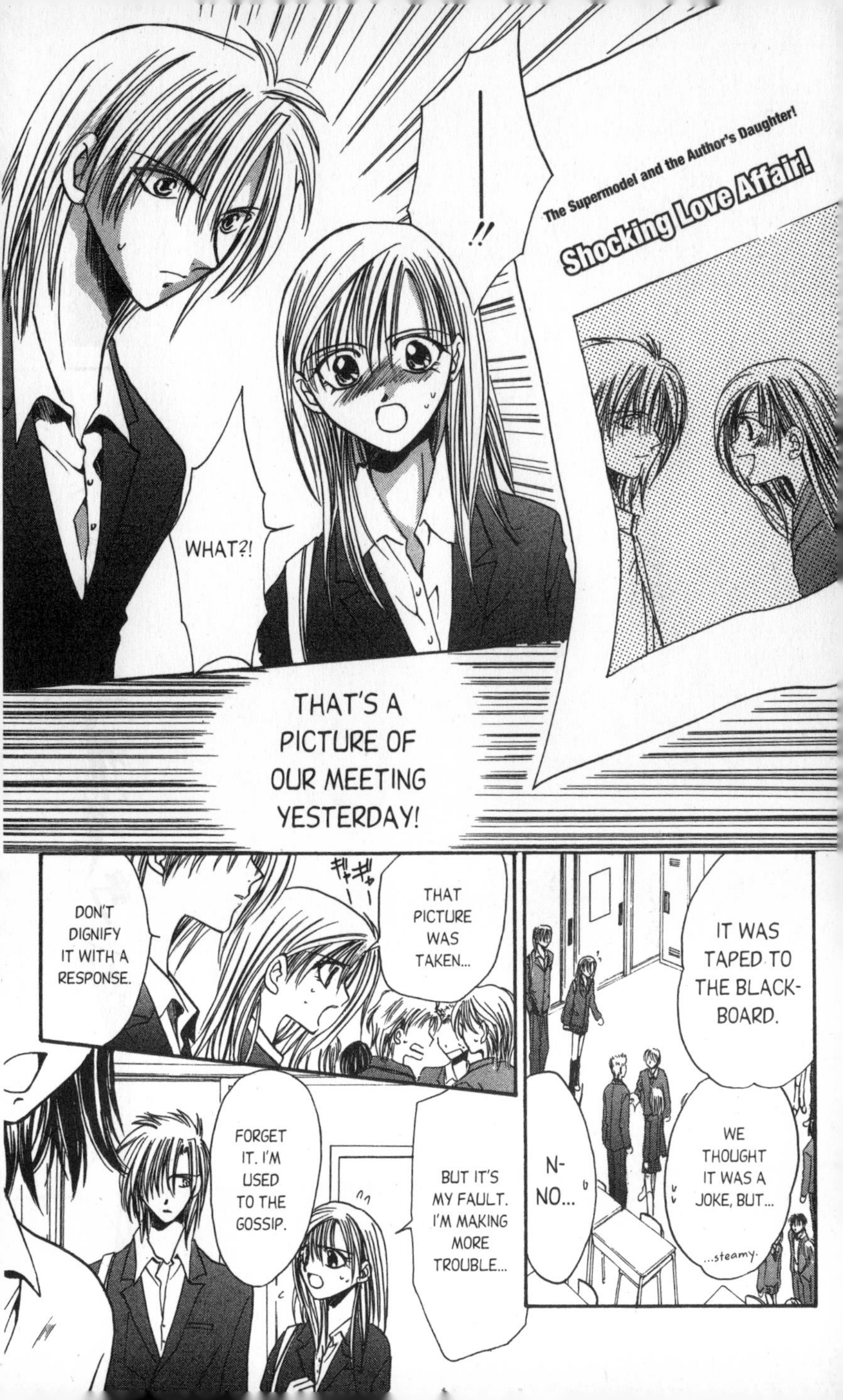
The Supermodel and the Author's Daughter!
Shocking Love Affair!
!!
WHAT?!
THAT'S A PICTURE OF OUR MEETING YESTERDAY!
IT WAS TAPED TO THE BLACKBOARD.
WE THOUGHT IT WAS A JOKE, BUT...
...steamy.
N-NO...
THAT PICTURE WAS TAKEN...
DON'T DIGNIFY IT WITH A RESPONSE.
BUT IT'S MY FAULT. I'M MAKING MORE TROUBLE...
FORGET IT. I'M USED TO THE GOSSIP.

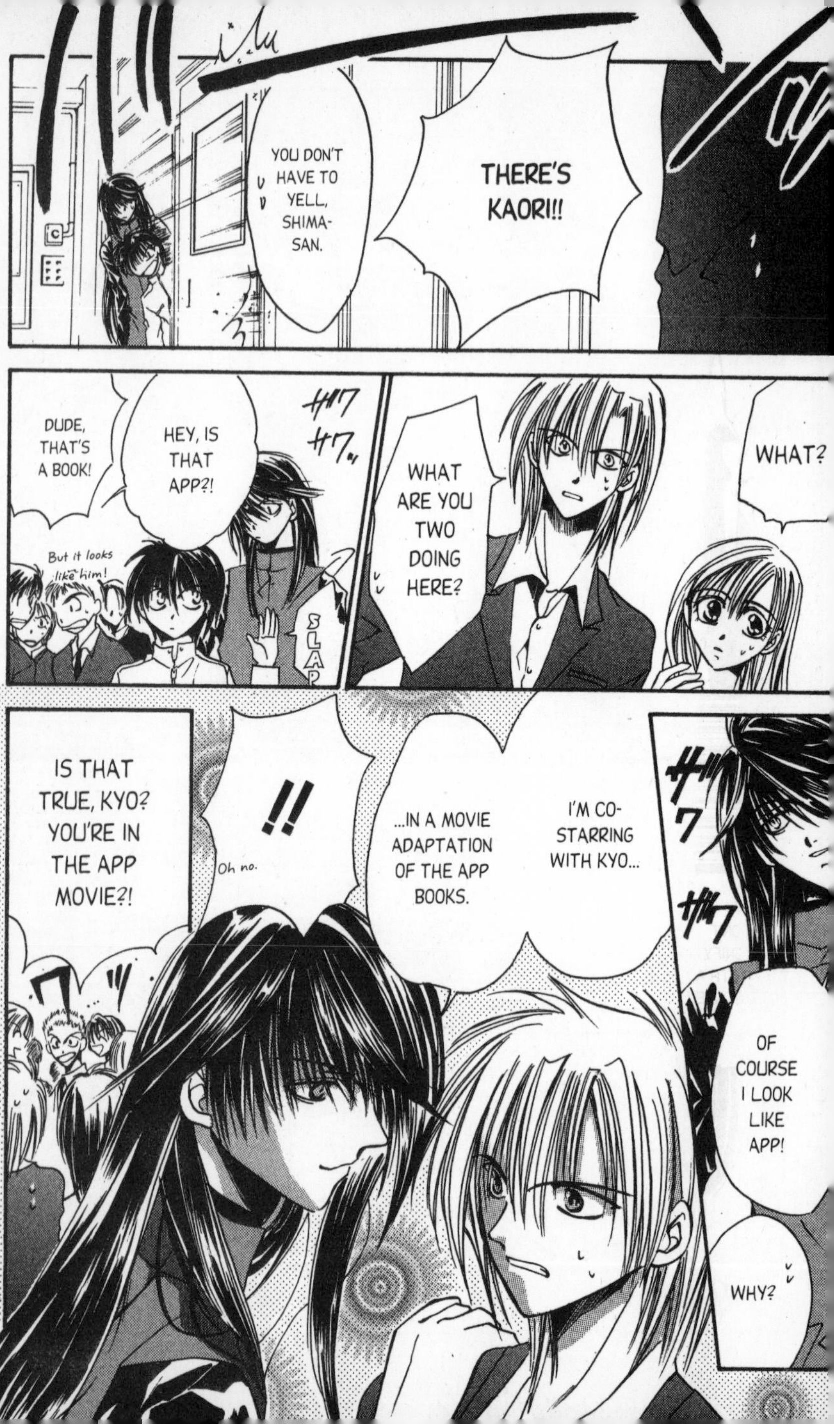
THERE'S KAORI!!
YOU DON'T HAVE TO YELL, SHIMA-SAN.
WHAT?
WHAT ARE YOU TWO DOING HERE?
HEY, IS THAT APP?!
DUDE, THAT'S A BOOK!
But it looks like him!
SLAP
OF COURSE I LOOK LIKE APP!
WHY?
I'M CO-STARRING WITH KYO...
...IN A MOVIE ADAPTATION OF THE APP BOOKS.
!!
Oh no.
IS THAT TRUE, KYO? YOU'RE IN THE APP MOVIE?!

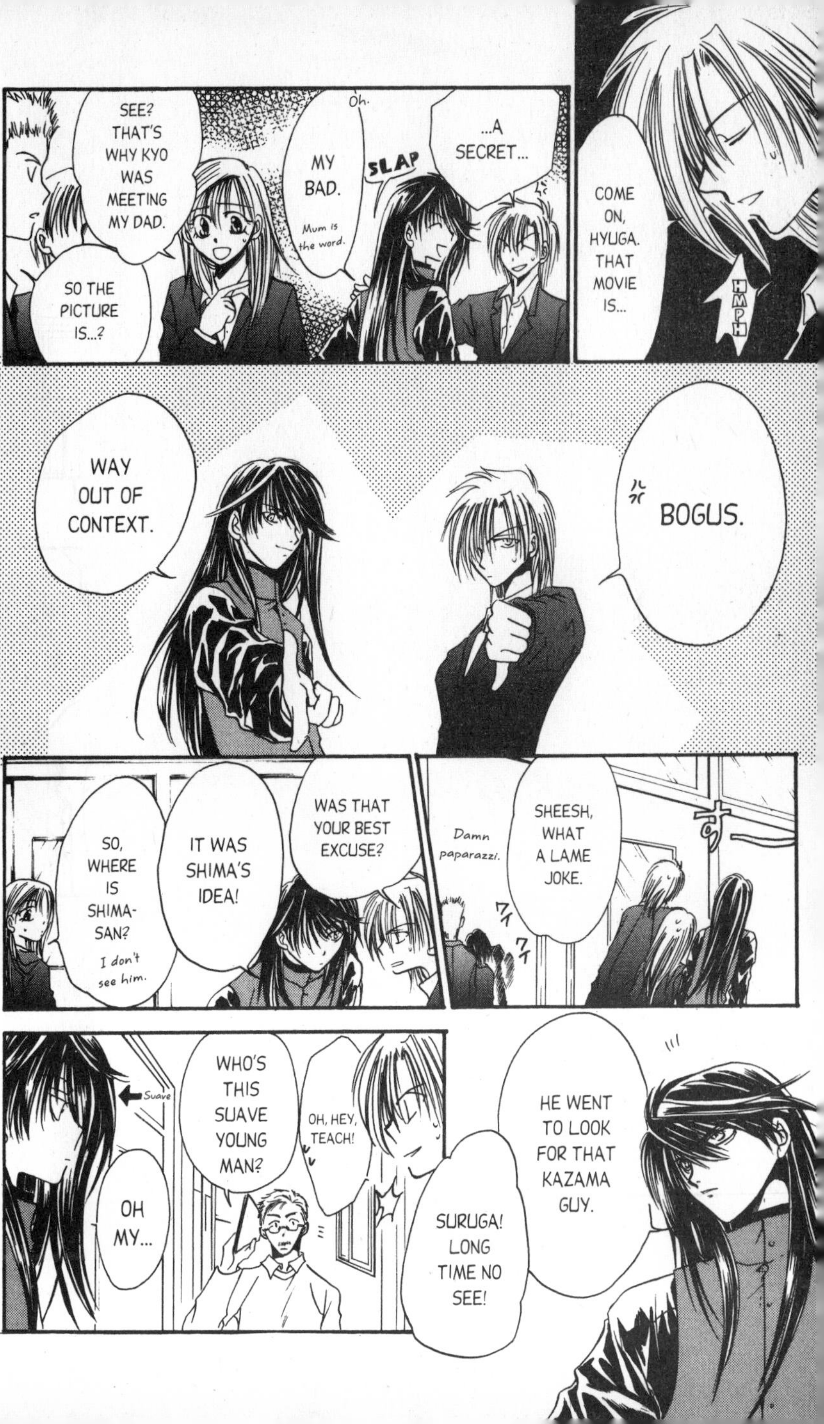
COME ON, HYUGA. THAT MOVIE IS...
HMPH
...A SECRET...
Oh.
MY BAD.
SLAP
Mum is the word.
SEE? THAT'S WHY KYO WAS MEETING MY DAD.
SO THE PICTURE IS...?
BOGUS.
WAY OUT OF CONTEXT.
SHEESH, WHAT A LAME JOKE.
Damn paparazzi.
WAS THAT YOUR BEST EXCUSE?
IT WAS SHIMA'S IDEA!
SO, WHERE IS SHIMA-SAN?
I don't see him.
HE WENT TO LOOK FOR THAT KAZAMA GUY.
SURUGA! LONG TIME NO SEE!
OH, HEY, TEACH!
WHO'S THIS SUAVE YOUNG MAN?
Suave
OH MY...

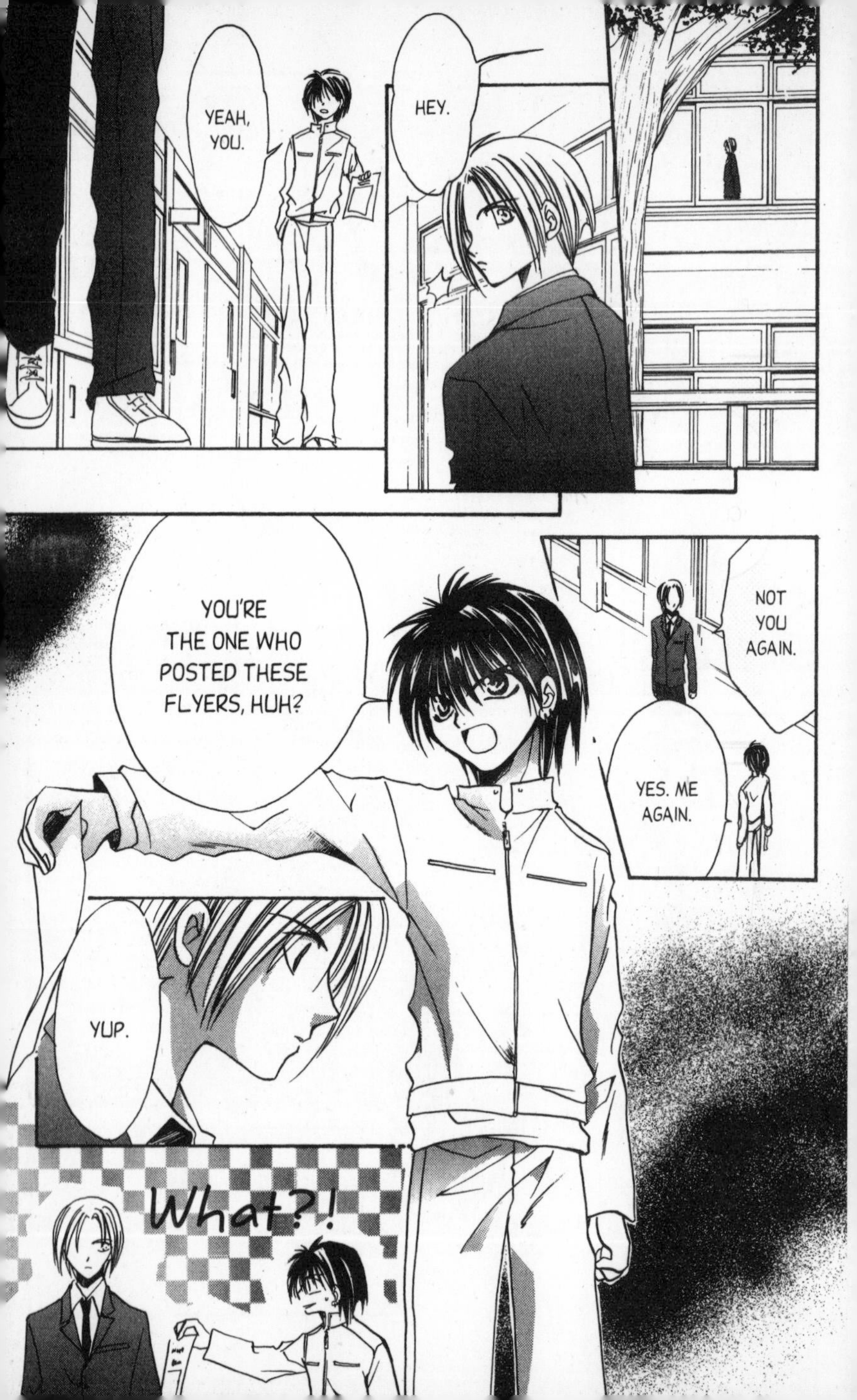
HEY.
YEAH, YOU.
NOT YOU AGAIN.
YES. ME AGAIN.
YOU'RE THE ONE WHO POSTED THESE FLYERS, HUH?
YUP.
What?!

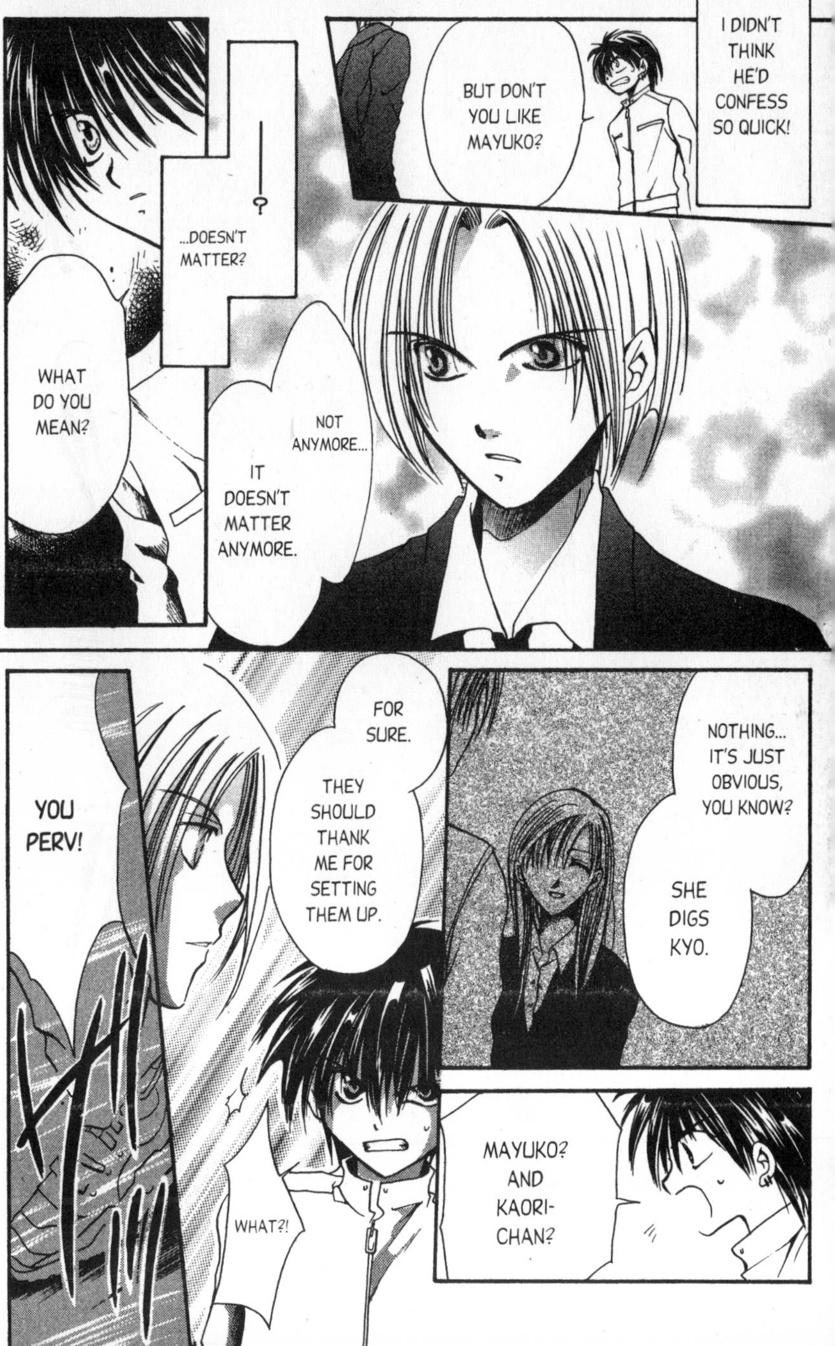
I DIDN'T THINK HE'D CONFESS SO QUICK!
BUT DON'T YOU LIKE MAYUKO?
NOT ANYMORE...
IT DOESN'T MATTER ANYMORE.
—?
...DOESN'T MATTER?
WHAT DO YOU MEAN?
NOTHING... IT'S JUST OBVIOUS, YOU KNOW?
SHE DIGS KYO.
MAYUKO? AND KAORI-CHAN?
FOR SURE.
THEY SHOULD THANK ME FOR SETTING THEM UP.
WHAT?!
YOU PERV!

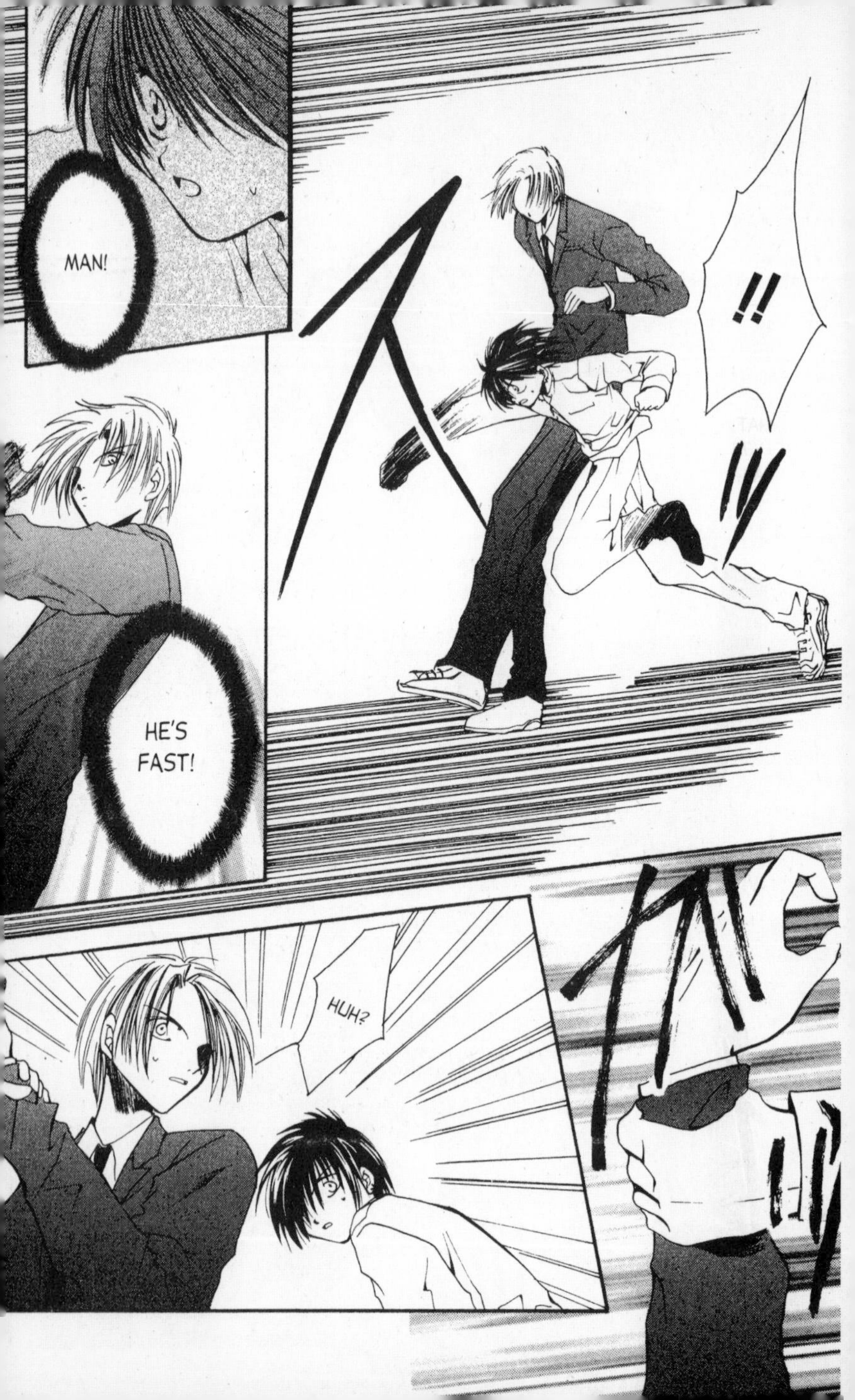
!!
MAN!
HE'S FAST!
HUH?

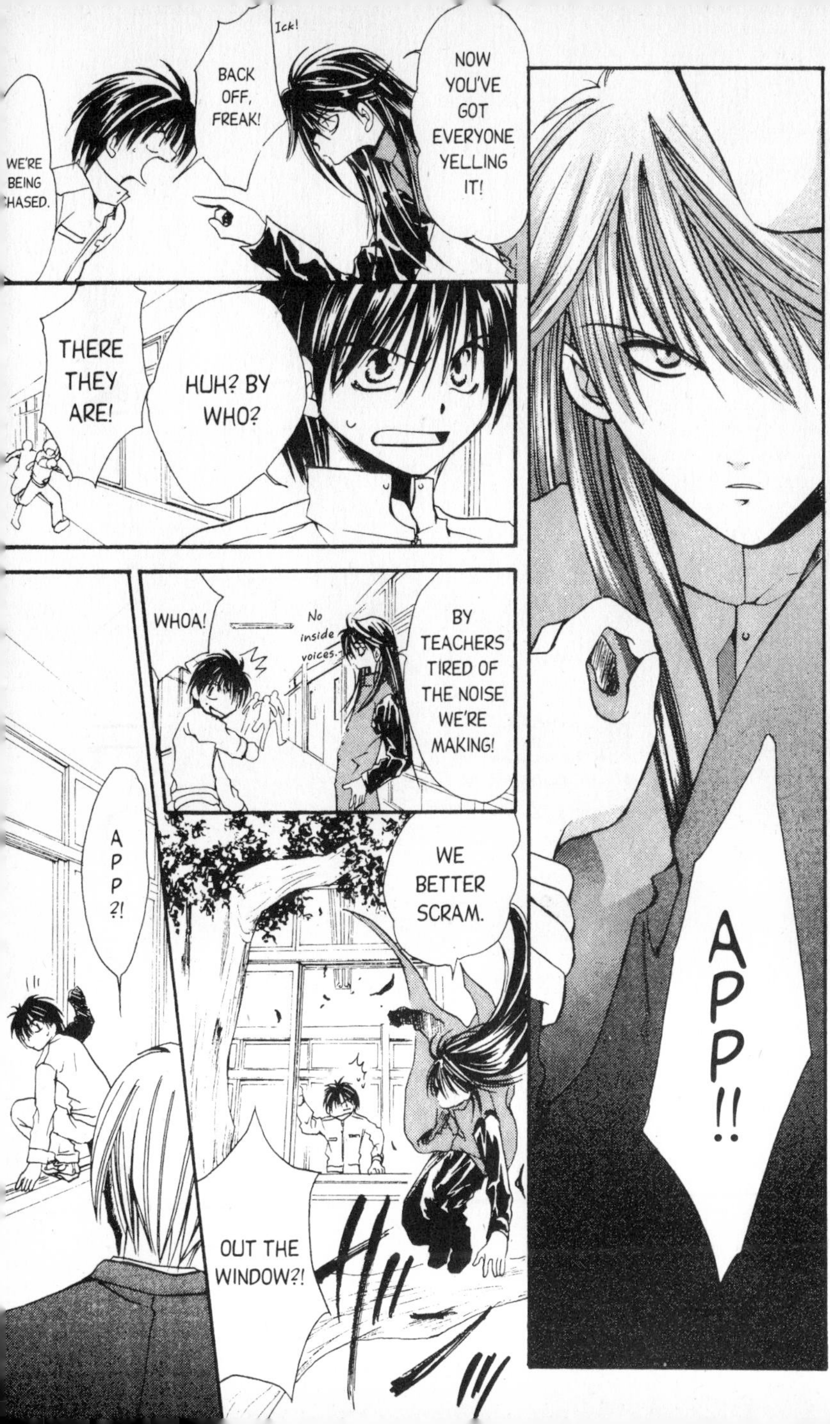
APP!!
NOW YOU'VE GOT EVERYONE YELLING IT!
Ick!
BACK OFF, FREAK!
WE'RE BEING CHASED.
HUH? BY WHO?
THERE THEY ARE!
BY TEACHERS TIRED OF THE NOISE WE'RE MAKING!
No inside voices.
WHOA!
APP?!
WE BETTER SCRAM.
OUT THE WINDOW?!

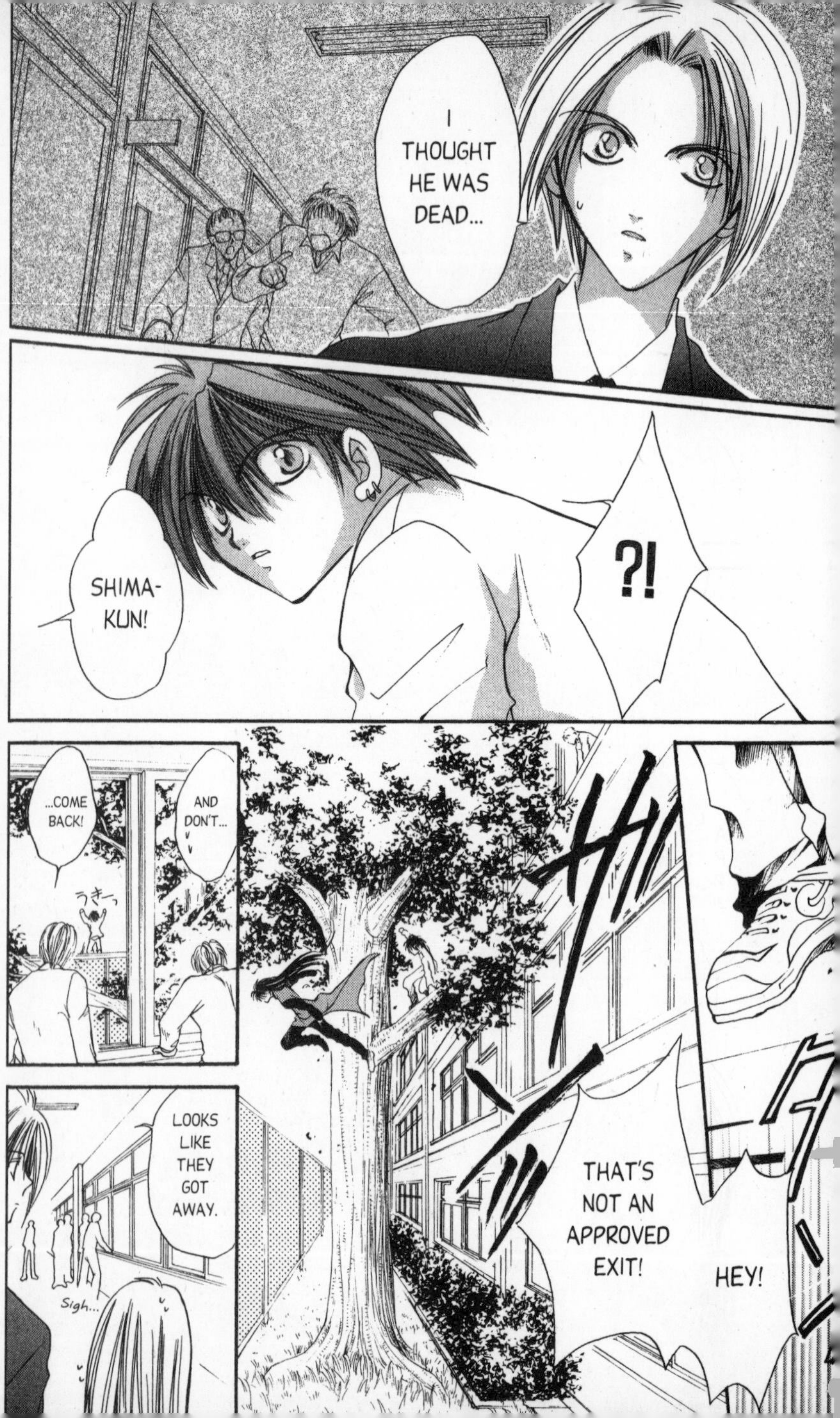
I THOUGHT HE WAS DEAD...
?!
SHIMA-KUN!
HEY!
THAT'S NOT AN APPROVED EXIT!
AND DON'T...
...COME BACK!
うきーっ
LOOKS LIKE THEY GOT AWAY.
Sigh...

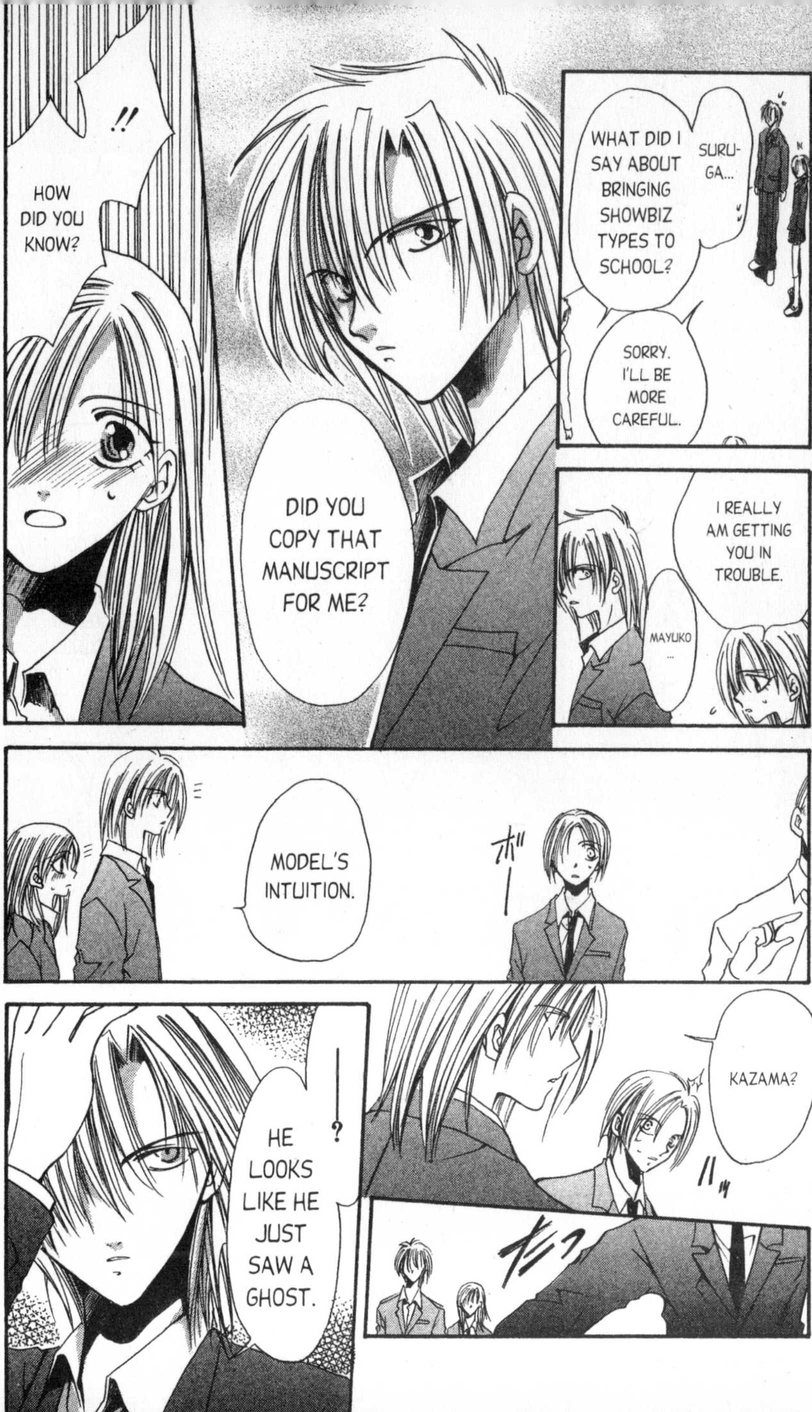
SURU-GA...
WHAT DID I SAY ABOUT BRINGING SHOWBIZ TYPES TO SCHOOL?
SORRY. I'LL BE MORE CAREFUL.
I REALLY AM GETTING YOU IN TROUBLE.
MAYUKO...
DID YOU COPY THAT MANUSCRIPT FOR ME?
!!
HOW DID YOU KNOW?
MODEL'S INTUITION.
KAZAMA?
?
HE LOOKS LIKE HE JUST SAW A GHOST.

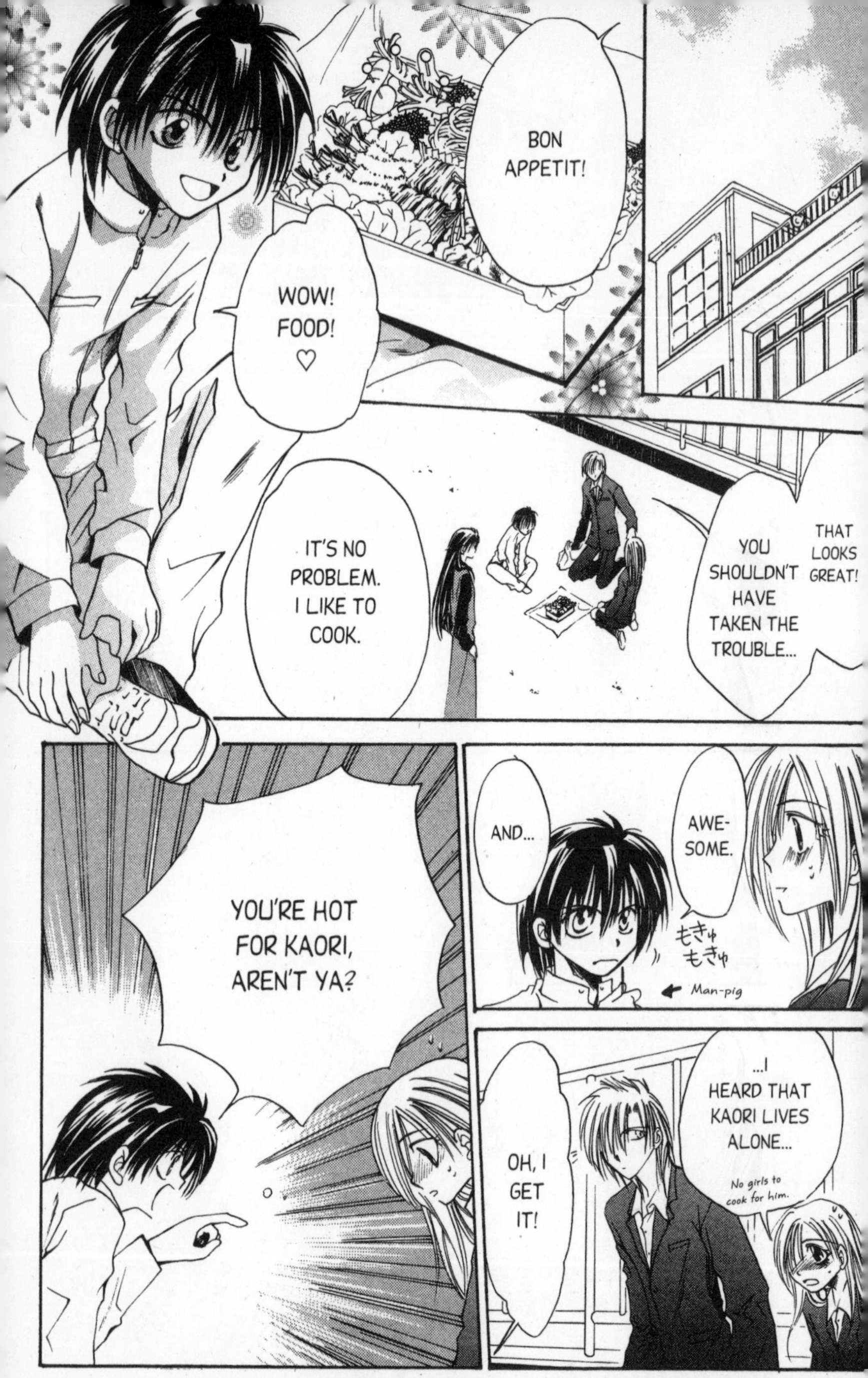
BON APPETIT!
WOW! FOOD! ♡
THAT LOOKS GREAT!
YOU SHOULDN'T HAVE TAKEN THE TROUBLE...
IT'S NO PROBLEM. I LIKE TO COOK.
AWE-SOME.
もきゅ もきゅ
AND...
Man-pig
...I HEARD THAT KAORI LIVES ALONE...
No girls to cook for him.
OH, I GET IT!
YOU'RE HOT FOR KAORI, AREN'T YA?

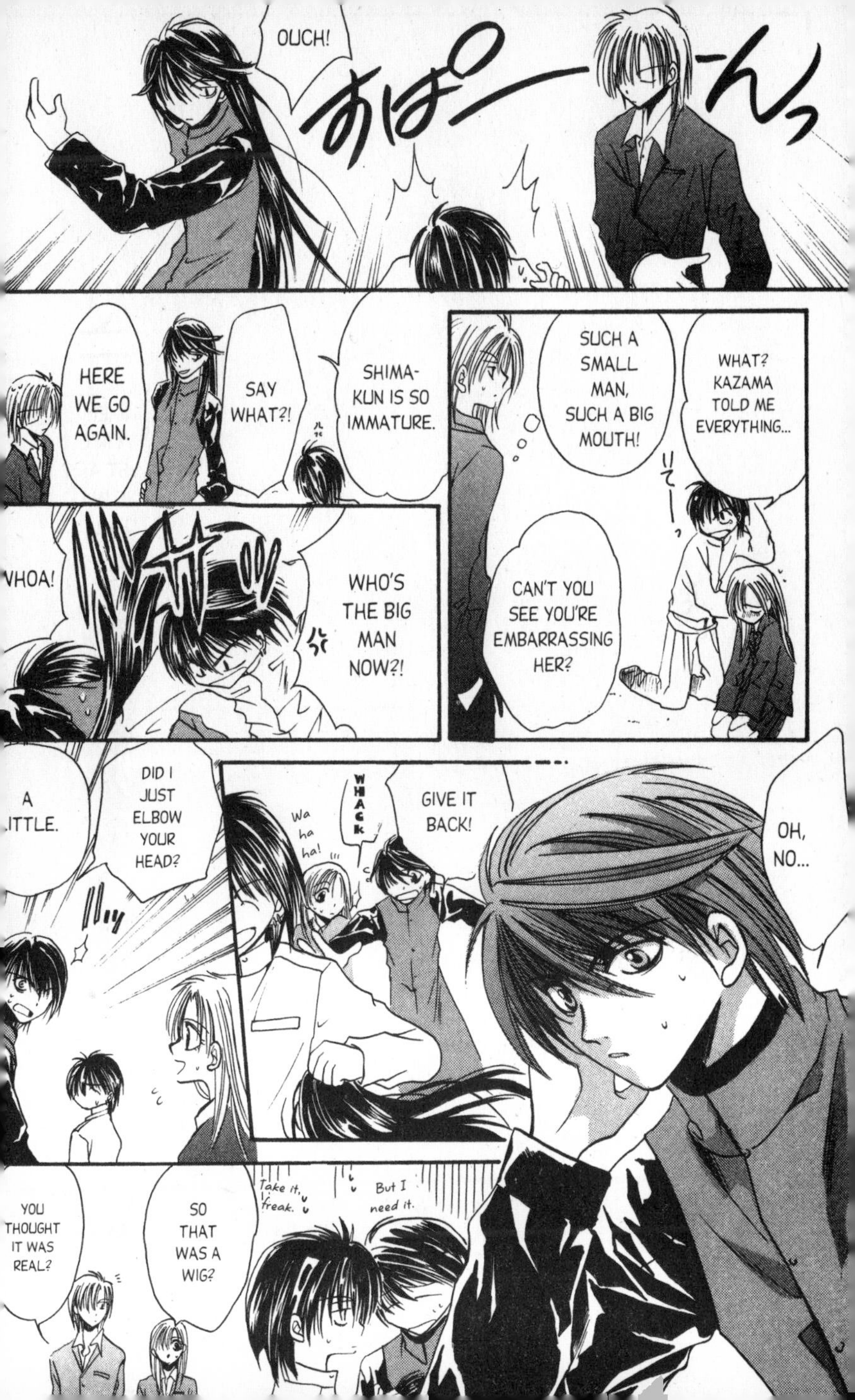

OUCH!
すぱーーんっ
WHAT? KAZAMA TOLD ME EVERYTHING...
SUCH A SMALL MAN, SUCH A BIG MOUTH!
CAN'T YOU SEE YOU'RE EMBARRASSING HER?
SHIMA-KUN IS SO IMMATURE.
SAY WHAT?!
HERE WE GO AGAIN.
WHO'S THE BIG MAN NOW?!
WHOA!
OH, NO...
GIVE IT BACK!
WHACK
Wa ha ha!
DID I JUST ELBOW YOUR HEAD?
A LITTLE.
But I need it.
Take it, freak.
SO THAT WAS A WIG?
YOU THOUGHT IT WAS REAL?

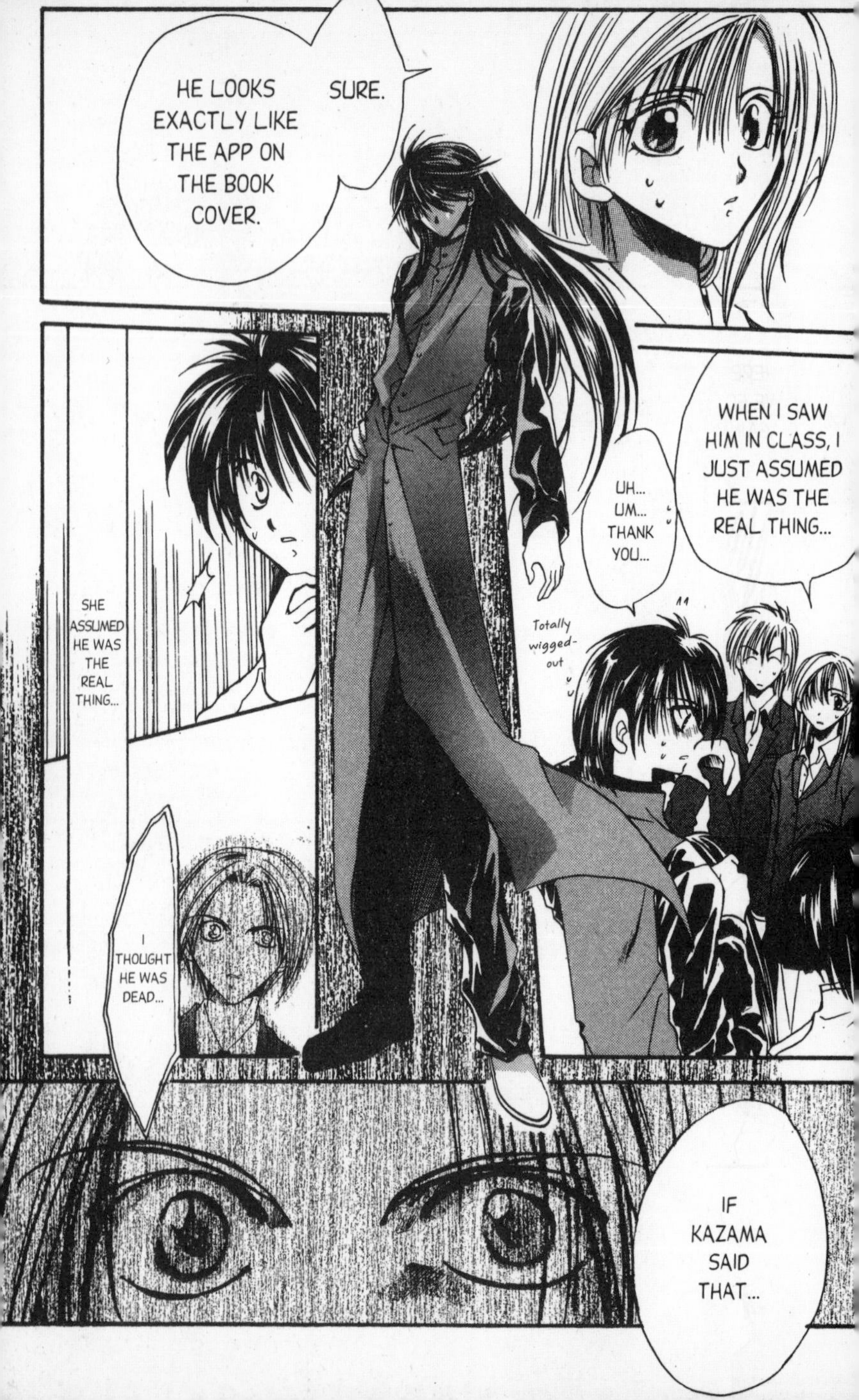

SURE.
HE LOOKS EXACTLY LIKE THE APP ON THE BOOK COVER.
WHEN I SAW HIM IN CLASS, I JUST ASSUMED HE WAS THE REAL THING...
UH... UM... THANK YOU...
Totally wigged-out
SHE ASSUMED HE WAS THE REAL THING...
I THOUGHT HE WAS DEAD...
IF KAZAMA SAID THAT...

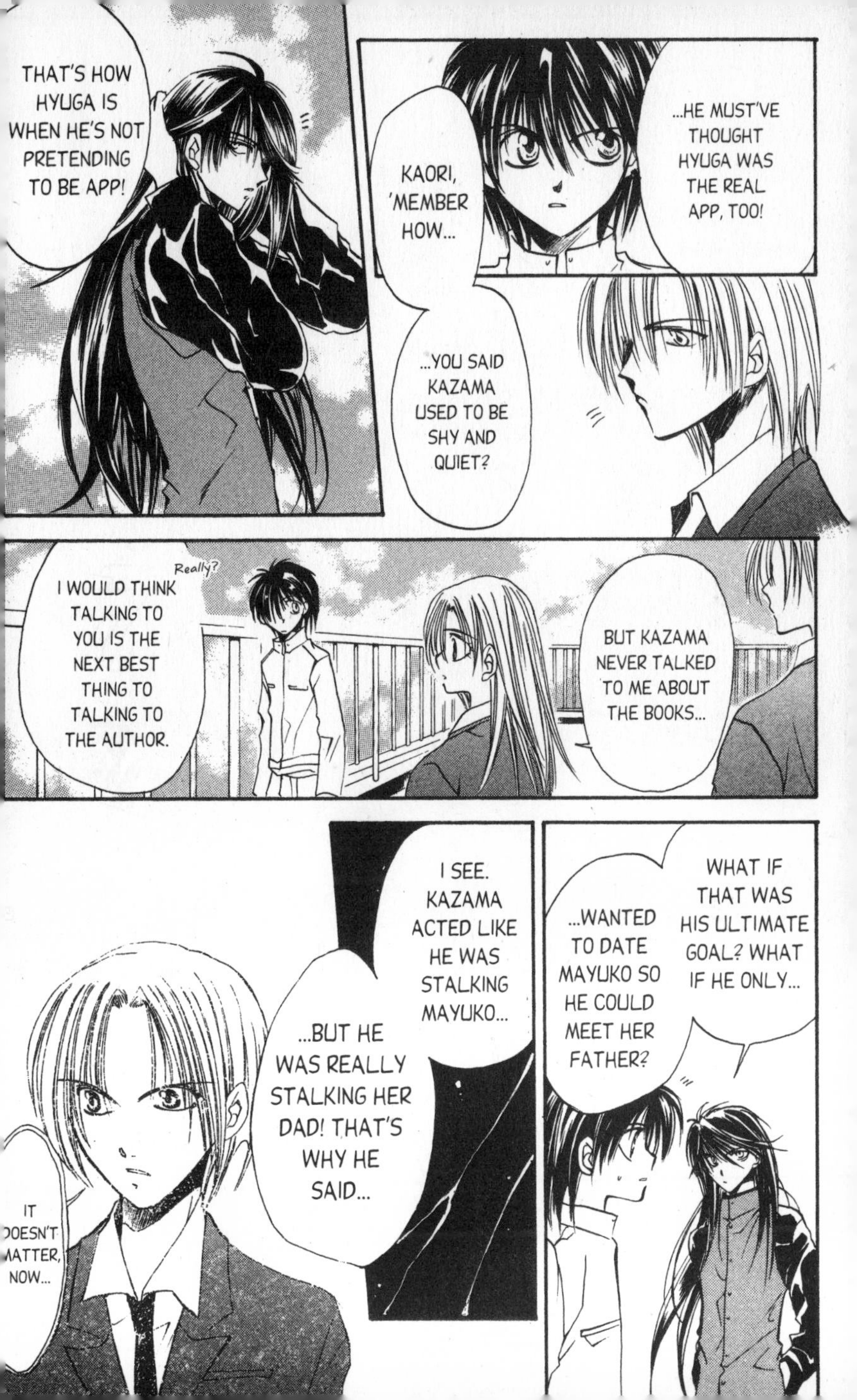
...HE MUST'VE THOUGHT HYUGA WAS THE REAL APP, TOO!
KAORI, 'MEMBER HOW...
...YOU SAID KAZAMA USED TO BE SHY AND QUIET?
THAT'S HOW HYUGA IS WHEN HE'S NOT PRETENDING TO BE APP!
BUT KAZAMA NEVER TALKED TO ME ABOUT THE BOOKS...
Really?
I WOULD THINK TALKING TO YOU IS THE NEXT BEST THING TO TALKING TO THE AUTHOR.
WHAT IF THAT WAS HIS ULTIMATE GOAL? WHAT IF HE ONLY...
...WANTED TO DATE MAYUKO SO HE COULD MEET HER FATHER?
I SEE. KAZAMA ACTED LIKE HE WAS STALKING MAYUKO...
...BUT HE WAS REALLY STALKING HER DAD! THAT'S WHY HE SAID...
IT DOESN'T MATTER, NOW...

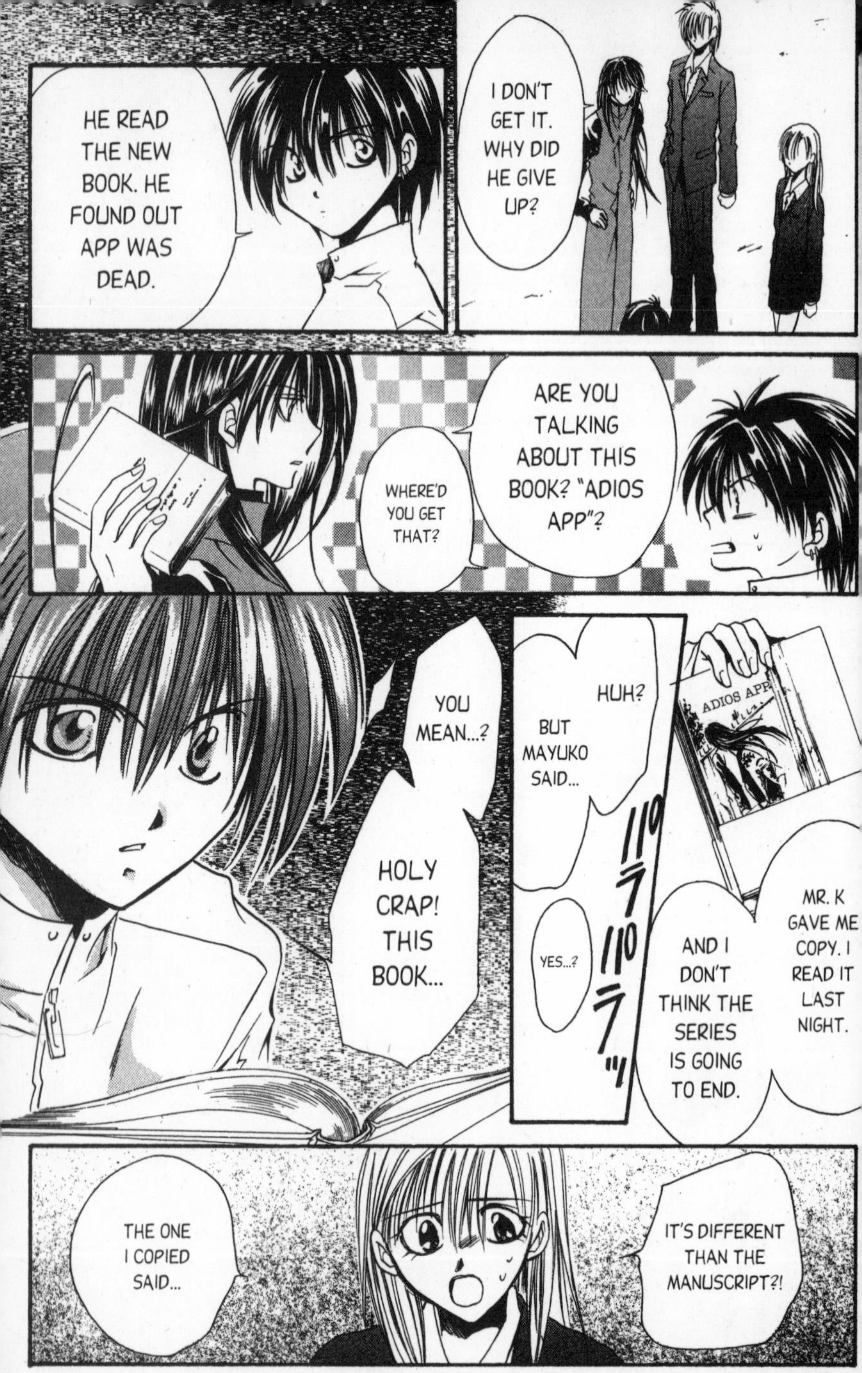
I DON'T GET IT. WHY DID HE GIVE UP?
HE READ THE NEW BOOK. HE FOUND OUT APP WAS DEAD.
ARE YOU TALKING ABOUT THIS BOOK? "ADIOS APP"?
WHERE'D YOU GET THAT?
HUH?
BUT MAYUKO SAID...
ADIOS APP
MR. K GAVE ME COPY. I READ IT LAST NIGHT.
AND I DON'T THINK THE SERIES IS GOING TO END.
YES...?
YOU MEAN...?
HOLY CRAP! THIS BOOK...
IT'S DIFFERENT THAN THE MANUSCRIPT?!
THE ONE I COPIED SAID...

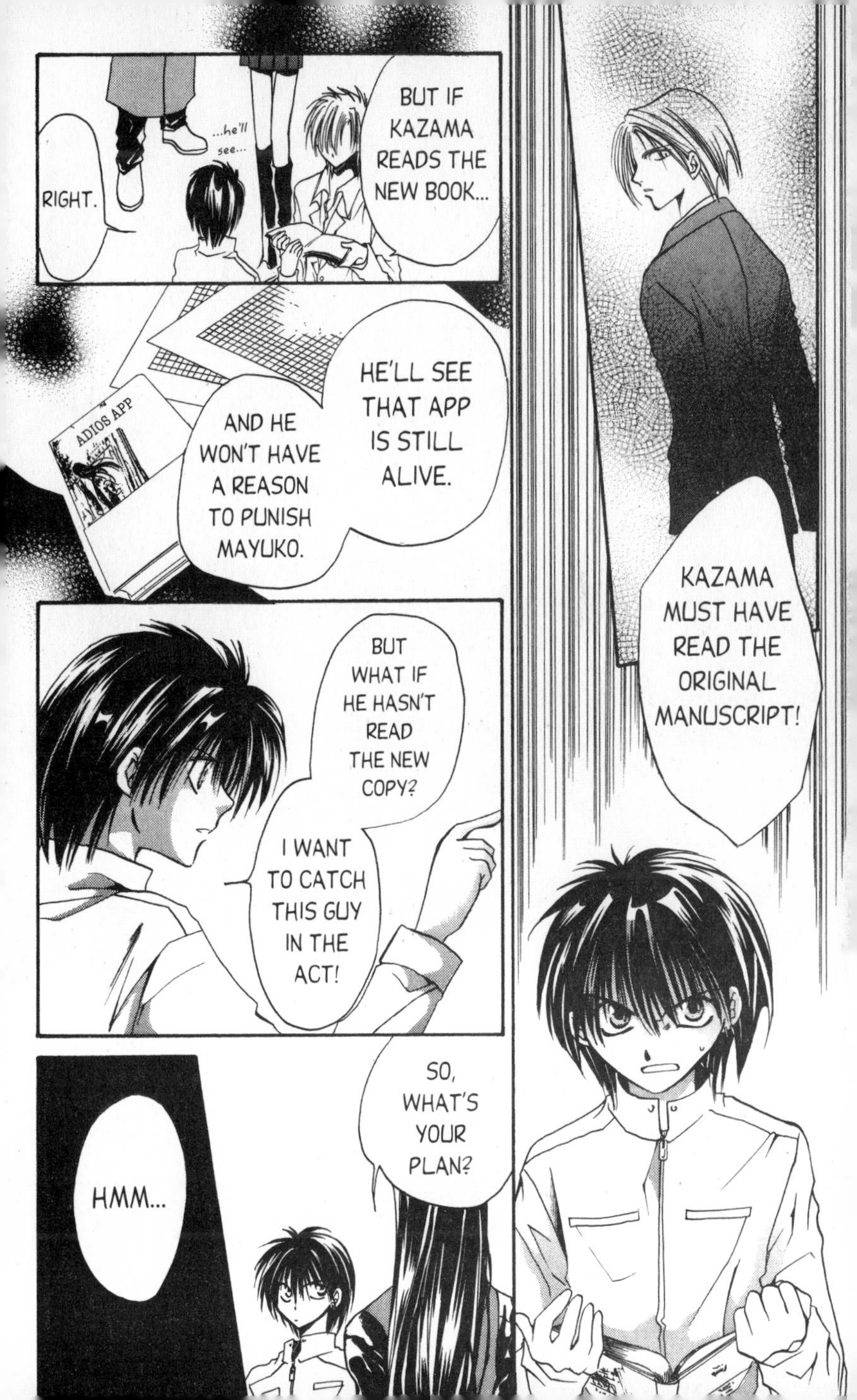
KAZAMA MUST HAVE READ THE ORIGINAL MANUSCRIPT!
BUT IF KAZAMA READS THE NEW BOOK...
...he'll see...
RIGHT.
HE'LL SEE THAT APP IS STILL ALIVE.
AND HE WON'T HAVE A REASON TO PUNISH MAYUKO.
ADIOS APP
BUT WHAT IF HE HASN'T READ THE NEW COPY?
I WANT TO CATCH THIS GUY IN THE ACT!
SO, WHAT'S YOUR PLAN?
HMM...

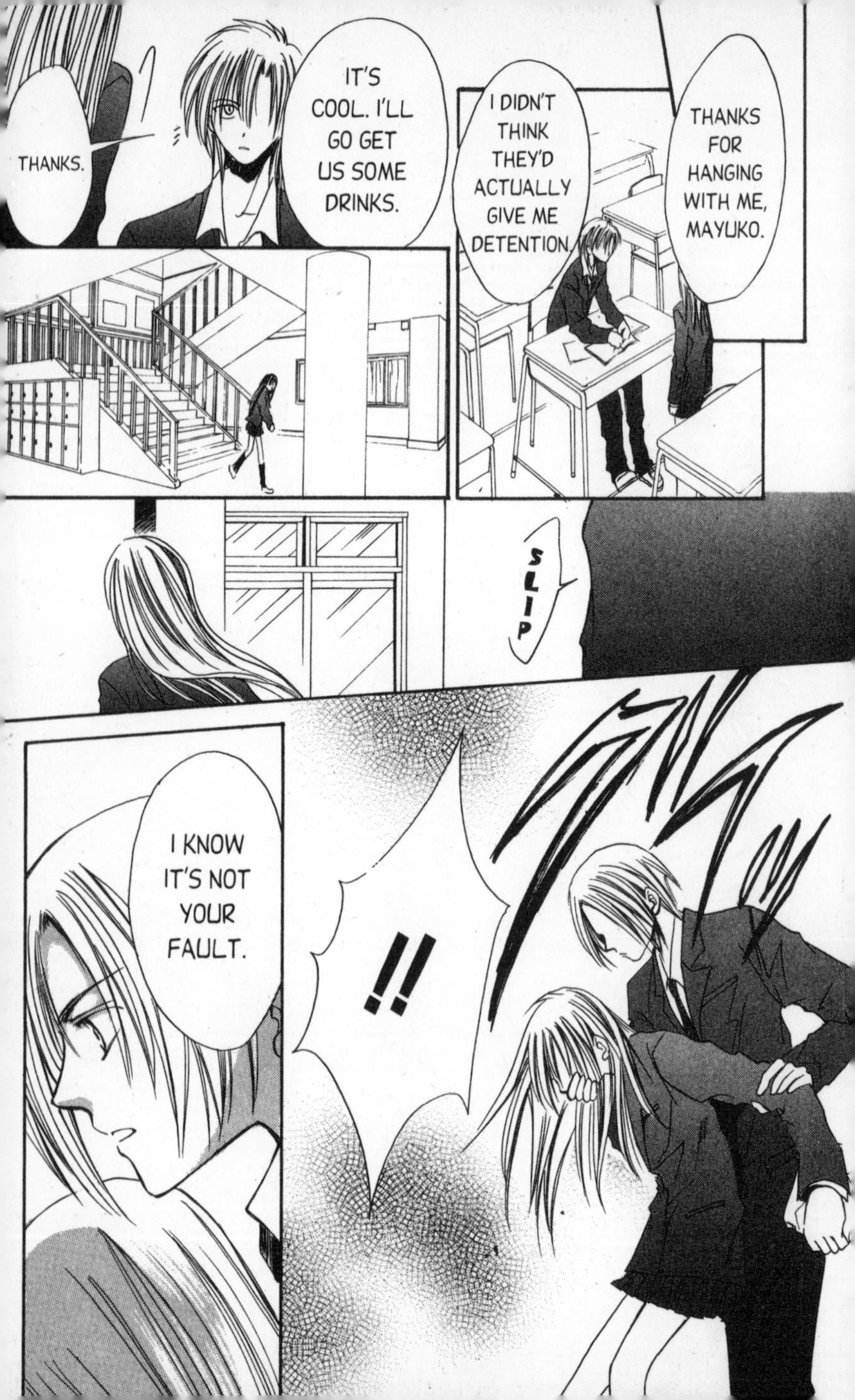
THANKS FOR HANGING WITH ME, MAYUKO.
I DIDN'T THINK THEY'D ACTUALLY GIVE ME DETENTION.
IT'S COOL. I'LL GO GET US SOME DRINKS.
THANKS.
SLIP
!!
I KNOW IT'S NOT YOUR FAULT.

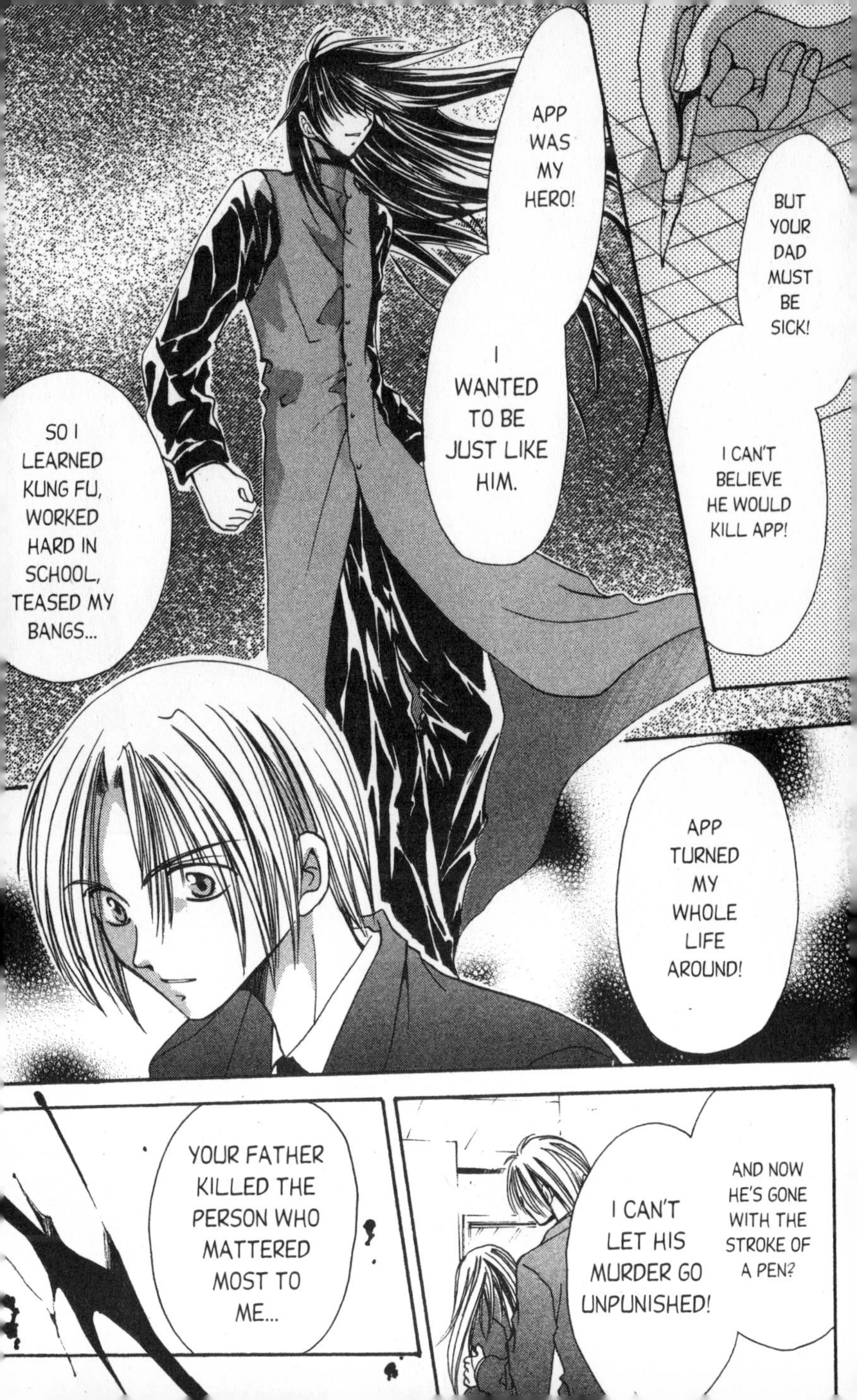
BUT YOUR DAD MUST BE SICK!
I CAN'T BELIEVE HE WOULD KILL APP!
APP WAS MY HERO!
I WANTED TO BE JUST LIKE HIM.
SO I LEARNED KUNG FU, WORKED HARD IN SCHOOL, TEASED MY BANGS...
APP TURNED MY WHOLE LIFE AROUND!
AND NOW HE'S GONE WITH THE STROKE OF A PEN?
I CAN'T LET HIS MURDER GO UNPUNISHED!
YOUR FATHER KILLED THE PERSON WHO MATTERED MOST TO ME...

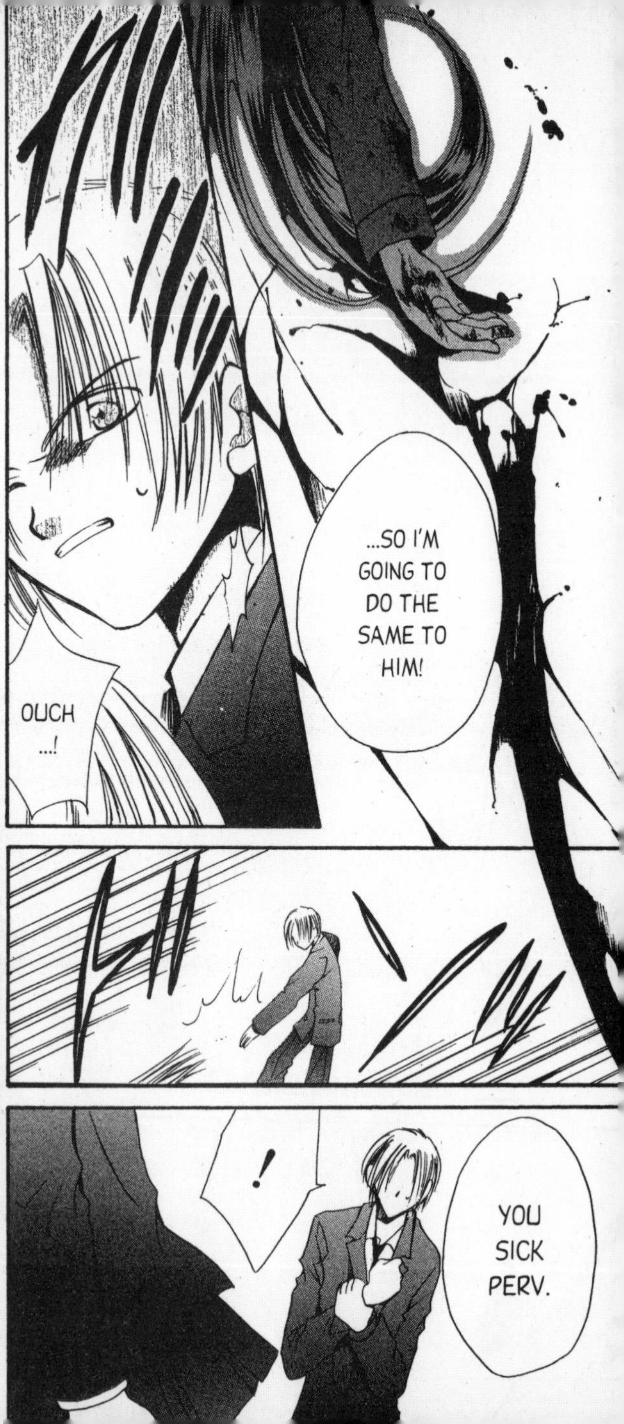
...SO I'M GOING TO DO THE SAME TO HIM!
OUCH ...!
YOU SICK PERV.
!

I didn't give you a birthday for Hyuga in volume 1, so here it is: August 31st. That's the birthday of a friend of mine, and it's also the day that marks the end of summer vacation. So it's good because it's easy to remember, but it's bad because nobody has time to celebrate. They're too busy catching up on summer homework! So, I would hereby like to proclaim...

B-DAY BASH FOR MR. HYUGA!!

...I accept cash or check!

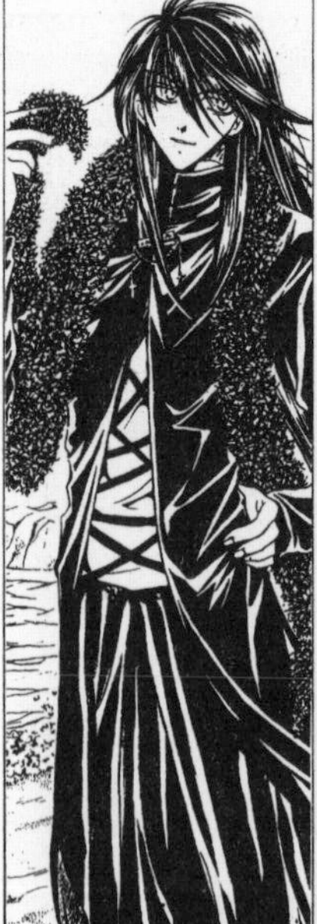

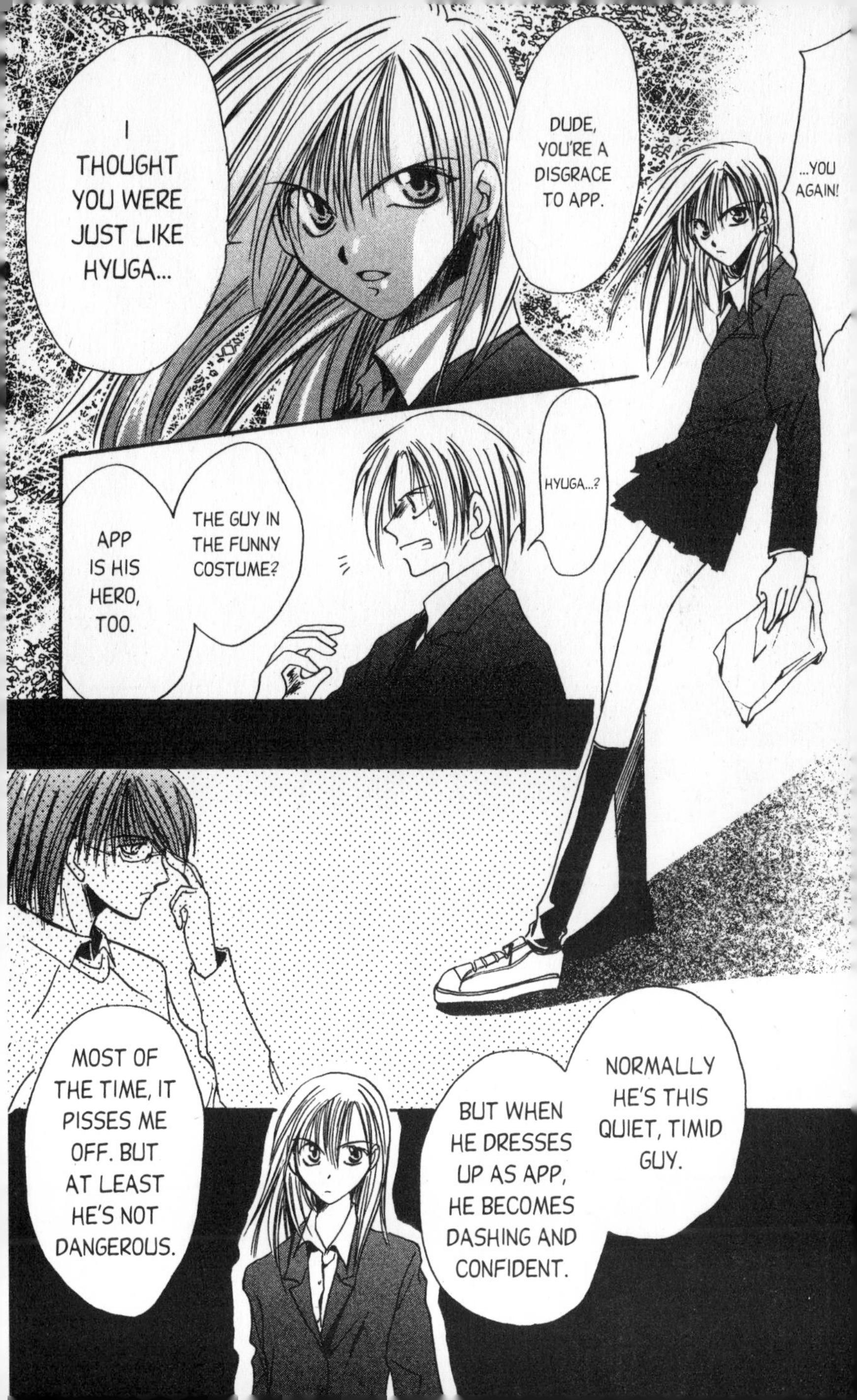
...YOU AGAIN!
DUDE, YOU'RE A DISGRACE TO APP.
I THOUGHT YOU WERE JUST LIKE HYUGA...
HYUGA...?
THE GUY IN THE FUNNY COSTUME?
APP IS HIS HERO, TOO.
NORMALLY HE'S THIS QUIET, TIMID GUY.
BUT WHEN HE DRESSES UP AS APP, HE BECOMES DASHING AND CONFIDENT.
MOST OF THE TIME, IT PISSES ME OFF. BUT AT LEAST HE'S NOT DANGEROUS.

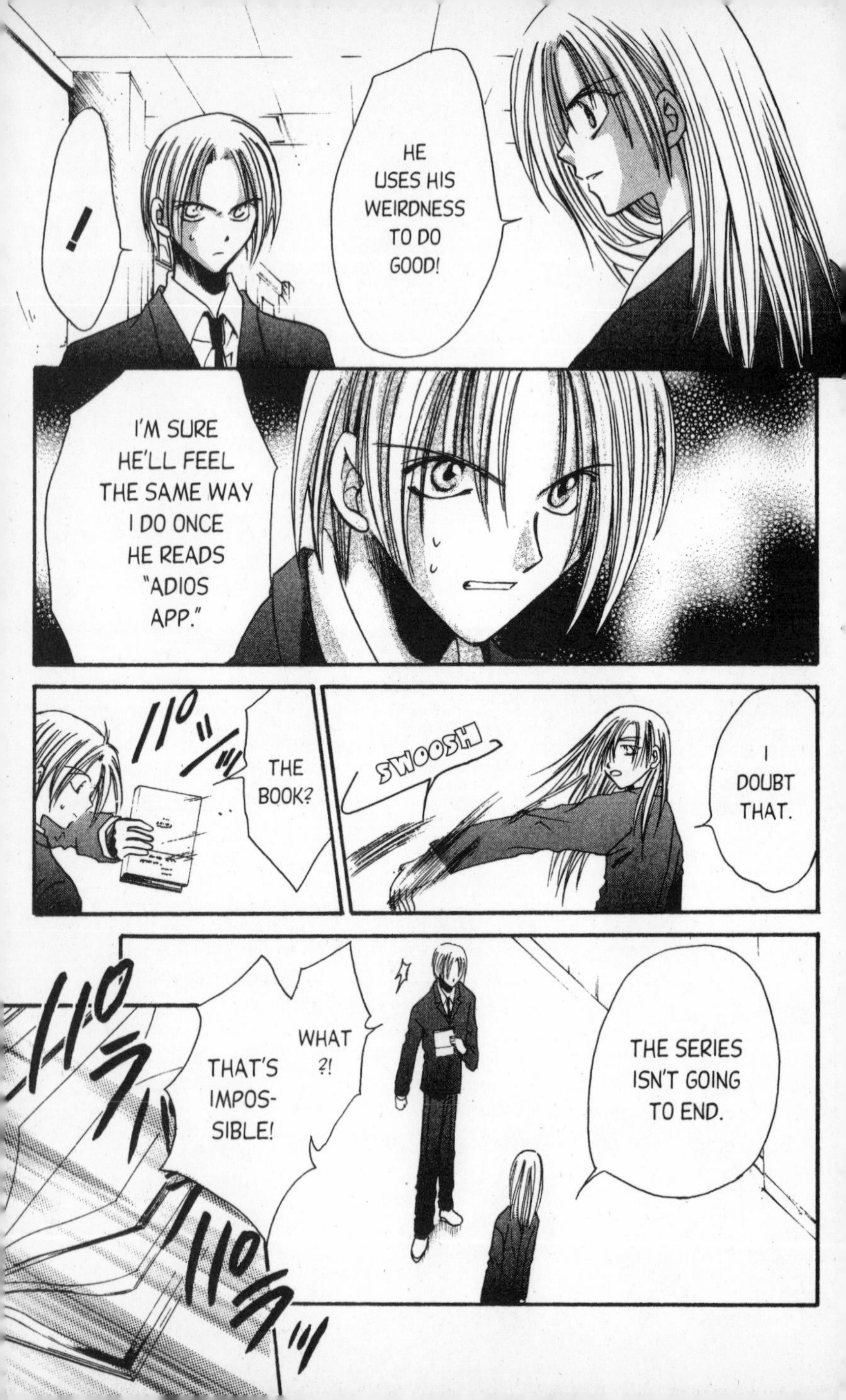
HE USES HIS WEIRDNESS TO DO GOOD!
!
I'M SURE HE'LL FEEL THE SAME WAY I DO ONCE HE READS "ADIOS APP."
I DOUBT THAT.
SWOOSH
THE BOOK?
THE SERIES ISN'T GOING TO END.
WHAT ?!
THAT'S IMPOS-SIBLE!

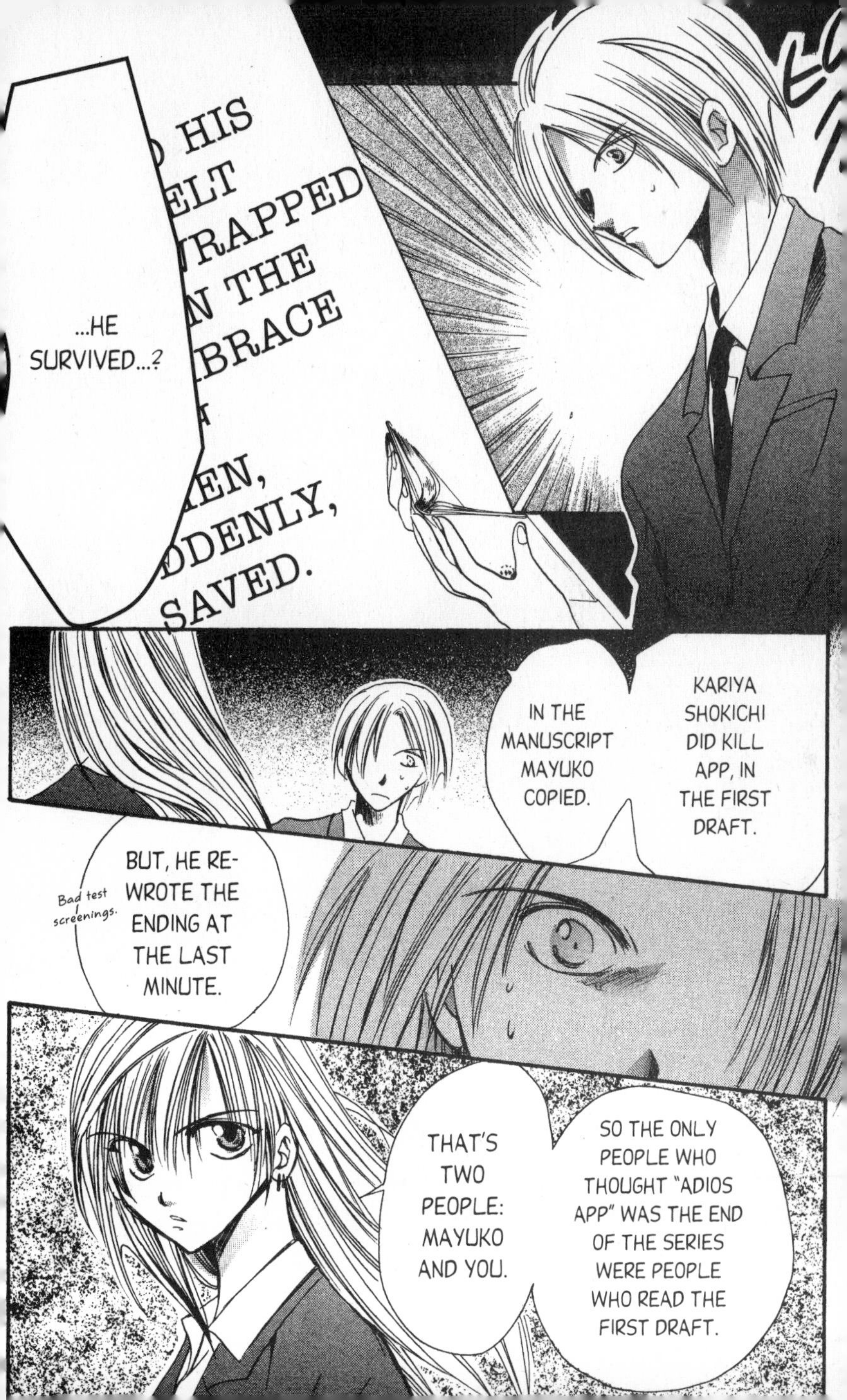
D HIS
ELT
RAPPED
N THE
BRACE
A
EN,
DDENLY,
SAVED.
...HE SURVIVED...?
KARIYA SHOKICHI DID KILL APP, IN THE FIRST DRAFT.
IN THE MANUSCRIPT MAYUKO COPIED.
BUT, HE RE-WROTE THE ENDING AT THE LAST MINUTE.
Bad test screenings.
SO THE ONLY PEOPLE WHO THOUGHT "ADIOS APP" WAS THE END OF THE SERIES WERE PEOPLE WHO READ THE FIRST DRAFT.
THAT'S TWO PEOPLE: MAYUKO AND YOU.

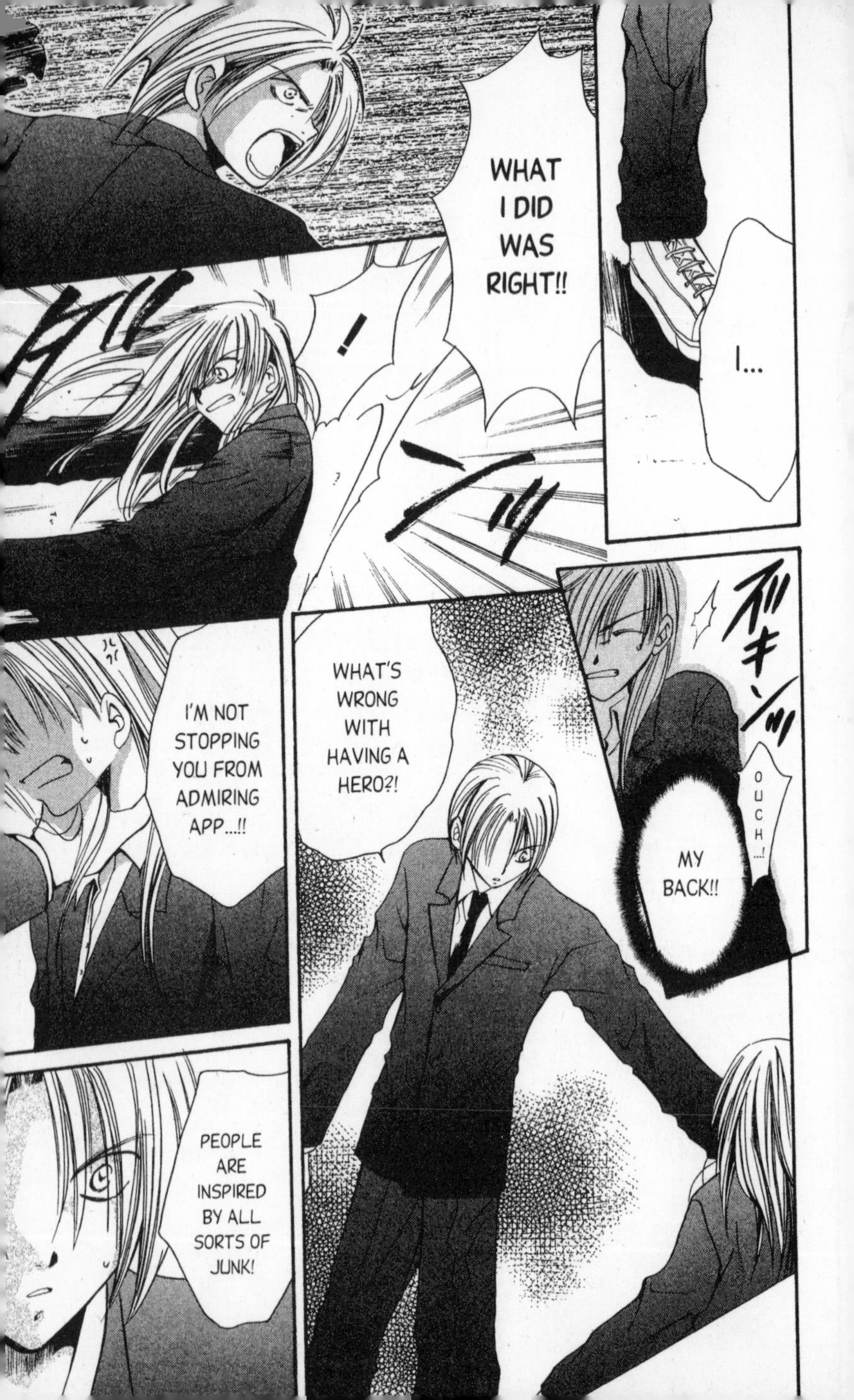
I...
WHAT I DID WAS RIGHT!!
!
OUCH...!
MY BACK!!
WHAT'S WRONG WITH HAVING A HERO?!
I'M NOT STOPPING YOU FROM ADMIRING APP...!!
PEOPLE ARE INSPIRED BY ALL SORTS OF JUNK!

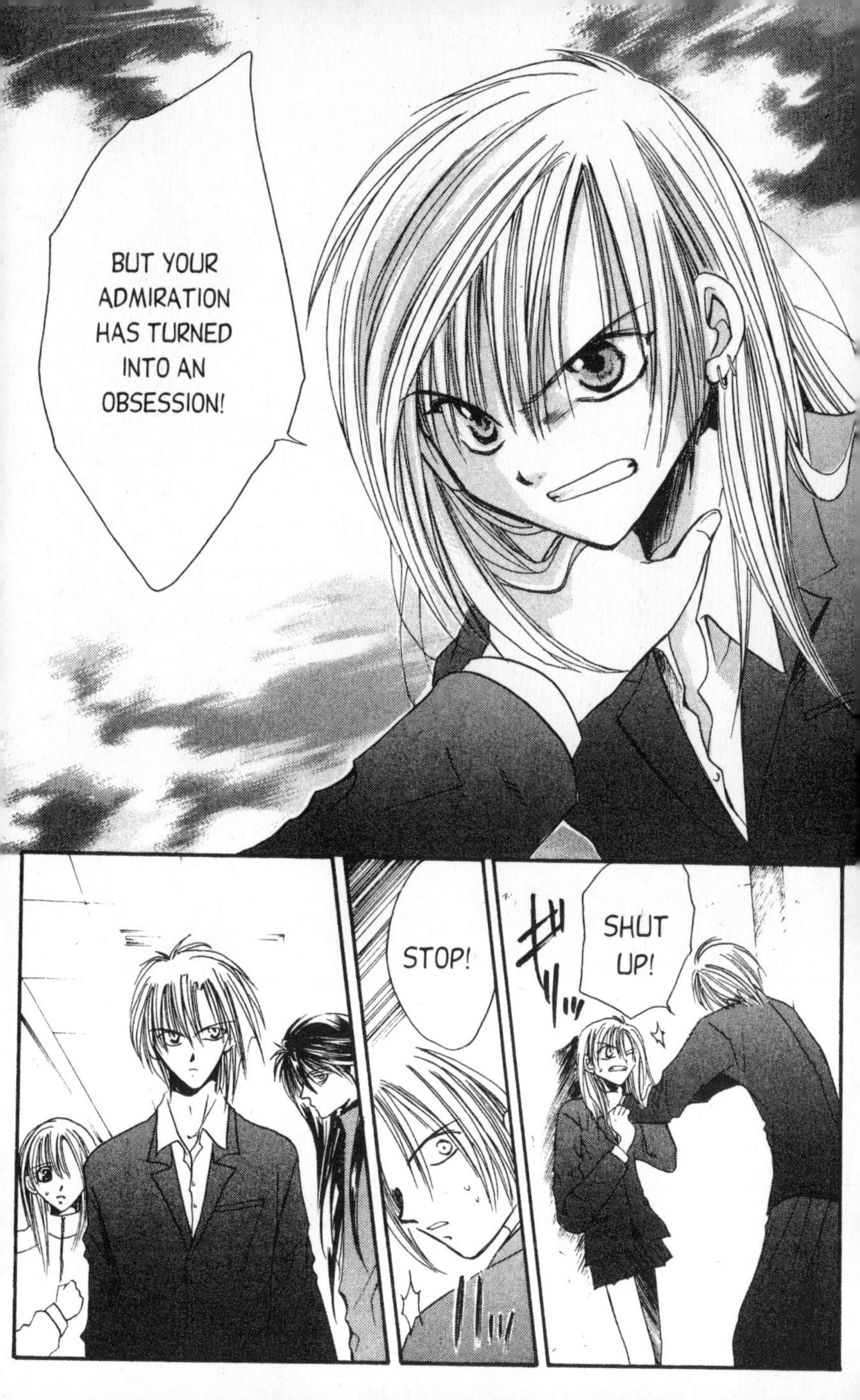
BUT YOUR ADMIRATION HAS TURNED INTO AN OBSESSION!
SHUT UP!
STOP!

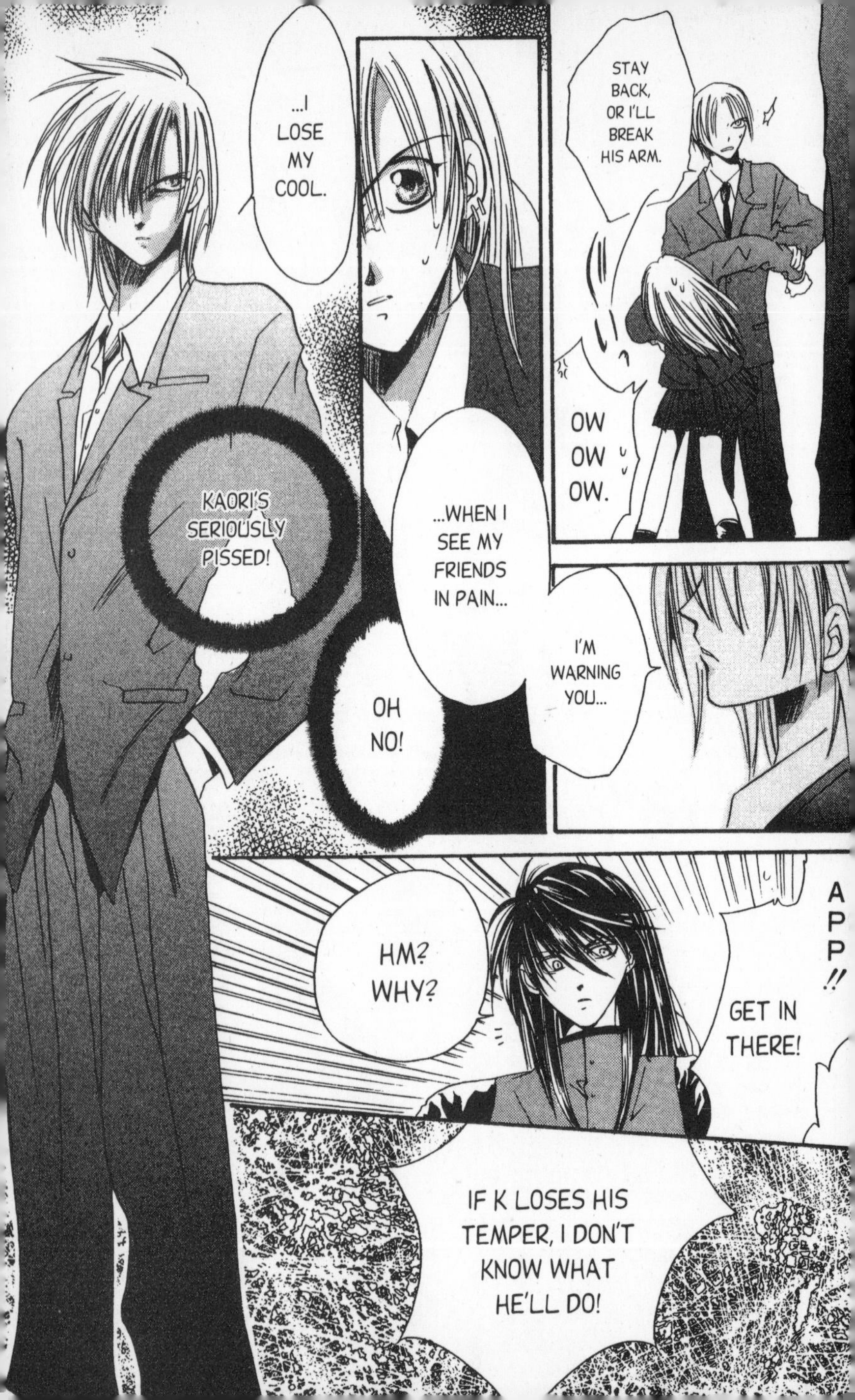
STAY BACK, OR I'LL BREAK HIS ARM.
OW OW OW.
I'M WARNING YOU...
...WHEN I SEE MY FRIENDS IN PAIN...
...I LOSE MY COOL.
OH NO!
KAORI'S SERIOUSLY PISSED!
APP!!
GET IN THERE!
HM? WHY?
IF K LOSES HIS TEMPER, I DON'T KNOW WHAT HE'LL DO!

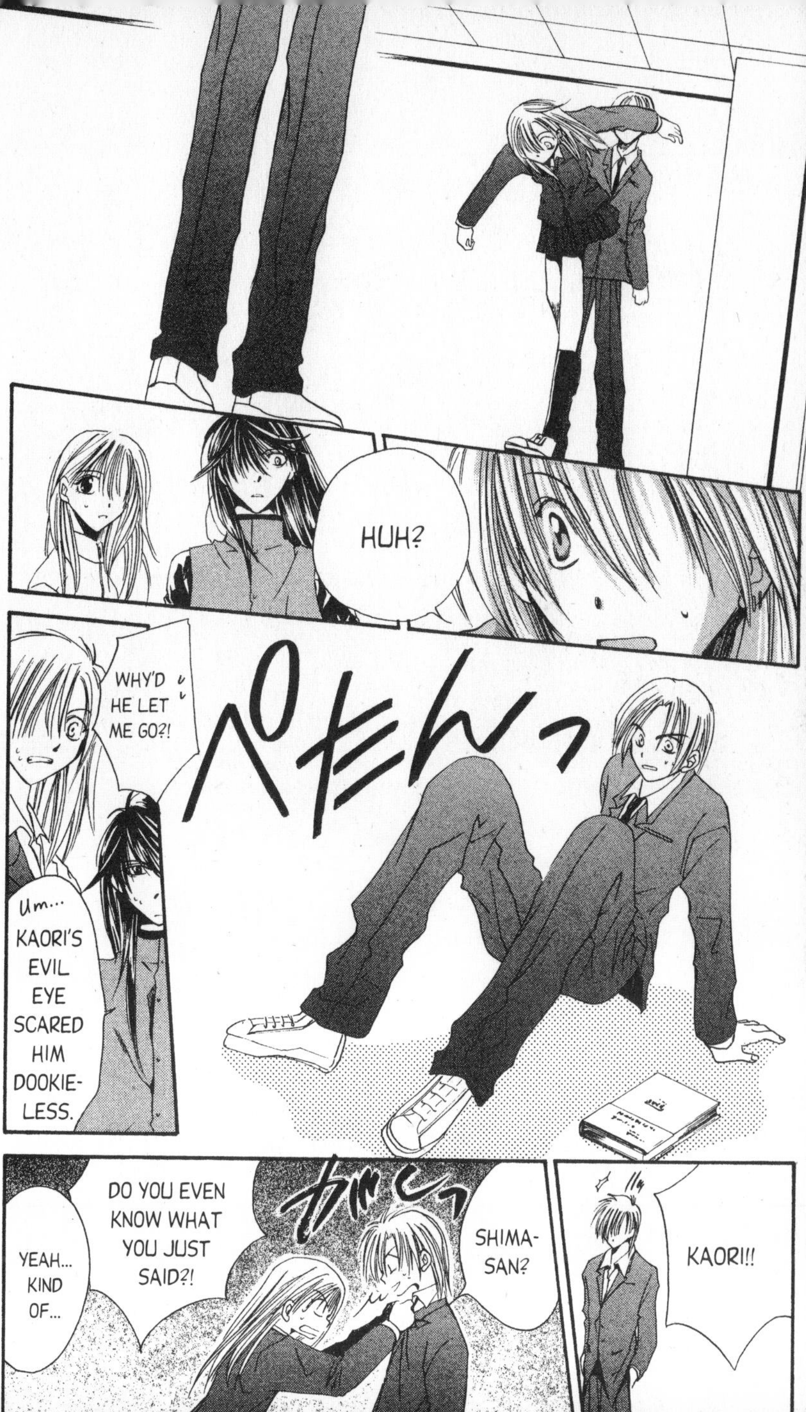
HUH?
ぺたんっ
WHY'D HE LET ME GO?!
Um... KAORI'S EVIL EYE SCARED HIM DOOKIE-LESS.
KAORI!!
SHIMA-SAN?
DO YOU EVEN KNOW WHAT YOU JUST SAID?!
YEAH... KIND OF...

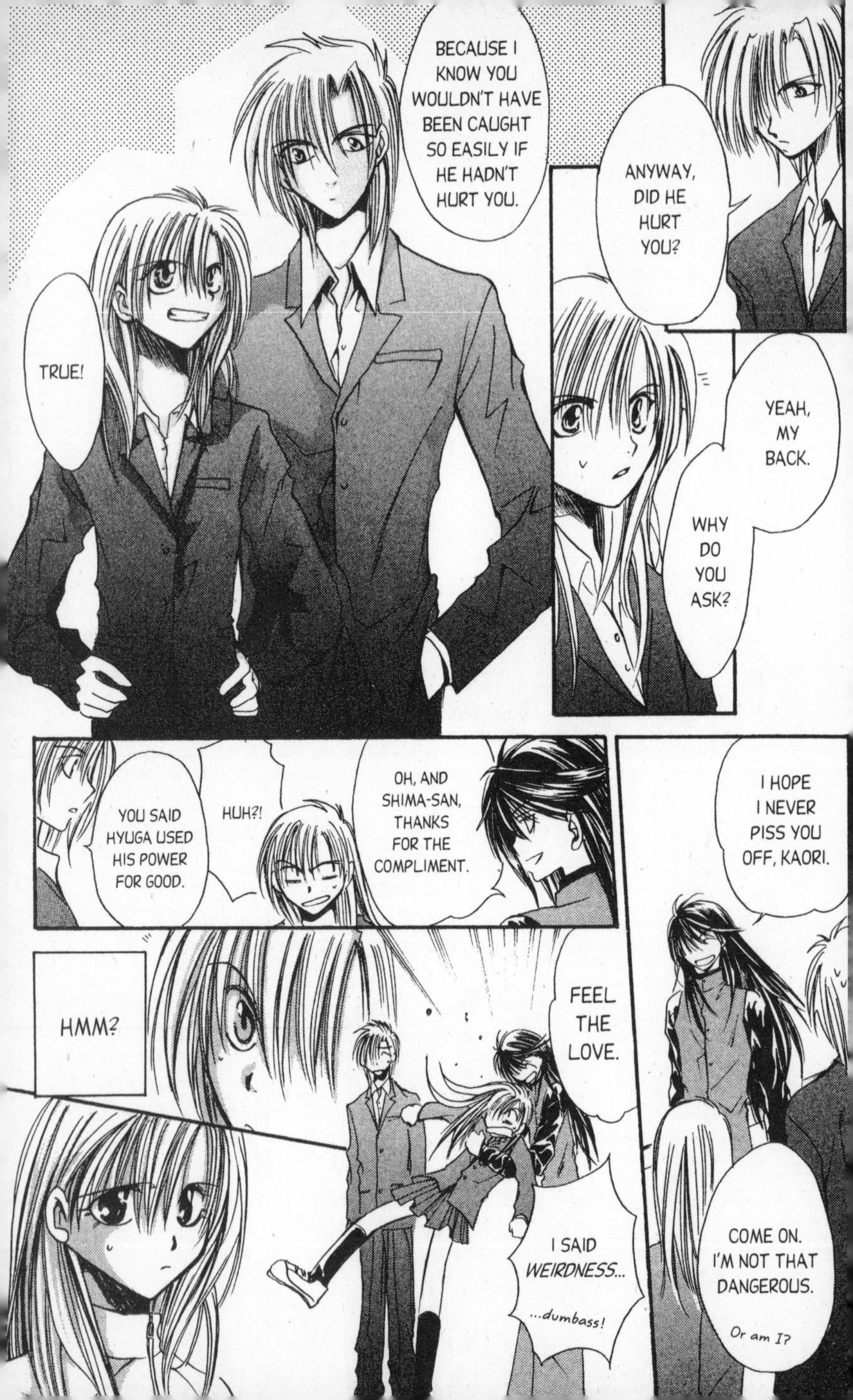
ANYWAY, DID HE HURT YOU?
YEAH, MY BACK.
WHY DO YOU ASK?
BECAUSE I KNOW YOU WOULDN'T HAVE BEEN CAUGHT SO EASILY IF HE HADN'T HURT YOU.
TRUE!
I HOPE I NEVER PISS YOU OFF, KAORI.
COME ON. I'M NOT THAT DANGEROUS.
Or am I?
OH, AND SHIMA-SAN, THANKS FOR THE COMPLIMENT.
HUH?!
YOU SAID HYUGA USED HIS POWER FOR GOOD.
HMM?
FEEL THE LOVE.
I SAID *WEIRDNESS*...
...dumbass!

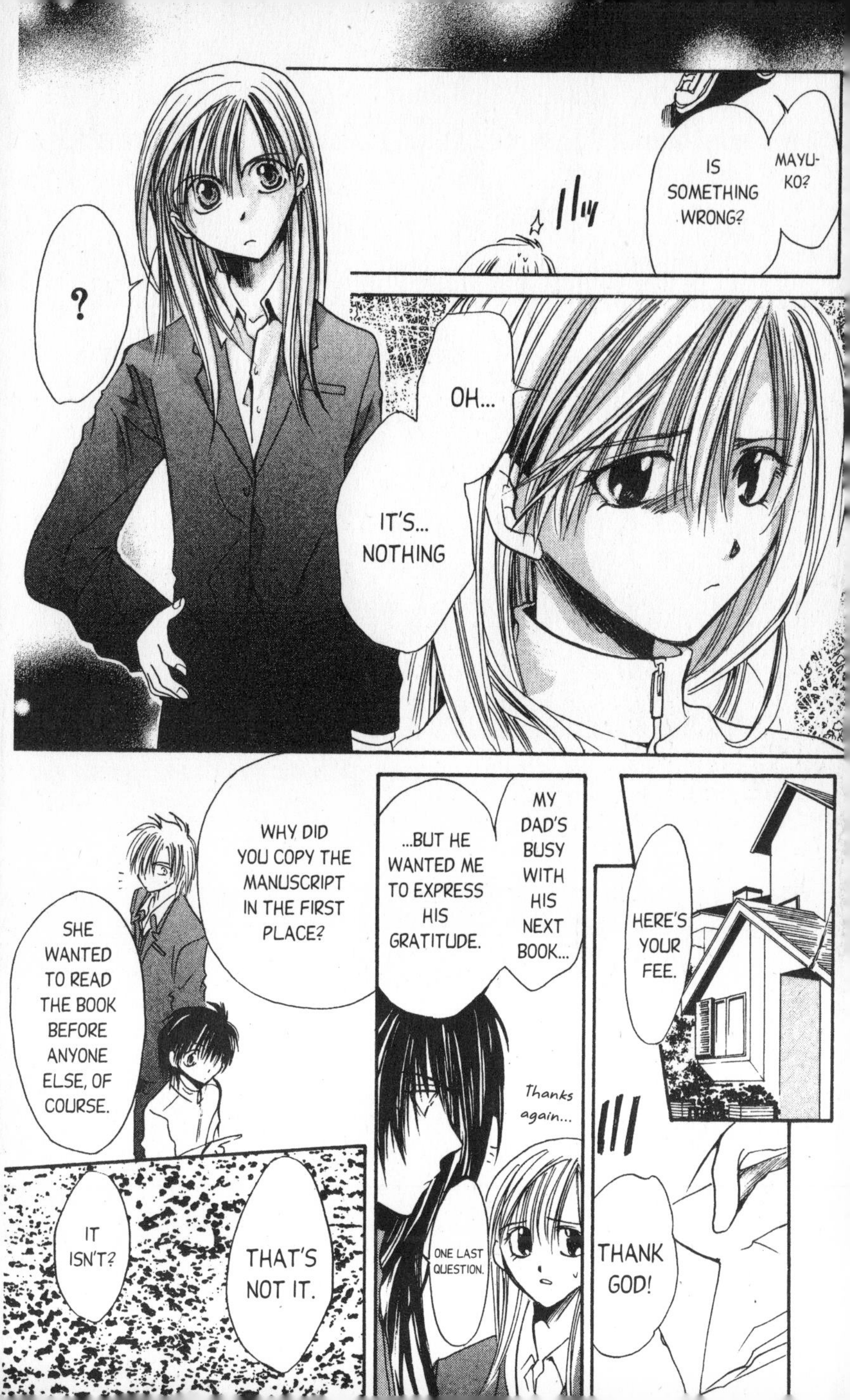
MAYU-KO?
IS SOMETHING WRONG?
OH...
IT'S... NOTHING
?
HERE'S YOUR FEE.
THANK GOD!
MY DAD'S BUSY WITH HIS NEXT BOOK...
...BUT HE WANTED ME TO EXPRESS HIS GRATITUDE.
Thanks again...
ONE LAST QUESTION.
WHY DID YOU COPY THE MANUSCRIPT IN THE FIRST PLACE?
SHE WANTED TO READ THE BOOK BEFORE ANYONE ELSE, OF COURSE.
THAT'S NOT IT.
IT ISN'T?

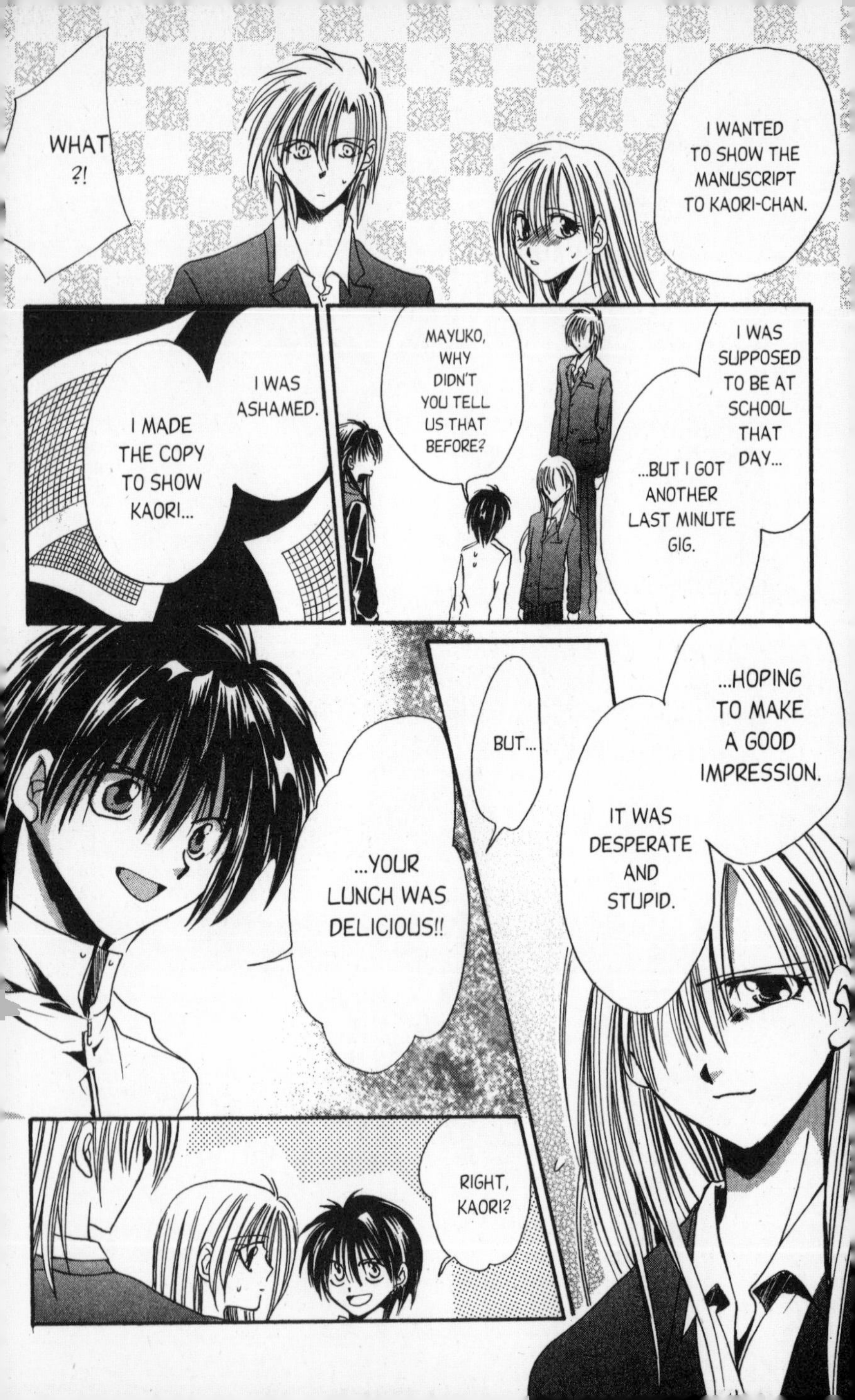
I WANTED TO SHOW THE MANUSCRIPT TO KAORI-CHAN.
WHAT?!
I WAS SUPPOSED TO BE AT SCHOOL THAT DAY...
...BUT I GOT ANOTHER LAST MINUTE GIG.
MAYUKO, WHY DIDN'T YOU TELL US THAT BEFORE?
I WAS ASHAMED.
I MADE THE COPY TO SHOW KAORI...
...HOPING TO MAKE A GOOD IMPRESSION.
IT WAS DESPERATE AND STUPID.
BUT...
...YOUR LUNCH WAS DELICIOUS!!
RIGHT, KAORI?

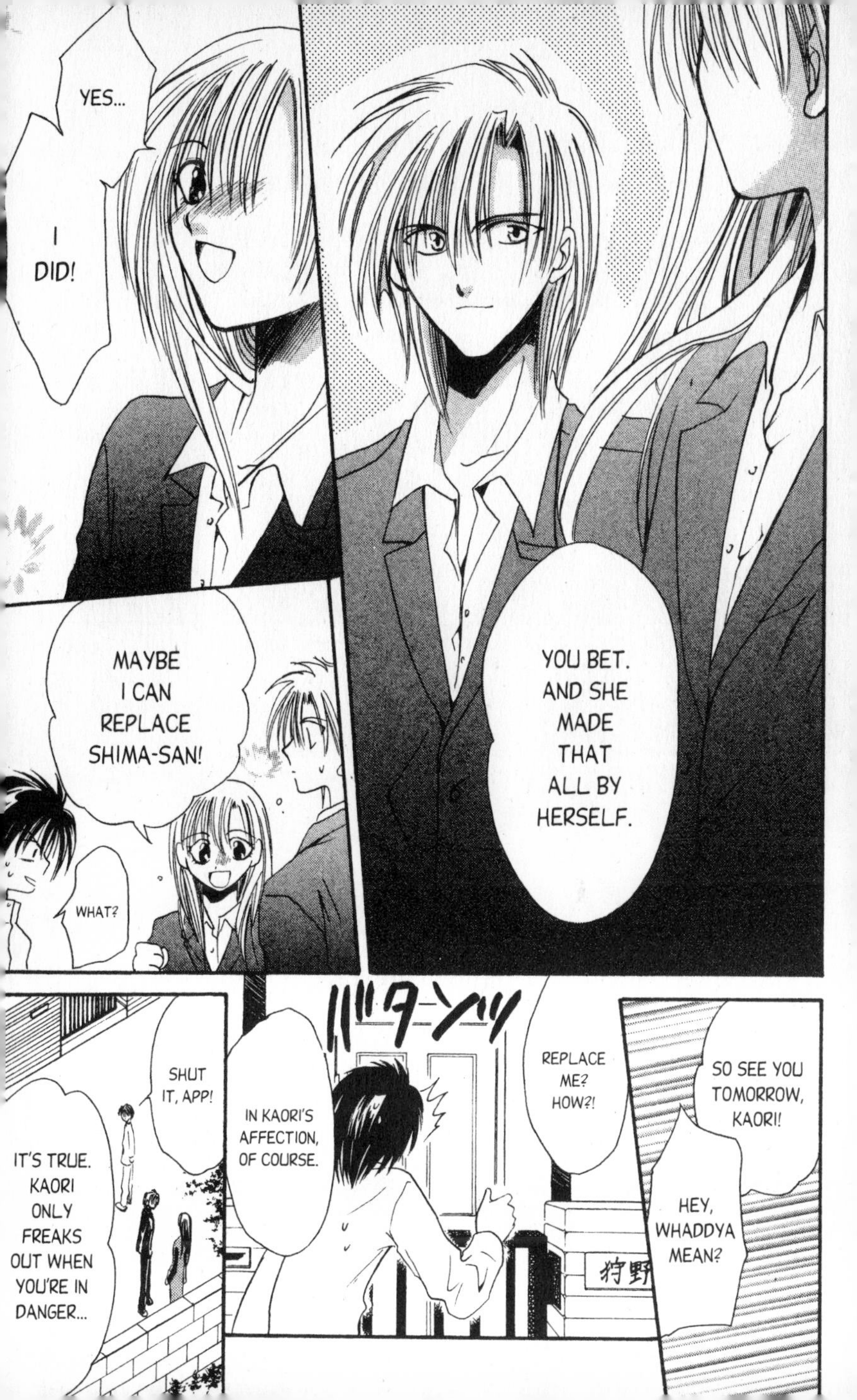
YOU BET. AND SHE MADE THAT ALL BY HERSELF.
YES...
I DID!
MAYBE I CAN REPLACE SHIMA-SAN!
WHAT?
SO SEE YOU TOMORROW, KAORI!
HEY, WHADDYA MEAN?
バターンッ
REPLACE ME? HOW?!
IN KAORI'S AFFECTION, OF COURSE.
狩野
SHUT IT, APP!
IT'S TRUE. KAORI ONLY FREAKS OUT WHEN YOU'RE IN DANGER...

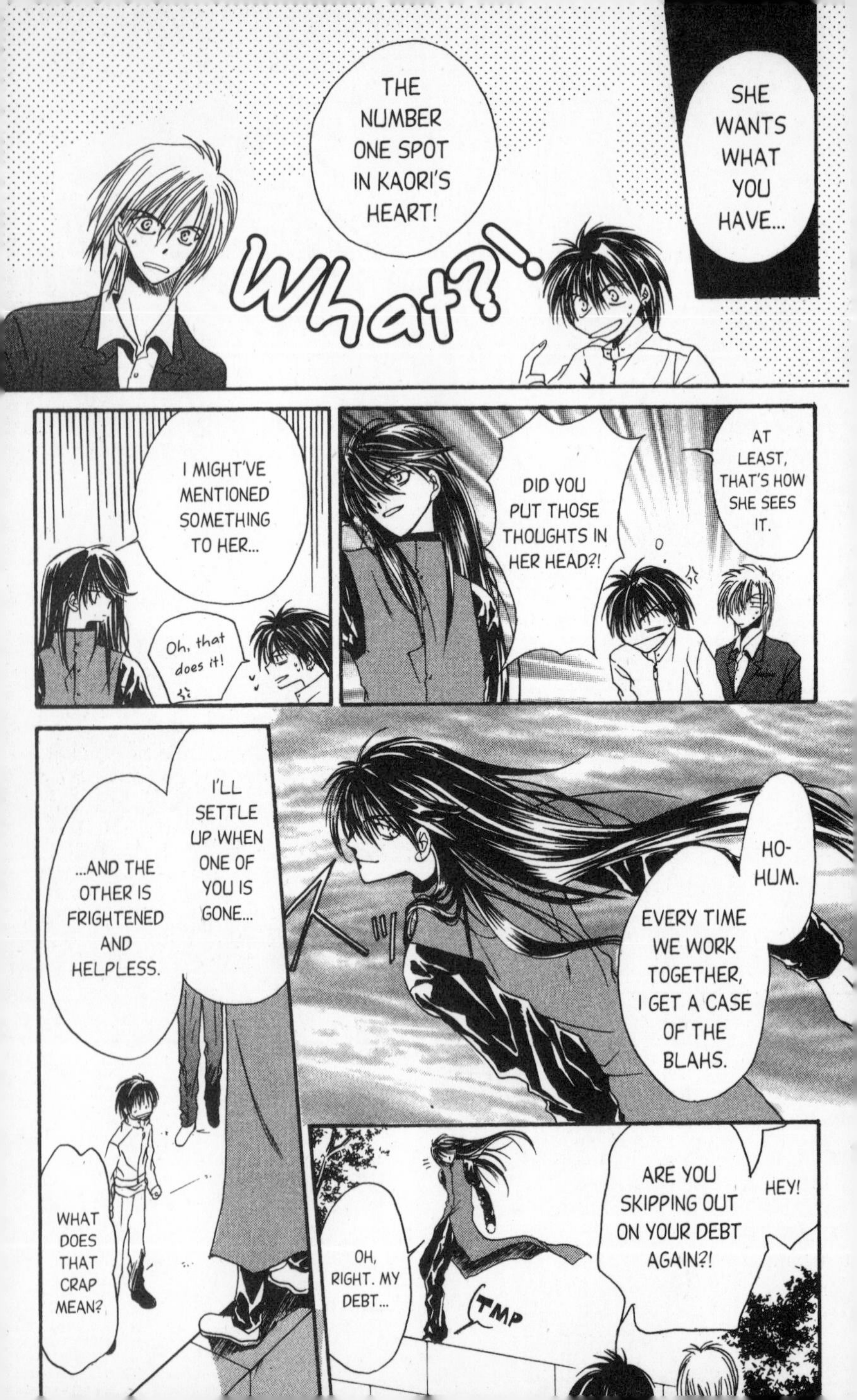
SHE WANTS WHAT YOU HAVE...
THE NUMBER ONE SPOT IN KAORI'S HEART!
What?!
AT LEAST, THAT'S HOW SHE SEES IT.
DID YOU PUT THOSE THOUGHTS IN HER HEAD?!
I MIGHT'VE MENTIONED SOMETHING TO HER...
Oh, that does it!
HO-HUM.
EVERY TIME WE WORK TOGETHER, I GET A CASE OF THE BLAHS.
HEY!
ARE YOU SKIPPING OUT ON YOUR DEBT AGAIN?!
OH, RIGHT. MY DEBT...
TMP
I'LL SETTLE UP WHEN ONE OF YOU IS GONE...
...AND THE OTHER IS FRIGHTENED AND HELPLESS.
WHAT DOES THAT CRAP MEAN?

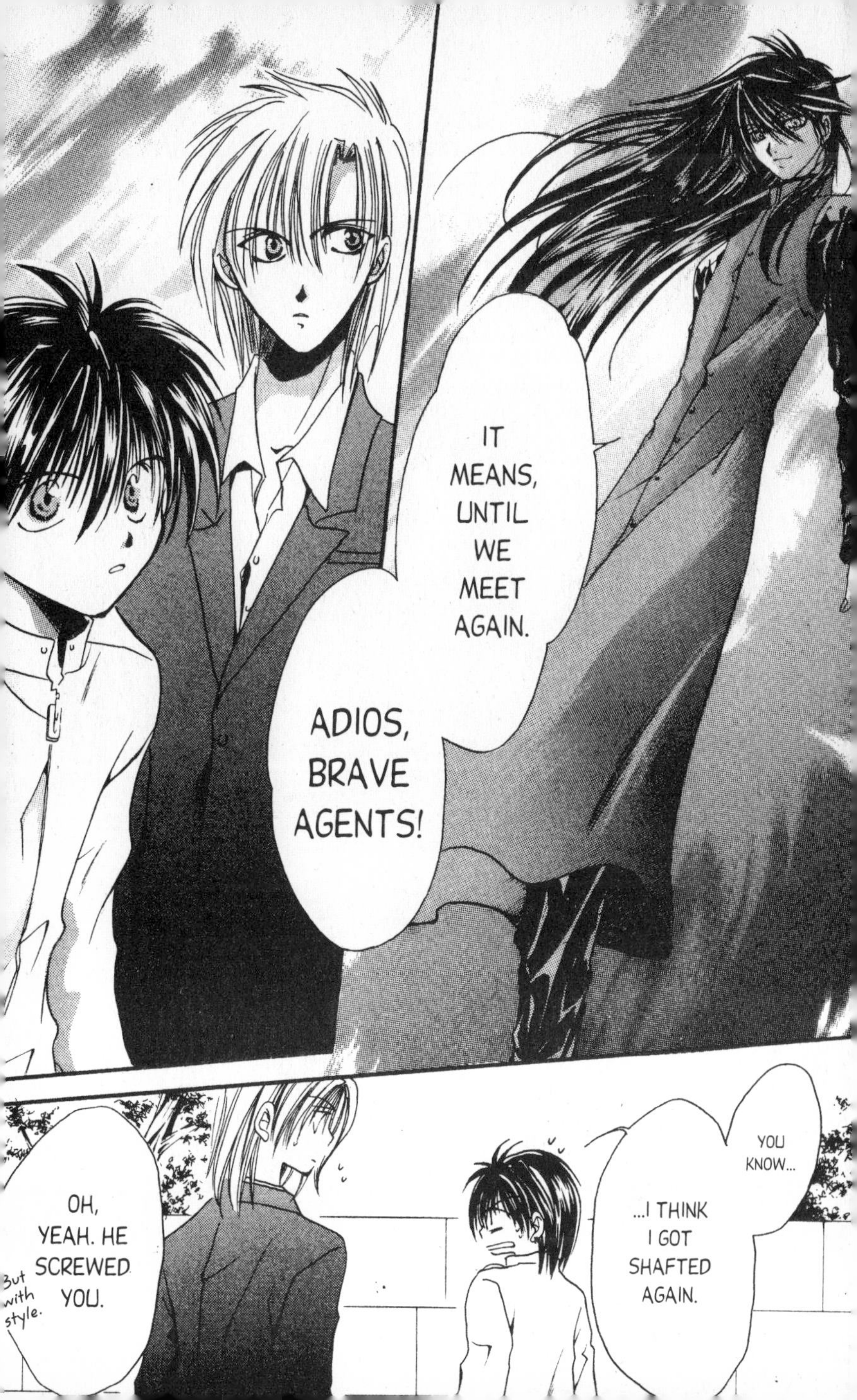
IT MEANS, UNTIL WE MEET AGAIN.
ADIOS, BRAVE AGENTS!
YOU KNOW...
...I THINK I GOT SHAFTED AGAIN.
OH, YEAH. HE SCREWED YOU.
But with style.

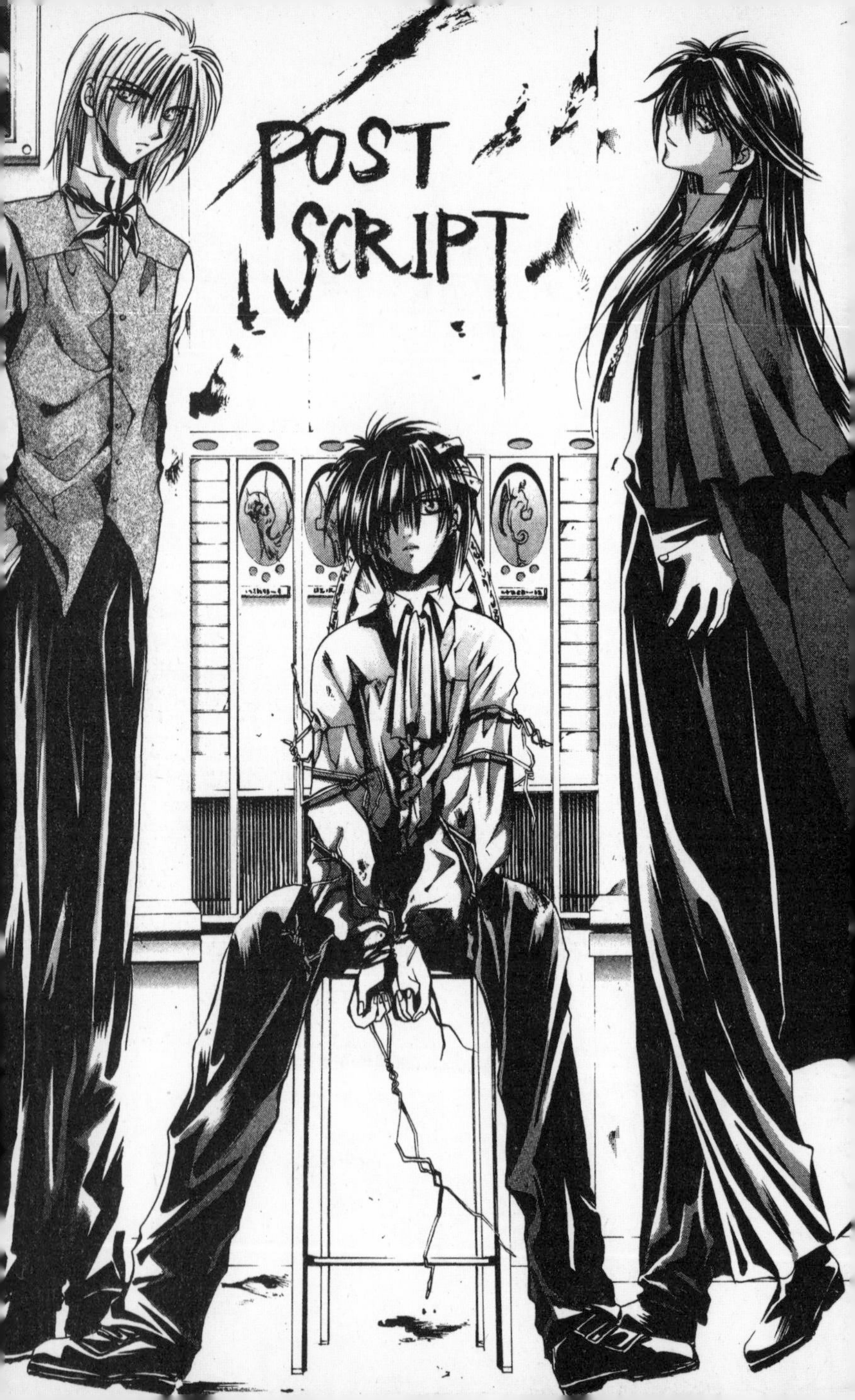
POST SCRIPT

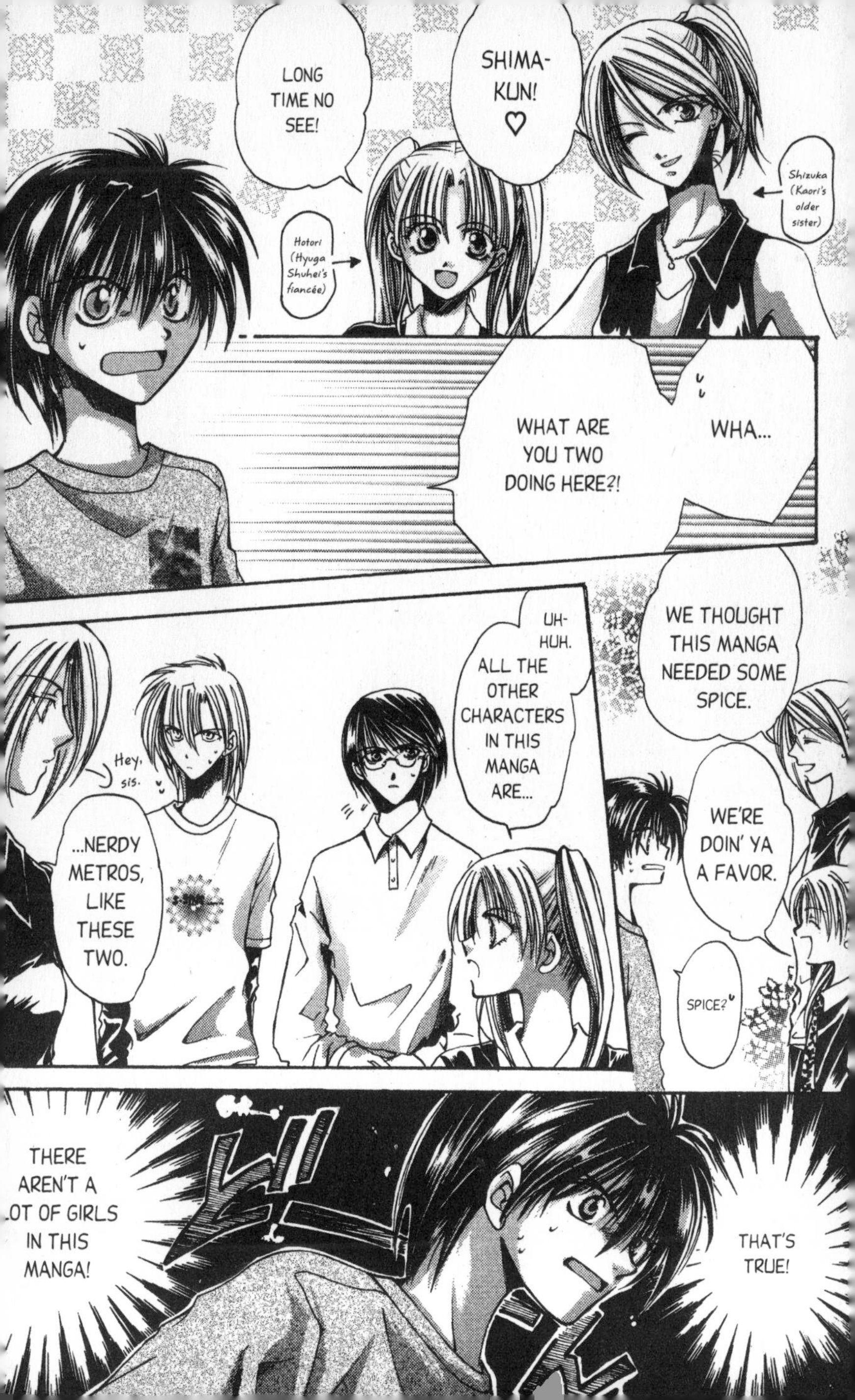
Shizuka (Kaori's older sister)
SHIMA-KUN! ♡
LONG TIME NO SEE!
Hotori (Hyuga Shuhei's fiancée)
WHA...
WHAT ARE YOU TWO DOING HERE?!
WE THOUGHT THIS MANGA NEEDED SOME SPICE.
WE'RE DOIN' YA A FAVOR.
SPICE?
UH-HUH. ALL THE OTHER CHARACTERS IN THIS MANGA ARE...
Hey, sis.
...NERDY METROS, LIKE THESE TWO.
THAT'S TRUE!
THERE AREN'T A LOT OF GIRLS IN THIS MANGA!

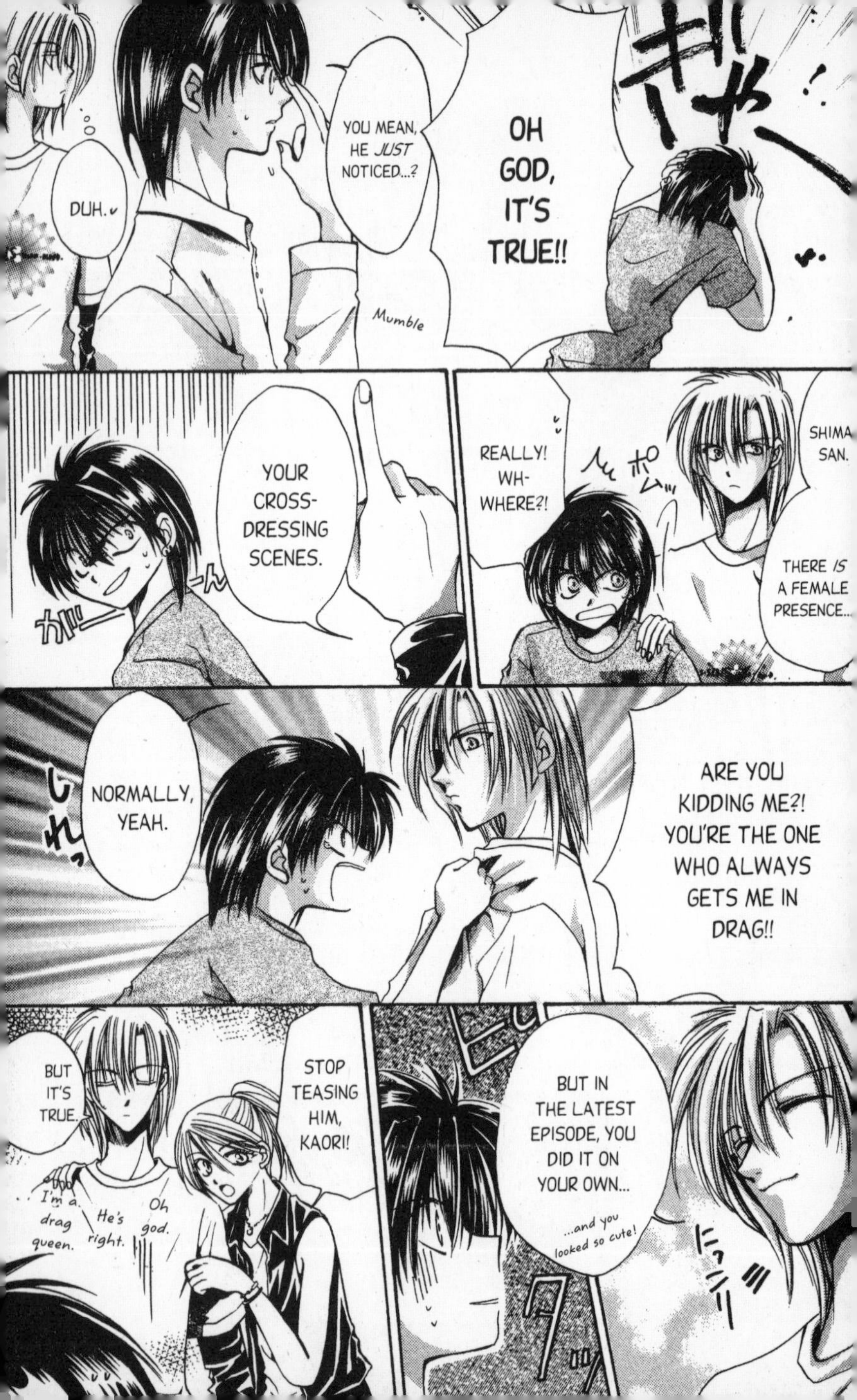
OH GOD, IT'S TRUE!!
YOU MEAN, HE *JUST* NOTICED...?
Mumble
DUH.
SHIMA SAN.
THERE *IS* A FEMALE PRESENCE...
REALLY! WH-WHERE?!
YOUR CROSS-DRESSING SCENES.
ARE YOU KIDDING ME?! YOU'RE THE ONE WHO ALWAYS GETS ME IN DRAG!!
NORMALLY, YEAH.
BUT IN THE LATEST EPISODE, YOU DID IT ON YOUR OWN...
...and you looked so cute!
STOP TEASING HIM, KAORI!
BUT IT'S TRUE.
Oh god.
He's right.
I'm a drag queen.

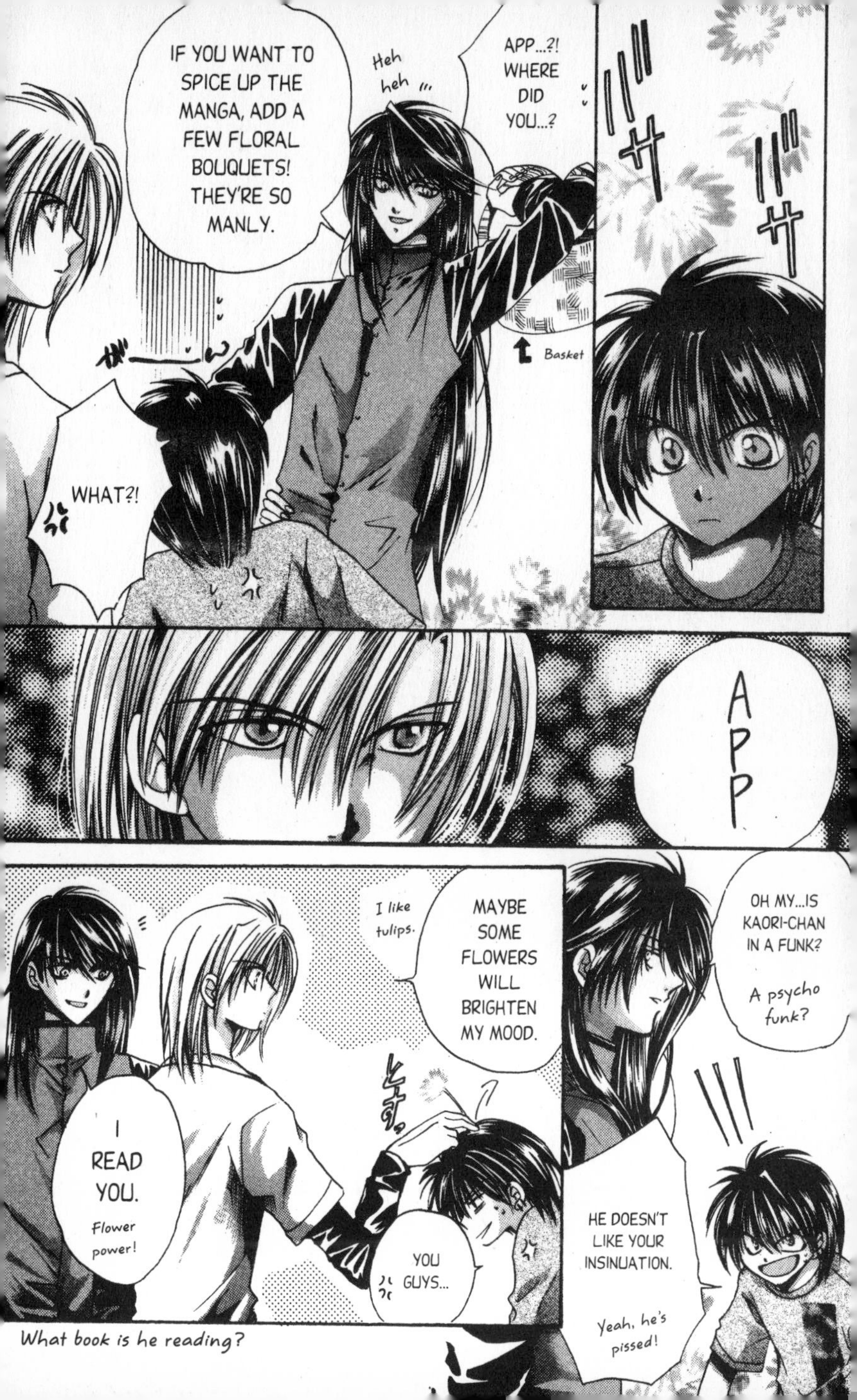
APP...?! WHERE DID YOU...?
Heh heh
IF YOU WANT TO SPICE UP THE MANGA, ADD A FEW FLORAL BOUQUETS! THEY'RE SO MANLY.
Basket
WHAT?!
APP
OH MY...IS KAORI-CHAN IN A FUNK?
A psycho funk?
HE DOESN'T LIKE YOUR INSINUATION.
Yeah, he's pissed!
MAYBE SOME FLOWERS WILL BRIGHTEN MY MOOD.
I like tulips.
YOU GUYS...
I READ YOU.
Flower power!
What book is he reading?

You might think I brought Shizuka and Hotori back because they're my favorite characters. I wanted to bring back the little boy from "Haunted by the Past" from volume 1, too, but that would have been too many people... Really, I just wanted to turn up my girl power!
And speaking of nostalgic characters, congratulations to anyone who noticed Edison ("Acting on Impulse", volume 1) hiding in the background of Mayuko's classroom.
On a different note, while I was working on volume 3, I got really sick and had to be hospitalized (for the first time in my life!). The doctors wanted me to stay for two weeks, but I was able to haggle them down to six days. It was a combination of stress and fatigue. Jeez, I guess I did work too hard...

And of course, I would like to thank my family, my friends and the people who helped me with my drafts. And my editor. And the readers who keep me going. I appreciate all your support!

So see you next time! Love, Ryo Saenagi!

※ I wanted to say goodbye, but I've got an extra page. Here's a short comic!

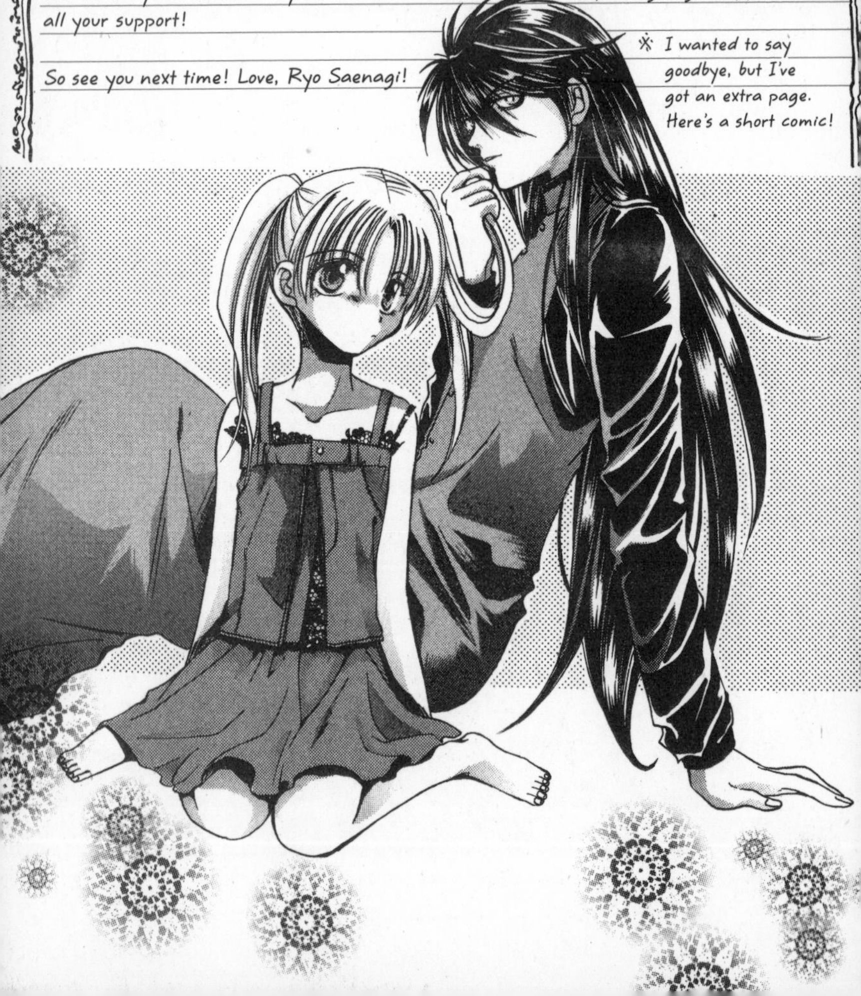

THE ROAD TO DESTRUCTION

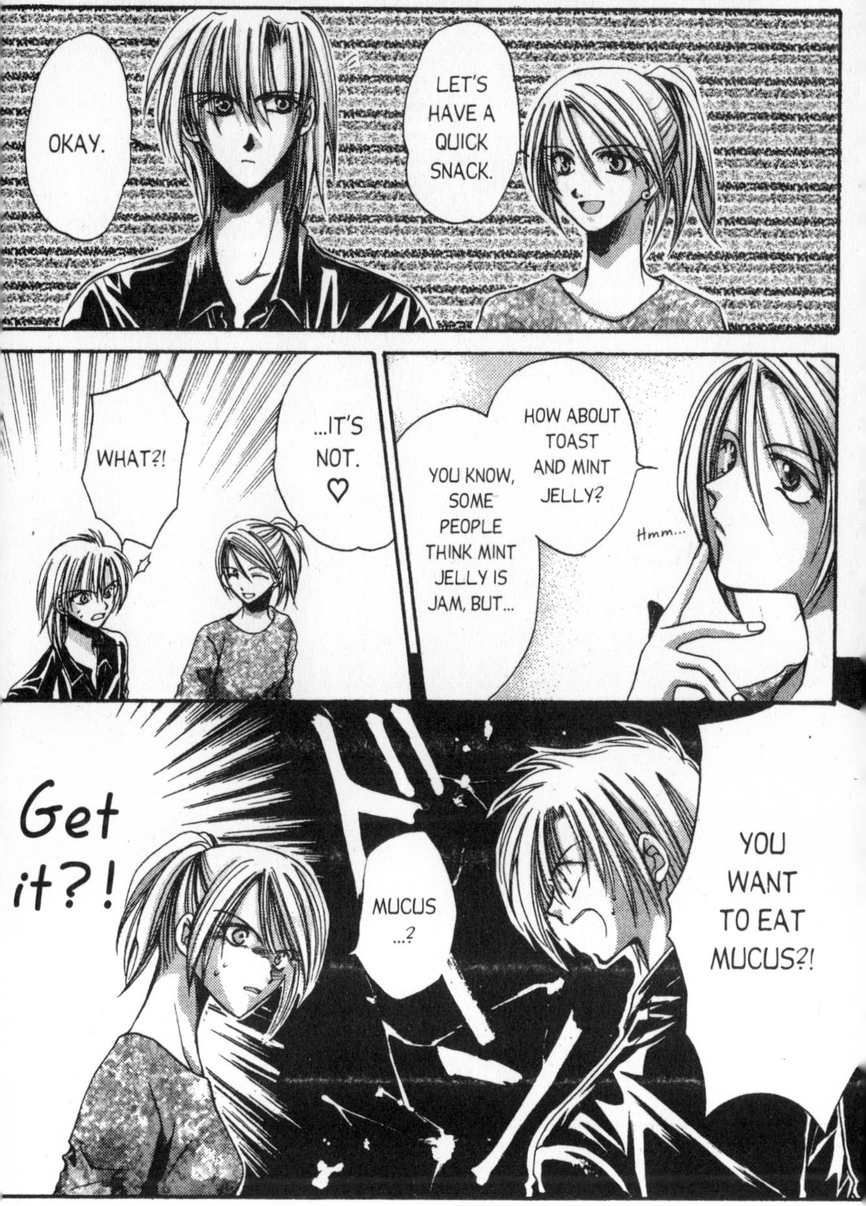
LET'S HAVE A QUICK SNACK.
OKAY.
HOW ABOUT TOAST AND MINT JELLY?
YOU KNOW, SOME PEOPLE THINK MINT JELLY IS JAM, BUT...
Hmm...
...IT'S NOT. ♡
WHAT?!
YOU WANT TO EAT MUCUS?!
MUCUS ...?
Get it?!

Say it out loud: Some people think it's jam, but-it's-snot. Now do you get it?

Hmm, I still don't get it.